The Ethical Challenge
of Auschwitz and Hiroshima

Apocalypse or Utopia?

Darrell J. Fasching

State University of New York Press

Published by
State University of New York Press, Albany

For information, address State University of New York Press,
State University Plaza, Albany, N.Y. 12246

Production by M. R. Mulholland
Marketing by Fran Keneston

Library of Congress Cataloging-in-Publication Data

Fasching, Darrell J., 1944-
    The ethical challenge of Auschwitz and Hiroshima : Apocalypse or Utopia? / by Darrell J. Fasching.
        p.   cm.
    Includes bibliographical references and index.
    ISBN 0-7914-1375-6 (alk. paper). — ISBN 0-7914-1376-4 (pbk. : alk. paper)
    1. Religious ethics.   2. Human rights—Religious aspects.
3. Technology—Moral and ethical aspects.   4. Utopias—Moral and ethical aspects.   5. Holocaust. Jewish (1939–1945)—Moral and ethical aspects.   6. Nuclear warfare—Moral and ethical aspects.
    I. Title.
BJ1188.F37   1993
241'.62—dc20   92-8118
                                                                                      CIP

10 9 8 7 6 5 4 3 2 1

For Gabriel Vahanian—
who first taught me to see
the utopian promise of Babel

Contents

Contents   ix

Preface

This book is dedicated to Gabriel Vahanian, mentor, friend and a theologian's theologian. His influence permeates each page. Every book, I am convinced has a surface structure and a deep structure. The surface structure draws upon the work of various authors in support of its argument. Their influence will be explicit and obvious. In this book the surface structure is built around the works of such figures as Jacques Ellul, Paul Tillich, Eric Voegelin, Bernard Lonergan, Irving Greenberg, John Dunne, Stanley Hauerwas, etc. The deep structure, however, is much harder to recognize. The deep structure reflects the way a book is organized—the types of questions that are asked and the way answers are sought. The influences on this deep structure will be less obvious but far more profound than those so obvious in the surface structure. It is not the quotations or references that define the deep structure but the very thought process through which the argument unfolds. While references to Gabriel Vahanian can be found in the surface structure, it is at the level of deep structure that his influence is so pervasive. This book simply would never have been conceived and would never have seen the light of day were it not for his influence on the deep structure of my own thought.

It is now a decade and a half since I completed my doctorate under the direction of Gabriel Vahanian at Syracuse University. I still remember the exhilaration of those graduate years. The intellectual atmosphere was filled with electricity and excitement. Graduate programs also have both surface and deep structures. The surface structure is made up of courses and requirements. Its focus is on content and method. And it is possible to walk away with a doctorate based on nothing more than that. But if one is very fortunate, as I was, one studies under a master who teaches far more than the particular contents and methods of a discipline. I entered Syracuse to study theology of culture and from Gabriel Vahanian I learned far more than content and method. I came to understand that theology is concerned not so much with the exegesis of sacred texts and traditions as it is an iconoclastic way of thinking about our humanity as a linguistic and culturally embodied reality—the word made flesh. I learned that which cannot be put down on the written page but which affects everything I write. I learned that which can only be absorbed by studying with a master. I learned to think theologically.

In saying this I do not mean to suggest that Gabriel Vahanian is somehow responsible for the weaknesses of this book. I am not at all sure that I have lived up to the gift that was given to me. It may be a weakness to fall short of such a high measure but it is no disgrace. It is in fact an honor. The deep structure of this book will be quite recognizable to those who are familiar with Vahanian's books. Many will be familiar with his books in English: *The Death of God, Wait Without Idols, No Other God,* and *God and Utopia.* But some may not be familiar with his two most recent works in French, which came out just as I was completing this manuscript: *Dieu anonyme* (God Anonymous) and *L'utopie chrétienne* (Christian Utopia).[1] The organizing themes of my own efforts can all be found in these works—the human as created in the image of a God without image, the dialectic of the sacred and the holy, and of technology and utopia vis a vis apocalypse; the experience of God or transcendence as the questioning of all our answers; the audacious protest against religion as itself religious; the utopian promise of Babel, etc. Even on those occasions when my own analysis departs from Vahanian's it is but a permutation which would have been impossible without his influence. Needless to say, the debt I owe to Gabriel Vahanian is immeasurable. I hope that in some modest way this book is a down payment on it.

I need to acknowledge a primary indebtedness not only to the living but to the dead. Two ghosts haunt the pages of this book. The surface structure is deeply indebted to Paul Tillich who pioneered the field of theology of culture and whose work first motivated me to consider theology as a profession. But there is another ghost which haunts these pages, namely, the ghost of Karl Barth. All my life I have been drawn to Tillich and have tried to escape the influence of Barth—but to no avail. As an undergraduate in Philosophy at the University of Minnesota my adviser was the distinguished scholar of Medieval Philosophy, Gareth Matthews. To my dismay I discovered in a conversation one day that he had read virtually everything Barth had ever written. When I finished my B.A. I went on to Syracuse University to study with Gabriel Vahanian. By some strange leap of intuitive insight I had decided Vahanian was a Tillichian. It was a considerable shock to discover that in fact it was not only Bultmann but Barth who deeply influenced his work. Then it came time to write my doctoral dissertation and Vahanian steered me toward Jacques Ellul—yet another Barthian. The result is that, although I have quite deliberately read very little of Karl Barth, I am afraid I have been unable to keep Barth from influencing my thought. I have absorbed his thought, it seems, by osmosis. For this I must both praise and blame Gabriel Vahanian above all.

Having said all this, I would like to acknowledge other debts as well. The total environment during my graduate days was the seed bed for this book. I cannot imagine having written it without the study of Job under Jim Williams, or Nietzsche and historical consciousness under Jim Wiggins, or the Bhagavad Gita and the Pali Canon under Dan Smith. Nor should I neglect to mention the influence of Dick Pilgrim's work in Japanese Buddhism or the seminars with Stanley Romaine Hopper, David Miller, D. B. Robertson and Ronald Cavanagh. Later, while I was writing my dissertation, Michael Novak, Huston Smith, and Alan Berger joined the faculty. Each left their mark and I would not wish it otherwise. To all of them I am deeply grateful.

There are others I need to thank as well. Bill Shea, my good friend and colleague, with whom I debated so many of the ideas found here. Also my graduate students: Tracy Stewart, Alice Hutton, Raul Canizares, James Massey, Diane Smith, Barbara Souders, and especially Robin Tuthill and Janet Nelson. Both Robin and Janet worked through two different drafts of this manuscript with me and their serious engagement with these drafts helped me to write a better book than it would have been otherwise. I am especially grateful for Janet Nelson's cogent criticisms which led me to significantly reorganize this manuscript. I also wish to thank two former students, Janet Bank and Susan Segal, for their careful reading of the manuscript and helpful suggestions which likewise affected the structure of this book.

I also owe special thanks as well to a former student, Jim David, who was instrumental in making it possible for me to attend the international conference on the Holocaust, "Remembering the Future," at Oxford University in the summer of 1988. It was the paper I prepared for that conference and the conversations I had there, especially with Alice Eckhardt, Richard Rubenstein, and Marc Ellis, which led me to conceive this book. Indeed, I drafted the first outline of this book while at that conference. Richard Rubenstein has had his own special impact upon this book. It is he who points out in his brilliant book, *The Cunning of History,* that we live in a world that is "functionally godless"—a world in which human rights and human dignity are reduced to civil rights which can be granted or withheld as societies choose. No theologian, he argues, has dealt with the fact that no crime was committed at Auschwitz. Moreover, no theologian has shown how the championing of human rights on the part of

religious communities in such a politicized world can make the slightest bit of difference. In this book I have tried to respond to his challenge and address these issues.

I also owe a debt to Max Stackhouse whose review and recom-
mendation of this project helped make it possible for me to get the
sabbatical I needed to complete it. And I would like to thank Stanley
Hauerwas for his willingness to look at a draft of this manuscript in its
earliest stages and offer words of encouragement. Finally I would like
to thank Rollin Richmond, Dean of the College of Arts and Sciences at
the University of South Florida, for his support and encouragement
which made it possible to complete this book in a timely manner.

Acknowledgments

I wish to expresss my appreciation for the assistance provided me by the University of South Florida, for this book was made possible in part by two University grants; a research grant for the summer of 1989 and a sabbatical grant for the fall of 1989. In addition, I wish to thank Fortress press for permission to utilize brief sections of my previous book *Narrative Theology After Auschwitz: From Alienation to Ethics* (Minneapolis: Augsburg Fortress, 1992) in order to complete the argument of this sequal. I also wish to thank the following for permission to adapt materials I have previously published elsewhere:

Soundings, for permission to adapt "Technology as Utopian Technique of the Human," Vol. LXII, No. 2, Summer 1980, pp. 135–158.

Horizons, for permission to adapt "Can Christian Faith Survive Auschwitz?", Vol. 12, No. 1, 1985, pp. 7–26.

Pergamon Press for permission to adapt material from "Faith and Ethics After the Holocaust: What Christians Can learn from Jews," in the proceedings of the Oxford international conference on the Holocaust entitled *Remembering for the Future*, Vol. 1, 1988, pp. 598–611. This was revised and reprinted in *The Journal of Ecumenical Studies* under the title "Faith and Ethics After Auschwitz: What Christian's Can Learn From the Jewish Narrative Tradition of Hutzpah" Vol. 27, No. 3, Summer 1990, pp. 453–479.

JAI Press for permission to adapt portions of two articles: "The Dialectics of Apocalypse and Utopia in the Theological Ethics of Jacques Ellul," which appeared in volume 10, 1990, pp. 149–165 and "Mass Media, Ethical Paradox, and Democratic Freedom: Jacques Ellul's Ethic of the Word," in volume 11, 1991, pp. 77–103 of *Research in Philosophy and Technology*.

The Journal of the American Association of Rabbis, for permission to adapt material from "Ethics after Auschwitz and Hiroshima: The Challenge of the 'Other' for Jews, Christians, Buddhists, and Other Strangers in a Technological Civilization," Vol. 6, No. 2, Summer, 1990, pp. 10–20.

Method, for material adapted from "Theology and Public Policy: Reflections on Method in the Work of Juan Luis Segundo, Jacques Ellul and Robert Doran," Vol. 5, No. 1, March, 1987, pp. 41–91.

I would also like to thank the following publishers for permission to use copyrighted material:

The Journal of Ecumenical Studies for excerpts from "Hutzpa K'lapei Shamaya: A Christian Response to the Jewish Tradition of Arguing with God," by Belden Lane, from Vol. 4, Fall 1986, pp. 567–586.

HarperCollins Publishers Inc., for excerpts from *The Cunning of History* by Richard Rubenstein, (New York: Harper, copyright 1975). Introduction copyright 1978 by William Stryon.

Crossroad/Continuum Publishing Group for excerpts from *The Tremendum,* by Arthur Cohen, (New York: Crossroad, copyright 1981).

Basic Books for excerpts from *The Nazi Doctors: Medical Killing and the Psychology of Genocide* (New York, Basic Books, copyright 1986) and *The Future of Immortality and Other Essays for a Nuclear Age* (New York, Basic Books, copyright 1987), both by Robert Jay Lifton. Basic Books is a division of HarperCollins Publishers Inc.

William B. Eerdmans Publishing Co. for excerpts from *The Naked Public Square* by Richard Neuhaus, (Grand Rapids: Eerdmans Publishing Co., copyright 1984) and for the reproduction of figure 1 from page 18 of *Creeds, Society and Human Rights: A Study in Three Cultures* by Max L. Stackhouse, (Grand Rapids: Eerdmans Publishing Co., copyright 1984.)

Macmillan Publishing Co. for excerpts from *The Secular City* by Harvey Cox (New York, Macmillan, copyright 1965).

University of Notre Dame Press for excerpts from *After Virtue* by Alasdair MacIntyre. (Notre Dame, University of Notre Dame Press, 1984, Revised Edition).

Beacon Press, for excerpts from *Ethics After Babel* (Boston, 1988) by Jeffrey Stout.

Word Books for excerpts from *Nuclear Arms: Two Views on World Peace* (Dallas: Word Inc., 1987) by Myron S. Augsburger and Dean C. Curry.

Orbis Books for excerpts from *The Emptying God: A Budhist-Jewish-Christian Conversation* (Maryknoll N.Y., Orbis Books, 1990), edited by John Cobb Jr. and Christopher Ives.

Prologue: The Challenge of Babel— From Alienation to Ethics After Auschwitz and Hiroshima

Now the whole earth had one language and the same words. And as they migrated from the east, they came upon a plain in the land of Shinar and settled there. And they said to one another, "Come, let us make bricks, and burn them thoroughly." And they had brick for stone, and bitumen for mortar. Then they said, "Come, let us build ourselves a city, and a tower with its top in the heavens, and let us make a name for ourselves; otherwise we shall be scattered abroad upon the face of the whole earth." The Lord came down to see the city and the tower which mortals had built. And the Lord said, "Look, they are one people, and they have all one language; and this is only the beginning of what they will do; nothing that they propose to do will now be impossible for them. Come, let us go down, and confuse their language there, so that they will not understand one another's speech." So the Lord scattered them abroad from there over the face of all the earth, and they left off building the city. Therefore it was called Babel, because there the Lord confused the language of all the earth; and from there the Lord scattered them abroad over the face of all the earth.

—Genesis 11:1–9[1]

The story of Babel is a tale for our times. It is a parable through which we might come to understand our situation. The citizens of Babel, it seems, sought to build a perfect city, a utopia whose technological prowess would make their name known throughout the earth. These citizens, we are told, sought to seize control of transcendence through the ideology of a single language and the common technological project of building a tower to heaven. God, however, upset their efforts by confusing their tongues, so that they could not understand each other. They became strangers to one another and so could not complete their task. They had to abandon all "final solutions" and settle for an unfinished city. The popular interpretation of this story is that the confusion of tongues was a curse and a punishment for the human sin of pride. But I am convinced that this is a serious misunderstanding of its meaning. For this story must be interpreted within the tradition of stories that make up the canon of the Tanakh (Old Testament), where the command to welcome the stranger appears more often than any other commandment.[2] In the light of that emphasis, I would suggest that the point of the story is that human beings misunderstood where transcendence lay, and God simply redirected them to the true experience of transcendence, which can occur only when there are strangers to be welcomed into our lives. The moral of this story, as I read it, is that utopian transcendence is to be found not in a "finished world" of technological and ideological conformity but in an "unfinished world" of diversity, a world that offers us the opportunity to welcome the stranger. Indeed, our attempts to define a world through technological prowess and ideological uniformity have led us, more than once, to the brink of MAD-ness (mutually assured destruction)—the brink of an apocalyptic nuclear annihilation. Our hope lies in seeing the utopian possibilities of a world of diversity—the latent possibilities that can be actualized through an ethic of welcoming the stranger.

This book follows upon and expands the argument of my previous book, *Narrative Theology After Auschwitz: From Alienation to Ethics* (Fortress, 1992). It is intended to be an experiment in theology of culture as an approach to comparative religious ethics through narrative. In *Narrative Theology After Auschwitz* I attempted to restructure the Christian narrative tradition in the light of Auschwitz through a dialogue with that strand of post-Holocaust Jewish theology and ethics that draws on the Jewish narrative tradition of chutzpah.[3] That volume culminated in an ethic of personal and professional responsibility proposed as a strategy for restraining the human capacity for the demonic.

This volume, *The Ethical Challenge of Auschwitz and Hiroshima: Apocalypse or Utopia?* continues the narrative ethics approach but extends the ethical focus of the discussion to encompass religion, technology, and public policy in a cross-cultural perspective. In this work, I attempt to do what narrative ethicists have said cannot be done; namely, construct a cross-cultural ethic of human dignity, human rights, and human liberation that is rooted in and respects the diversity of narrative traditions. Moreover, I have tried to do this without succumbing to either ethical relativism or ethical absolutism, even as I seek to directly confront the dominant narrative of our technological civilization. That narrative, I am convinced, is the Janus-faced myth of "Apocalypse or Utopia." This mythic narrative tends to render us ethically impotent, for, mesmerized by the power of technology, we become trapped in the manic-depressive rhythms of a sacral awe; that is, of fascination and dread. When we are caught up in the utopian euphoria created by the marvelous promises of technology we do not wish to change anything. And when, in our darker moments, we fear that this same technology is out of control and leading us to our own apocalyptic self-destruction, we feel overwhelmed and unable to do anything. The paradox is that the very strength of our literal utopian euphoria sends us careening toward some literal apocalyptic "final solution." In *Narrative Theology After Auschwitz* I argued that the demonic narrative theme that dominated Auschwitz was "killing in order to heal." In this book I argue that this theme became globalized when it was incorporated into the Janus-faced technological mythos that emerged out of Hiroshima. This mythic narrative underlies and structures much of public policy in our nuclear age. In response to this demonic narrative, I propose a cross-cultural coalition for an ethic of human dignity, human rights, and human liberation at the intersection of those holy communities whose narrative traditions emphasize the importance of welcoming the stranger. My goal is to construct a bridge not only over the abyss between religions, East and West, but also between religious and secular ethics.

The total project, then, is about religion, ethics, and public policy after Auschwitz and Hiroshima. It is about (a) rethinking the meaning of civilization and public order in an emerging pluralistic world civilization as we approach the end of a millennium—the year 2000 C.E.; (b) the need for a cross-cultural ethic in a world wracked by ethical relativism and ideological conflict; and (c) sacred and secular public narratives in a technological civilization and the appropriate role for religion in the shaping of public values in a "secular" world.

The perspective from which this book is written is that of theology. However, it is not "Christian" theology, although it is most certainly theology written by a Christian. It is not "confessional theology," but theology understood as an academic discipline within the humanities, whose purpose is the illumination of the human experience (individual and communal) of transcendence as self-transcendence. Needless to say, the same subject matter would be treated differently had this project been written by a Buddhist or some other more "secular" a-theist,[4] or by a Hindu, Jew, or Muslim rather than a Christian. And yet I intend it to be a theology that has something to say not only to Christians but also to Jews, Buddhists, and others—even to "secular" humanistic a-theists.

What I am engaged in is "theology of culture," a discipline first introduced by Paul Tillich in his 1920 essay, "On the Idea of a Theology of Culture," with which he inaugurated his career.[5] Theology of culture is an appropriate discipline for the "secular" university in an emerging world civilization. For, as Tillich insists, the theologian of culture is no "confessional theologian" but rather a "free agent" who takes as his or her task the identification and elucidation of the relationship between religion and culture in all its diversity. Theology of culture could equally be called "philosophy of religion," provided that discipline were able to break free of its nearly exclusive bias as a tradition of commentary on the logic of Western theism rather than on religion as a transcultural human phenomenon. Theology of culture, as I understand it, exists at the intersection of philosophy and the history of religions, as a form of comparative religious ethics. It separates itself from some forms of comparative religious ethics in that it goes beyond description to prescription. Its task is nothing less than a total critique of culture.

Doing ethics requires not just philosophical reflection but also historical, sociological, and psychological reflection. Tillich's proposal for a theology of culture draws these diverse elements into a unified whole that replaces traditional ethics with the new and uniquely modern task of the critique of culture. The critique of culture "as a whole" presents a unique problem. For if we live, move, and have our being within culture—how is it possible to transcend it so as to critique it? From what vantage point can we "stand outside it" so to speak? Such a critique presupposes the identification of values that, in some sense, transcend the cultures in which they are embodied. I believe such values can be identified. However, they do not exist in a vacuum. They are embodied in particular types of narrative carried by specific types of communal traditions that, in some sense, stand apart from the cultures in which they find themselves. The ultimate goal of theology of culture is to identify those religious experiences, forms of religious community and narrative traditions that have transcended the historical epoch and cultural milieu of their origin to influence other times and places. For these narrative traditions will have proven themselves culturally transcendent allies and therefore may offer possible norms for the critique of both religions and cultures.

Although I attempt to identify the positive and negative value of several types of religious experience in this book, I do not pretend to have written it from some neutral Archimedean vantage point. As Tillich insisted, no theologian of culture can escape his or her own religious and cultural history. Indeed, every scholar in the social sciences and humanities is a "participant observer" in the human condition being studied. There is no neutral vantage point from which to begin. As Alasdair MacIntyre and Stanley Hauerwas have both argued, no scholar lives in a storyless world, not even the Enlightenment rationalist who pretends to. One must acknowledge one's starting position and work outward from there. This is as true for the psychologist or anthropologist as it is for the political scientist, philosopher, and theologian. If we wish to speak of (or to) other storied worlds we must find a way to stretch our own narrative worlds to make a place for their otherness. That is in fact what I shall attempt to do. My own starting point is that of an alienated Christian, alienated from my own narrative traditions by my encounter with the Holocaust and the history of anti-Judaism that paved the way to it and by the processes of secularization in a technical civilization that led not only to Auschwitz but also Hiroshima. Confessionally, my stand in Christianity, like Tillich's, is that of a Lutheran. But like Tillich, I seek to be an objective scholar, making philosophically fair statements and evaluations about a wide diversity of religious and cultural phenomenon in order to construct a social ethic that can sustain a total critique of modern culture.

Nevertheless, I am only too aware how vulnerable are the arguments and methodologies that I use in this book. Many specialists will no doubt have serious questions about my grasp of materials that touch upon their areas. I too have such questions. But I see no point in playing it safe, I mean to provoke discussion, and I hope the dialogue that follows shall enrich and correct my perspective. Moreover, I confess my own perspective and its limitations at the outset because I believe that after Auschwitz and Hiroshima it is dangerous to write in the third person, as if no one in particular were having these thoughts. In our world we each need to take responsibility for our thoughts and their social consequences. I reflect further on these matters in the Epilogue, and some may find it helpful to read that concluding essay immediately after reading this Prologue to understand more clearly what I am attempting to do in the body of the text itself.

The best way to describe the "style" of the theology of culture proposed in these books is to suggest that it is a "decentered" or "alienated theology." Alienated theology is the opposite of apologetic theology. Apologetic theology typically seeks to defend the "truth" and "superiority" of one's own tradition against the "false," "inferior," and "alien" views of other traditions. Alienated theology, by contrast, is theology done "as if" one were a stranger to one's own narrative traditions, seeing and critiquing one's own traditions from the vantage point of the other's narrative traditions. It is my conviction that alienated theology is the appropriate mode for theology in an emerging world civilization—a civilization tottering in the balance between apocalypse and utopia. There are two ways to enter world history, according to the contemporary author John Dunne: you can be dragged in by way of world war or you can walk in by way of mutual understanding. By the first path, global civilization emerges as a totalitarian project of dominance that risks escalating into a nuclear apocalypse. By the second path, we prevent the first, creating global civilization through an expansion of our understanding of what it means to be human. This occurs when we *pass over* to an other's religion and culture and *come back* with new insight into our own.

Gandhi is an example, passing over to the Sermon on the Mount and coming back to the Hindu Bhagavad Gita to gain new insight into it as a scripture of nonviolence. Gandhi never seriously considered becoming a Christian but his Hinduism was radically altered by his encounter with Christianity. One could say the same (reversing the directions) for Martin Luther King Jr., who was deeply influenced by Gandhi's understanding of nonviolent resistance in the Gita. When we pass over (whether through travel, friendship, or disciplined study and imagination) we become "strangers in a strange land" as well as strangers to ourselves, seeing ourselves through the eyes of another. Assuming the perspective of a stranger is an occasion for insight and the sharing of insight. Such cross-cultural interactions build bridges of understanding and action between persons and cultures that make cooperation possible and conquest unnecessary. "Passing over" short circuits apocalyptic confrontation and inaugurates utopian new beginnings—new beginnings for the "postmodern" world of the coming third millennium. Gandhi and King are symbols of a possible style for a postmodern alienated theology.

To be an *alien* is to be a stranger. To be *alienated* is to be a stranger to oneself. We live in a world of ideological conflict in which far too many individuals (whether theists or a-theists) practice a "centered theology" in which they are too sure of who they are and what they must do. Such a world has far too many answers and not nearly enough questions and self-questioning. A world divided by its answers is headed for an inevitable apocalyptic destiny. However, when we are willing to become strangers to ourselves (or when we unwillingly become so), new possibilities open up where before everything was closed and hopeless. At the heart of my position is the conviction that the *kairos* of our time calls forth the badly neglected ethic of "welcoming the stranger" that underlies the biblical tradition and analogously "welcoming the outcast" that underlies the Buddhist tradition. This care for the stranger and the outcast, I shall argue, provides the critical norm for identifying authentic transcendence as self-transcendence.

Centered theologies, whether sacred or secular, theist or a-theist, are ethnocentric theologies that can tolerate the alien or *other*, if at all, only as a potential candidate for conversion to *sameness*. Centered theologies are exercises in narcissism that inevitably lead down apocalyptic paths like those that led to Auschwitz and Hiroshima. Why? Because such theologies, whether sacred or "secular," cannot permit there to be *others* in the world whose way of being might, by sheer contrast, cause self-doubt and self-questioning.

When as a student I read Paul Tillich, I found it hard to believe him when he said that the questions were more important than the answers. I was so taken with his answers that I was sure he was just trying to be modest. What really mattered were the answers. Since then, I have come to realize that answers always seem more important and more certain to those who have come by them without wrestling with the questions. I know now that Tillich was quite serious and quite right—the questions are indeed more important. I have come to find a fullness in the doubts and questions of my life, which I once thought could be found only in the answers. After Auschwitz and Hiroshima, I distrust all final answers—all *final solutions.* Mercifully, doubts and questions have come to be so fulfilling that I find myself suspicious of answers, not because they are necessarily false or irrelevant, but because even when relevant and true they are, and can be, only partial. It is doubt and questioning that always lures me on to broader horizons and deeper insights through an openness to the infinite that leaves me *contentedly discontent.*

Alienated theology understands doubt and the questions that arise from it as our most fundamental experience of the infinite. For, our unending questions keep us open to the infinite, continually inviting us to transcend our present horizon of understanding. In a like manner, the presence of the stranger continuously calls us into question and invites us to transcend the present horizon of the egocentric and ethnocentric answers that structure our personal and cultural identities. An alienated theology understands that only a faith which requires one to welcome the alien or stranger is truly a utopian faith capable of transforming us into "new beings" who are capable of creating a new world of pluralistic human interdependence.

To put it in terms closest to home for myself, as a Christian who

seeks to come to grips with Auschwitz in the light the history of
Christian anti-Judaism, I cannot be a Christian except as I am prepared to welcome Jews (and analogously Buddhists or secular humanists, etc.) into my life. The very attempt to convert them would be
to destroy the authenticity of my own faith by robbing me of the
chance to welcome the stranger (the one who is different from me and
a permanent witness of the Wholly Other in my life) who is given to
me as an invitation to self-transcendence. For the literal meaning of
transcendence is "to go beyond"—to go beyond ourselves (individually
and communally) as we are to become something more and something new. To be human is to have a utopian capacity to create new
worlds. When we deny ourselves that possibility, we set in motion
the seeds of our apocalyptic self-destruction. The tragedy of human
existence revealed by Auschwitz and Hiroshima is that we have continued to misread our situation. Given the opportunity for self-
transcendence, the opportunity to be carried beyond ourselves into a
new global human community, we have instead insisted on a "technological solution," a MAD (mutual assured destruction) solution.
This, at best, leads to a global stalemate between cultures and at
worst an attempt at global conquest. In either case we place ourselves
under the dark and threatening cloud of a nuclear apocalypse that
such a path risks.

Alienated theology is an attempt to critique one's own tradition
by imaginatively experiencing it through the eyes of the "other" who
stands outside one's tradition, as if one were the other who has been,
or will be, affected by it. This book is a project in, and an invitation to,
decentered or alienated theology. The task is not so much one of
getting correct what alien communities have thought about each other
as it is one of creating new insights and new meanings through a
process of shared insights. The task is not primarily the historical one
of recalling the past (although that must be done), but the ethical task
of constructing the future. We are engaged not so much in the description of being as in the making of being. We are not so much
interested in what Judaism, Christianity, Buddhism (and other a-
theisms) have been as what they will become as a result of engaging
in the process of alienated theology.

Living in an age of alienation, I used to think that the experience
of alienation was a problem in need of resolution. I have come to see
it, however, as a promising opportunity. For when we have become
strangers to ourselves we experience a new vulnerability and a new
openness to the other: other persons, other ideas, other cultures, and
other ways of life. To the degree that secularization alienates us from

our "sacred" traditions, it presents us with utopian possibilities. It also presents us with apocalyptic dangers. The greatest danger created by alienation seems to be that we shall become lost in a sea of relativism, of assuming one way is as good as another. This is just as destructive as those centered theologies that assume there is only one way.

Because culture, like nature, abhors a vacuum such relativism inevitably defaults in some arbitrary form of absolutism that refuses to tolerate the pluralism to which it is a reaction. When all values are viewed as equally arbitrary, no good reasons can be offered for one option over another. And when no good reasons can be offered, "the will to power" takes over. In a technological civilization, the autonomous secular rationality of technique, symbolized by Auschwitz and Hiroshima, expresses this arbitrary will to power. The notion that we live in a purely secular civilization needs to be qualified. All public order is structured by experiences of the sacred that, sociologically speaking, legitimate a given social order. The particular form of sacred order that dominates modern civilization simply assumes a secular guise. It is a demonic form rooted in the normlessness of modern cultural relativism and expressed in the paradoxical formula "nothing is any longer sacred not even human life."

It is my conviction, however, that a path lies between the extremes of relativism and absolutism, and that path is the way of doubt and self-questioning which accompanies *passing over* and *coming back* as a quest for insight through the sharing in the narrative traditions of the stranger. For as a permanent way I believe it prevents one from settling into either a self-complacent absolutism or a self-complacent relativism, replacing both with the experience of self-transcendence as a surrender to doubt and its social correlate, openness to the stranger.

In *Narrative Theology After Auschwitz*, I made the case for alienated theology as a way of doing comparative religious ethics by passing over into the narrative traditions of post-Holocaust Judaism and coming back to post-Holocaust Christianity to construct an ethic of personal and professional responsibility after Auschwitz. In the process of doing this I found myself forced to expand my vision of the project beyond Auschwitz and Western culture. I felt a second volume had to be written, because as I studied the post-Holocaust Jewish theologians who respond to the Shoah (i.e., the time of "desolation"), again and again, in the same breath with *Auschwitz*, the name *Hiroshima* kept coming up. The link between Auschwitz and Hiroshima turns out to be an inner link demanded by the analysis of those who were, directly or indirectly, the victims of the Shoah. It is as if those who know something of the "desolation" of Auschwitz recognize that in some sense they have a kinship with those who know the "desolation" of Hiroshima. Also, more than once I have encountered an awareness of a logical as well as psychological link between the two. This link is the progressive unfolding of a desacralized and desacralizing technological civilization that no longer holds anything sacred, not even human life—nothing that is except what Jacques Ellul calls the *technical imperative: If it can be done it must be done.* The death camps were technically feasible, and they came to pass. The atom bomb was technically feasible, and it came to pass. A final total apocalyptic nuclear annihilation of the earth is technically feasible . . . .

At Auschwitz technical power was still limited in scope and capable of being demonically directed at targeted populations such as Gypsies and Jews. However, with the coming of the bomb, technical power has become autonomous. It has outstripped human intentionality. If there is a next time after Hiroshima and Nagasaki, it will not matter who are the good guys and who the bad guys. The threat of apocalypse that erupted at Auschwitz is no longer limited to the West. Hiroshima symbolizes the globalization of the demonic in technological form, a globalization that forces a meeting of East and West.

The movement from Auschwitz to Hiroshima is psychological, logical, and finally mythological. For Auschwitz and Hiroshima have assumed the mythological status of sacred events that orient human consciousness. They have become transhistorical and transcultural events shaping a public consciousness of our common humanity. The horrifying irony of this is that they are not manifestations of the divine but of the demonic, and the common awareness they are creating is structured by dread. The task of theology in our time, as Arthur Cohen suggests, is to excavate the abyss of the demonic and build a bridge of transcendence over it. We need a common hope to unite us as a global human community, one that can carry us beyond our common dread. Perhaps excavating the abyss will motivate us to build a bridge—a bridge built by *passing over* the abyss and into other religions and cultures in order to *come back* with new insight into ourselves and our own religion and culture.

Auschwitz and Hiroshima warn of the danger of narrative traditions that divide the world into sacred and profane populations as the Nazis did with the categories of the "pure Aryan race" and the "subhuman races." For such divisions can lead to a *killing in order to heal* or the extermination of all who *are not worthy of life,* as the Nazis put it. In such a context the dialogue between Christians and Jews in response to Auschwitz, leads to the inclusion of Buddhists as inevitably as Auschwitz leads to Hiroshima. Despite their dramatic differences, these three traditions have an inner affinity with each other as holy communities, separated from society by their experiences of transcendence but united with each other in their complementary ethical traditions of welcoming the stranger and the outcast. The movement from Auschwitz to Hiroshima provides a prophetic warning of what the future holds if we fail to create a cross-cultural public order that can find unity-in-diversity.

When I began work on this book in 1988 it seemed as if we were living on the brink of nuclear annihilation in a cold war standoff between Russia and the United States. In the time that elapsed while writing it, the unimaginable happened—in the Fall of 1989 the Berlin Wall and the entire Iron Curtain collapsed. The dust had barely settled from these events when in December 1991 the Soviet Union itself ceased to exist, breaking up into a loose confederation of republics. It might seem, in the light of these events, as if the utopianism of history has overtaken the apocalyptic alarm I have sounded in this book. Indeed, there are genuine utopian possibilities latent in our new situation. However, there are also good reasons to be cautious. We should not equate dramatic changes in the surface structure of events with the needed changes in the deep structure of our world. Although the psychological tension of the cold war between Russia and the United States has thawed, we should not forget that enough nuclear weapons still remain at the ready to annihilate us several times over. I do not think the events we have witnessed can yet be counted as genuinely utopian. Instead, I fear that we have just shifted from the depressive apocalyptic phase to the manic utopian phase of the Janus-faced myth that governs modern life. And so we will assume once again that fundamentally nothing needs changing. But a closer examination of the evidence, I think, will reveal that the geography of the sacred and the profane is not so much giving way to utopia as it has simply shifted, splintering along new lines of apocalyptic dualistic confrontation that may disperse the control over nuclear weapons (both within and beyond the former Soviet Union) in ways that are perhaps even more dangerous than before. In any case, the threat of nuclear war is an extreme symptom—one that functions to draw our attention to the demonic tribalistic and technobureaucratic patterns of dehumanization at work in our emerging postmodern world. The point of this book is to analyze those patterns and suggest strategies for breaking them up so as to open up our world to its genuinely utopian possibilities—possibilities which lie beyond the sacral and demonic Janus-faced myth of apocalypse and utopia that presently governs our lives.

The apocalyptic threat of our time is that we shall be swallowed up in the abyss of the demonic. Our utopian hope lies in *passing over* and *coming back*. Our hope lies in creating a new world where strangers are welcome, a world where bonds of cross-cultural understanding could alter our relation to the technical order and at the same time make total destruction of "the other" unthinkable. I believe such a world is possible, based on a new social-ethical coalition of Jews, Christians, Buddhists, and other more "secular" a-theists—one that can have a transformative impact on the rest of the world. What is proposed is not so much a set of answers to the problems of the modern world as it is a process to be engaged in, through which, at the intersection of religions and cultures, we might find our way into the future together. It is not my intent to provide "final solutions" to the world's problems. "Final solutions" and "having a future," I fear, are incompatible goals. For my part, I prefer living in an unfinished world—one open to the utopian possibilities of our humanity as we approach the coming of the third millennium.

To make my case, I have divided the argument of this book into two parts. In Part I, I explore "The Promise of Utopia and the Threat of Apocalypse." In the first chapter, I explore the dialectics of the apocalyptic and utopian themes in our technological civilization through a philosophical analysis of technological utopianism and its apocalyptic distortions from Nietzsche to Jacques Ellul, Gabriel Vahanian, and Karl Mannheim. It examines the role religious experience plays in shaping the narrative imagination—a role powerful enough to give the same apocalyptic or utopian narrative traditions totally opposite linguistic and social meanings. Chapter 2 examines the way these apocalyptic and utopian themes have dominated the imagination of four major critics of culture, two Jewish and two Christian. They are Richard Rubenstein and Arthur Cohen, on the one hand, and Harvey Cox and Jacques Ellul, on the other.

In Chapter 3, I argue that the movement from Auschwitz to Hiroshima represents a demonic inversion of the experience of the holy and its narrative traditions. This movement begins in the rejection of the stranger and ends in a technological globalization of the demonic that forces a meeting of East and West, especially the Jewish-Christian-Buddhist encounter. In making my case for this globalization of the demonic, I draw on the work of Robert Jay Lifton, who argues that the demonic theme of the story used by the Nazi doctors, that is, *killing in order to heal,* reappears in the logic of the nuclear policy of mutually assured destruction that emerged after Hiroshima. This demonic logic, I suggest, has deep roots in a narrative theme common to almost all religions throughout history; namely the narrative theme of *life through death*.

In Part II, I propose a "Utopian Ethics for an Apocalyptic Age." In Chapter 4, I draw inspiration from the work of Paul Tillich, as I outline "theology of culture" as the shape that social ethics takes in a technological civilization, especially after Auschwitz and Hiroshima. I argue that theology of culture finds its norms for the utopian critique of the sacred stories of religions and cultures in the experiences of transcendence found in those holy communities whose narrative traditions have given rise to an ethic of two realms or two kingdoms with an emphasis on welcoming the stranger. Buddhism, Judaism, and Christianity are proposed as the main examples of such holy communities. Some may find it more useful to proceed directly from Chapter 3 to Chapter 5 and return to the theoretical and methodological concerns of this chapter upon completion of the book.

Chapter 5 suggests that the emergence of a human rights ethic since World War II, represented by the creation of the United Nations and its Declaration on Human Rights, is a cross-cultural response to the demonic as manifested at Auschwitz and Hiroshima. Drawing on the narrative tradition of audacity on behalf of the stranger (i.e., chutzpah) and the work of post-Holocaust Jewish theologians such as Elie Wiesel, Emil Fackenheim, and Irving Greenberg, the narrative tradition of *life through death* is rejected in favor of a cross-cultural nonviolent ethic of utopian audacity (chutzpah) on behalf of the stranger. It is further suggested that in Gandhi and Martin Luther King, Jr., we find a historical convergence of narrative traditions from diverse religions and cultures that share the spirit of this ethic of audacity. The narrative traditions that share this ethic have "separated" (as the Hebrew word for "holy" literally means) themselves from the sacred order of the larger society and critiqued that order in the name of the irreducible transcendence or dignity of the human. The notion of human rights, as it develops under the influence of such traditions, is grounded not in nature or "natural rights" but in a range of analogous experiences of our humanity (both religious and secular) as holy (that is, as fundamentally open to transcendence and therefore "empty," "imageless," or "undefinable") and in the shared narrative theme of such traditions—the theme of welcoming the stranger and the outcast. Aspects of the work of Jewish and Buddhist scholars such as Trevor Ling, Masao Abe, Robert Thurman, Irving Greenberg, Elie Wiesel, and Mordechai Rotenberg are reviewed and critiqued in the process of constructing an argument for a cross-cultural ethic of human rights and human liberation.

Chapter 6 views our modern technological civilization through the narrative of Babel, attempting to find ways to transcend the impoverishing vision of secular technobureaucratic rationality. Drawing on the work of Bernard Lonergan and Robert Doran, the myth of storyless technical rationality as the normative story of the secular city is critiqued in order to construct a model of secular reason which allows for pluralism and diversity and whose utopian norm is "welcoming the stranger." On the basis of this model, "human rights" are defended against the critique of Alasdair MacIntyre with the aid of Jeffrey Stout, John Dunne, and Stanley Hauerwas, in hope of promoting the utopian promise of the Babel for our emerging global technological civilization.

In Chapter 7, I construct a model of public policy in which diverse holy communities can cooperate cross-culturally to transform the naked public square of an emerging global civilization into a secular space defined by the "emptiness" of the holy—a space where welcoming the stranger as other, through a process of "passing over," is synonymous with surrendering to the transforming "otherness" of transcendence. The result would be the creation of a public order in which human dignity is normative and in which all political order is subordinate to a nonpolitical (in the technobureaucratic sense) public ethos defined by openness to the stranger. It would be a social order that, in welcoming the stranger, goes beyond tolerance (which forces us to privatize our religious differences) to create a new public order of *unity in diversity.* The construction of such an order requires us, I argue, to think of public policy formation as a process of telling and sharing stories and public policy ethics as the critique of the narrative imagination. The chapter ends with a critique of those narrative interpretations of the Book of Revelation that have fed the nuclear MADness of our recent history by supporting a sacral ethic of "life through death" (Lindsey and Curry) and favors an ethic of "life against death" such as that derived from Jacques Ellul's interpretation of the same narrative in terms of the experience of the holy. This chapter includes a discussion of aspects of the work of Richard Neuhaus, Michael Novak, Max Stackhouse, Alasdair MacIntyre, Stanley Hauerwas, Jacques Ellul, Dean Curry, Hal Lindsey, and Elie Wiesel.

The result, I hope, suggests the possibility of a common coalition of Jews, Christians, Buddhists and other kindred spirits, including more secular strangers in our technological civilization. This would be a coalition against any and all future eruptions of the demonic. Contrary to the usual critique of human rights launched by narrative ethicists as an attempt to impose a single universal storyless ethic on the whole human race, I argue then that an ethic of human dignity and human rights requires just the opposite; namely, a pluralistic coalition of the narrative traditions of holy communities that need to share only one thing in common—hospitality to the stranger.

Finally, in the Epilogue I reflect on the role of religious studies and theological ethics in the secular university after Auschwitz and Hiroshima in relation to the model of alienated theology I have articulated in this book. Here I draw inspiration from the work of Paul Tillich, Mircea Eliade, and Gabriel Vahanian in concluding my own argument.

The Promise of Utopia and the Threat of Apocalypse

Utopia displays the two faces we discerned in myth. On the one hand, it is a justification of the existing [technological] situation and, on the other hand, it is a recourse for man who is unable to change that situation, and who in this way gives himself reasons for continuing to live in it. Utopia . . . is a consolation in the face of slavery, an escape from something one is unable to prevent.

—Jacques Ellul, *The New Demons*

Hope . . . can be situated only in an apocalyptic line of thought, not that there is hope because one has an apocalyptic concept of history, but rather that there is apocalypse because one lives in hope. . . . Hope is the passion for the impossible. . . . What it calls for is not a person's last resort, nor some second breath, but a decision from without which can transform everything.

—Jacques Ellul, *Hope in Time of Abandonment*

In contrast to myth, for which apocalypse constitutes the supreme temptation, technology is tormented by a temptation which wears the mask of a newfangled ideology, namely technocracy, a sort of earthly paradise which no less than the lost paradise negates man. Where myth, allegedly concerned with nature alone, in fact ends up with apocalypse, technology, relentlessly charged with apocalypse (in every sense of the term), in fact constantly collides with that which we continue to call human nature.

—Gabriel Vahanian, *God and Utopia*

Since there is no language without society, from the utopianism of the individual body to the utopianism of the social body we find ourselves in one and the same trajectory, that of a technique of the human, of the humanization of man.

—Gabriel Vahanian, *God and Utopia*

Technology and the Dialectics of Apocalypse and Utopia

The Coming of the Millennium

The year 2001 is at hand, and the world as we know it is passing away. The decade we are in, the 1990s, is nothing less than the "countdown" to a new millennium. It may seem to us to be both the "best of times" and "the worst of times." Our technological genius has burst the boundaries of the earth to send a human being to the moon and relocate us in the infinitely expanded universe of Einstein, while at the same time we have split the atom and unleashed an awesome power capable of transforming our world. It is especially this splitting of the atom that gives rise to our own premillennial ambivalence. On the one hand, atomic power promises us a utopian world of abundance. Yet that very same power hangs over our heads like an apocalyptic cloud of impending doom—one that threatens the total annihilation of the human race. And if in other and more distant ages some dark and enigmatic god seemed to impose such an end on humankind, the irony in our new "secular" and technological age is that we now seem about to bring this end upon ourselves.

To deal constructively with the challenge of imagining our future as we approach the third millennium, it is important to be conscious of the fact that millennialism has played an important role in shaping the Western historical imagination.

On the last day of the year 999, according to an ancient chronicle, the old basilica of St. Peter's at Rome was thronged with a mass of weeping and trembling worshipers awaiting the end of the world. This was the dreaded eve of the millennium, the Day of Wrath when the earth would dissolve into ashes. Many of those present had given away all their possessions to the poor— lands, homes, and household goods—in order to assure for

themselves forgiveness for their trespasses at the Last Judgment
and a good place in heaven near the footstool of the Almighty.
Many poor sinners—and who among them was without sin?—
had entered the church in sackcloth and ashes, having already
spent weeks and months doing penance and mortifying the
flesh. At the altar the Holy Father, Pope Sylvester II, in full papal
regalia, was celebrating the midnight mass. . . . As the minutes
passed and the fateful hour was about to strike, a deathly silence
filled the venerable basilica.[1]

Looking back to the close of the previous millennium, the year 1000, it
appears from our modern vantage point as if we human beings were
still living in a dark age. We know that as the year 1000 approached,
anxiety levels rose throughout Europe. In a world deeply shaped by
the biblical vision of time and history, 1,000 years is a time span of
profound symbolic significance. The Book of Apocalypse, the last and
most enigmatic book of the Christian Bible, seems to suggest that
after a messianic reign of a thousand years God would bring this
world to its final judgment in an cataclysmic apocalyptic end. Nevertheless, the actual coming of that first millennium did not bring
final darkness but new light. In a feudal world that had survived the
collapse of Roman civilization and was still living in fear of barbarian
invaders from the North, it was hard to imagine the untold wonders
that lay ahead. Who could have anticipated that instead of an apocalyptic end, the millennium would bring a utopian new beginning?

The year 1001 brought a millennium not of darkness but of light
and *enlightenment*. A *renaissance* of civilization, a new age of progress,
science, secularization, economic and technological innovation. If the
first millennium was dominated by an apocalyptic sense of doom, the
millennium that followed has been dominated by a utopian euphoria.
This euphoria expressed a growing conviction that the future of the
earth was not so much in the sacred hands of a divine power as in the
secular hands of an increasingly scientific and technologically sophisticated humanity.

If the ancient world saw time as cyclical and without a final
direction, the medieval world was heir to the great cosmic vision of
Augustine, who argued that, although the secular history of the "city
of man" was indeed cyclical, nevertheless hidden within this history
was another, more linear history that moved forward toward a final
and glorious end—the "city of God." Augustine's book, *The City of
God*, definitively shaped the medieval imagination of time and space.
Humanity lived caught in the tension between two cities and two

histories—the one, secular, of little or no final significance, and the other, sacred, promising meaning, purpose, and a glorious destiny. Even as Augustine dismissed pagan cyclical time as an inadequate representation of human destiny so he also dismissed the more enthusiastic apocalyptic expectations of some of his fellow Christians who felt the end was near at hand. The reign of a thousand years spoken of by the Book of Revelation, he argued, refers to no final utopian age of glory and spiritual enthusiasm but rather to the reign of Christ through the church in history.[2] If Augustine's argument successfully dampened the apocalyptic enthusiasm of his peers it did so only at the cost of deferring this enthusiasm until a millennium had come to pass. Never mind that "1,000 years" was a symbolic number for Augustine, referring to an unknown and indefinite amount of time. This subtlety was lost on the average medieval individual facing the coming of the millennium.

For Augustine, the trinitarian reality of God was to be understood, in so far as God could be, by analogy with our human capacity for the word that enables us to experience self-consciousness: a consciousness in which, he argued, knowledge of self and knowledge of God are inextricably intertwined. The Trinity, one yet three, is fundamentally unimaginable (i.e., un-image-able) in a way analogous to the un-image-ableness of the human self. Through the mediation of the word, the mind comes to know itself as both one and yet three (one consciousness yet three—memory, intelligence, and will). "Trinity" was a concept that resulted from the reworking of Greek metaphysical categories in relation to self-consciousness so as to express by analogy the Hebraic notion of a God who can act in time without losing transcendence; that is, without collapsing into pure immanence or pantheism. Thus, even as the human word can proceed from the speaker to effect changes in the world without compromising the integrity of the speaker, so, even more so, God retains transcendent integrity (i.e., is not absorbed by the world) when God sends both Word and Spirit into the world. *Trinity* referred to the God who is revealed through the action of Word and Power (Spirit) in history. But not in all the events of history, only in those events that make up the history of the "city of God" (biblical and church history) hidden within the "city of man." *Trinity* affirmed the presence of God in history but it did not dictate the direction of the history of the human city. That history continued to manifest its relatively meaningless cyclical patterns of advance and decline.

Augustine shaped the biblical narrative into "a tale of two cities," a symbolic universe within which medieval humanity could dwell. But the elapse of the first millennium brought a new prophet with a new vision of time and space—a Cistercian monk and abbot from southern Italy, Joachim of Fiore (1132–1202). Whereas Augustine required human beings to live in two separate narratives (i.e., two kingdoms) at the same time, Joachim offered humanity to chance to live in one. Whereas Augustine's vision demanded that one accept the relative meaninglessness of the secular order even as one embraced the meaningfulness of sacred history, now Joachim offered humanity one history in a vision that would unite both in a single narrative of spiritual and material progress. The vision of the three ages of history offered up by this eccentric monk and mystic shaped the utopian mythos that came to dominate the second millennium— the myth of progress. Joachim is to the millennium that gave birth to modernity what Augustine was to the medieval vision of the previous millennium—the great foundational architect of a new symbolic universe.

In his *Everlasting Gospel,* Joachim offered a vision that undid Augustine's. Joachim offered his own trinitarian vision that dismantled the Augustinian trinitarian symbolism of self-consciousness and applied the symbols to a three-stage vision of history. Resurrecting the very apocalyptic tradition Augustine had suppressed, he spoke of history as having three ages: the age of the Father (beginning with Abraham), which was superseded by the age of the Son (beginning with Christ), and finally he predicted the coming of a third age— that of the Spirit whose leader would appear by the year 1260. Later, the radical Franciscans identified Francis of Assisi as that leader. As with the apocalypticism of the Montanist tradition in early Christianity, in this third age the institutional church would give way to direct guidance by the Holy Spirit. This direct infusion of the Spirit would create a natural spontaneous harmony between all individuals and render all institutions superfluous. Thus this tradition was anticlerical, antiinstitutional, and anarchistic in its apocalyptic intensity. The third age would be an age of perfection, of perfect freedom and harmony, which was destined to last a thousand years.

Eric Voegelin has argued that the Joachimite symbolism of the three ages provides the fundamental mythos for the unfolding of modernity in the West. The symbolism of history as three ages captured our historical imagination (e.g., the division of Western history into ancient, medieval, and modern with its implied vision of progress). For Joachim the third age was identified with the triumph of a mystical monasticism over the institutional church. But his three ages became increasingly secularized into the myth of *history as progress.* So we find it reappearing in Gotthold Lessing's Enlightenment vision of the three ages of the education of the human race: childhood, adolescence, and adulthood. The last or third age is identified of course with the age of Enlightenment, in which the emergence of the autonomy of reason would lead to a natural and rational harmony among human beings. The vision of three ages is also foundational to the nineteenth century, where Auguste Comte divided history into the ages of *myth, philosophy,* and *science,* with the third age again promising fulfillment. Hegel provides yet another version with his three stages of freedom in history, a vision Marx revised to culminate in his own version of the third age—the classless society. And we find the third age myth also underlying Hitler's vision of the *Third Reich,* or third kingdom, which he proclaimed would last a thousand years. The myth of the third age has incontestably fueled diverse visions of history as progress.[3]

The modern mythos is at one and the same time both apocalyptic and utopian. It is apocalyptic in that it demands a decisive break with the past, a break that in its more radical manifestations is conceived of as requiring a revolutionary apocalyptic battle between the forces of light and of darkness. It is utopian in that what is imagined to follow this radical break with the past is a new utopian order of harmony and perfection that reverses all the trials, tribulations and suffering of history. Its radical historical power comes from the fact that, unlike Augustine's myth of two cities, Joachim's vision leads to the fusing of the spiritual and material into one history in which spiritual progress is identified with material progress leading to an explosion of energy directed toward the political, scientific, and technological transformation of the earth and its societies into the various imagined visions (divine and demonic) of the utopian perfection of the third age.

Technological Utopianism á la 1965: Of Madmen, Astronauts, and the Death of God

In 1965, a human being walked in space for the first time in history. On March 18 of that year, cosmonaut Alexei Leonov stepped into space for a ten minute walk. He was followed in less than three months by the American astronaut Edward White. What is striking about the human exploration of space is that unlike all earlier pioneering efforts in human history, the whole world was able to participate, to see what was happening virtually as it happened, thanks to modern mass media. Thus on millions of TV sets around the world an image was cast up of our contemporary situation of virtually mythic proportions. Cut loose from the earth's atmosphere, floating free at the end of a tether linking him to his space craft, the space walker symbolized the technological utopianism of an apocalyptic age. The optimism of the decade that would put a human being on the moon saw the astronaut as the symbol of our technological capacity to transcend all limits, to both create and discover new worlds without limit. Yet this symbol was not without ambiguity. Floating in space, without a clear sense of direction, the astronaut was also a reminder of the demonic normlessness of a technological civilization. This is the very normlessness predicted by Nietzsche's madman at the end of the nineteenth century.

Modern human beings, Nietzsche suggested, had committed a deed of world-historical import. And yet they remained ignorant of its reality because they had not yet experienced its earth-shaking consequences. As Nietzsche tells it, a madman entered the public square crying "I seek God, I seek God." Many who did not believe in God began to chide him—"Did he lose his way? . . . Is he hiding? . . . Has he gone on a voyage?"

> The madman jumped into their midst and pierced them with his glances. "Whither is God" he cried. "I shall tell you. We have killed him—you and I. All of us are his murderers. But how have we done this? How were we able to drink up the sea? Who gave us the sponge to wipe away the entire horizon? What did we do when we unchained this earth from its sun? Whither is it moving now? Whither are we moving now? Away from all suns? Are we not plunging continually? Backward, sideward, forward, in all directions? Is there any up or down left? Are we not straying as through an infinite nothing? Do we not feel the breath of empty space? Has it not become colder? Is not night and more night coming on all the while? Must not lanterns be lit in the morning? Do we not hear anything yet of the noise of the gravediggers who are burying God? Do we not smell anything yet of God's decomposition? Gods too decompose. God is dead. God remains dead. And we have killed him. How shall we, the murderers of all murderers, comfort ourselves? What was holiest and most powerful of all that the world has yet owned has bled to death under our knives. Who will wipe this blood off us?

> What water is there for us to clean ourselves? What festivals of atonement, what sacred games shall we have to invent? Is not the greatness of this deed too great for us? Must not we

ourselves become gods simply to seem worthy of it? There has never been a greater deed; and whoever will be born after us— for the sake of this deed he will be part of a higher history than all history hitherto."

Here the madman fell silent and looked again at his listeners; and they too were silent and stared at him in astonishment. At last he threw his lantern on the ground, and it broke and went out. "I come too early," he said then; "my time has not come yet. This tremendous event is still on its way, still wandering—it has not yet reached the ears of man. Lightning and thunder require time, the light of the stars requires time, deeds require time even after they are done, before they can be seen and heard. This deed is still more distant from them than the most distant stars—*and yet they have done it themselves.*"[4]

What is astonishing about the imagery of this passage, originally published in 1882, is how uncannily it corresponds to the image of our space walker in 1965. It is as if Nietzsche's prophecy of the deed that was yet light years away from being acknowledged had now finally entered human consciousness. It is as if, in some uncanny way, Nietzsche had seen our astronaut floating in space and had grasped with utter lucidity the implication of that experience. "Who gave us the sponge to wipe away the entire horizon? Whither are we moving now? Away from all suns? Are we not plunging continually? Backward, sideward, forward, in all directions? Is there any up or down left?" It is as if he could foresee that the modern secular, scientific, and technological civilization which was coming to birth in his time would lead inevitably to the death of God; that is, to a normless world "cut loose from its sun," cut loose from the bonds of gravity, adrift in deep space—floating and tumbling, without a sense of direction, suffering the consequences of the disappearance of the horizon as one breaks free of the earth.

Auschwitz and Apocalyptic Madness: From the Death of God to Genocide

Scarcely more than half a century after Nietzsche's madman had unleashed his prophecy the Nazis came along to embrace his vision of a normless *will to power.* Nietzsche had offered a vision of a new type of individual who would have to take charge of human history after the death of God; namely, the *Übermensch* or self-transcending person. Such individuals would have the courage to "transvalue all values" and remake the world in their own image. Nietzsche, of course, had a somewhat aristocratic vision of these new individuals. But his vision was easily usurped by the Nazis who imagined themselves, the pure Aryan race, as the natural embodiment of this superior human being who would recreate the world through a *will to power.* The Nazi program of attempted genocide of the Jews is a logical outcome of this new normless situation expressed in Nietzsche's parable of "the Death of God." In a world where power is the final arbiter of values and *might makes right,* deicide is inexorably followed by genocide.

It is not the will to power itself which is unique to the modern situation. The will to power has been present in every age and every culture. What is unique is the presence of the will to power in a culture without counterbalancing norms to hold it in check. In traditional or premodern societies religion played a central and public role in influencing the social order. What all traditional societies have in common is the belief that the order of society is part of a normative order of nature as structured by the sacred ancestors, gods or God. Because the order of society was considered part of the order of nature as divinely established, such societies were conservatively ordered. Society, like nature, was viewed as fixed and given and not an object to be manipulated and changed.

Modern society differs fundamentally from all traditional societies in that in the modern world we now understand society as artificial rather than natural. We now see society as a construct, shaped by human decisions, rather than as an extension of nature. The essence of technological civilization is not the transformation of nature, nor is it the proliferation of machines. It is, rather, the awareness of self and society as human constructs that can be shaped and changed. Neither astronomy nor chemistry nor even physics has produced the revolution in self-understanding in which we are caught up. These sciences were revolutionary for an industrial society. The revolutionary sciences for a technological civilization are the human sciences—especially history, sociology, and anthropology. It was the new comparative sociohistorical consciousness accompanying the emergence of the social sciences in the nineteenth century that gave birth to a consciousness of society as a human product rather than an extension of nature. Society, so understood, is the expression of modern technological consciousness. Industrial society, which attempted to shape and change nature, has been superseded by a technological civilization that seeks to shape and change not only nature but the human self and society.

The problem is that the very process by which human beings

have come to think of society as capable of being shaped and changed is a secularizing or desacralizing process. The public order of traditional societies was stabilized by the firm belief that this order was part of a value-laden natural order determined by the gods and ancestors. Each society saw its social order through the lens of a sacred myth or story, what Peter Berger calls a *sacred canopy,* which made its social order appear to be a direct expression of the natural order. But with the emergence of sociohistorical consciousness in the nineteenth century, the variety of cultures strung out through time and across cultural boundaries came to be compared. As a result the natural order of each society came to be seen as an artificial construct and all cultural values came to be thought of as relative. These values no longer appeared, as they had from within each society, as firmly fixed in a cosmic order. Now they appeared as subjective, culturally relative, human options.

This is the point at which the fundamental crisis of modern society appears. Because human values in premodern societies were typically embedded in normative myths of natural order, their demythologization, which made it possible to think of changing society at the same time undermined the very norms by which such decisions could be made. Precisely at that point at which human beings became conscious of their ability to shape and change society they lost access to the norms needed to make those decisions. It is this situation, which Nietzsche addresses with his parable of the *death of God,* that unchained the earth from its sun so that we now drift aimlessly in space without any sense of up or down. We have lost our sense of moral direction.

The world we have made for ourselves seems to be the embodiment of Babel—a confusing pluralism of voices and values. We live, it seems, in a sea of cultural and ethical relativism in which all ethical choice is reduced to arbitrary personal preference. With no rational way to adjudicate moral disputes such disagreements are reduced to ideological struggles based on the will to power. It is the tragic paradox of our time that the increase of our power over nature and society has been in inverse proportion to our capacity to discover a normative consensus by which to govern the exercise of this power.

We are faced now with what I believe to be the most serious and pressing problem of our time: the discovery and articulation of the philosophical and theological foundations of a normative social ethic whereby culture itself can be critiqued and hence shaped and changed through those public policies and personal commitments that truly promote the human good.

From Auschwitz to Hiroshima: A Prophetic Warning
of Global Apocalypse

Our modern technological civilization offers us seemingly infinite utopian opportunities to recreate ourselves (e.g., genetic engineering, behavioral engineering) and our societies (social engineering) and our world (chemical engineering, atomic engineering). But having transcended all limits and all norms, we seem bereft of a normative vision to govern the use of our utopian techniques. This normlessness threatens us with demonic self-destruction. It is this dark side of technical civilization that was revealed to us not only at Auschwitz and but also at Hiroshima.

Auschwitz represents a severe challenge to the religious traditions of the West: to Christians, because of the complicity of Christianity in the anti-Judaic path that led to Auschwitz renders its theological categories ethically suspect; to Jews, because their victim status presses faith in the God of history and in humanity to the breaking point. But the path to Auschwitz, and from Auschwitz to Hiroshima, represents a challenge, equally severe, for the scientific and technical, secular culture of the Enlightenment. We do not seem to have fared any better under a secular ethic than we did under a religious one. Indeed we have fared worse. Genocide it seems is a unique product of the modern secular world and its technically competent barbarians.

Auschwitz stands for a demonic period in modern Western civilization in which the religious, political and technological developments converged to create a society whose primary purpose was the most efficient organization of that entire society for the purpose of exterminating all persons who were regarded as aliens and strangers—especially the Jews. The Nazi vision of the pure Aryan society represents a utopian vision of demonic proportions—a vision that inspired an apocalyptic revolutionary program of genocide. It reveals at once both a time of "The Death of God" in the Nietzschean sense and yet the resurgence of religion, that is, a demonic religiosity that creates a new public order in which all pluralism is eliminated from the public square and in which virtually nothing is sacred—not even human life. The period of the Holocaust stands as prophetic warning to a technological civilization that has no other norm than the *will to power*.

If Auschwitz embodies the demonic use of technology against targeted populations to commit genocide, Hiroshima and Nagasaki represent the last such use of technology. For with the coming of Nuclear warfare, technology has outstripped human intentionality so that if the bomb is ever used again, genocide will be transformed into

collective suicide or *omnicide*—the destruction of all life. Having enemies is a luxury no community on the face of the earth can any longer
afford. If there is a next time, it will not matter who is right and who is
wrong, we shall all perish in the flames. Auschwitz and Hiroshima
suggest that the millennium which brought us the utopian age of
progress threatens to bring itself to an abrupt apocalyptic conclusion.
The age of the bomb seems to have shattered and restructured the
millennial myth. No longer can we imagine that apocalypse will be
followed by utopia. The myth of unfolding stages seems to have
broken apart into an absolute Either-Or: either Apocalypse or Utopia.
Not wishing to face the terror of the first option we enthusiastically
(although uneasily) embrace the second. Through a somewhat forced
utopian euphoria we try to repress the prophetic warnings of Auschwitz and Hiroshima which remind us that a normless world will
inevitably end in apocalyptic self-destruction.

The Visions of Two Madmen: Apocalypse or Utopia?

> When he [the Lamb] opened the sixth seal, I looked, and there came a
> great earthquake. . . . The sky vanished like a scroll rolling itself up
> and every mountain and island was removed from its place.
>
> (The Book of Revelation 6:12–14)

The mythic and metaphorical complexity of our situation, captured in our TV image of the spacewalker and in Nietzsche's parable
of the death of God, is further complicated by the fact that the visions
of apocalypse and utopia are rooted in the biblical tradition. There is a
relationship between Nietzsche's madman, our space walker, and
John of Patmos, the visionary author of the *Apocalypse* (i.e., The Book
of Revelation). The former two are dependent on the later. John, too,
is a kind of madman who in his own way has an extraterrestrial
vision. He envisions the disappearance of the horizon as the sky is
rolled up like a scroll and the normal order of things is brought to an
end. John's vision is also both apocalyptic and utopian. The apocalyptic disappearance of the earthly horizon presages the coming of a new
horizon, the horizon of a new city—a New Jerusalem. Like our modern technological world, it too, is a kind of secular city, for there is no
temple in this city (Rev. 21:22). Yet it is marked not by the absence of
God but rather a universal presence in which God is both "nowhere"
and "everywhere," being "all in all." The paradox of John's apocalyptic vision is that, although he too experiences the loss of horizons, he
does not experience the normless vertigo of our Nietzschean space
walker. On the contrary, the loss of horizons is for him a sign of hope

because it presages the destruction of the demonic that subverts the utopianism of creation by promoting a literal and nonutopian apocalyptic destiny for the earth.

The narrative of mythic proportions that dominates our technological civilization is the Janus-faced myth of *apocalypse and utopia*. This narrative is ethically paralyzing. Convinced that technology is the ultimate power governing our destiny we have surrendered ourselves into its hands, and having made this decision we vacillate between moments of utopian euphoria, when all seems so promising that we wish to change nothing, and apocalyptic despair, when all seems so threatening that we do not believe we can change anything. The paradox is that it is our utopian euphoria that sends us careening toward an apocalyptic final solution. As a result, a kind of autonomous techno-logic takes hold whose demonic face was disclosed at Auschwitz and again at Hiroshima. Technology has replaced nature as that realm of power that has become our fate.

While technological utopianism seems to transform all new beginnings into tragic and demonic endings, the ancient seer of the Apocalypse, whose vision still remains with us, dreamt of a normative utopian world, a world of new beginnings and new creation delivered from all demonic powers. Our narratives of *apocalypse* and *utopia* are complex and ambiguous. At the popular level of our technological culture the human imagination is lured into embracing the infinite utopian possibilities of our civilization as symbolized by our astronaut breaking free of the earth. Yet our psyches unconsciously nag us daily with apocalyptic images of technological self-destruction. At some level we are all mad, aware that the technological powers we hope will deliver us are the very ones that may destroy us. And yet another possibility is hinted at in the apocalyptic vision of this other madman, John of Patmos. If our technological utopianism seems inherently apocalyptic, still perhaps in our history is yet another kind of apocalypticism, which is inherently utopian. If the demonic normlessness of the former would lead us down the path to oblivion, it may be possible that the iconoclasm of the demonic in the latter may yet offer genuinely utopian possibilities.

Language, Technique, and the Utopianism of the Body

In spite of our attempts to sustain our utopian optimism by repressing the memories of Auschwitz and Hiroshima, our hope now seems to have become the victim of its own inner contradictions—a world of plenty becomes a world of pollution, a world made secure by

"Star Wars" becomes the most insecure world of all. We are attracted by the utopian possibilities of technology only to find ourselves faced with an apocalyptic future. The more we seek the first the closer we come to the second. Our hope paradoxically seems to create a hopeless situation. It is becoming apparent that we are indeed the victims of the technological, Janus-faced mythos of Apocalypse and Utopia.

It is not a matter of one single coherent myth but rather of diverse fragments that, each in its own way, reinforces the sacral experience of technical power. It is only necessary to recall the diverse myths of the gods of nature in ancient Greece or ancient India to realize that myth is inherently pluralistic and fragmentary. Nor will you necessarily find the words *apocalypse* and *utopia* explicitly expressed in these diverse narrative fragments. Rather, these words name fundamental attitudes expressing countless hopes and fears in an endless variety of imagined scenarios found in the mass media (news, advertising, drama, etc.) and in our private dreams and fantasies. At some level, conscious or unconscious, we are awed by the power of technology and this awe expresses itself in the ambivalence of the *awesome* and the *awful,* the ambivalent fascination with a technological world that promises utopian abundance yet threatens an abrupt apocalyptic end to the human race. This mythos enchants us with its bright side, the visible and alluring face of utopia, while its dark apocalyptic side remains largely out of sight. The dark side lurks in the half conscious fears that sporadically raid the borders of our consciousness or attack us through the subterranean passages of our dark dreams, occasionally erupting with a paralyzing force into full consciousness. It is our enchantment by this mythos that is ethically paralyzing. It renders us unable to act, for when we are in a utopian mood we do not wish to change and when we are in an apocalyptic mood we do not believe we can.

In the light of Auschwitz and Hiroshima and of our contemporary circumstances, the first step of our ethical task is to discover how we might conceive of the relationship between our humanity and technology so as to render technology the servant of human freedom. What we are seeking is a philosophical anthropology that is able to locate the common denominator between our humanity and technology so that it suggests a course of action effective in subordinating technology to human freedom.

We might begin by suggesting, as Jacques Ellul has, that the essential characteristic of technology is not the machine, but rather technique. As the ideal of efficient management overtakes every human activity, it produces a social transformation in which society as a whole becomes the object of efficient management. Such a society, Herbert Richardson suggests, is governed by "sociotechnics—that new knowledge whereby man exercises technical control not only over nature, but also over all the specific institutions that make up society."[5] Society is integrated into a single rational system, a totally artificial environment. If the classical Greek term *techné* suggested an art or technique that followed or idealized nature, modern technique reverses this order. Now nature must follow art; reality is subordinated to the transforming activity of imagination.[6]

Technology may represent a triumph of human freedom over nature, but nature has only yielded to a law equally harsh—that of efficiency. In a technological society personal preference inevitably must yield to the criterion of efficiency, the rational calculation of the best means to be used to achieve the maximum results with a minimum of cost and effort. Such means render obsolete all those techniques that are less efficient. Actions that do not conform to the requirements of efficiency simply cannot compete.

If we recognize that technology is essentially technique, then the horizon of our considerations is defined not so much by the encounter between human beings and machines but is more intimately associated with our humanity, with what Gabriel Vahanian aptly calls the "techniques of the human."[7] Technique is, after all, simply method; the means or ensemble of means selected for the realization of a given end. But the raising of the question of means and ends is a uniquely human ability given with our capacity for speech. If our humanity was once defined by the capacity for "reason" (*homo sapiens*), today it is more typically defined by the capacity for toolmaking and tool using (*homo faber*). But toolmaking hardly renders "reasoning" superfluous in defining the human. Rather both are rooted in our capacity for speech.

The capacity for speech is the capacity to symbolize and conceptualize. It is the capacity to experience a moment of hesitation between what we have been and what we shall be. This capacity is created by the ability to abstract from the immediate rush of experience and represent to ourselves not only what is but also what might have been. Language enables us to represent to ourselves the felt contrast in our experience between actuality and possibility.

This capacity of language, then, introduces the essential ambiguity that uniquely characterizes our humanity, namely, the freedom that emerges with the capacity to envision possibilities yet to be realized. As Sartre would say, *we are what we are not and are not what we are.*

The human alone is defined by the capacity to become what it is not. Insofar as our humanity is characterized by the capacity for language, we can say that the human is essentially technique; that is, the human person as a linguistic animal is essentially his or her own "means" for realizing "ends." Language, as the capacity of the human, is the metatechnique of which every specific technique is but a specialized instance. Every technology is a specialized language or technique for the realization of human possibilities.

When Thomas More coined the word *utopia,* he cleverly drew upon the meanings of two possible Greek prefixes attached to the word for "place" (i.e., *topos*). In transliteration, the choices would appear as *ou-topos,* meaning "no place" and *eu-topos* meaning "good place." Certainly both meanings apply. Utopia is the vector of human hope for a better world, a "good place." But utopia must never be definitively identified with any particular place. To do so would be a premature closure of history. In a sense, then, utopia must always remain "no place."[8]

Ordinarily *utopia* should not be used as a noun, but, more correctly, as an adjective. Its valid application is as a description of the human condition in its linguistic, or more precisely, its verbal condition as possibility ever to be realized.[9] The human occurs through the realization of new possibilities, in the creation of new worlds. Human beings are utopian in so far as they move along the vector of their hopes to create a new world; and they remain utopian only in so far as they are able, ever and again, to transcend the given horizon of the present world to imagine a new one. Therein lies the ultimate freedom that makes us human. It is the freedom to define a world rather than be defined by and confined to one.

The human occurs wherever nature gives voice to its utopian possibilities. It is "through language," says Gabriel Vahanian, "that man transcends the mute horizon of his body."[10] The body is that place where nature ceases to be mute and by some miracle is delivered into the condition of speech. That the human occurs as a bodily condition means that the body is our most intimate and immediate experience of nature. Our primary experience of nature is not that of "something out there," but of the body as the condition that makes the "self" possible. "The human body," says Alfred North Whitehead, "is that region of the world which is the primary field of human expression."[11] Through the techniques of language the body gives birth to "self"; that is, the utopian capacity to become what it is not. We are those beings who are able to imagine a world before it exists and then devise the means for its realization. Through our humanity, nature is transformed into culture, the natural into the artificial, and the earth is humanized.

The Technological City as the Utopian Horizon of the Body-Self

The human occurs on the boundary line between the natural and the artificial. It occurs where nature transcends itself and gives voice to its utopian possibilities. Where nature is delivered from its muteness through the act of speech, there you have in one and the same moment the appearance of community and individuality. Indeed our individuatlity presupposes community. This is true first of all because our humanity occurs through the body, and every body exists in a condition of ecological interdependence with its environment. In this sense the whole universe is one body, a community of becoming characterized by unity in diversity. Second, our humanity occurs only through language—the communal reality out of which the uniquely human dimension of individuality emerges. In this respect Merleau-Ponty has observed, "we begin reading a philosopher by giving the words he makes use of 'common meaning' and, little by little, through what is at first imperceptible reversal, his speech comes to dominate language, and it is his use of words which ends up assigning them a new and characteristic signification."[12] Language as the common human reality inherited from the past is the medium through which the individual experiences himself or herself, first as communal and then through the creative addition of his or her own living speech, as uniquely individual in contributing to the common linguistic condition.

There is no such thing as a private language. How could a language understood only by the speaker be a language? Would we not say that the individual simply babbles, that he or she has not yet learned to speak? Because language is the utopian technique of our humanity, the utopian imagination always manifests itself in a vision of a new community. The human city is the symbol of the linguistic condition of the body-self. Even as the body can be individual only through an ecological interdependence, the body-self in its individuality can only occur through a dialectical interdependence with the ecology of his or her cultural-linguistic universe, which is the city.

The city is essentially a utopian phenomenon because through it, nature becomes what it is not, that is cultural or artificial. The city as the communal condition of the human is the midwife of all techniques of the human. Civilization is said to begin with the city precisely because in the city the languages (i.e., techniques) of the human are liberated from their ethnocentric tribal roots to converge to create a common human future that transcends all "natural" differences.

It is in the cities that the various technologies, that is, techniques of the human, proliferate and gradually find themselves coordinated into a technological system in which every technical specialization heightens the condition of ecological interdependence through which the utopian possibilities for a common future are realized. Every technology is a specialized language for questioning nature in the hope that it might yield its utopian possibilities. Every technology is rooted, first of all, in the scientific question, "What is the structure of matter, of life, of mind, of society?" This question is then followed by the technological question, "What are the techniques for the appropriation of these structures for human purposes?"[13] So the human realizes itself, for example, in a movement from physics to engineering, from biology to medicine, from psychology to psychiatry, from sociology to politics, etc. Wherever the human occurs, nature puts itself in question to transcend itself toward its utopian possibilities. Wherever the human occurs, the natural gives way to the artificial, and human beings transform themselves through the transformation of their utopian horizon—the city.

When the engineering mentality, with its commitment to the appropriation of the structures of nature to manipulate and transform nature according to human purposes, is combined with sociological consciousness of the malleability of self and society, the result is the technological city as the first consciously utopian city. Now the city is systematically and self-consciously organized to apply the most efficient techniques for the transformation of human beings and society toward the realization of that which it is not, toward the realization of its utopian future.

It is no accident that in a technological society the meaning of the human undergoes its most radical challenge. On every front nature is forced to give way to the artificial. No longer are such claims as "men are naturally superior to women" or "whites are naturally superior to blacks" or "heterosexuals are naturally superior to homosexuals" consonant with the experience of the human. The emergence of the technological society is radically utopian precisely because it demythologizes human self-understanding as a construct of nature. We no longer experience our humanity as a fixed order of nature, but as radically technological, as utopian, as that which is human precisely because it is able to transcend the horizon of the given to realize a new self and a new society.

As historical and sociological consciousness came to clear expression in the nineteenth century, this utopian understanding of the self was definitively articulated by Friedrich Nietzsche through his vision of the *Übermensch*. In Nietzsche's *Übermensch* we find conjoined the Dionysian freedom of the will and the Apollonian orderliness of reason. That is to say, the *Übermensch* is characterized by the "inexorable solar will."

By combining into one unitary principle the narrative identities of Dionysus (the god of the ecstatic and tranformative will) and Apollo (the sun god or god of rational order), Nietzsche symbolizes the newly emerging utopian self, the technological self, whose reality consists in overcoming, going beyond; that is, in continually creating ever new rational orders through an act of will that transvalues all values. Although Nietzsche's *Übermensch* has been variously translated as "overman" and "superman," his meaning is probably made clearer by translating it as "the self-transcending self." The key to this self-transcending self for Nietzsche is "style," which is the art or skill (*techné* or technique) of creating one's own rational order through self-creation. "One thing is needful. *'Giving style' to one's character*—a great and rare art! It is exercised by those who see all the strengths and weaknesses of their own nature, and then comprehend them in an artistic plan until everything appears as art and reason and even weakness delights the eye."[14] The self is an artificial reality, a self-transcending reality, which reworks and redefines nature until even weakness becomes strength. For Nietzsche, the human occurs in the self-transcending overcoming of "human nature," in the utopian freedom to create an artificial self, a new and unique creation that exists only in the realizing of its self-transcending freedom.

"Style," says Whitehead, "is an aesthetic sense, based on admiration for the direct attainment of a foreseen end, simply and without waste."[15] Style is the essence of technique, the "exclusive privilege of the expert." Indeed, "with style you attain your end and nothing but your end. With style the effect of your activity is calculable, and foresight is the last gift of gods to men. With style your power is increased, for your mind is not distracted with irrelevancies, and you are more likely to attain your object."[16] Style is the essence of modern technology. It is the efficient use of means to realize the new and artificial. With style the dual meanings of *techné* as *art* and *skill* are joined in the utopian task of realizing a new self through the creation of a new society. Style is what characterizes the technological city as a self-consciously utopian reality.

The Apocalyptic Deformation of Utopianism: Procrustean and Protean Distortions

If the utopianism of modern technology is rooted in our linguistic capacity for self-creation through the recreation of our world, why is it that technology is so widely experienced today as our fate—an autonomous power out of control? The answer, Manfred Stanley suggests, has to do with the technological nature of language.[17] Language is a "form of consciousness, (and false consciousness), and . . . an instrument of world creation, destruction, corruption, and control."[18] The first, primary and metatechnological feat of the human, we might say, is the creation of a symbolic universe, a cultural world through which the human realizes itself. What causes the linguistic reality of the technological society to become our fate is the deformation of the utopianism of "technique" into the linguistically opaque condition of "technicism."

Technicism is the linguistic "mystification" of the human world that obscures the "free and responsible nature of human action" through "metaphorical misapplication" of scientific and technical imagery.[19] It is a form of the Procrustean myth that seeks to truncate reality to fit one's a priori categories. It is the creation of a symbolic world of discourse dominated by the theoretical explanations of "experts" who characterize the world as a universe of global forces, processes and transformations entirely unrelated to human agency. "The person as agent" is "made to disappear almost entirely from theoretical attention when moral preoccupation with collective survival and social engineering induces the humanistic disciplines to be unduly influenced by models drawn from physical sciences."[20] When the explicit connections between human agency and our cultural universe are not clearly articulated within this symbolic universe, the ethical imagination is deprived of the means of arriving at those insights by which human action could be effectively guided to intervene in the processes of our world to define it rather than be defined by it.

The technicist objectification of the world results in the atrophy of our ethical imagination and the abdication of our utopian self-transcending freedom before an apparently autonomous technological phenomenon. The technological world is reduced to a "natural phenomenon" understood on the basis of models drawn from the

physical sciences. These models still interpret reality through a Cartesian (mechanical) view of nature that separates mind (self) and body
and thereafter can find no connection between them and hence no
place for the self within the world that science describes. There is no
hint, in such models, of our humanity as the linguistic-utopian technique or expression of nature. When nature is no longer understood
as capable of giving birth to the human, it loses its utopian capacity
and becomes our fate. It is at this point, as Karl Mannheim's work
suggests, that the utopian becomes ideological, and that which masquerades itself as an instrument of new creation becomes, in fact,
guarantor of the "status quo."[21] When the utopian becomes ideological, technology becomes a fate beyond human control headed toward
some literally apocalyptic destiny.

The ideological mystification of technique does not by itself explain the power that technicism exercises over human beings. Insofar
as every person exercises a linguistic capacity, each and every person
must be induced to participate in the linguistic game of technicism
and thereby legitimize it. To explain this further power of technicism
over human beings, Stanley, finds it necessary to appeal to the religious function of technique. The power of technicism comes from its
appeal to profound human needs and hopes. In so doing it becomes
more than an objectification and mystification of the experienced human world. It becomes a full-scale mythology, a utopian representation of human destiny that satisfies the human needs and hopes for
security, abundance, and meaning. Stanley, in fact, suggests that the
inducement for acquiescence in the linguistic game of technicism is
the millennial hope it holds out; namely, that technology will make
possible the conquest of scarcity and all the uncertainties of life, thus
creating a paradise of abundance capable of fulfilling all desires. In
this respect technicism becomes "a myth of the fullest eschatological
stature." As such it is nothing less than a "reconstitution of a world
metaphor . . . a supremely religious, as well as social phenomenon."[22]

Technicism is a reduction of our humanity to a fixed and autonomous order of nature in a Cartesian mode. As Jacques Ellul has suggested, the technological or technicist society has come to serve the
role nature once did in human experience. Even as nature once was,
so now the technicist society is experienced as that all-encompassing
environment which provides human beings with life and abundance
and also threatens them with the possibility of capricious annihilation
and death. The technicist society, like nature, is experienced as the
object of both fascination and dread, Rudolf Otto's classical descrip-

tion of the sacred.²³ Even as technique is uprooting and transforming our humanity, its technicist deformation permits it to appear as our new nature, in the sense of a new, fixed, autonomous, sacralized order to which we must conform in order to survive. Unable to imagine existence "outside" the technicist society, experiencing an absolute dependence on it in life and death, acquiescent to its autonomous requirements because of the hope that it will ultimately fulfill all human desires, human beings in the technicist society are seduced into embracing technicism and giving up the utopian freedom to transcend and define our world. We settle for the pseudo-utopian ideology of a technicist society that, although promising the new, ever more securely conforms us to the status quo.

Nietzsche's *Übermensch* is unlikely to become a dominant cultural type in this technicist society, for in Nietzsche's view, human beings prefer the comfortable and secure morality of "the herd." Rather than face the reality of the artificiality of the human, the terrifying freedom of self-creation, people cling willingly to the illusion that their values represent the fixed and natural order of human existence. In this way human beings *cosmicize* their world, imputing to it the sacred status of an unchanging cosmological order. This is the first manner in which the utopianism of technology is transformed, or rather deformed. By this process technology becomes an autonomous and unchangeable reality subject to the apocalyptic destiny of the technicist imperative—*If it can be done it must be done.*

This cosmological order with its "herd" morality protecting the status quo seemed to Nietzsche to be legitimized by the "pathetic" God of Jews and Christians as mediated through bourgeois mediocrity in nineteenth-century Europe. In this context, the advent of the technological self, that is, of the *Übermensch*, to transcend and transvalue the world could only mean the death of God. This death, Nietzsche insisted, was in fact an act of murder, the necessary act of the self-transcending self in the exercise of its "solar will." If God's existence legitimizes the fixed order of the present, then the overcoming of this order means overcoming God. The self-transcending *Übermensch* replaces God as creator of the world. "*If* there were gods, how could I endure not to be a god! *Hence* there are no gods."²⁴ The loss of "human nature" that occurs with the appearance of the self-transcending self and the murder of God renders the universe a void that must be filled by the autonomous creativity of the self-transcending self, alone and without guidance.

This rejection of the "cosmological" status of the world in favor of the "transvaluation of all values" by Nietzsche's *Übermensch* represents the other extreme in the apocalyptic distortion of utopian free-dom. It is one we could call the *existentialist* distortion of technological utopianism. If it rejects technicism, it does so only in the name of a *countertechnicism*. It does so only with the intention of delivering on the promise of technological utopianism that technicism both offers and subverts. It is in effect a total rejection of the cosmological status of the world implied by the Procrustean mythos of technicism in favor of the countertechnicist mythos of Proteus—the myth of our infinite capacity to transform our selves and our world into whatever we desire.[25] Contrary to the technicist myth, the Protean myth sees the world not so much as "the cosmos writ small" but rather as "the human writ large." If the cosmological distortion of utopianism would smother human freedom and creativity in a world of necessity and secure mediocrity that invites an apocalyptic totalitarianism, the existential distortion of technological utopianism, at the other ex-treme, threatens the stability required by every human society with the danger of an anarchistic-apocalyptic conflict of opposing Nietz-chean wills to power. If the cosmological distortion would impose an absolute normative order on society, the existentialist distortion threatens to submerge the human city in a sea of anarchic freedom and nihilistic ethical relativism.

In reflecting on the murder of God, Nietzsche asks: "How were we able to drink up the sea? Who gave us the sponge to wipe away the entire horizon? What did we do when we unchained this earth from its sun? Whither is it moving now? Whither are we moving now? Away from all suns? Are we not plunging continually? Back-ward, sideward, forward, in all directions? Is there any up or down left?"[26] Replacing God as creator of the world is a terrifying experi-ence, for suddenly there is no frame of reference, no guiding star, no direction from which one can get one's bearings and begin.

In the heroic world of the *Übermensch*, where the fixed order of the world has been overcome with the murder of God, self-creativity becomes an unrelenting burden, for without it the world would dis-solve into the void. Nietzsche speaks of this burden in the confession of "The Night Song" from *Zarathustra*:

Light am I; ah, that I were night! But this is my loneliness that I am girt with light. Ah, that I were dark and nocturnal! How I would suck the breasts of light! . . . But I live in my own light; I drink back into myself the flames that break out of me. I do not know the happiness of those who receive; and I have often dreamed that even stealing must be more blessed than receiv-

ing. This is my poverty, that my hand never rests from giving. . . . My happiness in giving died in giving; my virtue tired
of itself in its overflow. . . . Alas ice is all around me, my hand is
burned by the icy [sic]. Alas, thirst is within me that languishes
after your thirst. Night has come: alas that I must be light! And
thirst for the nocturnal![27]

"The Night Song" is a moving confession of the isolated ego of the
technological *Übermensch*, the Protean self burdened with the task of
continuous self-transformation, in its striving to "overcome." The
movement of overcoming is the hand that "never rests from giving."
It is the confession of one imprisoned in the icy light of one's own
existence: "But I live in my own light; I drink back into myself the
flames that break out of me." The *Übermensch* can no longer know the
happiness of those who receive. The eros of the "inexorable solar
will" must never stop from creating and overcoming. It can never
leave off from asserting itself. The *Übermensch* can never enter into the
"mystic night" nor experience a noetic encounter with the *otherness* of
being (or more precisely, with the *otherness* of the becoming of the
beings that compose the universe) through which one might receive
light as a gift out of the darkness. Such a gift would be an insight as to
the direction of the path that lies ahead. But for Nietzsche there can
be no path, no order of being (or becoming), only an overcoming
through self-creation.

     For Kant the phenomenal world might not be knowable "in
itself," but its facticity, its otherness, must be respected. In Fichte the
will of practical reason overcomes the rationality of pure reason and
its respect for the otherness of the phenomenal and moves toward a
philosophical idealism. In Nietzsche this idealism seems to be reduced to an ego function of the *Übermensch* who lives in his or her
own light. The self-transcending project of the *Übermensch* renders
him or her incapable, or rather unwilling, to "receive." There can be
no dialogue with the strange and alien otherness of the world. This
dialogue is incompatible with the self-transcending freedom of the
Übermensch, who must always define the real and never be defined by
it. Nietzsche's *Übermensch* exists only through a conscious refusal to
be put in question, to be open even to the possibility of the reality of
this otherness. Undoubtedly it is because of a fear that such openness
means the disappearance of self-transcending or utopian freedom
and a reduction to the condition of the false consciousness of the
"herd." For Nietzsche, it seems, an order of being beyond the self
means a fixed order, destructive of human freedom.

Doubt and Utopian Transcendence

If, however, the body is our most intimate experience of the otherness of the world through which the intentionality or verbal condition of nature is delivered into speech, then our humanity, that is, our utopian capacity for speech, begins in a receiving of being. If, as Merleau-Ponty has suggested, our perceptions are openings of the flesh filled by the inpouring flesh of the world, then giving voice to a thought is not a pure act of creation but begins rather in an experience of discovery in which the body gives birth to the words that "surprise me, myself and teaches me my thought."[28]

To experience this surprise, I would suggest, is to undergo the "aha" experience of insight. It is the experience of receiving an answer to a question put to the otherness of the world. There is, Bernard Lonergan suggests, an invariant set of operations that belong to the experience to knowing.[29] The intentionality of consciousness oriented by an unrestricted passion to understand and pursued toward the horizon opened up by a specific question operates dynamically, moving from experience to insight (i.e., understanding) to judgment to decision (or action).

In moving from experience to understanding to judgment, the subject finds himself or herself constrained to acquiesce to an inner demand for objectivity. This constraint brings to light the moral quality of the act of knowing as the subject raises all the possible objections to the insight that may show it to be an oversight. But if all the possible objections are answered, the judgment, "it is so," becomes inescapable and the subject has no choice but to assent or fall into a condition of self-deception.

In overcoming all the hazards of knowing, the subject experiences the "virtually unconditioned" objectivity of (not absolute but rather) contingent truth that suggests a direction of appropriate action and defines the horizon of new questions that may lead to additional insights.[30] It would seem, then, that the question defines the horizon of possibilities to be exhausted through the pursuit of insight. In the very act of arriving at insight one overcomes the existing horizon, but only to discover a new one, and with it new possibilities and new questions.

For Nietzsche, there seem to be only two options. Either there is a fixed order of being with a fixed horizon in which there is no freedom (i.e., the Procrustean or cosmological myth) or there is self-transcending freedom and no fixed horizon (i.e., the Protean or existential myth). But as Lonergan's work suggests, there is a third option, namely, that transcendence occurs through a shifting of horizons.[31]

If so, then the quest for understanding is like a journey in which the arrival at what is perceived as the horizon from one viewpoint occasions the discovery of a new horizon and the further direction for one's journey. On this model it would appear that the otherness of reality is itself utopian and that utopian transcendence occurs through the dialectic of the question and answer between the inquiring subject and the otherness of the world.

If this be the case, then the self-transcending project of the technological self need not proceed as Nietzsche envisioned, by way of the murder of God, that is, the destruction of the horizon of being and the sense of direction it provides. Rather, if our humanity gives voice to the utopian condition of nature, then self-transcending freedom occurs through the receiving of insight by which the given horizon is transcended and a new horizon of possibilities is opened up. We realize our humanity then through a realization of that which it is not, as a movement toward the ever-shifting horizon of our journey.

On the premise of this third option, the historical and sociological relativity experienced by the technological self as a "knower" need not lead one into the void of pure relativism and nihilism as it seems to do with Nietzsche. Rather than falling into a world without horizons, the technological self exercises its self-transcending freedom by moving from horizon to horizon. By putting the world in question and being put in question by the world, one experiences insight as a guide to action toward the realization of the utopian in which the given horizon is transcended and redefined in an act of new creation. But unlike that of Nietzsche's *Übermensch,* this act of new creation emerges out of a dialectic of the self and the otherness of the world. It emerges out of the experience of giving and receiving in which the ego is relativized and in which the noetic process borders on a mystical participation in the ecological integrity of the utopian becoming of all things.

Doubt is a condition of the body-self, a kind of suspended animation that, in giving voice to its implicit question, realizes its utopian freedom to transcend a given horizon. Doubt emerges whenever the body-self confronts a limit that appears as integral to the given horizon of possibilities. At that point the body-self must either be conformed to the "real" or else transcend and transform the horizon of its possibilities. In that moment when the self experiences doubt that the limit is identical with the real, there the self-transcending character of freedom is realized as a possibility.

In the moment of doubt the self-transcending and dialectical relation between the knower and the known, self and society (i.e., the reflecting self and its social roles), the body-self and its symbolic universe is disclosed. Doubt reveals a gap, an infinite qualitative distance. It reveals the priority of the utopian self to the horizon of its universe. It is doubt that reveals that our humanity is not defined and confined by its given horizon.

Doubt gives rise to the question that guides the utopian self on its quest for insight as guide to action toward the overcoming or transcending of the limit given with the present horizon. This doubt is a received condition. Existentially, a person does not choose whether or not to doubt. Doubt, it seems, comes over the self and raises its own question—demanding integrity and self-transcendence. Doubt arises out of the body, insistently seeking a voice through which to put "reality" in question.

Every technology is the result of a quest for insight that begins with a doubt about the limit of human possibilities and moves toward the utopian transcendence of that limit and the opening of a new horizon of possibilities. In that utopian act of freedom the essential technological reality of the human is revealed. The technological essence of our humanity is realized through realizing of the utopian possibilities of the earth.

Procrustean technicism and Protean countertechnicism are two potentially fatal forms of narrative distortion that threaten our utopian possibilities by creating linguistic worlds that have no place for either *otherness* or doubt. Procrustean technicism renders opaque the relation between the self-transcending creativity of our humanity and the products of that creativity. It sunders the relation between nature and our humanity as well as between our humanity and technology in order to exclude the human and assimilate technology to a "dehumanized" nature. The result is the appearance of both technology and nature as our fate. This technicism, although promising the new, in fact conforms us to the status quo, a fixed horizon of possibilities. Technicism, by excluding the question of the human, renders opaque the human act of free creativity by which the technological universe is sustained and thereby renders scarce those linguistic resources necessary for the realization of self-transcending freedom. But Protean countertechnicism is equally problematic. If Procrustean technicism overwhelms the autonomy of the self with the massive reality of the *otherness* of the cosmos, so that the self virtually disappears, Protean countertechnicism commits an error of equally momentous proportions in the opposite direction. In the Protean mythos the self is the "massive reality" and the world virtually disappears, so as to become invisible.

An essential task, necessary for the recovery of freedom in a technological society, is the systematic dismantling and reconstruction of our symbolic universe (i.e., the technological city) piece by piece (just as it was constructed), by putting into question the specific technicist and countertechnicist theoretical characterizations of the world that have emerged in every field of human endeavor. In their place we must articulate a theoretical account of a genuinely utopian technological world. Such an account is one which takes seriously both the self and the otherness or alienness of the world. This account makes the links between human freedom and its products explicit and clear and enables the ethical imagination to grasp the kinds of acts that could modify and control these products.

Both technicism and countertechnicism break apart the authentic utopian dialectic given with our capacity for speech. For if speech arises out of the body under the condition of doubt, it does so to test its primal experience of the otherness of reality. Moreover, if there is no such thing as a private language, then again our very capacity for speech suggests a primal experience of the reality of other speakers. It is this experience of otherness that lures us beyond ourselves and into the authentically utopian task of becoming what we are not, through a process of questioning and answering which is at the same time a process of giving and receiving. It is this dialectical or dialogical process of doubt and questioning, I am convinced, that provides a suggestive model for a genuinely utopian social ethics—one capable of demythologizing the apocalyptic distortions of the utopian mythos in both its Procrustean and Protean narrative forms and desacralizing the technical order that gives rise to these myths. Such an ethic has as its goal, not so much the destruction of either apocalyptic or utopian narratives as a liberation of both from their Procrustean technicist and Protean countertechnicist distortions. For despite the overwhelming apocalyptic dangers of our emerging global technopolis, I believe it offers genuinely utopian possibilities for the coming millennium. Despite the apocalyptic distortions of technicism and countertechnicism, I remain convinced that the apocalyptic narrative theme is not inherently antithetical to utopianism. Indeed, when both the apocalyptic and utopian narrative themes are desacralized and freed from the influence of what I would call "the sacral imagination," they turn out to be, not diametrical opposites but a dialectical unity.

The Dialectics of Apocalypse and Utopia

The task I have set for myself is to recover this dialectical unity, obscured by all sacral dualisms, so as to articulate a cross-cultural social ethic of human dignity, human rights, and human liberation. The insight that false sacral divisions disrupt the essential dialectical unity of apocalypse and utopia first came to me after I struggled for a number of years to reconcile the positions of two contemporary theological critics of technicism who have profoundly influenced me, Jacques Ellul and Gabriel Vahanian. For Jacques Ellul utopian thought is the problem for which apocalyptic thought is the cure. For Gabriel Vahanian it is just the opposite. My own reading of their arguments led me to believe each was largely right in what they affirmed and wrong in what they denied.

In the chapters which follow I intend to show that the narratives of apocalypse and utopia which have their origins within the horizons of the biblical tradition have in fact become a global public myth—one intimately shaped by the experiences of Auschwitz and Hiroshima. At the same time, I intend to show that the insight gained from sorting out the disagreement between Ellul and Vahanian can be related to the larger horizons of our emerging global civilization, teaming with narrative diversity, in such a way as to illuminate the possibility for a cross-cultural ethical coalition in defense of human dignity, human rights and human liberation—a coalition which can be entered into by all those narrative traditions, East and West, which emphasize the importance of welcoming the stranger.

Few claims about Jacques Ellul would seem more paradoxical (that is, "contrary to appearances") than the claim that he is a "utopian thinker." You do not have to read very far in Ellul before you discover that he considers utopian thought the primary myth of our technological civilization, whose sole function is to render human beings totally subservient to its necessities. We will put up with any dehumanization, he argues, we will accept any demand for efficiency and give up any freedom, as long as we believe we shall be rewarded with utopia. If there is such a thing as fate or necessity in a technological society, if technology has a certain autonomy, it is because we have been seduced into surrendering ourselves to its demands in return for the promise that it will fulfill our wildest utopian dreams for comfort, for pleasure, and for success.

Ellul considers utopian thought to be an escapist reaction to that which cannot be prevented.[32] Constructing utopian fantasies, he says, is the favorite passtime of intellectuals. But the fantasies of a

Campanella, a More, or a Fourier "do not seem to have played the slightest historical role in the past nor foretold any future reality. . . . I fail to see a positive value in utopian views. They do humanity no good. Whenever men have taken utopian descriptions seriously, the result has been disastrous."[33]

Yet, despite this, Ellul's own theological ethics is oriented toward a utopian transformation of society. But that utopianism gets drowned in the rhetoric of apocalypse. Ellul's phobia about the word *utopia* has prevented him from seeing that his unique appropriation of apocalyptic tradition is utopian. In fact Ellul inverts the popular meanings of *apocalypse* and *utopia* in his own theological writings. *Where the world embraces utopian hopes and fears apocalyptic scenarios, Ellul embraces apocalyptic hopes and fears utopian scenarios.* This reversal is intimately tied to the distinction he makes between the sacred and the holy. Contrary to popular usage, Ellul treats the terms *sacred* and *holy* not as synonyms but as antonyms. Thus, the sacred is, for him, the reverse image of the holy. And whereas the sacred encloses society in a fixed order, the holy introduces that element of transcendence which opens society to the future.

For Ellul, utopia is an expression of the sacral imagination of our technicist society and the apocalyptic mode of thought expresses the transforming power of the sanctified imagination. As a sociologist, Ellul argues that the sacred is simply an inherent element in the psychosocial structure of our human world that legitimates the structure of a technicist society so that it becomes totalitarian, demonic and dehumanizing. Only by breaking with the seductive allure of this sacral world, he argues, can a self-transcending freedom be reintroduced into the technological city whereby it can become an anticipation of a new city—the New Jerusalem. For Ellul, the theologian, *apocalyptic hope* is hope in the God who is Wholly Other. That hope ruptures one's psychological and spiritual dependency on the sacral structures of this world. It is a hope which is not conformed to this world and therefore able to transform the world.

The key to Ellul's thought is his exegesis of Apocalypse—the Book of Revelation (which we shall examine in some detail in the last chapter). Ellul separates this apocalyptic narrative from others of the genre, arguing that it is not a book that despairs of history. Rather than announcing the catastrophic end of history, the Apocalypse is the revelation of God's freedom at work in history as mediated by radical human hope. In Ellul's view, the Apocalypse is to be taken seriously, but not literally, for its speaks in the language of exotic symbol precisely because it speaks of the ultimate paradox of the presence "of the Eternal in Time, of the action of the End in the Present, the discovery of the New Eon, not at the end of time, but in this present history" through which all things can be transformed and made new.[34]

The thrust of Gabriel Vahanian's theological critique of Ellul, especially in *God and Utopia,* was precisely to chide Ellul for not recognizing that there is such a thing as a biblical form of utopianism, an iconoclastic form of utopianism that Vahanian would take to be normative.[35] Unlike the dualistic ideologies of apocalyptic thought that afflict "man with visions of another world," he argues, "utopia, like the kingdom, is moved by the vision of a new world, [that is] radically other. . . . Echoing, as it were, the biblical view of the world as creation, utopia holds that only the *novum* [i.e., the genuinely new] is realizable, everything else being nothing but repetition."[36]

If Ellul is phobic about *utopianism,* Vahanian is phobic about *apocalypticism,* which he equates with an ideological dualism more concerned with changing worlds than changing the world. Ellul's work, however, should serve as a reminder to Vahanian (who already acknowledges a large indebtedness to him) that biblical apocalypticism is not about *changing worlds* but precisely about *changing the world.* Ellul's understanding of the apocalyptic narrative tradition sounds suspiciously like Vahanian's understanding of the utopian narrative tradition. The problem is that Ellul fails to appreciate the utopianism of the very apocalyptic tradition that stands at the center of his thought. By the same token Vahanian fails to appreciate that Ellul's apocalypticism really does draw on the authentic utopianism of the biblical tradition. Despite their seeming opposition it does not seem to me that the disagreement between them is substantive. For Vahanian's eschatological novum like Ellul's apocalypse of the eschaton is nothing other than the presence of the Wholly Other in the here and now that calls into question the sacred order of "reality," making all things possible and all things new.[37]

Like Ellul, Vahanian would claim that, if our world has been desacralized, the sacred has disappeared in one form only to reappear in another. It is as "supernaturalism" that the sacred has met its demise, but only to give way to the sacred as "the utopian arena of transcendence."[38] Our humanity, which becomes a possibility through the word, is limited neither to nature nor history but transforms both through speech—the word made flesh, a new creation (novum). It is as a creature of language that our humanity comes to expression as technological and utopian.

In Vahanian's view we must not reject the language of technological utopianism but appropriate it so that we might *expropriate* technological utopianism as a language of faith.[39] This is a move Ellul has been reluctant to make. Like Vahanian, Ellul endorses Barth's theological distinction of the three stages or moments in the relation between the Word of God and our culturally human words. First the Word *appropriates* our words (i.e, speaks to us by using our language) then the Word *contradicts* our words (i.e., the *No* of judgment that brings about a transformation of meaning) and then finally the Word *expropriates* our words to convey the freedom of the Gospel (i.e., the *Yes* of God to our words now transformed so as to communicate transcendence).[40] However, there are times when it seems as if Ellul has abandoned this dialectic and the *No* he pronounces has become an absolute no. The question is, Is Ellul's No truly dialectical, as Barth advocates, or is it a nondialectical negation? If there is an important difference between Vahanian and Ellul it is that Vahanian has followed through on the Barthian dialectic precisely at that point where Ellul remained reticent, at the point of transition from negation to expropriation. In a way that Ellul has not, he has been willing to imagine what it would be for the word to become flesh in a technological civilization, an imaginative act at once both eschatological and utopian.

Far more than the medieval world, which imagined the human in terms of nature, our contemporary technological civilization is open to the linguistic utopianism of the Gospel narratives. For both the Gospels and technological utopianism speak of the human through the language of new creation. Indeed, argues Vahanian, "there is no humanity without technology. The human itself depends on techniques, and utopia is ultimately nothing other than a technique of human technologies."[41] "Far from being a robot, technological man is the man who makes himself."[42] It remains for utopianism only to be linked with the biblical eschatological experience of the holy, Vahanian argues, to give birth to the novum, a genuinely new creation of the human in which we discover our utopianism in the image and likeness of the God who has no image (Deut. 4:15).[43] The Christ event, the word made flesh, is but the affirmation of the coming of the human, the affirmation that human destiny is tied to neither nature nor history nor the utopian techniques through which it comes into being but to the eschaton.[44] In Christ the human person is not trapped in a "human nature" but experiences a truly utopian invitation to become a new creature, here and now.[45] One should not be misled however, for Vahanian is not identifying biblical utopianism with technological utopianism but relating them to each other dialec-

tically. "Utopia is not the kingdom. Utopia is to the kingdom as nature is to creation, or as history is to redemption, or, simply as the
flesh is to the spirit. If there is a relationship between them, it is one
of radical otherness."[46] It is this relation of radical otherness that gives
to faith its iconoclasm, that pivotal no of the Barthian dialectic that
makes a revolutionary expropriation of technological utopianism possible.

As I struggled with these seemingly opposing viewpoints I began to believe that Ellul and Vahanian each had grasped half of a
Janus-faced myth that was in fact a unity—the myth of Apocalypse-
Utopia. What is really occurring between them is a conflict of the
narrative imagination in which for Ellul the language of apocalypse is
understood as the language of transcendence or the holy through
which all things can be transformed, whereas utopian language is
viewed as a sacral ideological language that legitimates the technicist
status quo. For Vahanian the categories are reversed: apocalyptic language is sacral and ideological, and utopian language is the language
of the holy-transcendence that calls all things into question to make
all things new. Putting two and two together, I realized that there
were in fact two forms of the "Janus-faced" narrative of Apocalypse-
Utopia. The first expresses the nondialectical dualism of the narrative
imagination under the influence of the experience of the sacred that
divides all things into the irreconcilably opposing categories of sacred
and profane. The second Janus-faced language expresses the dialectical relationship of the holy and the secular. For the holy, as both Ellul
and Vahanian insist, desacralizes and hence secularizes the sacred,
opening the human world to transcendence and transformation.

Reading Karl Mannheim, one of the founding fathers of the
sociology of knowledge, enabled me to grasp this dialectical unity of
apocalypse and utopia. Mannheim constructs a very interesting argument, in *Ideology and Utopia,* for the roots of utopianism in the apocalyptic tradition and of the importance of that tradition for the making
of history.[47] Utopias, he argues, introduce a tension into the present
order of things that is creatively disruptive. Without this tension we
would live "in a world in which there is never anything new, in which
all is finished and each moment is a repetition of the past. . . . With
the relinquishment of utopias, man would lose his will to shape history and therewith his ability to understand it."[48]

In tracing the history of utopianism, Mannheim identifies the
apocalyptic tradition as the most important source for this kind of
radical utopianism. He cites the apocalypticism of Thomas Munzer as

an example and argues that this kind of apocalypticism embodies a radically utopian mode of transformative consciousness in which "the impossible gives birth to the possible and the absolute interferes with the world and conditions actual events."[49] This utopian consciousness introduces an attitude of "tense expectation" in which "the promise of the future which is to come is not . . . a reason for postponement, but merely a point of orientation, something external to the ordinary course of events from where he [i.e., an individual] is on the lookout, ready to take the leap." Such apocalyptic utopianism "sees the revolution as a value in itself, not as an unavoidable means to a rationally set end."[50]

For Mannheim the utopian mentality is revealed in those "hopes and yearnings" that give rise to an inherently iconoclastic mode of consciousness "incongruous with the state of reality within which it occurs." This mode of consciousness inspires those actions that tend to "shatter, either partially or wholly, the order of things prevailing at the time. . . . [and] break[s] the bonds of the existing order."[51] The problem as Mannheim sees it is that utopias get confused with ideologies, and for good reason, because an ideology deliberately masquerades as a form of utopian consciousness but actually serves to maintain the status quo. Ideologies promise change but deliver more of the same old thing, whereas the utopian mentality unmasks such ideologies and forces transformative change. The relationship between ideology and utopia is rendered extremely problematic by the fact that in the "real world" the two are almost always found intertwined. Every ideology contains utopian elements and every utopia contains ideological elements. However, one sure sign of an ideology is its propensity for making absolute claims for the social structure— claims that suggest that it is unquestionably sacred. To the degree that these claims are relativized, to that degree the apocalyptic-utopian elements can be liberated from their ideological straightjacket and shatter and transform the existing order of things.

Mannheim's analysis makes it possible to see both Ellul and Vahanian as sharing the same narrative tradition. Mannheim's analysis of apocalyptic and utopian narrative themes offers the opportunity of dispelling the illusion of fundamental disagreement between them. Vahanian needs to recognize that there is more than one kind of apocalyptic narrative, and Ellul needs to recognize that there is more than one kind of utopian narrative. The kind of utopianism Ellul wishes to renounce is ideological (Procrustean) utopianism, the ideology of a technological civilization that promises change and substitutes the illusion of change. And the kind of apocalypticism Vahanian wishes to renounce is the ideological (Protean) apocalypticism intent on changing worlds rather than changing the world. Both could be understood as distortions of a genuine *apocalyptic utopianism*— distortions produced by a sacral imagination. An apocalyptic utopianism would be a utopianism stripped of its ideological components under the impact of an imagination shaped by the experience of the holy. Such a utopianism would desacralize technological utopianism, liberate it from its ideological straitjacket, and unleash its transformative potential.

What the argument between Vahanian and Ellul helps us understand is that the popular "mythological" meanings of the terms *apocalypse* as cataclysmic total destruction and *utopia* as an ideal world of total perfection are really fragments and distortions of a biblical eschatology that underlies the historical imagination of Western civilization. The result of this fragmentation has been to break apart the dialectical unity of realism and transcendence in the biblical proclamation resulting in the nondialectical dualistic opposition of apocalypse and utopia expressing a pessimistic Procrustean realism on the one hand and a naive Protean optimism on the other. The one expresses a cosmological orientation that tells us "that's the way things are and we can't change them." The other reflects an anarchical existentialist orientation that insists "we can become whoever we wish to become and do whatever we wish to do." These fragments are the result of dismantling of the dialectical unity of biblical eschatology that holds realism and openness to transcendence and transformation in a tense unity—one that enables those eschatological holy communities which embody this unity to be a fermenting and transforming utopian presences *in* but not *of* the world.

Nietzsche's madman proclaimed his message in the marketplace, that new *secular* arena of modern society which Richard Neuhaus has called *The Naked Public Square*.[52] This secular public square has come to be recognized as perhaps the distinctive characteristic of modernity. Nietzsche's madman entered this square to announce the death of God and the emergence of a new public order whose utopianism (i.e., a world where all values can be transvalued) is inherently demonic and apocalyptic (a world in which the all values are transvalued by the will to power). We need to explore the implications of the Janus-faced myth of apocalypse and utopia in relation to the problem of public order, ethics, and social policy in the naked public square. Is there an alternative to a public order torn asunder by the value pluralism of our modern technological civilization in which ideological conflict seems to be resolved only by a will to power? In the chapters which follow, I shall argue that there is indeed a utopianism capable of transcending the literalism of our Janus-faced *mythos*, one capable of embracing our religious and cultural value pluralism in a public ethic which is normative without being totalitarian.

2

The Narrative Ambivalence of a Technological Civilization: Apocalypse or Utopia?

The Janus-faced myth of apocalypse and utopia underlies the ambivalent evaluations of modern technological civilization typical of our century. In this chapter, beginning with the utopian euphoria of 1965, the year of the first space walk, we shall trace these narrative themes through key works from four theological critics of culture: Harvey Cox, Richard Rubenstein, Jacques Ellul, and Arthur Cohen. Through their work I believe we can come to a clearer understanding of the dynamics of the apocalyptic threat to the utopian promise of our technological civilization—dynamics that, if left unchecked, will link our destiny to that of Auschwitz and Hiroshima.

Technopolis: The Secular City as Utopian

In the same year that an astronaut first walked in space, Harvey Cox's *The Secular City* was published. This provocative book celebrated the utopianism of technopolis, the modern secular city. This city, he argued, was the logical outcome of the secularizing impact of the biblical world-view on Western civilization. The publication of *The Secular City* was one of those rare, almost unheard of, occurrences where a scholarly book on religion became a popular best seller. Although the book deserved the attention it received, its tremendous popularity was in large part due to fortunate timing. It captured the mood of technological euphoria sweeping the United States, a mood that seemed to be vindicated by astronauts breaking free of the earth to walk in space.

The Secular City was both popular and controversial. It took many in the churches by surprise for it did not celebrate American society with the civic-religious enthusiasm of the 1950s, which had embraced a vision of Christian America. On the contrary, it celebrated this society precisely for its secularity, the very thing people in the pews were used to hearing condemned as the enemy of God and country. Cox saw *technopolis,* as he called this new order, as both liberating and humanizing, rather than dehumanizing as the conventional wisdom of technological critics had proposed. He was prepared to praise the bureaucratic and technological order that secularization had brought about. Cox offered a bold utopian thesis for a new generation of pragmatic and secular individuals who were about to put a human being on the moon; namely, that technopolis was the historical outcome of the secularizing freedom of the Gospel.

To enable his readers to grasp the significance of his thesis, Cox presented a view of history as unfolding in three ages, symbolized by the tribe, the town, and technopolis (or cosmopolis). These three ages were said to have been dominated by myth, metaphysics, and scientific technology, respectively. In this schema we find the narrative tradition initiated by Joachim of Fiore's myth of the three ages of history clearly at work.

The ancient city essentially clung to a town mentality. Drawing an analogy with Marx's three stage theory of history as moving from primitive communism through capitalism to socialist communism, Cox suggested that the town is only a transition stage on the way to a third possibility—technopolis as cosmopolis. Unlike the citizens of the ancient polis, who saw the world as the city of the gods, and the residents of the medieval manor, who saw the world as the city of God, the modern cosmopolitan sees the world as the city of humanity. "The world has become . . . [a] city and . . . [the] city has reached out to include the world."[1] In the emerging modern technopolis, where human beings have finally come of age, all religious self-understandings are relativized and privatized, and all religious absolutes are replaced with pluralism and tolerance.

Tribal individuals danced and chanted their religion, merging with the *daemon* of their group. By contrast the citizen of the town reads the word, hears it preached and addressed to him or her as an *individual.* "The age of the towns gave us printing and books, rational theology, the scientific revolution, investment capitalism, and bureaucracy"—all of which fall under the category Max Weber called *rationalization.* Finally, in the modern technopolis this rationalization seems to have reached a certain critical mass that appears to be transforming human identity in preparation for a new cosmopolitan age.

Secularization, as a process that rationally organizes human life, appears to have two sources which work in tandem. The first is the process of urbanization. Urbanization, Cox told us: "means a structure of common life in which diversity and the disintegration of tradition are paramount. It means a type of impersonality in which functional relationships multiply. It means that a degree of tolerance and anonymity replace traditional moral sanctions and long-term acquaintanceships. The urban center is the place of human control, of rational planning, of bureaucratic organization—and the urban center is not just in Washington, London, New York, and Peking. It is everywhere."[2] The second source is the biblical tradition. Indeed "the rise of natural science, of democratic political institutions, and of cultural pluralism—all developments we normally associate with Western culture—can scarcely be understood without the original impetus of the Bible."[3] This is true, in Cox's view, because, echoing Max Weber's thesis, biblical religion is a desacralizing and disenchanting form of religion. As a result secularization is "an authentic consequence of biblical faith."[4]

The biblical view of creation by a single transcendent God had the effect of sweeping away the polytheistic gods who inhabited nature, desacralizing the world and making it the secular arena of human action, where humans are given dominion over nature allowing science and technology to emerge and flourish. Even as Genesis desacralizes nature, we are told, so Exodus desacralizes politics. Exodus desacralizes the ancient polytheistic views of political order as represented by the Egypt of the Pharaohs. Egypt represents the hierarchical order of traditional sacred societies, the divinely sanctioned order of nature established by the gods of nature. The Exodus is the story of deliverance from the static order of nature into the dynamic order of history, where the God of transcendence opens the path of historical change and transformation. The Constantinian temptation of Christianity was always to close the chasm between the world and this God, resacralizing the world and the political order. But the biblical tradition, Cox argued, requires Christians to call into question all religiopolitical orders. Christians should exemplify a "holy worldliness" that demands that the world remain secular and not pretend to claim the status of the holy.

Neither nature nor society and its values can any longer be seen as "changeless expressions of a divine will." "Both tribal man and secular man see the world from a particular, socially and historically conditioned point of view. But modern secular man knows it, and tribal man did not; therein lies the crucial difference."[5] Thus modern human beings are peculiarly aware of the cultural particularity and relativity of their values and world-views. The result is a pluralistic society tolerant of differences and wary of absolutes. "Secularization places the responsibility for the forging of human values, like the fashioning of political systems, in man's own hands. And this demands a maturity neither the nihilist nor the anarchist wishes to assume."[6]

The danger, Cox admitted, is that such relativism will lead to nihilism. His response to that threat was to suggest that nihilism is an adolescent reaction to freedom that can and must be replaced by a new maturity in which human beings accept that their values are not absolute and yet recognize that every society needs a set of cohesive values to survive. As a result they will set about creating a conscious cohesion of values based on consensus. "Thus it is now possible for the United Nations to develop a Declaration of Human Rights based on a consensus of all the nation-states involved. It does not, like the American founding documents, rest on affirmations concerning the inalienable right with which men are 'endowed by their Creator. . . .' Nor is it based on some theory of natural law. It is the expression of a consensus which draws together several cultural and religious traditions including those which believe neither in a Creator nor in any form of natural law."[7]

Critics saw technopolis as impersonal and dehumanizing. In contrast to the "I-Thou" relationships of traditional communities (*Gemeinschaft*), technopolis seemed to have substituted mechanical and impersonal (*Gesellschaft*) "I-It" relationships. Cox responded by suggesting that far from being dehumanizing, the new social order was liberating. It offered opportunities for new and deeper patterns of humanization. Anonymity and mobility did not so much reduce human interactions to "I-It" relations as "I-You" relations. These relationships actually freed one to selectively engage in deeper "I-Thou" relationships. The liberating mobility and anonymity of modern life is in fact, Cox argued, a direct consequence of the liberating and desacralizing message of the Gospel. The lesson of the parable of the Good Samaritan is that anonymity does not preclude caring.

Critics also argued that technological civilization creates a society of "organization men," of individuals in gray flannel suits who are little more than mechanical interchangeable parts. But Cox insisted that it need not be so. Although we have become a society of corporations governed by managers whose collective influence and power is often more extensive (and ominous) than that of government, the challenge, Cox argued, is to extend "the mechanism of political democracy . . . to the ponderous economic structures that have developed."[8] This will require an "unsentimental" understanding of how organizations are structured and how they function. And it will also require "demythologizing our sacred economic theologies."[9]

Indeed, there is good reason to see modern corporations and service bureaucracies as uniquely open to transformation. This is because, unlike traditional social orders that were thought to be sacred and unchangeable, the modern managerial society is "flexible, future oriented, secularized and limited in its scope. . . . In contradiction to its bucolic critics' claims, the organization offers many more possibilities for choice and creativity than were available in the age of the sacral order."[10] In fact modern organizations reflect the eschatological and desacralizing impact of the biblical tradition on society in four essential characteristics: (1) They are flexible, capable of being organized and reorganized. (2) They are future oriented, functionally organized for the purpose of reaching future goals. (3) They are secular. Neither organizational structures nor the functional roles they create for managers and other employees are sacred and unchangeable. All are evaluated according to performance. (4) They make a limited claim on their members. That is, we live in a society of pluralistic institutions, each of which have limited purposes and make only limited claims on our lives. No organization seeks "to endow him [the employee] with a total identity or life meaning."[11] These characteristics, Cox suggested, are the result, in large part, of the impact of the church on Western civilization. For the church introduced into the sacred order of the ancient world a new model of social organization based on free association, even as it played a role in desacralizing the institutions of the ancient world and reorienting human consciousness toward the future.

The task of the church, Cox proposed, is to discern the action of God in historical events and cooperate in promoting the work of God in history. The action of God was to be discerned in those historical events that bring about social change in the form of secularization, because the activity of God is always to be recognized by its secularizing impact. Therefore, Christians have an obligation to embrace and promote secularization. At the same time Cox also insisted that *secularization* not be confused with *secularism*. For secularism is an ideology, "a new closed world-view which functions very much like a new religion."[12] Secularism is the very antithesis of secularization and thus the very antithesis of the biblical tradition as well. It is the denial of the relativity of one's own world-view that seeks to make that view into a new absolute, resisting all further historical movement of change and transformation. By contrast, the ideal of the *secular city* is a utopian openness to social change.

> There is no reason why Christians cannot make use of the aspi-
> rations set forth in these fictional cities [i.e., utopias]. As an
> interpretive model, the city usefully complements the freedom
> and liberation of secularity with the idea of reciprocity and inter-
> dependence. But the city too is an open-ended image. No street
> plan is provided. Every utopia which does prescribe specific
> remedies quickly becomes an impediment to change rather than
> a spur. The emerging city signifies a purposeful process, not an
> achieved goal. The pattern of the secular city is not revealed
> from on high. It must be painfully worked out by man himself.[13]

To this end Cox urged Christians to embrace a new social and political ethic of revolution in which the call to conversion must be depri-vatized so as to manifest its social dimensions. Conversion can make a difference only when it expresses a willingness to abandon the dehumanizing social patterns of the past and embrace a secularizing and humanizing process of social change. To bring about such a social and cultural conversion, the church must be willing to become a cultural exorcist, "ready to expose the fallaciousness of the social myths by which the injustice of a society are perpetuated and to suggest ways of action which demonstrate the wrongness of such fantasies."[14] Through such change the old order of creation is trans-formed into a new creation in which human beings let go of their adolescence and assume an adult sense of responsibility for their world.

Auschwitz: The Secular City as Apocalyptic

A decade after the appearance of *The Secular City* Richard Rubenstein's *The Cunning of History: The Holocaust and the American Future* was published. If Cox, as a WASP (White, Anglo-Saxon, Prot-estant) read the history of secularization (urban and biblical) as liber-ating and humanizing, Richard Rubenstein read that very same histo-ry through Jewish eyes and came to some very different conclusions. If the mood of Cox's book was essentially utopian, the mood of Rubenstein's was essentially apocalyptic, reflecting perhaps the dif-ferent experiences of the two historical traditions they represent. In less than 100 pages, Rubenstein provided a brilliant and devastating analysis of the "deep trends" of Western civilization in the light of the Holocaust.

The thrust of his analysis was to demonstrate that the Holocaust is not an anomalous accident but rather the logical outcome of the "cunning of history"—the secularizing history of urbanization and of the biblical tradition. It is a history, he argued, that begins with the invention of the city and ends in the death camps. "Perhaps it was no accident," he wrote,

> that the most highly urbanized people in the Western world, the Jews, were the first to perish in the ultimate city of Western civilization, Necropolis, the new city of the dead that the Germans built and maintained at Auschwitz. Auschwitz was perhaps the terminal expression of an urban culture that first arose when an ancient protobourgeoisie liberated its work life from the haphazard, unpredictable, and seasonable character of agriculture and sustained itself by work which was, in the words of Max Weber, "continuous and rational." In the beginning, removed from immediate involvement in "the vital realities of nature," the city was the habitat of the potter, the weaver, the carpenter, and the scribe; in the end, it houses the police bureaucrat and his corporate counterpart coldly and methodically presiding over the city of the dead.
>
> There is always the danger that Metropolis will become Necropolis. The city is by nature antinature, antiphysis, and, hence, antilife. The world of the city, *our world*, is the world of human invention and power; it is also the world of artifice, dreams, charades, and the paper promises we call money. . . . Whenever men build cities, they take the chance that their nurturing lifeline to the countryside may someday be severed, as indeed it was in wartime Poland. . . . The starving inmates of Auschwitz, consuming their own substance until they wasted away into nothingness, may offer a prophetic image of urban civilization at the end of its journey from the countryside to Necropolis. . . . Unless current economic, social and demographic trends are somehow reversed, there will be other citizens of the city of the dead [beside the Jews], many others.[15]

Rubenstein, then, read the Holocaust as nothing less than a prophetic disclosure of the apocalyptic destiny of civilization.

If history begins in the tribe and ends in technopolis, that history, according to Cox, is a utopian history of progressive liberation and humanization. Rubenstein, however, seems to have read that history in just the opposite direction. The tribe was the high point and it has been all downhill since then. Tribal human beings, he suggested, lived in a world of sacred limits, a world in which warfare was largely a ritual activity that resulted in a minimum loss of life. Urbanization began a process of dehumanization, a process whereby humans were cut off from the sacred rhythms of nature and began to break all natural limits. This dehumanization begins when tribal community is broken and people become strangers to one another in large impersonal cities, where life is held together by the rule of vast impersonal bureaucracies. Bureaucracy is a rationalizing process for the organization of human effort that mechanizes and dehumanizes life. It establishes a rhythm of life that is alienated from nature and oriented toward the efficient and effective organization of human effort to accomplish the purposes of the city-state. The city essentially creates an artificial and impersonal environment in which life becomes less and less sacred and more and more secular until finally, in the twentieth century, nothing is any longer sacred, not even human life. Our century witnesses this with over 100 million deaths in two major world wars (and countless minor ones), heightened by the atrocities of Auschwitz and the devastation of Hiroshima, foretelling, perhaps, a final and total apocalypse or nuclear annihilation.[16]

The death camps represent the breaching of a "hitherto unbreachable moral and political barrier in the history of Western civilization . . . henceforth the systematic, bureaucratically administered extermination of millions of citizens or subject peoples will forever be one of the capacities and temptations of government."[17] The genocidal program of the Nazis was a "thoroughly modern exercise in total domination" that required the efficient bureaucratic organization of an entire nation-state for the systematic purpose of totally exterminating an unwanted portion of its population. It started with the bureaucratic definition of who a Jew is, then proceeded to a bureaucratic process of systematically stripping those so identified of their citizenship and property rights, and finally subjected them to a systematic bureaucratic process of extermination in the gas chambers.

As an act against the Jews, the Holocaust cannot be compared to anything that preceded it. Although persecution, expulsion, and violent pogroms mar the history of Christian-Jewish relations, violence against the Jew had always occurred at the level of popular and spontaneous uprisings. Such violence was typically held in check at official levels by both church and state. It was only with the emergence of the modern technically and bureaucratically organized secular state that the possibility of an official, state organized program of genocide came to be realized for the first time.

The destruction process required the cooperation of every sector of German society. The bureaucrats drew up the definitions and decrees; the churches gave evidence of Aryan descent; the postal authorities carried the messages of definition, expropriation, denaturalization, and deportation; business corporations dismissed their Jewish employees and took over "Aryanized" properties; the railroads carried the victims to their place of execution. . . . The operation required and received the participation of every major social, political, and religious institution of the German Reich.[18]

Although the history of religious anti-Judaism played a tragically decisive role in preparing the way for the Holocaust, it was not finally religious anti-Judaism but post-Enlightenment secular racial anti-Semitism that crossed the line to genocide.

The Holocaust, Rubenstein insisted, cannot be reduced to historical accident and must not be treated as if it is fundamentally irrational and unexplainable. On the contrary, the Holocaust is "an expression of some of the most significant political, moral, religious and demographic tendencies of Western civilization in the twentieth century."[19] The tendencies Rubenstein had in mind included the long historical trends of urbanization, bureaucratization, rationalization, and desacralization that culminate in ethical relativism—with the privatization of values on the one hand and the absolutization of the power of the state on the other. The catalyst that organized these trends into something far more ominous, Rubenstein identified as population growth; namely, the problem of what to do with "surplus population."

The tremendous population growth since the late middle ages, we are told, placed a severe strain on Europe. For a time the discovery of the Americas acted as a safety valve, siphoning off excess population. But as we moved into the twentieth century the option of emigration began to be severely restricted. At that point, Rubenstein suggested, Europe turned to war as a solution. The tremendous loss of life in two world wars and beyond is one way civilization resolves such ecological pressures.

Especially significant is the problem of "stateless persons." In the 1920s and 1930s as national boundaries were being redefined many countries ended up with unwanted minorities, many of which ended up being denationalized or denaturalized; for example, the White Russians, the Spanish republicans, the Armenians, the Jews. Individuals belonging to these groups became stateless persons without legal rights. The *apatride* were technically outlaws, that is, those not covered by the law. They were subject to "unrestricted police domination" and were often detained in camps under "protective custody." "The unifying bond between the *apatrides* and the first prisoners in the German concentrations camps was that both groups were outlaws. Neither the *apatrides* nor the German political prisoners [at first primarily communists and socialists] were outlaws because of any crime they had committed, but because their status had been altered by their country's civil service or police bureaucracy. They had been deprived of all political status by bureaucratic definition. As such they became *superfluous men.*"[20]

In the years prior to World War II the numbers of stateless persons grew rapidly. There seemed to be no solution as to what to do with these surplus populations. No solution, that is, that was thinkable—until Hitler and Stalin came along. "We who live in the post-World War II era have seen the birth of an altogether different moral universe."[21] In this moral universe people who are socially useless or politically problematic have no value and no rights. Their existence or nonexistence is of no importance. The Jews of Germany fit this category. They were a people nobody wanted. When Lord Moyne, the British high commissioner in Egypt, was offered a chance to save a million Hungarian Jews his response was "What shall I do with those million Jews?"[22] In such a moral universe the Nazis felt free to believe they were doing the world a favor by ridding it of the Jews. "In the moral universe of the twentieth century, the most 'rational' and least costly 'solution' of the problem of disposing of a surplus population is unfortunately extermination. . . . From a purely bureaucratic perspective, the extermination of the Jews of Europe was the 'final solution' for the British as well as the Germans."[23]

The implications of the Holocaust for human rights are ominous. The horrifying truth to be faced, Rubenstein argued, was that "the Nazis committed no crime at Auschwitz since no law or political order protected those who were first condemned to statelessness and then to the camps."[24] That is the chilling power of state bureaucracy—by stripping individuals of their citizenship they were stripped of all human rights. The most devastating fact of the Nazi era is that even when it was over and the "perpetrators" were brought to judgment at the Nuremburg trials, "Justice Robert Jackson, the presiding American judge . . . expressed the opinion that the Nazis involved in the extermination of the Jews could not be prosecuted for murdering Jews of German nationality. He argued that no state can sit in judgment of another's treatment of its minorities. Jackson felt compelled to assert the ultimacy of national sovereignty over all conflict-ing claims, even the right to life itself."[25] The Nazis were basically tried and condemned for war crimes against the citizens of other sovereign nations. Rubenstein concluded therefore that "the Nurem-berg trials were not a giant step forward in international law. They were in all likelihood an elaborate exercise in national vengeance."[26] Nor was Rubenstein comforted by the notion that there may be a higher law of natural human rights which can be appealed to in the case of such crimes. "The dreadful history of Europe's Jews demon-strated that *rights do not belong to men by nature.* To the extent that men have rights, they have them only as members of the polis, the political community, and there is no polis or Christian commonwealth of na-tions. . . . Outside of the polis there are no inborn restraints on the human exercise of destructive power."[27]

"To the best of my knowledge," Rubenstein argued, "no theo-logian has attempted to deal with the problems implicit in the fact that the Nazis probably committed no crime at Auschwitz." Even if one could prove that atrocities violated some divine law, "it is difficult to see what practical difference that would make in the arena of contem-porary politics."[28] Even if the leaders of major religions could agree on such a transcendent law what penalties would be forthcoming to enforce it? The Holocaust demonstrates that "there are absolutely no limits to the degradation and assault the managers and technicians of violence can inflict upon men and women who lack the power of effective resistance. . . . We live in a world that is functionally god-less . . . [in which] human rights and dignity depend upon the pow-er of one's community to grant or withhold them from its mem-bers."[29]

For Rubenstein the process of secularization does not end, as for Cox, in some technological utopia but rather in a technological apoca-lypse.

> The process of secularization ends where it began. In the begin-
> ning secularization involved the demystification of and the lim-
> itation of the sovereign's power. In the end, the secular state has
> dethroned all mystifications of power and morality save its own.
> The state becomes the only true god on earth with the power to
> define realistically what is good and will be rewarded and what
> is evil and will be punished; this truly sovereign god also has the
> ultimate power of divinity, the power to decide who shall live
> and who shall die. No cold-blooded contemporary David need
> worry about a modern Nathan the prophet proclaiming the ulti-

macy of God's law. That day is over, never to return, unless some apocalyptic catastrophe destroys Western civilization as we know it and compels mankind to begin again out of the nuclear ruins.[30]

Moreover, Rubenstein argued, the solution to our problems cannot simply be a return to that good old-time religion of the "Judeo-Christian" tradition. Why? Because as Max Weber pointed out, the biblical tradition is a desacralizing form of religion that helped to create the very secular world we live in. Like Cox, Rubenstein is prepared to embrace Max Weber's thesis, but with Weber and against Cox, Rubenstein shares a profound pessimism about the social and historical consequences of this biblical and urbanizing history.

The devastating fact is that, "It was the land of the Reformation that became the land in which bureaucracy was first perfected in its most completely objective form."[31] "The very same secularization process which led to Jewish emancipation [under Napolean] led to the death camps one hundred and fifty years later. . . . The process of secularization that led to the bureaucratic objectivity required for the death camps was an essential and perhaps inevitable outcome of the religious traditions of the Judeo-Christian West."[32] The Nazi project cannot be reduced to an "explosion of pagan values," but was rather an outgrowth of Judeo-Christian values. Weber's linkage of the Protestant work ethic with secularization, capitalism, and the development of bureaucracy "are important in demonstrating how utterly mistaken is any view that would isolate Nazism and its supreme expression, bureaucratic mass murder and the bureaucratically administered society of total domination, from the mainstream of Western culture."[33] And for those who might think that these trends might be blamed exclusively on the Reformation, one might remember that it was the bureaucratic organization of the Roman Catholic Church that Hitler admired and took as a model to be emulated in building his own hierarchical order of authority.

Although "the Judeo-Christian tradition is said to proclaim an ethic in which every man is possessed of an irreducible element of human dignity as a child of God, nevertheless, beyond all conscious intent, it has produced a secularization of consciousness involving an abstract, dehumanized, calculating rationality which can eradicate every vestige of that same human dignity."[34] The world was made secular to protect the uniqueness of a God who alone is holy. But by the dialectical logic of a Hegelian "cunning of history" (in which every historical situation tends to generate its opposite), once that secularization process was unleashed it took on a life of its own. Reaching a point of full autonomy during the Enlightenment, the process was turned back on the very traditions that initiated it, bringing about not only the desacralization of the world but the death of God—rendering the world functionally godless, a realm in which nothing is any longer sacred, not even human life.

If the biblical religious traditions embody such a cunning and deadly dialectic so does the urbanization process that also contributed to secularization.

It is an error to imagine that civilization and savage cruelty are antitheses. On the contrary, in every organic process, the antitheses always reflect a unified totality, and civilization is an organic process. Mankind never emerged out of savagery into civilization. Mankind moved from one type of civilization involving its distinctive modes of both sanctity and inhumanity to another. In our times the cruelties, like most other aspects of our world, have become far more effectively administered than ever before. They have not and they will not cease to exist. Both creation and destruction are inseparable aspects of what we call civilization.[35]

Both civilization and religion, Rubenstein argued, have a dark side. The Nazis could think of themselves as a "chosen race" because Judaism invented such a category. And Luther's intolerance and hatred is thoroughly biblical. "There is no escape from the self-defeating ethos of exclusivism and intolerance . . . as long as our fundamental culture is derived from a religious tradition that insists upon the dichotomous division of mankind into the elect and the reprobate."[36] The only cure for such a civilization, Rubenstein argued, is worse than the disease—it is nothing less than an apocalyptic "world-wide catastrophe in which hundreds of millions of human beings are destroyed and civilization as we know it disappears. . . . [And] we have the weaponry to bring it about."[37]

Surveying the paradox of Western civilization, the creation of surplus populations through increased technological efficiency on the one hand and the creation of the technological capacity for total self-destruction on the other hand, Rubenstein ended his book with a final apocalyptic question.: "Is there not," he asked, "a measure of madness in a system of technological rationality that first produces masses of surplus people and then holds forth extermination as the most 'rational' and practical solution to the social problems they pose?"[38]

Technopolis: The Sacralization of the Secular City

For Harvey Cox secularization offered humanity a utopian hope for a new and more fully human city. For Richard Rubenstein it offered only demonic dehumanization leading to a final apocalyptic destiny. For Cox, the demonic and threatening aspects to the secular city were attributed to the vestigial remains of earlier sacral stages of society. Thus the cure is further and more complete secularization. For Rubenstein, further secularization would mean only further dehumanization. If anything, what may be called for is a new sacralization of society, which might reestablish sacred limits on human behavior. For the French theologian and sociologist Jacques Ellul, the paradox of the technological society is that the secular itself is but a new manifestation of the sacred.

Jacques Ellul, first gained attention in this country for his books *The Technological Society* and *The Political Illusion,* both of which appeared in English translation in the United States in the mid-1960s, about the same time as Cox's *The Secular City.*[39] Then a decade later when Rubenstein's book was published, a translation of Ellul's pivotal work on the sociology of religion in a technological society, *The New Demons,* also appeared.[40]

In a world that, according to Harvey Cox, had "come of age" to embrace secularism with hopeful enthusiasm and that Richard Rubenstein saw as hopelessly secular and demonic, Ellul offered an analysis suggesting that the sacral character of the secular society produced both the illusion of utopianism and the very real threat of apocalyptic self-destruction. Ellul set out to show, especially in *The New Demons,* that the secularity of technopolis was but a reversion to a very ancient religiosity in a new guise. The secularity of the technological society, he argued, is structurally and functionally of the same type as the ancient mythologies and their religiosities of nature. We are fooled only because now it is no longer nature but technology that induces this religiosity. So, he insisted, in the midst of this secular world we find ourselves "at the sacred heart of a technical universe."[41] Secularization is dehumanizing rather than liberating not because nothing is any longer sacred but precisely because the impersonal technical-bureaucratic order of technopolis is the new embodiment of sacral value.

Although Ellul acknowledged Marx as the decisive influence in his sociological work, much of his critique of contemporary society, as with Cox and Rubenstein, appealed to themes found in Max Weber's theory of the rationalization and bureaucratization of society. What makes a society technological, he argued, is not the presence of machines but rather techniques that rationalize all areas of human endeavor. Hence it is more accurate to speak of a technical civilization than a technological one.[42] Ellul focused on the inherent dynamic of technical decisions as carried out by the professionals in the myriads of bureaucracies that structure life in a technical civilization. In such a civilization, human freedom becomes an illusion, he argued, because all decisions are made on the basis of the most technically efficient solution. Unlike traditional societies in which techniques were embedded in custom and tradition and made to conform to a larger complex of nontechnological values, modern society is dominated by a complex of techniques, each of which is rationally calculated to produce maximum efficiency. Modern technique totally rationalizes society. Now custom and culture are expected to adjust to the rational requirements of efficiency.

A technical society, differs from all previous societies, including industrial society, by virtue of its application of the most efficient techniques, not only to nature but also to society and the human self. A technical civilization is in essence a managerial civilization. We know we have arrived at a technical civilization when society itself is the object of efficient management, organized according to "the totality of methods rationally arrived at and having absolute efficiency . . . in every field of human activity."[43]

Cox argued that modern bureaucratic organizational structures are more flexible and open to change than traditional societies and suggested that it was only a matter of democratizing them or making them more humanizing. In Ellul's view Cox was a victim of the peculiar kind of political illusion a technical civilization creates. For the politician more and more finds that the issues to be faced have become so complex and technical that his or her only recourse is to consult technical experts. These experts, made available by government and corporate bureaucracies, in turn suggest the most efficient solutions to political problems.

The result is the reduction of political decisions to technical ones while creating the illusion of political freedom (i.e., of political control over technology).[44] This illusion is created by mass media that portray our politicians as dramatic figures taking charge rather than amateurs dependent on bureaucratic experts. Thus the illusion that we are able to govern the shape of our technological society politically is the result of a diversion of attention. Mesmerized by the television screen and its bias for the superficially dramatic in political life, the individual in our society remains oblivious to the underlying trends and direc-

tions set by the geometrically progressive growth of technical decisions.

The media feed us utopian illusions—illusions that tell us that
we can be in control of technology and that our surrender to the
demands of efficiency will bring about a utopian world of abundance.
Media, especially television, not only generate the political illusion
via the evening newscast but also, through both entertainment and
advertising. They sell us a style of life that promises us utopian abundance as the payoff for accepting the demands technical rationalization make upon us. Moreover, Ellul argued, if there are individuals
who have trouble adjusting to the demands of efficiency, never fear,
for a variety of professional technicians—counselors, psychologists,
social workers—are standing by ready to use the latest techniques to
help them adapt.

Cox argued that secularization and technology increased human
options. Ellul however argued that it is no longer possible to choose a
technique for reasons other than efficiency, for the less efficient simply cannot compete with the more efficient. It is not a matter of
technicians imposing their own political values on others, for they
have no freedom to choose anything but the most efficient solution if
they want to keep their jobs. It is rather, to paraphrase Rubenstein, a
matter of the "cunning of technique." Technique has become autonomous. It has taken on a life of its own. What emerges in a technical
civilization is a spontaneous convergence of efficient techniques. The
result is that technique dictates the mechanistic ethos of modern society, an ethos intended by no one and yet to which everyone is forced
to conform. Hence, the techniques that we once thought would be
the instruments of our liberation have turned out to be the new masters that we must serve if we wish to survive. Once we are committed
to the use of the most efficient techniques, said Ellul, we must accept
the fact that "our own desires and aspirations can change nothing."[45]

Ellul therefore found Cox's thesis, that the technical-bureaucratic
order of the secular city is liberating, to be false, even as he also
challenged the thesis both Cox and Rubenstein shared, that the modern technopolis is a secular city. "The sacred," said Ellul, "is not one
of the categories of religion. Religion, rather, is one possible rendition
of the sacred."[46] Just because a phenomenon does not fit our usual
definitions of religion does not mean that the sacred is absent. As a
sociologist Ellul argued that the ethos or institutional infrastructure of
every civilization prior to the modern period was legitimated by a
mythos or superstructure grounded in the experience of sacral power,

and the modern period is no exception. If one finds a phenomenon that fulfills "exactly the same function" that myth and ritual fulfilled in previous societies, then the vocabulary may have changed but the "reality is identical and . . . [we are] really in the presence of a religion or of a myth."[47]

The experience of the sacred is elicited by whatever form of power human beings believe themselves to be dependent on for their existence and well being. Thus in ancient societies nature was that all-encompassing power on which human beings experienced themselves as absolutely dependent for life and the goods of life, even as it could arbitrarily threaten them with death and destruction. So they responded to nature with fascination and dread. They experienced it as a milieu of sacred forces to which one sought to conform through religiopolitical myth and ritual. But then science and technology emerged and desacralized the forces of nature, bringing them under human control. Any power great enough to desacralize the sacred, said Ellul, will itself be experienced as the true ultimate power that governs life and death, and it will stir in us the same primitive religious emotions of fascination and dread that nature once did. Today it is no longer nature but technique and the all-encompassing environment of the technological society that promises us life and abundance and yet can capriciously threaten us with death and destruction. Thus technology unconsciously elicits from us these same emotions and causes us to seek to conform to its demands through our own forms of myth and ritual. It is no accident then that, having always understood ourselves in terms of the sacred, we have now come to identify the evolutionary emergence of human beings with the power to make tools.[48]

We fail to see the religiosity of our civilization, according to Ellul, because we identify religion with monotheistic traditions like Judaism and Christianity, traditions that make a distinction between religious community and political society. Because these communities have lost hegemony over Western culture we assume that this makes the West secular. In fact, however, what has happened is a reversion to pre-Judaic and pre-Christian religiosity, a religiosity originally embodied in polytheism with its worship of the forces of nature and the attribution of sacredness to the very political order of society itself.

In the tradition of Durkheim, Ellul argued that no society can function without the legitimation of the sacred. Sacred order is both essential and yet a constant demonic and dehumanizing threat to human life, for it inevitably absolutizes some particular values at the expense of others while wrapping itself in an aura of unquestionability. Every society generates a morality grounded in its experience of the sacred, and it promotes this as its ethic. The sacred provides the fundamental parameters of moral order by which life is oriented and lived between the dichotomies of the sacred and the profane and its permutations: pure-impure, permitted-forbidden, good-evil. The sacred defines the arena of freedom and the forbidden limits that humanity may not safely transgress. Sacralization defines good and evil (i.e., sacred and profane) in a corresponding hierarchy of social values. The resulting morality is always rooted in the natural, social, and technical necessities of life expressed through a defining symbol and center. In the ancient world that center was nature, its myth was formulated in terms of the god[s] of nature and its ethic took the form of natural law. Today that center is technical efficiency as the criterion of good and evil, its myth is explicitly utopian (and implicitly apocalyptic), and its societal ethic is an ethic of efficiency. It is an ethic driven by a technical imperative—*if it can be done it must be done.* In such an ethic "good and evil are synonyms for success and failure."[49] And as both Ellul and Rubenstein have noted, in modern society the good is identified with the surpassing of all limits; that is, the biggest, the fastest, the best, the most powerful, and so on. The logical direction of such an ethic lies along the path that leads from Auschwitz to Hiroshima and on to a final nuclear apocalypse.

An ethic based on such foundations masquerades as an ethic of realism. The technological system becomes a given, like the order of nature. To do without it becomes unimaginable, like trying to do without nature. Morality, in this situation, is the promotion of those virtues by which individuals and social-political systems can be made to function successfully within the social order as given. In Ellul's view, such an ethic thrives by promising what it cannot deliver— utopia. The ultimate mythological expression of this ethic is the demonic myth of utopia. Even as nature once seduced peoples into sacrificing human lives in exchange for its promised benefits, so today technology exacts these requirements. So we are led into ever deeper levels of subservience to the technological phenomenon by the shining hope of a utopian future, and yet our hope paradoxically seems to create a hopeless situation in which each person feels unable to act, unable to make a difference, "unable to make history, and . . . knows that now there is no other person making it either, only blind mechanisms, obscure powers, inexplicable interactions."[50]

Even our most desperate attempts at revolution find themselves integrated into the sacred order. The profanation of the sacred, Ellul argued, is itself inherent in the dialectic of the sacred. Like the ancient Babylonian new year festival, every revolution that seeks to profane the sacred order is only one more ritually permitted plunge into disorder, an orgiastic regression to chaos whose purpose is returning to the primal sources of life and power in order to recreate sacred order—a sacral renewal of the cosmos. Whereas the sacred defines the socio-cosmic order within which human action can occur (i.e., sacred space), the profane manifests itself as "the sacred time . . . inserted into the sacred order as a period of legitimate disorder, of transgression included in order,"[51] whose real purpose is renewing sacred order. Thus Ellul observed that every revolution since 1789 has only succeeded in reinstituting the nation-state.[52] The names may change with the revolution but the sacral order of society remains essentially unchanged. The success of every revolution requires that the "revolutionary" give way to the "manager" and the reestablishment of an even more rigid sacralized society.

Yet the technical society will "not be a universal concentration camp," Ellul insisted, "for it will be guilty of no atrocity. . . . Our deepest instincts and our most secret passions will be analyzed, published and exploited. We shall be rewarded with everything our hearts ever desired. And the supreme luxury of the society of technical necessity will be to grant the bonus of useless revolt and of an acquiescent smile."[53] It will be guilty of no atrocity, that is, until that fateful moment when we are awakened from our utopian bliss by the nightmare of the ultimate nuclear "final solution" to the uncertainties of the human condition.

According to the biblical narrative, Ellul argued, the first murderer in history, Cain, is the creator of the first city and with it technology.[54] The city became the place of human rebellion against God, the place where human beings sought to take charge of their destiny. "The cities of our time are most certainly that place where man can with impunity declare himself master of nature. It is only in an urban civilization that man has the metaphysical possibility of saying, 'I killed God.'"[55] The spirit of conquest and war dominates urban life: "What world could better demonstrate the parallel between urban civilization and warring civilization than our own, a world where the city and war have become two of the poles around which the entire economic, social and political life of our time move."[56] Despite their differences, Ellul shared much of Rubenstein's vision of the genocidal cunning of the history of civilization. There is something about the sacred order of urban civilization that is demonic, even and especially when that order assumes a secular and technological guise.

From Auschwitz to Hiroshima: Technopolis and the Abyss of the Demonic

In Nazi Germany, according to Elie Wiesel, "there was . . . a technique, a science of murder, complete with specialized laboratories, business meetings and progress charts."[57] The politics and business of genocide was carried out by cultured and highly educated professional and technical experts. One is forced to ask, in the light of Auschwitz, if the logic of efficiency that governs technical civilization is not inherently demonic. Is not the technicist state of mind inherently immune to all ethical considerations other than its own technical imperative. Was not Rubenstein closer to the truth than Cox when he recognized that the cunning of secularization was that, although it began as a protest against sacred absolutes, political and otherwise, it ended in the absolutization of the state. And is not Ellul's analysis even more cogent when he observes that the nation-state itself has become a technical nation-state, subservient to an emerging universal technical order and logic, a sacred order and logic that devalues the value of life itself? If we live "at the sacred heart of a technical universe," it is a universe of demonic proportions. According to Irving Greenberg:

> The strain of evil is deeply embedded in the best potentials of modernity. The pollution is in the liberating technology; the uniformity in the powerful communication and cultural explosion; the mass murder in the efficient bureaucracy. This suggests a desperate need to delegitimatize the excessive authority claims of our culture. Yet some of its most attractive features may be the ones to lead us into the path of no return.
>
> The Holocaust was an advance warning of the demonic potential in modern culture. If one could conceive of Hitler coming to power not in 1933 but in 1963, after the invention of nuclear and hydrogen bombs, then the Holocaust would have been truly universal. It is a kind of last warning that if man will perceive and overcome the demonism unleashed in modern culture, the world may survive. Otherwise the next Holocaust will embrace the whole world.[58]

Greenberg, in an essay "Cloud of Smoke, Pillar of Fire: Judaism, Christianity and Modernity After the Holocaust," published in the same year as Ellul's *The New Demons,* provided a chilling example of the demonic logic of efficiency. The Nazis, he explained, had arrived at the technique of gassing the Jews with Zyklon B after experimenting with a variety of other techniques (firing squads, engine exhaust fumes, etc.) that had proved inefficient and too costly. In the summer of 1944 the Nazis halved the volume of Zyklon B gas used in each gas chamber because of short supplies. The result was to more than double the time and the agony of dying. Using surviving Nazi records, Greenberg calculated that in 1944 it cost less than half a cent per person to gas each victim. And despite this, in an apparent attempt at further economic efficiency, children were thrown into the crematorium fires alive. The alleviation of a child's agony in death was apparently not worth the half cent it would have cost to gas him or her first.

Arthur Cohen in his book *The Tremendum,* published in 1981, argued that the Holocaust is the occasion for a new revelation for all humankind. Only this time what is revealed is not the divine but the demonic. Cohen deliberately adapted the language of the holy, forged by Rudolf Otto, to speak of this revelation. Otto spoke of the awesome and awful power of the divine as a fascinating and yet terrifying *mysterium tremendum.* God, as Cohen interpreted Otto, is "the enormous mystery, . . . the terror-mystery."[59]

The phenomenology of the Holy begins with the perception of the terror-mystery of God and radiates from there, qualified and moderated and textured by the traditional modes of mercy, love, justice, until the utter God becomes the Father God of *Tatenu,* until the shattering presence becomes the still, small voice, until the terror-mystery becomes a God with whom human beings can coinhabit the universe. . . . The ferocity of God appears to resemble the demonic. It is no less the case if one listens, as the [biblical] text unfolds its narrative, that what begins in ferocity ends in a bird with an olive branch and a rainbow. The terror-mystery of the Holy becomes the love-mystery of the Holy and the terror dissolves into grace.[60]

However, "we of the modern age are no longer able to deal with the Holy," Cohen argued, for we "regard ourselves as alone and autonomous in the universe, unbounded by laws except as conventions of power, unhedged by moralities except as consent and convenience dictate."[61] The infinite power of God once denied to humans now is claimed by humans and denied to God.

There was a time when a consciousness of the holy lead human beings to acknowledge two histories, the secular and the holy. In the Middle Ages the tension between these two orders, "the city of man" and "the city of God," was manifest between king and bishop and the tension between these two orders "maintained a healthy imbalance. . . . All this delicate tension dissolved with the victory of the secular state . . . which could conceive, administer, and propagate any viewpoint throughout its realm quickly and efficiently, employing the press, the clergy, the law, the army, and the civil service as instruments of disseminating policy."[62]

A new *tremendum*, a demonic counter-*tremendum*, has appeared upon the face of the earth. "It is the human *tremendum*, the enormity of an infinitized man" who seeks to conquer death by building a "mountain of corpses," that is, by the "magic of endless murder."[63] The *tremendum* is the inversion of life in "an orgiastic celebration of death." "The Jew may well be the ideal victim because his mere persistence, his sheer endurance, his refusal to die throughout four millennia until the *tremendum*, was a celebration of the tenacity of life."[64]

Even as the appearance of the holy separates events in time into before and after, argued Cohen, so does the demonic. In reflecting on Jewish history, one can construct not only a history of divine events such as Exodus and Sinai, but it is also possible to construct a history of demonic events, revelations of the dark side of history. These events Cohen described as "caesuras" that reveal the "abyss of history" opened up by the *tremendum*. "The abyss of history is . . . a gap in normal time, no less a decisive gap than would be the messianic redemption. In the time of the human *tremendum*, conventional time and intelligible causality is interrupted. In that time . . . the demonic tears the skein of events apart and man (and perhaps God no less) is compelled to look into the abyss."[65] In Jewish history, Cohen identified three such events: (1) the destruction of the first Temple, (2) the expulsion of the Jews from Spain, and (3) the Nazi death camps. Each threatened to destroy Jewish faith, hope, and a sense of meaning. In the first two this threat was transcended. In the first case the abyss opened up was closed by rabbis affirming (as the prophets had done after the fall of the first temple) that "we are being punished for our sins." In the second caesura, the abyss was closed by "transforming the event into an end-time of ordinary history and the beginning-time of mystic gnosis." Finally with the Nazi death camps the abyss opened once more and "one-third of the Jewish people fell in."[66] This time, it seemed to Cohen, neither guilt nor mystic hope was able to find meaning in the midst of tragedy and so close the abyss of the demonic. Thus this caesura remains an open wound. There can be no question of closing the abyss this time, he argued. At best, one can hope to build a bridge over it, allowing life to go on even as the wound remains exposed.

When Cohen spoke of this *tremendum* he spoke deliberately of an event that defines Jewish consciousness. "There is no way of making the genocidal totality of the death camps meaningful to the non-Jew as such."[67] For each Jew is a survivor, either in fact or by accident. As with the Exodus and Sinai, so now with the *tremendum*, each Jew must say "I was really, even if not literally, present." And yet Cohen insisted that the *tremendum* is a reality of the twentieth century that neither Jew nor non-Jew can avoid. For in this century there have been more than one caesura opening into the abyss. Non-Jews have their own names for the *tremendum*.

> Auschwitz or Hiroshima or Vietnam or Cambodia or Uganda—what does it matter as long as each person knows the *tremendum* that bears his name; and it is one name only, for the rest what endures beyond the name and binds each human being in abjectness and torment to the other is that the configurations overlay, the *tremendum* of the Jews becomes the *tremendum* of the nations. Over the abyss which each hollows out of history, human beings renew their sense of themselves as creatures beleaguered by their destinies as Jews or Christians or Africans or Buddhists or whatever name is called victim and murderer.[68]

Cohen denied that the uniqueness of the Holocaust is somehow compromised by drawing such analogies. "Every genocidal *tremendum* is unique to the victims." Only those hounded by guilt seek to hide in generalities. "The Cambodian does not tell the Jew that Auschwitz is not unique—it is the calm West that makes such announcements."[69]

Cohen was convinced that if we are to find a way beyond our apocalyptic future, it is essential that the *tremendum* which cannot be circumvented must be excavated. "The task of excavating the demonic is no metaphor. How can we regard the atomic bomb, or Vietnam, or the revelations of Solzhenitzyn's *Gulag*, if not as modalities of the abyss, excavations and elaborations of the human penchant to self-infinity, to the ultimate *hubris* which brings not only Jews but all creatures to the borderlands from which there is return for none. It begins with the Jews and it may end with the habitable world."[70] The demonic, revealed by the holocaustal desolation of the Shoah, can and must be excavated and understood. If the Holocaust is treated as a *mysterium* "unavailable to thought, unsusceptible of any intellectual seizure and identification, the profound risk is run that an historical event is made absolute and therefore necessary, overturning all other historical events whose occurrence is contingent and whose meaning is tributary."[71]

Treating the Holocaust as a *mysterium* would effectively remove it from history and make it impossible to learn anything from it. Although the immensity of it is shattering, Cohen argued, the Holocaust is no mystery for it has its roots in "the triumph of technics by which procedures of dehumanization and distanciation were brought to their perfection. The evil is remarked less in its passion than in its coldness."[72] It is the outcome of history

> stripped of sacral implication for more than two centuries. . . .
> The profane has passed its judgment; whether Church or Syna-
> gogue manipulate the saeculum, not the Holy but the profane
> triumphs. . . . The human in the human being counts for little.
> Submitted to anonymous, manipulative, depersonalized con-
> trol, the individual and his free imagination are flayed raw.
> Within a stripped and naked saeculum the holocaust can be only
> relatively situated. An historical order without prevenient limits
> set by the Holy is, at most, relatively disastrous; absolute disas-
> ter to be meaningful occurs only within a perspective that con-
> tinues to acknowledge the absolute. . . . Given a historical vi-
> sion or social doctrine which allows of no transcendence, no
> openness before absolute claim[s]; no nexus between the human
> and the divine, what has occurred as *tremendum* is, at best, a
> malign fortuity which, . . . we force upon the world's attention
> as though it were of significance to everyone or, abashed, we
> deny it meaning, hoping from the benign indifference of secular
> toleration that the accident will not become normative.[73]

The danger is that the *tremendum* will become either a new absolute or else succumb to pure relativism—either that we shall make it the measure of all things or else simply relegate it to the category of the long history of tragedies generated by "man's inhumanity to man." To evaluate the *tremendum* appropriately requires more than intellectual understanding. It requires the kind of insight that comes through emotional and spiritual identification with the victims.

The Holocaust can and must be understood and yet there are dimensions of such experiences that thought cannot fully penetrate. One need only remember the children burned alive at Auschwitz to know that in being understood in historical terms the reality of the Holocaust is not exhausted, for there is something terrifyingly incomprehensible about the reality of its evil that "exceeds the discernible causalities of history. . . . It gathers up the premises of history, but exceeds them."[74] That is perhaps why Cohen insisted that the *tremendum* requires more than understanding, it requires excavation. One must "subscend" into the abyss, one must be immersed in its sacral and mythical reality in order, it would almost seem, to be born again. But that is not quite right, for one does not so much become a "new being" as a "wounded being." "The wound of the survivor is as permanent as is his redemption by clarification. Illusion is stripped away."[75] Cohen did not think this wound could be healed. All Jews could do was build a bridge over the *tremendum* so as to go on with life.

Cohen's understanding of the Holocaust shared a great deal with Rubenstein's. Both saw the Shoah as a convergence of the demonic in its universal and particular forms—the universal being the triumph of technicism over humanity through the secular bureaucratic state; and the particular, the triumph of the ethnocentric tribal values embedded in the anti-Judaism of Western civilization. What is common to these two forms of the demonic is what Cohen calls the *self-infinitizing* of the human. Self-infinitizing is the penchant of human beings for transforming the secular and relative into the sacred and absolute—in the one case the absolutizing of tribal identity and in the other the absolutizing of the human capacity for technique. And when the secular and relative becomes sacred and absolute the world becomes closed and demonic—headed for some literal apocalyptic destiny. By excavating the demonic Cohen contributed to mapping those dark subterranean passages that link both religion and urbanization to secularization and both to Auschwitz and Hiroshima. Mapping the terrain of the demonic is the first step, not only to building a bridge over it but also a wall around it.

At this point Cohen's project complements that of Jacques Ellul. Where Cohen began with an analysis of the particularity of the Holocaust as a religious revelation that shed light on the demonic nature of technicism, Ellul began with technicism and located its propensity for the demonic in its sacralization. Of course Cohen spoke from a Jewish theological perspective whereas Ellul spoke from a Christian point of view. And yet it should not surprise us that these two perspectives seem to converge in their understanding of the demonic. When Cohen described the demonic power of the human *tremendum* as rooted in the human propensity for self-infinitizing action he could well be quoting Jacques Ellul's exegesis of the book of Revelation.

In the apocalyptic vision of the book of Revelation, the earth is viewed as under the power of the demonic, which takes the appearance of a beast bearing the enigmatic number 666. Probably no other number has been so much speculated upon in the history of exegesis. And yet Ellul's exegesis is as disarmingly simple as it is illuminating. The number 7, he argued, symbolizes the completeness of creation in unity with God. That is, $4 + 3 = 7$, where 4 signifies the four directions of the created order and 3, the trinitarian reality of God. In this context, 666 symbolizes the incomplete created order (symbolized by the sixth day) attempting to multiply itself and its power, to infinitize itself (pretending to be the seventh day); that is, to make itself sacred and therefore, complete, absolute, and unquestionable.[76] Cohen and Ellul offered converging insights into the self-infinitizing human project of the technical nation-state, in which the demonic in its racist particularity merges with the universal demonic propensity of secular, bureaucratic technical ordering. In so doing both substantially agreed with Rubenstein's analysis without succumbing, as both Cox and Rubenstein had, to the myth of the secular. By grasping the sacred and demonic character of the technical nation-state both Cohen and Ellul succeeded in illuminating just why the technological utopianism of the second millennium seems headed for some inevitable apocalyptic destiny. It remains to be seen, therefore, whether the technological utopianism of the secular city can ever be rescued so as to realize Harvey Cox's vision of the humanizing promise of technopolis.

3

From Auschwitz to Hiroshima:
The Apocalyptic Dark Night

Doubling and the Demonic Narrative of Auschwitz:
Killing in Order to Heal

A new public form of religiosity is coming to birth in our time—an essentially demonic form, disclosed by the events of Auschwitz and Hiroshima that have dramatically shaped the world we live in. These events have brought about a demonic inversion of the narrative traditions of the holy. The task at hand is to review the path that led to Auschwitz and from Auschwitz to Hiroshima and beyond to our own MAD (mutually assured destruction) world. As we conclude Part I, the goal is to identify and illuminate the common narrative theme which these events share—*killing in order to heal and slaying to make alive*. For if we can understand the dynamics of this narrative theme we might then begin to imagine an ethical strategy by which to subvert it. That is in fact what I shall attempt to do in Part II.

The Path to Auschwitz

In 381 C.E., under Theodosius, the first Christian emperor (Constantine was not baptized until his deathbed), Christianity was declared the only legal religion of the empire. At this time all pagan traditions were suppressed and forbidden, and Judaism came under severe legal restrictions. Within that same decade an ominous event occurred that was to set the pattern for the next millennia and a half of Jewish-Christian relations. In 388 C.E. the bishop of Callinicum in Mesopotamia led a mob in burning a Jewish synagogue. Theodosius, in an attempt to administer justice, ordered the bishop to rebuild the synagogue. At this time the emperor's throne was in the city of Milan. The bishop of Milan was the great church father and teacher of Augustine, Ambrose. Ambrose rebuked Theodosius for his attempt to have the synagogue rebuilt by the errant Mesopotamian bishop, saying that if the opportunity arose he too would be happy to burn any dwelling where Christ is denied. He then threatened Theodosius with divine punishment if the emperor forced the restoration of the synagogue. Theodosius, in an effort to find a compromise, offered to pay for the restoration out of state funds. Still Ambrose refused his approval. And then Ambrose exercised a new and unheard of power over the emperor who was, of course, also a member of his congregation. Ambrose refused him the sacraments until Theodosius acquiesced to his demands.[1]

This event set the pattern for the treatment of Jews in Western civilization from the fourth century onward. The state became an instrument of the church for the suppression of Judaism in particular and heretics in general. Behind this event already lay more than 300 years of theological anti-Judaism in the writings of the church fathers. Justin Martyr (100–165 C.E.) accused the Jews of killing Christ. Origen (185–254 C.E.) taught that the Jews had committed a crime against the savior of the human race and can never be restored to their "former condition." John Chrysostom (344–407 C.E.), who worried about his Christian flock at Antioch fraternizing with the Jews and attending synagogue services on Jewish holidays, wrote a series of vicious and ugly sermons against the Jews. In these sermons he suggested that God hates and rejects the Jews who cannot be forgiven for their "crime" and who will remain for all time without a temple or a nation as their just punishment. They are, he suggested, "animals fit for slaughter." And Augustine (354–430 C.E.), according to Edward Flannery, was the first to develop the "negative witness" theory to resolve *the Jewish problem.* What is that problem? It is the problem of why God allows Jews to continue to exist at all after the coming of the Messiah, Jesus of Nazareth. The sheer continued existence of those who "denied Christ" had to be explained. Augustine's answer was that as a punishment for killing Christ, God had decreed that they would carry the sign of Cain, condemned to wander the earth forever without a home as a negative witness to the truth of Christianity.[2]

Based on the myth of supersession, which has roots in some of New Testament narrative traditions, the Christian claim has been that Christ brought a new covenant that replaces the old (e.g., Hebrews 8).[3] Therefore the people of the Mosaic covenant have no right to exist as God's chosen people. By claiming that election was transferred from the people Israel to the community of the new covenant, Christians have engaged in a process of spiritual genocide. We have said to the Jew: "You have no right to exist as God's chosen because God has rejected you and chosen us instead. We are the true Israel."

It is hardly coincidental that the legal status of Jews suffered increasingly as these teachings took hold, first under the Theodosian law code and then later under Justinian's revision of that law code. Justinian's code, in fact, revoked the legal status Judaism had enjoyed under the Romans, which had been continued, with restrictions, under Theodosius. In essence Judaism no longer was afforded any legal rights. And as its legal status crumbled the vulnerability of Jews to prejudice and violence increased: synagogue burnings, Jewish children forcibly taken away from their parents and baptized, expulsions of Jews from country after country, and especially from the time of the Crusades, repeated mob violence or pogroms with extensive loss of life. Indeed, in the first six months of the first crusade between a quarter and a third of the Jews of Germany and northern France were slaughtered.[4] Throughout Europe, right into the modern period, Jews lived in fear of their lives every year as holy week came around and the entire history of negative stereotypes about Jews would once more be rehearsed in Christian ritual and sermon.

When Hitler told two Catholic bishops that he was only finishing what the church had started, he knew whereof he spoke. Indeed one of Hitler's favorite German authors was Martin Luther, for he could be quoted without editing to justify Nazi policies.[5] And the yellow badge that the Nazis made the Jews wear was adapted from the Medieval Catholic church. No wonder Hitler could say in *Mein Kampf*, "I believe that I am acting in accordance with the will of the Almighty Creator: by defending myself against the Jew, I am fighting for the work of the Lord."[6] The historian Lucy Dawidowicz describes Hitler's mental world as apocalyptic and Manichaean. He saw his struggle with the Jews in religious terms, as a cosmic battle between the children of light (the Aryan race) and the children of darkness (the Jews), and he saw himself as the messianic figure who would bring this struggle to a successful conclusion on behalf of God's "chosen people"—the German-Aryan race. "Two worlds face one another," said Hitler, "the men of God and men of Satan! The Jew is the anti-man, the creature of another god. He must have come from another root of the human race. I set the Aryan and the Jew over and against each other."[7]

Hitler's identification of the Jews as "children of the devil" and "creatures of another god" draws on a long and popular tradition in Western Christendom, one that can be traced back through Luther and the Medieval tradition to church fathers such as John Chrysostom, but the ultimate source is finally biblical—the Gospel of John, where Jesus is portrayed as saying to his Jewish audience: "Why do you not understand what I say? It is because you cannot accept my word. You are from your father the devil, and you choose to do your father's desires. He was a murderer from the beginning and does not stand in the truth, because there is no truth in him . . . for he is a liar and the father of lies" (John 8:43). Whether or not such statements in the New Testament are correctly interpreted as anti-Judaic in terms of their original context, it is a historical fact that such narrative traditions embedded in the New Testament have, century after century, incited anti-Judaic prejudice.

Unquestioning Obedience and the Two Kingdoms

When Christianity went from being a minority and sometimes persecuted religion to being first the favored religion under the Roman emperor Constantine (313 C.E.), and finally the only legal religion of the empire under the emperor Theodosius (381 C.E.), Christians of the fourth century were extremely impressed by this reversal of fortunes. Men such as Eusebius of Caesarea, author of the first history of the church, and Augustine, perhaps the most influential theologian in the shaping of Western Christianity, took this amazing victory of the church over the empire as a sign of God's will and God's favor. The emergence of the Roman empire came to be seen as the will of God for the establishment of a universal order of peace to facilitate the spread of the Gospel. It was a mutually beneficial interpretation. The empire gained stability from a new legitimating religion, and Catholic Christianity gained a favored and protected ascendancy over its Christian and non-Christian rivals.

With the acceptance of the linkage between church and state as providential came the implication that unquestioning obedience to Christ requires obedience to the state. The key scripture that seems to have promoted this occurs in Paul's letter to the Romans:

Let every person be subject [i.e., obedient] to the governing authorities; for there is no authority except from God, and those authorities that exist have been instituted by God. Therefore whoever resists authority resists what God has appointed, and those who resist will incur judgment. For rulers are not a terror to good conduct, but to bad. Do you wish to have no fear of the authority? Then do what is good, and you will receive its approval; for it is God's servant for your good. But if you do what is wrong, you should be afraid, for the authority does not bear the sword in vain! It is the servant of God to execute wrath on the wrongdoer. Therefore one must be subject, not only because of wrath but also because of conscience. (Romans 13:1–5)

Such a statement, carrying the weight of scriptural status, especially from one as prominent in the Christian tradition as Paul, naturally promoted an identification between obedience to God in Christ and obedience to Caesar, that is, the state. To be sure there were various qualifications on this obedience. Both Aquinas and later Calvin, for instance, allowed for revolt against unjust rulers under very specific conditions. Luther, however, took the most extreme position, suggesting that in fact under virtually no conditions is revolt permissible. That extreme ethic of obedience goes a long way toward explaining the cooperation of the churches with the Nazis. But even in its less extreme Catholic and Calvinist forms the presumption is still on the side of obedience to the state.

It was to Romans 13 that Luther appealed in formulating his extreme position in response to the peasant revolts of his time. The peasants responded favorably to Luther's message of the freedom and equality they had in Christ. They felt encouraged by it to revolt against the nobility, whom they believed abused and ignored their freedom and dignity. Luther was then forced to clarify his position on the two kingdoms through which God rules the world: the spiritual inner kingdom of God expressed through the lives of the faithful in the church and the outer physical kingdoms of the world expressed through established rulers. Through the first God rules with the right hand of grace and compassion and through the second God rules with the left hand of justice and wrath.[8] The freedom of the Gospel, it seems, is only an inner spiritual freedom. The equality of all in Christ is to be realized only in the next life. Here in this world there can never be equality. God acts through the state to establish order, and all must learn to accept their assigned places in that social order. Only God can establish rulers and only God can remove rulers. It is not permissible for human beings to revolt, even against a vicious and unjust ruler.

The need to be obedient to the rule of God through both the right and the left hands leads Luther to formulate an ethic of paradox. One must live in the world, he insisted, with the knowledge that one is always, at the same time, both a saint and a sinner. Even a Christian society of saints would remain a society of sinners in need of both God's gracious compassion and just wrath. For Luther, one must clearly distinguish between one's personal life under the rule of God's right hand and one's public life which is under the rule of the left hand of God. Although one should be loving and forgiving in one's personal life, one may also have to perform harsh acts of justice for the good of others in the public realm. The paradox of the ethical life is that one can be both a loving and forgiving Christian and at the same time perform the role of public executioner or hangman, for example, without inconsistency or moral culpability.[9] In fact, although the Medieval Catholic tradition required a public executioner to do penance, Luther insisted there was no need for this, because it is God who takes the life and not the executioner, who only acts in obedience to his duty and hence accrues no personal guilt.[10] In both realms (public and personal) one who acts in unquestioning obedience is carrying out the will of God.

As painful as it may be, it is necessary to acknowledge that it was not only Luther's adoption of traditional anti-Judaic theology that paved the road that led to Auschwitz but also his understanding of faith as unquestioning obedience. Neither of these aspects originated with Luther. Both have deep roots in the first century origins of Christianity. But it was especially through Luther that they were mediated to Nazi Germany so that Hitler could see himself as finishing what the church started. Both aspects contributed directly to the human capacity for the demonic during the Shoah.

Doubling and the Demonic at Auschwitz

When one stands back and takes in the sum total of evil during the Shoah it is overwhelming. When one looks at specific deeds of cold atrocity, it is overwhelming. But when one examines the personal histories and day-to-day life of persons who committed such deeds one is struck with how ordinary most of these persons are. The Shoah, says Eli Wiesel, demonstrated that, "it is possible to be born into the upper or middle class, receive a first-rate education, respect parents and neighbors, visit museums and attend literary gatherings, play a role in public life and begin one day to massacre men, women and children, without hesitation and without guilt. It is possible to fire your gun at living targets and nonetheless delight in the cadence of a poem, the composition of a painting. . . . One may torture the son before the father's eyes and still consider oneself a man of culture and religion."[11]

Robert Jay Lifton's recent study *The Nazi Doctors: Medical Killing and the Psychology of Genocide*[12] offers some insight into how such things are possible. Lifton's interviews with physicians who served in the death camps provides an intimate look into the lives and psyches of the professional physicians who played a major role in operating the camps. Lifton tells of commenting to a survivor of Auschwitz how he was struck by the "ordinariness of most Nazi doctors . . . neither brilliant nor stupid, neither inherently evil nor particularly ethically sensitive, they were by no means the demonic figures—sadistic, fanatic, lusting to kill—people have often thought them to be."[13] To which the survivor commented: "But it is *demonic* that they were *not* demonic." The lesson of Auschwitz is that "ordinary people can commit demonic acts."[14]

What made it possible for these doctors to kill with a good conscience was a certain kind of narrative theme. The underlying narrative theme of Nazi mythology was cosmological. Through this narrative the Nazis were able to promote their ideology as objective truth based in the very structure of nature. As Lifton noted, "the nation would now be run according to what Johann S. [a Nazi physician] and his cohorts considered biological truth, 'the way human beings really are.' That is why he had a genuine 'eureka' experience— a sense of 'That's exactly it!'—when he heard Rudolf Hess declare National Socialism to be 'nothing but applied biology.' "[15] The Aryan race was *by nature* the superior race. The Nazi vision was a "biocracy" in which the state was "no more than a means to achieve *'a mission of the German people on earth'*: that of *'assembling and preserving the most valuable stocks of basic racial elements in this* [Aryan] *people . . . raising them to a dominant position'*."[16] It was this biological-racist narrative that legitimated surgical excision of the Jews by means of the death camps. The Jews were viewed as "agents of 'racial pollution' and 'racial tuberculosis,' as well as parasites and bacteria causing sickness, deterioration, and death in the host peoples they infested. . . . The cure had to be radical: that is, (as one scholar put it), by 'cutting out the *canker of decay* . . . ' "[17]

If, as the tradition of narrative ethics argues, the rationality of our actions is determined by the narrative we understand ourselves to be in, then this story gave rationality and even a sense of moral duty to the Nazi physician's task of having to kill in order to heal. "In terms of actual professional requirements, there was absolutely no need for doctors to be the ones conducting selections: anyone could have sorted out weak and moribund prisoners. But if one views Auschwitz, as Nazi ideologues did, as a public health venture, doctors alone became eligible to select."[18] The Nazi myth put them in charge of both nature and history, making them the authors of their own story. In this story, the physician played a key role as the representative embodiment of modern science and technology whose societal role as a healing professional gave legitimacy to the Nazi genocidal program against the Jews.

How is it that ostensibly quite ordinary men and women, well-educated persons, medical professionals dedicated to healing and giving life, could so totally and completely embrace this demonic genocidal process? The answer, Lifton's work suggests, lies in a process he calls *doubling*. Doubling is "the division of the self into two functioning wholes, so that a part-self acts as an entire self."[19] Doubling originates in the extreme form of self-deception that occurs when the self is placed in an environment radically discontinuous with its previous environment in its values and practices, so that one's previous self becomes dysfunctional. In the doubling process, the Auschwitz physician developed a second self "both autonomous and [yet] connected to the prior self that gave rise to it."[20] He needed his first self to continue to think of himself as a good man and a good physician, and he needed the second self to perform his new responsibilities and duties in his new Auschwitz environment. The physician created a second separate "killing self" as a means of psychological survival to keep his or her "true self" unstained by the guilt of his or her duties.

The double, Lifton insists, should not be confused with multiple personalities. Whereas both multiple personalities and doubling are responses to extreme environmental conditions, in the multiple personality these conditions occur in childhood as the personality is developing, and the personality splinters into selves that may be totally unaware of each other. In doubling the splintering occurs in the adult personality, and the two selves are very much aware of each other. Nor should doubling be equated with a psychosis such as schizophrenia. Metaphorically speaking, Lifton argued, in schizophrenia the self is like a tree in which the self has splintered and shattered near its roots. In the case of multiple personality, the trunk is essentially sound and the split is higher up. In doubling the split "takes place still higher on a tree whose roots, trunk, and larger branches have previously experienced no impairment; of the two branches artificially separated, one grows fetid bark and leaves in a way that enables the other to maintain ordinary growth, and the two intertwine sufficiently to merge again should external conditions favor that merging."[21] This impairment is temporary and "occurs as part of a larger institutional structure which encourages or even demands it."[22]

For the doctors of Auschwitz, the change from their family and professional environment in the larger society to the death camps produced a demonic form of doubling. Doubling, however, is not inherently demonic. Indeed Lifton argues that it is a fundamental human phenomenon. The root of doubling is the mysterious experience of reflexive self-consciousness (i.e., the reflecting self's [as subject] capacity to reflect upon itself [as object]. Doubling becomes demonic only when the reflecting self refuses to accept responsibility for its role-defined public self through which it expresses itself. The fundamental ethical choice is whether the reflecting self will accept responsibility for the self as actor (i.e., the self that performs its role) or whether it will refuse to accept responsibility for the public role-defined self's actions. In such a case the reflecting self surrenders its will to some higher authority who absolves that self of responsibility for its public self's actions. In that situation the public self has no personal deciding center but is rather possessed by some outside or heteronomous authority.

Although Lifton did not explicitly make the distinction, I think it is useful to distinguish between the *primary doubling* of reflexive self-consciousness (i.e., our ability to step back and watch ourselves) and the *secondary doublings* through which we create role-defined selves in response to different institutional environments. I suspect that doubling first occurred when human beings made the move from the tribe to the city. The complex roles required of the urban self tends to produce multiple personalities. Urban individuation forces the self into self awareness, requiring the self to deal with the conflicts among the multiple selves created by the multiple roles of urban life. If these selves are consciously related to each other in an integrated ethical ecology answerable to the inner demands for self-transcendence and self-knowledge, the result will be life-enhancing. But if these selves remain sociologically and psychologically compartmentalized, the result will be Manichaean, demonic, and dehumanizing.[23]

Essential to the process of demonic doubling found among the Nazi physicians was being confronted with the social reality of Auschwitz as a massive unchangeable fact. As one physician reported: "One couldn't . . . really be against it. . . . That is, mass killing was the unyielding *fact of life* to which everyone was expected to adapt."[24] The ritual initiation of a doctor into the process of making the selections included a routine of heavy drinking and socializing, during which the new doctors would be helped to accept what they were expected to do by those who were already adapted to the process. When a physician raised the question of how these things could be done, a process of *reality therapy* would set in, in which the newcomer would be brought to see that the very fact that these camp inmates had been sent to Auschwitz meant that they were already dead. It was simply a matter of how and when. As one Nazi physician put it, "What is better for him [the prisoner]—whether he croaks . . . in shit or goes to heaven in [a cloud of] gas?"[25] The massive, everpresent, all-encompassing bureaucratic process already had determined their fate unchangeably and therefore the physician was encouraged not to feel personally responsible. Indeed, under the conditions of war, it was argued, physicians' have a duty to select. Why should the physicians' responsibilities be any less demanding than those of the soldiers at the battlefront? One must not shirk one's duty, no matter how unpleasant. In fact the more unpleasant, the more morally praiseworthy it was to have the courage to perform it.

The doctor's professional identity also helped facilitate his or her acceptance of the paradox of having to kill in order to heal. For Lifton argues that becoming a medical student itself creates a form of doubling. "That doubling usually begins with the student's encounter with the corpse he or she must dissect, often on the first day of medical school. One feels it necessary to develop a 'medical self,' which enables one not only to be relatively inured to death but to function reasonably efficiently in relation to the many-sided demands of the work."[26] Although anyone might undergo the process of doubling, says Lifton, nevertheless, "professionals of various kinds— physicians, psychologists, physicists, biologists, clergy, generals, statesmen, writers, artists—have a special capacity for doubling. In them a prior, humane self can be joined by a 'professional self' willing to ally itself with a destructive project, with harming or even killing others."[27] The temptation of the professional, he argues, is to suppose that whatever one does as a professional is always healing.

The process of doubling did not eliminate conscience but rather transferred conscience to the new Auschwitz self "which placed it within its own criteria for good (duty, loyalty to group, 'improving' Auschwitz conditions, etc.), thereby freeing the original self from responsibility for actions there."[28] Doubling is a kind of shifting of narrative horizons—a migration into a new world, in which what would be unethical within the first world is perfectly ethical and rational within the second. The new self exists within a new cosmos (a new institutionally embodied narrative), and that cosmos has built into it its own ethical norms to which the self must conform as long as it exists in that cosmos. Doubling is the coward's alternative to questioning the legitimacy of the new world one is asked to inhabit—in this case the world of Auschwitz.

In doubling, one part of the self 'disavows' another part. What is repudiated is not reality itself—the individual Nazi doctor was aware of what he was doing via the Auschwitz self—but the meaning of that reality. The Nazi doctor knew that he selected, but did not interpret selections as murder. One level of disavowal, then, was the Auschwitz self's altering of the meaning of murder; and on another, the repudiation by the original self of *anything* done by the Auschwitz self. From the moment of its formation, the Auschwitz self so violated the Nazi doctor's previous self concept as to require more or less permanent disavowal.[29]

"Doubling," Lifton argued, "is the psychological means by which one invokes the evil potential of the self. The evil is neither inherent in the self or foreign to it. To live out the doubling and call forth the evil is a moral choice for which one is responsible, whatever the level of consciousness involved. By means of doubling, Nazi doctors made a Faustian choice for evil: in the process of doubling, in fact, lies an overall key to human evil."[30] In this process doubling begins not through an act of commission but of omission. The demonic double overtakes the personality not when that person wills to do evil. No, the will to evil is a secondary parasitic act that depends on a prior *lack* or *absence* of a will to truthfulness and self-knowledge. It is out of that *absence* and *lack* that the demonic double is born in self-deception. What makes self-deception possible is that the self does not have to do anything. The double emerges through "not doing." Thus the self can say to itself—"How can I be responsible, I didn't do anything?" In that moment of refusal to heed the inner doubts and questions, the inner demand for truthful self-knowledge, there is a failure of self-transcendence. In that moment the demonic assumes flesh and evil becomes a real ontic presence.

Demonic doubling can be short-circuited if the reflecting self reclaims and reintegrates the double, assuming responsibility for the actions of its public self. This would require the reflecting self to use its capacity for doubling (i.e., for self-alienation and self-reflection) not to distance itself and disown the actions of its public self but call itself into question. Unlike the case of demonic doubling, this reflecting self remains dialectically related to its public role identities and is prepared to accept responsibility for all its public selves (i.e., social roles). The demonic double, by contrast, is a substitute for genuine self-transcendence. Instead of surrendering itself to its own doubts and self-questioning, which would open the self to the infinite inner demand for truthfulness, the demonic double confines both itself and its victims to the hell of the closed totalitarian world created by its self-deception.

Nietzsche's madman wondered what games and rituals would have to be invented to be worthy of the death of God. The double, with his or her professional scientific and technical expertise, discovered the appropriate ritual—the archetypal ritual of recreating the world, recreating it, of course, in his or her own image, which means eliminating from the world all who are *different* or *alien*. Finite beings imagine being infinite to mean having absolute power over life and death. The Holocaust, Cohen argued, is the product of "an infinitized man" who seeks to conquer death by building a "mountain of corpses."[31]

Using this analysis of the Nazi doctors as our guide, we can say that the demonic emerges in society with the critical conjunction of three factors. First, there must be the creation of mythological narrative that divides humanity into two camps: the children of light and the children of darkness, sacred and profane, good and evil, saved and damned—those who are the *same* and the those who are *different* (i.e., aliens or strangers). This myth demands and justifies that the forces of evil and chaos be removed to save the cosmos as the dwelling place for the true children of light. Such a division of humanity into opposing camps, moreover, must not appear arbitrary. It must be cosmicized, so that these divisions appear, not as the work of human invention or judgment, bias, or prejudice, but rather simply as reality or *the way things are*. In the case of the Shoah, this mythic narrative has a long history of development going back at least to the Christian myth of supersession. But the cosmicization of this myth occurred only with the Enlightenment when being a Jew was redefined, from religious terms to secular, scientific, racial-biological terms.[32]

Second, at some critical point an institutional revolution must occur to give massive social embodiment to this myth. In Nazi Germany this revolution began in the National Socialist Party (NSDAP) as an unholy community that succeeded in *transforming* German society through the process of *Gleichschaltung* or "coordination." Without this second step, the Nazi myth of the Aryan race would have remained an impotent fringe phenomenon. Again the institutional precedents for this can be found in the earlier institutional history of Christendom, religious and political, that stripped Jews of their citizenship and rights. (Hitler especially admired the bureaucratic authoritarianism of the Catholic church.)

The third and final factor necessary for the demonic is largely a response to the first two; namely, the process of doubling. Doubling is undoubtedly incipiently present from the beginning, but once the myth has been embodied in the total institutional structure of society, doubling becomes a pervasive social phenomenon, not only in the death camps but in society at large as well. The massive institutional embodiment of the demonic, legitimated by the mythic narrative, makes its bureaucratic structures appear to be impenetrable and un-changeable. They become part of the natural order and thus simply a given that is not a matter for ethical reflection any more than trees and mountains. One is simply faced with reality and must learn to accommodate by being "realistic." Realism is the language of the de-monic whose purpose is to seduce us into thinking we have no other choice. Again and again, the Nazi doctors justified what they "had to do" with the thought that nothing could be changed, that once the bureaucracy had selected the Jews for the camps they were already dead. Everything that followed was a mere formality, fulfilling their *predestination*. Hence, the Nazi doctors did not see themselves as do-ing the selecting at all—that, in a sense, was already complete.

Doubling and Luther's Two-Kingdom Ethic

Although Robert Lifton does not explore the role that Luther's two kingdom ethic may have played in the development of this doub-ling, I would argue that the influence of Luther's ethic on German culture directly contributed to the propensity of the Nazi doctors to develop a demonic double.[33] Luther's ethic demands that one devel-op a double self through which one's personal life is kept separate from one's public life. Luther's ethic suggests that every Christian must live with the paradox of being in two stories at the same time—the right-handed story of the sacred inner and personal kingdom ruled by God's gracious mercy and the left-handed story of the outer kingdom, the secular and public world ruled by God's just wrath.

The combination of Luther's insistence that one may be obli-gated in one's public role to carry out unpleasant duties (e.g., the hangman) and his emphasis on unquestioning obedience, even to an unjust ruler, forces the self to double when it performs its public duty. It is hard to imagine Luther's good Christian hangman performing his duty without doubling. Doubling may be a universal psychological phenomenon in response to radical changes in institutional contexts, as Lifton suggests, but, given the formative role of Luther's ethic in German culture, doubling may have been built into the culture. Christian ethics, I believe, played a preparatory role in promoting the eruption of the demonic capacity for doubling and self-deception in Nazi Germany.

But it is not only the two kingdom aspect of the Christian story, as Luther interpreted it, that contributed to the legitimation of the demonic double among the Nazi doctors. There is also a fundamental flaw in the narrative that accompanies and authorizes his two kingdom ethic—the narrative that portrays the life of faith as a paradoxical *wrestling with God*. The way in which Luther appropriated the biblical story of Jacob wrestling with the stranger (Genesis 32:23–32) to express his understanding of faith departs from and inverts the meaning of the biblical story, authorizing unquestioning obedience to a God who is the archetypal model of the one who kills in order to heal.

Luther speaks of God as a hidden God with whom he wrestled in an inner struggle. This God reveals himself paradoxically through opposites which come dangerously close to breaking the unity of God into a Manichaean-Gnostic duality. Thus Luther tells us that:

> *When God brings to life, he does it by killing*; when he justifies, he does it by making guilty; when he exalts to heaven, he does it by leading to hell. . . . And finally, God cannot be God unless he first becomes a devil and we cannot go to heaven unless we first go into hell, and cannot become the children of God, unless we first become the Devil's children. . . . We have spoken in extreme terms of this, and we must understand what is just as startling, that God's grace and truth, or his goodness and faithfulness, *rule over us and demand our obedience*. . . . For a little while I must accord divinity to the Devil, and consider our God to be the Devil. But this does not mean that the evening lasts for the whole day. Ultimately, his steadfast love and faithfulness are over us [Psalms 117:2].[34]

This theme of bringing to life through death did not originate with Luther but goes back to Augustine of Hippo, who in his *Confessions* interpreted his wrestling with his own inner *other* self, as a wrestling with the God *"who gives wounds in order to heal, who kill[s] us lest we should die away from you"* (*The Confessions*, Book II, 2).[35]

Both Luther and Augustine, who stands behind Luther's piety, invert the meaning of the biblical story in which Jacob is told his new name will be Israel (Genesis 32:23–32). In this story Jacob is accosted by a stranger who wrestles with him until daybreak. Jacob demands that the stranger identify himself but he will not. Instead he requires

Jacob to do so and then blesses Jacob and promptly changes his name to *Israel*, meaning wrestler with God, "for you have striven with God and with humans, and have prevailed" (Genesis 32:28). And as the sun rises and the stranger flees, Jacob walks away limping, resolving to call the place *Peniel*, meaning "I have seen God face to face and yet my life is preserved" (32:31). The biblical version, as Jewish interpretation has faithfully recorded, emphasizes that although the stranger (God) is not defeated, Jacob prevails. He is the victor. Within Judaism, this story is understood to authorize an audacious faith that dares to question God and demand that God keep the covenant promises (as we shall see in the chapter 5).

The Augustinian-Lutheran interpretation of Jacob wrestling with the stranger (i.e., God), by contrast, requires that God be the victor and the self be defeated. Conversion is the defeat of the human self that, Augustine says, sweeps away all doubts and Luther says, demands total obedience. It is as if, in the Christian narrative imagination, somebody has to win and somebody has to lose. Moreover, it is imperative that the human self be the loser, for by dying the self is raised up to new life. Healing comes through killing, life comes through death. But the Genesis story, as Judaism has rightly seen, presents another possibility, namely, that both God (the stranger) and Jacob can the be the victor. In the Genesis story God does wound in order to heal (Jacob's thigh is injured yet he is blessed by the stranger and given a new name) but he does not slay in order to make alive.

In the light of the Shoah and Lifton's study of the ethic of the Nazi doctors, with their two-kingdom ethic of doubling and absolute obedience so as to be able to kill in order to heal, this strand of Augustinian (Catholic) and Lutheran (Protestant) narrative tradition and its understanding of *two-kingdom* ethics that has dominated the Christian tradition must be recognized for what it is: totally demonic, morally bankrupt, and permeated with the stench of death. Few have seen the pagan[36] and demonic possibilities that lurk beneath the surface of the biblical narrative traditions with more clarity than Richard Rubenstein, when in *After Auschwitz* he confessed that he had abandoned belief in the prophetic-rabbinic God of history in favor of a belief in the pagan deity, the holy nothingness, that is witnessed to in the biblical preprophetic narratives of Judaism. When this pagan dimension of the biblical deity becomes dominant, the holiness of God, he argued, becomes "more than a moral force. He who makes alive is also He who slays by His very presence. . . . I believe few men knew the truth about God in His holiness as did Martin Luther."[37] The difference between the God of transcendence and the idol (even if the idol is a biblical one) is captured in these alternate narrative interpretations. The idol demands the total annihilation of our individuality, requiring our total obedience and conformity, whereas the living God invites our disputation and affirms each of us in our dignity as an *other*. This God only demands that we do the same for those *others*, those strangers, sent into our lives as an invitation to self-transcendence.

From Auschwitz to Hiroshima: The Demonic Inversion of the Narrative Traditions of the Holy—East and West

On July 16, 1945, at 5:30 in the morning the first atomic bomb was exploded in the desert of New Mexico at a site named Trinity. A fireball "infinitely brighter than the sun, its temperature 10,000 times greater, began an eight-mile ascent . . . turning night into day."[38] The awesomeness of the experience inevitably elicited a religious response from among the observers. One reporter, overwhelmed by this tremendous display of power, said he thought of "the Lord's command, 'Let there be light.'" His response was in tune with the human response to power throughout the ages. Power over life and death has always been both fascinating and terrifying, awesome and awful. Whenever human beings encounter a power they believe governs their destiny, Rudolf Otto suggests, they respond religiously with the ambivalent emotions of fascination and dread. The power of the bomb evoked emotions analogous to those evoked by the holy. But the symbols of "light" and "life," drawn from the book of Genesis were not really appropriate for this event was no life-giving act of creation. It was rather a demonic inversion of the holy, revealing a power meant to produce total annihilation. J. Robert Oppenheimer, the scientist who orchestrated the Manhattan Project, captured its meaning most accurately. He remembered the line from the Bhagavad Gita, spoken by Krishna in his manifestation as the cosmic deity Vishnu, the lord of life and death: *"I am become death, the shatterer of worlds."* Here, it seems, the inner telos of the normless technological will to power revealed its logical outcome.

The technological utopianism of the secular city, embodied in the Manhattan Project, revealed itself at Trinity to be leading toward an apocalyptic and suicidal destiny for the whole human race. We found ourselves in the presence of a new sacred power. The demonic nature of the sacral power of technology that first manifest its true face at Auschwitz, as Irving Greenberg put it, in a "cloud of smoke and a pillar of fire," now reared its ugly head again at Hiroshima.[39]

Like all manifestations of the sacred, it separated itself from ordinary time and space. It was not, however, an intrusion of the divine into time and space but rather, as Arthur Cohen put it, a *caesura*, an opening up of the abyss of the demonic. It was an abyss whose fault line ran from Auschwitz to Hiroshima. The division of history into a new before and after, which began at Auschwitz, found its completion in the movement from Trinity to Hiroshima. On August 6, 1945, at 8:16 a.m., the bomb exploded over Hiroshima and the *millennium of utopia*, the millennium that gave rise to science, technology and the myth of progress, came to a premature apocalyptic end.

Although they stand side by side in the mythic imagination, Auschwitz and Hiroshima cannot be equated as historical events. Auschwitz expresses the linkage of the technological mythos to the intentionally demonic tribalism of the Germans. Hiroshima represents the halting of a similar linkage of technology and demonic tribalism among the Japanese by the United States, which for all its failures was shaped by a narrative tradition of welcoming, not annihilating, the alien and the stranger.[40] Hiroshima stands as a warning, reminding us that if the Germans or Japanese had had the bomb, demonic tribalism and genocide would have won the day.

The parallel between Hiroshima and Auschwitz is only partial, and yet it is critical to understand, for it highlights the apocalyptic and demonic trajectory of technological efficiency. In sheer numbers, Auschwitz overwhelms Hiroshima and Nagasaki combined. At Auschwitz the death toll is in the range of 2 million, whereas the death toll from Hiroshima and Nagasaki combined may have reached 400,000.[41] But the true measure of the immensity of Hiroshima is not in the total number killed but rather the technical efficiency of the bomb. The bomb makes it possible to recreate the desolation of the Shoah at a level of mind-boggling efficiency the Nazis could scarcely imagine. It took the Nazis several years to create their cities of the dead, but our technological genius now makes it possible to do so almost instantaneously. On average Auschwitz, as I calculate it, exterminated 2,000 to 3,000 people per day. A record day might see the extermination of 10,000.[42] But at Hiroshima, tens of thousands died instantly. And even more died from the after effects of the bomb. The atomic bomb makes the gas chambers seem pathetically inefficient by comparison.

The Hiroshima bomb was an eschatological phenomenon, offering an apocalyptic promise of yet more terrifying things to come. Today, a single one megaton hydrogen bomb equals eighty Hiroshima bombs. Before the thaw in US-Russian relations Jonathan Schell estimated a nuclear attack on the United States might be in the range of 10,000 megatons or the equivalent of 800,000 Hiroshima bombs.[43] The total number of bombs in existence around the world was estimated by Schell to be approximately "50,000 warheads . . . possessing the explosive yield of roughly . . . 1,600,000 times the yield of the bomb that was dropped by the United States on the city of Hiroshima."[44] The United States and the Soviet Union could destroy each other with "a fraction of available megatonnage."[45] And while political tensions have eased our weapons are still poised. An all out nuclear war would in all likelihood bring down a nuclear winter, a socioecological catastrophe which would make life virtually impossible and death preferable to life, even for survivors. Indeed, by some calculations, the exploding of as little as 1 percent of the current megatonnage could bring on such a winter.[46] As an eschatological symbol, Hiroshima reminds us that our technological power now exceeds all human intentions, whether benevolent or demonic. If there is a next time for the use of the bomb it will not make any difference who the good guys or the bad guys are. The bomb now dwarfs human intentions and engulfs us all in a mythic pattern of collective suicide.

From the vantage point of our post-Auschwitz and post-Hiroshima experience it must be said that we live in an age of apocalyptic desolation. We live in the "in-between time"—the time between the first and second coming of The Bomb. We await the coming of the millennium fearing the beast that W. B. Yeats saw "slouching toward Bethlehem."[47] It appears as if our present millennium (1000 to 2000 C.E.), which was dominated by utopian hopes, could be headed for an apocalyptic end—if not with the bang of nuclear annihilation then with the wimper of radioactive waste and other forms of pollution. We live in a world in which nothing appears to be sacred any longer, not even human life. Civilization, the world created by urbanization, says Richard Rubenstein, ends not in utopia but in the necropolis of the death camps. The human city may be destined to become the city of the dead.

If Auschwitz provided the first prophetic warning of the destiny of an emerging world civilization, Hiroshima provided the second. Hiroshima is the sign that the demonic inversion of the holy embodied in modern technological society will not be confined to the Western world. The invention of the atomic bomb foretells that the final apocalypse will be a global one—an act of collective global suicide. We live in an apocalyptic age, a time of Shoah, that is, of desolation—a time whose symbols are Auschwitz and Hiroshima.

Once silence was the language of the mystical encounter with the source of life. But after Auschwitz and Hiroshima silence has become the language of the encounter with the kingdom of death. In the mystical encounter with the holy, the symbolic imagination was transcended and individuals were left only with the emptiness and imagelessness of transcendence. As Robert Lifton's comparative analysis of the survivors of both Auschwitz and Hiroshima (especially of artists and writers) confirms, today another kind of immensity defeats the imagination—the immensity of the demonic. Moreover, every attempt to capture, in either word or image, the experience of immersion in the kingdom of death, Elie Wiesel has suggested, seems totally inadequate. Or as one Japanese author-survivor put it "there is . . . no category for the atomic bomb experience. . . . One can find no words to describe it."[48] And another confessed that the immensity of the grotesque reality of death—the dead bodies, the smell—left him blocked "by a sense of the experience as sacred."[49]

Auschwitz and Hiroshima are the formative religious events of our world. The formative religious events of our secular world are paradoxically, at one and the same time, both sacred and profane. They have a profane, even demonic, face and yet they elicit religious responses. Like the great classical events of religious history, they are historical events that arise out of history and yet transcend history to divide time into *before* and *after*. But unlike the events of the Buddha's Enlightenment, the Exodus led by Moses, or the Resurrection of Jesus, these sacred events are demonic—a demonic inversion of the holy.

August 6, the day the bomb was dropped, was the date for the feast of Transfiguration in the Christian calendar, a day that celebrates the revelation of the divinity of Jesus and provides a foretaste of his resurrection, recalling how Jesus and his disciples climbed to the top of a high mountain where he was transformed before their very eyes. In that moment, "His face shone like the sun, and his clothes became dazzling white," so bright that his disciples covered their eyes and fell down (Matthew 17:1–8). The telling of this event in the New Testament itself alludes to Moses coming down the mountain with the ten commandments—commandments that offer life. Here too, "the skin of his face was shining and they [the people] were afraid to come near him."(Exodus 34:29–35) These events recall formative moments in the history of Western religious experience. They recall the power of the Jewish God of history whose reality Christians sought to affirm with the doctrine of the trinity. But after Auschwitz and Hiroshima it seems as if the God of history has died. The symbols of "light" and "life" have been coopted by the demonic and undergone an inversion of meaning.

This is no less true for the Buddhists than it is for Jews and Christians. Once enlightenment meant to bring the light of insight that liberates the self from suffering and death through the experience of *anatta* or no-self. But the total annihilation of all selves at Hiroshima, brought about a demonic inversion of the experience of *no-self*. The *hibakusha* (literally, "explosion affected person") or survivors of Hiroshima and Nagasaki speak of themselves as *mugamuchū*, meaning "without self, without center."[50] However, they speak not of the humanizing experience of liberation or no-self that comes with Buddhist enlightenment but the experience of total desolation that comes with total immersion in the kingdom of death of which the survivors of Auschwitz were the first to speak. The dark night of Hiroshima brings no mystical fulfillment only total immersion in a shoah, a time of desolation.

Thus *light* and *enlightenment* no longer symbolize the giving of life. The *cloud* and the *pillar of fire* by which Israel was led through history no longer remind us of liberation and salvation but rather of the gas chambers of Auschwitz and the mushroom clouds of Hiroshima and Nagasaki. Trinity no longer names the God of life but the place where planetary death was born. We live in a time of the demonic inversion of the holy. Now when a commanding voice speaks from a burning fire it speaks not the language of being, *I Am Who Am*, but of not-being, *I Am Become Death*.

From Trinity to the Bhagavad Gita: Wounding in Order to Heal, Slaying to Make Alive

The Meeting of East and West

Oppenheimer's recalling the words of the Bhagavad Gita at the Trinity test site is very revealing. It is as if in a moment of inverse enlightenment or revelation, the religious symbols of East and West clashed and exploded within his psyche and he grasped the experience of the sacred as the demonic inversion of the holy. It seems he chose the name, *Trinity*, for the experimental bomb site under the influence of the seventeenth century poet John Donne, known for his poetic exploration of religion, death, and suicide. General Groves, Oppenheimer's superior, wrote him to ask why he chose the code name *Trinity* for the site. Oppenheimer answered: "Why I chose the name is not clear, but I know what thoughts were in my mind. There is a poem of John Donne, ['Hymn to God My God, in My Sicknesse'] written just before his death, which I know and love. From it a quotation:

> As West and East
> in all flatt Maps—and I am one—are one,
> So death doth touch the Resurrection."[51]

The poem, says Richard Rhodes in his recounting of the event, suggested to Oppenheimer the paradox that as "dying leads to death but might also lead to resurrection, . . . the bomb for [Niels] Bohr and Oppenheimer was a weapon of death that might also end war and redeem mankind."[52] Oppenheimer, in his letter, admitted that " 'that still does not make a trinity.' But in another, better known devotional poem Donne opens, 'Batter my heart, three person'd God.' Beyond this, I have no clues whatever."[53]

Oppenheimer was not fully conscious of the connection between the two poems which haunted him, but the link is clear when the two are compared. For, as Rhodes points out, like the first passage, a reading of Donne's *Holy Sonnets* shows that it also explores the theme of redemption through destruction.

> Batter my heart, three-personed God; for You
> As yet but knock, breathe, shine, and seek to mend;
> That I may rise and stand, o'rthrow me, and bend
> Your force to break, blow, burn, and make me new.[54]

Donne's fourteenth "Holy Sonnet" describes a theme which we should readily recogize—wrestling with the God who wounds in order to heal and slays to make alive. It is the metaphorical appropriation of the story of Jacob, wrestling with the stranger. But notice, it is the Christian version of that story, the version we encountered in Augustine and Luther. It is the version that inverts the meaning of the biblical narrative—the version in which God not only "wounds in order to heal" but also "slays in order to make alive." It is the version that allows the self (in this case, Oppenheimer) to deal with its uneasy conscience by doubling, that is by assuming a two-kingdom ethic, in which the second or professional self, through an ethic of unquestioning obedience, *will do what it must do* no matter how distasteful this is to the first self.

For the scientists who worked on the Manhattan Project, a central motivation had been the defeat of Hitler and urgency was added to their task by the belief that the Germans might succeed in building such a bomb first. But once Germany was defeated it became a more problematic ethical question as to whether the bomb should be used against Japan. There was absolutely no danger that Japan was even close to building such a bomb. And yet whenever the ethical question came up it was quickly buried by the technobureaucratic skill of General Groves and Oppenheimer.

In December of 1944, Dr. Samuel Goudsmit, head of an Allied intelligence team, reviewed the German scientific papers discovered in Strasbourg. It was clear to him that the Germans had failed to develop the bomb. Pleased at this discovery, he commented to a military assistant, "'If the Germans don't have the bomb, then we don't need to use ours.' 'You don't know [General] Groves,' said the officer. 'If we have such a weapon, then we'll use it.'"[55] Groves, who headed up the project for the Pentagon, and Oppenheimer, who was directly in charge of the Manhattan Project, were enthralled with the technical imperative: If it can be done it must be done.

Just as the Germans had produced a demonic inversion of the holy community and its two-kingdom ethic by separating the Nazi doctors from the world to bring them into unquestioning obedience to the demonic purposes of the bureaucratic state, so was it the case with the Manhattan project. In the monastic traditions of Christianity and Buddhism it was thought that the city was the place where conscience is corrupted and withdrawal from the world (into the desert or the forest) was necessary to wrestle with oneself and save one's conscience. In the age of Auschwitz and Hiroshima, however, the inverse of that assumption proved to be true. The Nazis isolated their camp physicians in order to bring them into conformity to the sacred bureaucratic will and its categorical imperative—to kill in order to heal. Likewise, the scientists of the Manhattan project were isolated in the desert of Los Alamos, New Mexico. Initially Groves tried to bureaucratically compartmentalize the work of the scientists (for security reasons, he argued) to such a degree that most of them would have no occasion to talk to each other. Oppenheimer had to confront him immediately and point out that as scientists they simply could not do the job they were being asked to do without the free exchange of ideas. A compromise set of bureaucratic procedures were worked out.

In this environment the ethical question of the use of the bomb came up for discussion only once. An attempt was made to hold a meeting of the scientists involved in the project at the desert location in Los Alamos, New Mexico. Only fifty of the scientists out of a population of approximately 5000 showed up.[56] Oppenheimer made a point of being there and succeeded in squelching any further questions. Oppenheimer, as a fellow scientist, was able to inspire trust in the military and political bureaucracy and induce the scientists to believe that "Once you know how to make the bomb it's not your business to figure out how not to use it."[57] Robert Wilson, who had called that meeting, reflected in later years that it was as if they were automatons. Further questioning "simply was not in the air. . . .Our life was directed to do one thing, it was as though we'd been programmed to do that. . . . We were the heroes of our epic . . . and there was no turning back."[58] Indeed, when the presidential committee, appointed by Truman to decide the issue of the use of the bomb on Japan, met on May 31, 1945, the possibility of not using it was never raised. Even the option of a demonstration use of the bomb or the dropping of the bomb on a nonurban target never came up for discussion, except in an unofficial ten minute discussion by four members of the committee over lunch. Groves, was very pleased to see the "mounting momentum for unquestioned use of the bomb."[59]

It was not the scientists in the desert whose conscience was awakened but those scientists who had been working out of Chicago. There Leo Szilard and James Franck both made desperate attempts, on behalf of the protesting Chicago scientists, to awaken the conscience of the President and the Secretary of War. Szilard sent around a petition to be sent to the president, which got sixty-seven signatures in Chicago, eighty-eight in Oak Ridge, "and many more were ready to sign when the military authorities stepped in" and stopped the petition for "security reasons."[60] At Los Alamos, Oppenheimer prevented the petition from ever being circulated. Special reports were also written only to end up in deadend files, subverted by a bureaucratic process intent on reaching a preordained conclusion. The petitions, thanks to bureaucratic procedure, were never seen by Truman. Not one of the four scientists at the May 31 meeting in Washington communicated any of the questions and ethical doubts of the Chicago scientists. Here, as in Germany and Japan, the bureaucratic procedures of decision making proved themselves impervious to the demands of conscience. Equally frightening was the fact that the political and military decision makers were totally unable to understand the technical details of the scientific reports on the bomb. Secretary of War Stimson told Groves, in the middle of a briefing, "I don't understand a word you are saying." And General Marshall sent back his briefing papers after three hours, "because he could not penetrate them. For the first time in history decision makers had become so helplessly dependent on the arcane wisdom of specialists that they could no longer inject relevant questions."[61] In the end, the logic of technical autonomy would not be defeated—if it can be done, it must be done.

No doubt the unconscious, or barely conscious, apologetic that Oppenheimer had worked out in his own mind to justify the preordained conclusion of the Manhattan Project was expressed in his gravitation to the poems of John Donne and the code name Trinity. Although the bomb would do unheard of damage and unleash a terrible new power in the world, still the very awesomeness of the power of the bomb was seen as the necessary lethal force that would bring an end to the war allowing the renewal of life. But when, on the day of Trinity, the moment came and the experiment became the *reality* of the bomb, it was not the words of Christian trinity but the words of Vishnu, one of the deities of the Hindu trinity, that seemed most appropriate—for in the Hindu trinity (unlike the understanding of transcendence in Judaism, Christianity, or Buddhism) the divine and the demonic are one.

Vishnu is a member of the Hindu trinity of Brahma, Vishnu, and Shiva. This is not the Trinitarian deity of history as found in Christianity but rather a Hindu trinity of nature, governing the infinite cycles of death and rebirth. It is as if, between Auschwitz and Hiroshima, Oppenheimer's psyche was overwhelmed by what Mircea Eliade called the *terror of history.*[62] His experience reflected a cosmic event—the death of the God of history, the God whose goodness transcends evil. It is as if the "Manhattan Project" of secular and technological utopianism had been assimilated back into the order of nature and nature's gods, who are impervious to human feeling and human destiny. Like, Nietzsche's *Übermensch,* Oppenheimer's own technological self, which found its self-expression in the Manhattan Project, created no utopian future but rather found itself locked into the endless cycles of eternal return, cycles ruled by an apocalyptic and demonic will to power.

If we turn to the Gita passage Oppenheimer quoted from memory, we discover that the more typical translation is "Time am I" rather than "I am become Death."[63] Either, however, is a legitimate translation of the Sanskrit.[64] As the context makes clear time is the power of death, the destroyer of worlds. But what follows is especially interesting. Vishnu says to Arjuna:

> Do what thou wilt, all these warriors shall cease to be,
> Drawn up [there] in their opposing ranks.

> And so arise, win glory,
> Conquer thine enemies and enjoy a prosperous kingdom!
> Long since have these men in truth been slain by Me,
> Thine is to be the mere occasion.[65]

We must remember that Arjuna is a Kshatriya, a warrior who chooses not to go to war against his own relatives even though the war is just. He wishes neither to kill nor be killed. Krishna, his chariot driver, has been teaching him the four yogic paths to enlightenment to convince him that his caste duty as a warrior is to fight and that, as long as he is not "attached to the fruits of his actions" [i.e., as long as he does not act from personal motives such as ambition or greed] but rather does his duty selflessly, he will not accrue any negative karma. Indeed "though he slay these thousands he is no slayer."[66] And now, in Chapter 11 of the Gita, Krishna reveals his true identity as Vishnu. And what is his message? He is the real slayer of all men. All he asks of Arjuna is that he do his duty selflessly and in unquestioning obedience. He need not feel any guilt for killing his kinsmen for he is not really their slayer. Here we have an archetypal example of the logic of demonic doubling. We found this same demonic logic at work in Luther's hangman and among the Nazi doctors, only for the latter, instead of God it was nature and bureaucracy who decreed life and death and absolved these physicians of responsibility for their actions by declaring: "Long since have these men in truth been slain by Me, Thine is to be the mere occasion."

The point I wish to make is certainly not that the Gita is somehow directly responsible for the behavior of the Nazi doctors. Hardly. What I am suggesting is that the unconscious link Oppenheimer made between Trinity and Vishnu is more than accidental. It symbolizes the meeting of East and West at Hiroshima, religiously and culturally, in the eruption of the demonic. The first of Donne's poems to be recalled by Oppenheimer, not only links death and resurrection but also "East and West." For Donne goes on to say:

> Is the Pacific Sea my home? Or are
> The Eastern riches? Is Jerusalem?
> Anyan, and Magellan, and Gibralter,
> All straits, and none but straits, are ways to them,
> Whether where Japhet dwelt, or Cham, or Shem.[67]

The allusions to East and West reverberate throughout the poem. Japhat, Cham (Ham), and Shem are the three sons of Noah, whose descendants were believed to have been dispersed to Europe, Africa, and Asia. What they evoke for Donne, however, is not so much our concern as what they evoked for Oppenheimer (and for us) after Auschwitz and Hiroshima.

Two Ways of Dealing with Responsibility and Guilt

The point to be grasped is that, whether we speak of the Hindu trinity or the Christian trinity, we are speaking of mythologies that sacralize death. Both Vishnu and the Christian trinitarian God differ from the Jewish God of history in one important respect. The God of Arjuna as well as that of Augustine, Luther, and Donne "wounds in order to heal and slays to make alive" whereas the God who comes as a stranger to wrestle with Jacob (Genesis 32:23ff) "wounds in order to heal" but does not slay to make alive. The God of Jacob wins not by defeating the human but by enabling the victory of the human. Israel, we are told, means "he who wrestles with God and man and prevails." For such figures as Augustine, John Donne, and Martin Luther, the trinitarian God with whom they wrestled was the divine slayer who must defeat the person wrestled with. In the Christian imagination, in contradiction to the biblical story of Jacob wrestling with the stranger (Genesis 32:23ff), God must be the victor and human beings must be defeated.

In this story there is a profound transformation of identity, a conversion or enlightenment—Jacob becomes Israel. In the Christian narrative imagination this can occur only if there is a total death of the self and a total surrender of will in unquestioning obedience. But in the Jewish imagination, God seeks not the total annihilation of the self but rather the discovery of its inalienable dignity. Jacob is wounded but neither he nor the stranger is defeated. The stranger flees with the dawn and Jacob is blessed and enabled to walk away with only a limp. Judaism alone seems to have grasped the decisive criterion of transcendence, the inalienable human dignity of the self created in the image of the God without image. No God worthy of the name would ask for the total sacrifice of that dignity, for it would be the same as asking for the giving up of one's being created in the image of God.

These two ways of interpreting this story represent two ways of dealing with guilt and responsibility. The first leads to violence against the stranger and absolves the self of personal guilt through a total surrender to a higher will. The second requires the self to take responsibility for its past through a repentance that wounds and heals and, in so doing, leads to the path of nonviolent struggle that

allows both parties to walk away with their dignity. Jacob was wrestling with his guilt for the ways in which he had cheated his brother
Esau in his youth (Genesis 25:19–33:17). And now, after many years,
they would soon be face to face. "The text says it clearly," Elie Wiesel
tells us,

> Jacob is afraid. And Rashi, in his elegant manner, hastens to add
> that Jacob [like Arjuna] is afraid for two reasons: he is afraid of
> being killed and of having to kill. For he knows that one does not
> kill with impunity; whoever kills man, kills God in man. For-
> tunately, he is assaulted by an angel before he is assaulted by
> Esau. Who is the angel? Is it an angel at all? The text says "Ish,"
> a man, but Jacob speaks of God. And though he emerges victo-
> rious from the struggle, his victory does not imply his adver-
> sary's defeat. Thus Israel's first victory teaches us that man's true
> victory is not contingent on an enemy's defeat. Man's true victo-
> ry is always over himself.[68]

When approaching ethics through narrative, we need to realize
that everything depends on how the narrative is interpreted. The
Christian interpretation of the Jacob story requires a total death of the
self, a total surrender of will in unquestioning obedience to the God
who slays. Out of this surrender then emerges a totally new self.
Through the despair of the dark night of the soul or the sickness unto
death, the individual's own will is finally extinguished in a spiritual
death experience. This is not fundamentally different from that which
is expected of Arjuna by the God Vishnu in the Bhagavad Gita. Bhakti
yoga and Karma yoga also require a total surrender of the self. Christianity and Hinduism are, in this sense, common embodiments of
mythologies that sacralize death. If there is a universal narrative
theme in the history of religions from the primal myths of eternal
return in tribal and early urban societies on through the great myths
of Christianity, Islam (whose very name means "to surrender"), Hinduism, and Buddhism, it is that of life through death—death as total
surrendering of the self becomes the pathway to life. The one who is
willing to embrace the God who is slayer will be led through death
into new or eternal life. There is a fundamentally demonic fascination
in these traditions with the need for a total surrender to death—a
surrender that is essentially pagan. It is most dangerous in the cosmological religions that demand the sacrifice of the self to its sacred
caste or class duty. But even among such anthropological religions as
Christianity and Buddhism, it creates a propensity to fall back into a

cosmological posture. Only the Jewish narrative tradition of audacity or chutzpah, as we shall see in chapter 5, stands as a bulwark against this temptation.

The fascination with life through death or killing in order to heal bears an uncanny resemblance to the obsession with death the suicidal person often exhibits. There is something in the psyche of the suicidal person that desires death, that experiences a religious or numinous fascination with death and surrenders to that fascination under the influence of an almost magical belief that death will provide an experiential answer to the problems that could not be answered in life.

The suicidal person, A. Alvarez confessed, knows what it is to be possessed by *The Savage God*.[69] Even as falling in love remains the root experience of what the ancients called possession by the goddess of love, so the strange obsession with death that can overtake the suicidal person is also a kind of *falling*—a falling into a dreadful fascination with the god of death. Suicidal consciousness, like erotic consciousness, is an extraordinary state of mind that creates its own myth and ritual, its own sense of reality. Entrance into this state of mind is like a conversion that alters or even inverts one's previously held values and creates its own morality. One who has made the decision for suicide often has about him or her the calm of religious assurance—it is as if he or she already belongs to another world and can no longer be touched by the things of this world. Death becomes more than an end, it becomes a *wholly other* reality and *the only* reality compared to which all else is unreal.

The great world religions can usefully be understood as a response to an emerging urban consciousness of individuality and mortality—a consciousness that calls the meaning of life into question and makes suicide a tempting option. Such religions pursue the paradox of the art of dying as the secret to living. In effect they seek to transmute the suicidal impulse, diverting the impulse to physical self-destruction in the face of meaninglessness into a spiritual act of self-destruction that opens the self to the abyss of infinite meaning. This point can be illustrated with the story told by the Buddhist Zen master Hakuin about a man who hung over an abyss and was urged to "let go."

> If you wish to attain the true Non-ego [the Buddhist state of no-self or enlightenment] you must release your hold over the abyss. If thereafter you revive you will come upon the true ego of the four virtues. What does it mean to release one's hold over

the abyss? A man went astray and arrived at a spot which had never been trodden by the foot of man. Before him there yawned a bottomless chasm. His feet stood on the slippery moss of a rock and no secure foothold appeared around him. He could step neither forward nor backward. Only death awaited him. The vine which he grasped with his left hand and the tendril which he held with his right hand could offer him little help. His life hung as by a single thread. Were he to release both hands at once, his dry bones would come to nought. Thus it is with the Zen disciple. By pursuing a single *koan*[70] he comes to a point where his mind is as if dead and his will as if extinguished. This state is like a wide void over a deep chasm and no hold remains for hand or foot. All thoughts vanish and in his bosom burns hot anxiety. But then suddenly it occurs that with the *koan* both body and mind break. This is the instant when the hands are released over the abyss. In this sudden upsurge it is as if one drinks water and knows for oneself heat and cold. Great joy wells up. This is called rebirth (in the Pure Land). This is termed seeing into one's own nature. Everything depends on pushing forward and not doubting that with the help of this concentration one will eventually penetrate to the ground of one's own nature.[71]

Hakuin taught that true spiritual enlightenment occurs through a process which begins with the *great doubt* proceeds to the *great death* and ends in the *great joy.* In the first stage you are "overcome by a feeling of anxious, horrendous fear" as you doubt that life has any meaning, that there is a state of religious liberation. Even if there is such a liberation, you doubt that you can achieve it. In such a state you are stalemated and cannot proceed any further. The only way out is the great death, which in turn opens the gate to the great joy.

If there is such a thing as a generic religiousness to human existence, I suspect it is rooted in the universal impulse to suicide. That impulse I think has two sources, which Freud saw as being in opposition but which I see as complementary—eros and thanatos. The negative source of the impulse, thanatos, is grounded in the lonely burden that the urbanized individuated self is for its bearer. Being able to anticipate old age, sickness, and death as a loss of self can make life seem an intolerable burden and without hope. From this experience emerges the impulse to escape the burden of life by attacking its biological roots (i.e., physical death through suicide). But at the same time there is also the experience of the erotic-religious fascination with death as a transforming experience. There is an erotic drive or lure within the self (but which is not the self) that seeks to transcend (i.e., go beyond) the self. The ambivalent religious emotions of fascination and dread, which are intimately related to our reactions to suicide have their roots in these two types of experience: (1) the self's dread or *great doubt* about the burden of life and (2) the *fascination* with the death of the self as the abyss of transformation. Rather than working against each other, these two sources of the suicidal impulse can work together—for *thanatos* inaugurates the quest for an answer to the burden of self (i.e., of old age, sickness and death), but *eros* transmutes the quest from the biological to the spiritual level (i.e., the level of language, mind and self). The fascination with death drives the self to want to enter the experience of death prematurely (i.e., before one's biological life actually fails because of age or illness, etc.). But the danger, as A. Alvarez argued from his own personal experience with attempting suicide, is that the fascination with death will be understood literally rather than symbolically and spiritually. Thus Alvarez noted that it was not until his near-death experience that he realized that the death experience he hungered for was one of psychological transformation and not literal biological annihilation.

One can find examples of this language of transformation in Western religion as well as in the Asian traditions—Kierkegaard's sickness unto death, for instance, or John of the Cross's dark night of the soul. The common wisdom of these traditions is that the path from anxiety to despair is crucial to bring about a saving transformation that rescues one from the abyss of meaninglessness. The paradox is that one must will to plunge into that abyss, one must abandon oneself to despair and will one's own death. The way to the great joy of nirvana is through a great death just as the way to union with God is through the despair that is the dark night of the soul. Even the preaching of predestination and the grim vision of hell and damnation in the Calvinist tradition of Protestantism can be viewed as a form of skillful means, like the Zen *koan,* whose purpose is to bring one to the edge of despair about salvation through one's own efforts and so afford the opportunity to let go and "take the plunge"—to become, as William James put it, twice born.

The paradox that is communicated is that one must willingly enter into the great death to transcend old age, sickness, and death. It is as if the great death were a kind of vaccination against the real thing (i.e., biological death). Spiritual suicide becomes a cure for death and religion becomes the practice of the art of dying. A profound religious insight is contained in this tradition, but it is rendered dangerous by the religious propensity for literalism, on the one hand, and symbolic hyperbole, on the other. The death of the self is needed, but it requires neither a literal death nor a total surrender or total replacement of the old self by a new self. As the spiritual autobiographies of individuals as diverse as Augustine of Hippo and Gandhi make only too painfully clear, much of the old self survives the transformation to continue in the new self. The decisive point to be made, as Irving Greenberg reminded us, is that after Auschwitz there must be no total surrender, no total loyalty, no unquestioning obedience, not even to God, for such a spiritual attitude opens the possibility of SS loyalties.

The Bushido Ethic and the Path to Hiroshima

Evidence for the truth of Greenberg's assertion can be found in the Bushido ethic of the Samurai warrior, with its deep roots in the Zen Buddhist tradition, that shaped the militaristic ethos of Japan. This ethic did for Japan what Luther's ethic of unquestioning obedience did for Germany. In his study of Tokugawa Religion, Robert Bellah argued, that the "ethic of the Bushido became in Tokugawa and modern times the national ethic, or at least a large part of it."[72] Although it began as a warrior ethic, through its amalgamation with Confucian morality it became "the cornerstone of national morals."[73] Its central themes were militarism, especially absolute obedience to one's feudal lord, and a preoccupation with death and the ethic of honor as found expressed in the traditional ritual of *seppuku* (ritual suicide). "It is said, '*Bushido* means the determined will to die.'" A Bushido manual, the *Hagakur,* offers the following instruction: "Every morning make up thy mind how to die. Every evening freshen thy mind in the thought of death. And let this be done without end. Thus will thy mind be prepared. When thy mind is always set on death, the way through life will always be straight and simple."[74] Meditation on death is meant to purify the self of all selfish desires and prepare one for the total sacrifice of oneself, if necessary, for one's lord. Thus, the warrior is instructed: "As our Imperial Throne is endless from the beginning, so we should let this thought sink deeply, that our loyalty must be endless. . . . 'He who dies for the sake of his lord does not die in vain. . . . This is the way of loyalty."[75] In the Bushido ethic, says Bellah, "injunctions to be upright and fulfill one's duty are frequently met with, and absolute obedience is enjoined. . . . [even to] accept an unjust death if it were so decreed."[76]

The military emphasis is crucial. . . . It typifies selfless devotion to the collectivity and its head, even to the point of death. Death indeed in a military context can come to symbolize that very devotion. . . . It is, then, to its symbolic importance for the central value system, I believe, that we can attribute in large part the very high valuation placed on the military in Japan even after two hundred and fifty years of peace. . . . Certainly the leaders of the Restoration were strongly moved by the *samurai* spirit, and their ability to command the loyalty and obedience of the nation with so little opposition was in considerable part due to the fact that they did embody the ideal values not only of the *samurai* but of all Japan.[77]

Bellah made some interesting comparisons and contrasts between Japan and the West, especially Germany. The "society of Anglo-Saxons," he tells us, "had the same high regard for loyalty that the ancient Japanese had. . . . Such attitudes [i.e., the warrior ethic of loyalty] were by no means new among the Germanic peoples. . . . In both Japan and the West these semitribal conceptions of the lord and follower relation persist in the Middle Ages and form one source for the "feudal" values of the respective cultures."[78] Beginning in the early modern period these values were largely displaced by Renaissance and Enlightenment values of human autonomy in the West. In Japan, however, these values continued on into the modern period. The one exception in Europe was Germany. Although countries like England and France had become national entities by the end of the fifteenth century, it was only in 1871 that Germany became a nation.

Throughout the nineteenth century, Germany like Japan, remained essentially a feudal culture. Both countries experienced modernization as an intrusion of outside cultures (e.g., Commodore Perry's landing in Japan in 1853 and Napoleon's invasion of the German territories in 1805) and reacted with a paradoxical combination of modernizing and antimodernizing attitudes. That is, both sought to use the modern (especially technology) to overcome the modern. Both viewed modern Enlightenment attitudes of universalism as a degenerative force, eroding sacred cultural histories and identities. As Bellah noted, both Germany and Japan responded by developing a romantic nationalism as a countermodernist strategy. This nationalism, stresses the

primordial identities of language, ethnic origin, or religion. . . . Where religion is a divisive issue within the society or its univer-

salism appears to threaten national particularism, religion may
not be a primary theme in the ideology, or some primitive national religion may be emphasized or created for the occasion.
Germany, where religious divisions between Lutherans, Calvinist, and Catholics went very deep, is such an example, though
the attempt to resurrect early German mythology, . . . was never entirely successful. In Japan, where the old national religion,
Shinto, was still functioning, the artificial revival of old religious
symbolism was considerably more effective. . . . In general the
technique of romantic nationalism in the face of the disturbances
and disruptions of modernization has been to reemphasize the
real or supposed unity and solidarity of the hallowed past.[79]

Thus we find in Japan, as in Germany, a social order legitimated
by a cosmological type of religiosity. In Japan, antimodernization took
the form of resuscitating the tradition of the emperor of Japan, giving
it a central political importance out of all proportion to the role it had
played in the prior history of Japan. The new emphasis on the sacred
role of the emperor was used to legitimate the new Japanese state.
Indeed, the throne of the emperor is described as "coeval with heaven
and earth." According to the *Kokutai No Hongi, The Fundamental
Doctrine of the National Entity,* issued by the Ministry of Education in
1937:

Our country is established with the Emperor, who is a descend-
ent of Amaterasu Ohmikami [Heaven Illuminating Great God-
dess], as her centre, and our ancestors as well as we ourselves
constantly behold in the emperor the fountainhead of her life
and activities. For this reason, to serve the Emperor and to receive the Emperor's great August Will as one's own is the ratio-
nale of making our historical 'life' live in the present; and on this
is based the morality of people.

Loyalty means to reverence the Emperor as (our) pivot and
to follow him implicitly. By implicit obedience is meant casting
ourselves aside and serving the Emperor intently. To walk this
Way of Loyalty is the sole Way in which we subjects may "live,"
and the fountainhead of all energy. Hence, offering our lives for
the sake of the Emperor does not mean so called self-sacrifice,
but the casting aside of our little selves to live under this August
Grace and the enhancing of the genuine life of the people of a
State.[80]

Through her Shinto, Confucian, and Buddhist narrative traditions the Japanese saw Japan as a country with a destiny decreed by nature to rule the world. In an 1858 memo to the Shogun from his chief counselor on foreign affairs Masayoshi Hatta, relations with foreign countries is recommended in conjunction with military preparations so that "Our national prestige and position thus ensured, the nations of the world will come to look up to our Emperor as the Great Ruler of all the nations, and they will come to follow our policy and submit to our judgment."[81] Kosuke Koyama, describes the Japanese mentality that led to World War II in terms reminiscent of the Germanic Aryan mythology. "The nation was paralyzed under the tyranny of the divine mythology. When the best of Japanese scholars were banned the exercise of reason was condemned and the people were fed with unreasoned slogans which proclaimed that Japan was the righteous nation and her enemy was devilish. The world seemed divided into two camps, that of good people and that of the bad. The Japanese were good and the United States was the focus of all evil."[82]

When one inserts the Bushido ethic into such a cosmological-mythological ethos, the results are not dissimilar to those that occurred with Luther's ethic of obedience in Nazi Germany under the myth of the pure Aryan race. The Bushido ethic of unquestioning loyalty and obedience and its Buddhist version of the myth of life through death lends itself too readily the sacrifice of self to a false infinite, namely, the sacral-political order of society. Indeed, as in Nazi Germany, this myth and its ethic of obedience can lead an entire society to embrace an ideal of suicidal behavior. Even as the suicidal person undergoes a conversion experience that inverts the values of life and death, so it can be for a whole society. When this occurs, the sacred and transforming values which govern human action are no longer those that promote life but those that promote death.

In an essay on Confucian ethics in China, Robert Bellah made a point that is transferable to Japan as well. He noted that what is missing from the Confucian [and Bushido] Asian ethic of filial piety and loyalty is the tragic dimension.

In East Asia there is no literary genre that we might call tragic. . . . There are no tragic heroes in the Western sense, men whose agony calls into question the justice of the cosmos itself; in a word, there is no Chinese [or Japanese] Job. . . . The particularly tragic note in the West seems to require a double motion that never quite gets started in China [or Japan]. In the first motion the world is criticized from the point of view of God, but then by a subtle reversal it is God himself who is questioned. Christianity, it is claimed, overcomes the tragic. Perhaps so, but as long as it carries near the heart of its critical narrative the words, "My God, My God, Why has thou forsaken me?" it does not destroy the tragic. . . . The capacity to ask questions of the ultimate is perhaps a consequence of shifting the locus of ultimacy from the natural social order to a transcendent reference point.[83]

Bellah is right to see Jesus' challenge from the cross as standing the narrative tradition of Job, but that narrative strand of the Christian tradition has been almost entirely ignored in Christianity. Judaism (as we shall see in chapter 5) has kept this radical ethic of human dignity alive, standing with Job, in the breach between human dignity and the myth of life through death.

The Apocalyptic Dark Night and the MAD-ness of Planetary Suicide

After Auschwitz and Hiroshima we are in danger of transforming the myth of life through death into a literal apocalyptic myth of our collective destiny. This kind of pagan religiosity must be abandoned. Oppenheimer's trinitarian mythic consciousness in which East and West converge is playing a dangerous game. The god of Auschwitz and Hiroshima manifests itself as the "savage god"—the sacred technological power that "has become death." The symbolism of death and rebirth that has nearly universally governed the religious imagination can have meaning only within the context of a self-renewing natural order. But technology, especially nuclear technology (whether peaceful or military), breaks with the rhythms of nature, threatening not only total destruction of the human race but also a near total collapse of the life-sustaining ecology of our natural environment. The death-dealing potential of nuclear technology overwhelms its own capacity to give life. The very racism that led to the cataclysms of Auschwitz and Hiroshima is rendered superfluous by the bomb. In the bomb there is neither East nor West. All races will be destroyed. All will become equal in their desolation, victims of the great equalizer—death.

Even within the confines of traditional natural order, however, the call for total surrender and total obedience led to the death camps and the denial of a transcendent human dignity. Our unconscious surrender to the sacral power of technology has as its training ground the conscious surrender of one's will and one's whole being advocated by virtually all religions East and West. After Auschwitz and Hiroshima, we can longer afford the luxury of an unadulterated pagan mythology of life through death, not even when it is sublimely transmuted, by Buddhist or Christian spirituality, into a language of self-transformation. We need not an ethic that sacralizes death but one that sanctifies life. We need not a sacral ethic but an ethic of secular holiness that champions human dignity, human rights, and human liberation against all mythologies of death with audacious tenacity.

We live in an apocalyptic world that has developed a dangerous collective suicidal consciousness. Robert Lifton, in his work, both in relation to Auschwitz and Hiroshima, has come to recognize the danger of the apocalyptic consciousness that guides our nuclear public policies. It is as if we have a collective longing for death as a final solution to the ambiguities of the human condition, as if through our collective death we could force a transcendence of death and an encounter with ultimate reality. Thus Lifton explains:

> I have come to recognize an awesome spiritual battleground in responses to [the] nuclear threat, sometimes involving contending groups of people and sometimes struggles within individual minds. Put most simply, the issue is whether ultimate virtue derives from preserving the world or from destroying it.
>
> Those we may call the world-destructionists (Armageddonists) are not always clear on exactly *who* would be committing the ultimate act of annihilation (it is sometimes man, sometimes God). Yet that does not so much matter to them because ultimately God would be responsible: he, and he alone would be carrying out his promise, as prophesied in Revelation and other biblical texts. However dubious the theology, it conjoins nuclear holocaust with the evangelical Christian impulse toward world cleansing in the name of achieving the ultimate spiritual moment (the Second Coming or the Kingdom of God). Integral to that world cleansing is *self*-cleansing. What takes on greatest moral urgency for the Armageddonist is not the prevention of nuclear holocaust but the individual's spiritual preparation for his or her transport (via the "Rapture") to a higher state. One is urged to make that religious preparation immediately, "while there is time to do it, not put it off"—and then (as A. G. Mojtabai quotes an "end-time" minister) one will be literally carried

away in joy: from one's automobile . . . one's home, . . . and, as one proceeds on up, from everything else. . . . Though I speak of an absurd psychic extreme, one should not underestimate the broader appeal of end-time ideology as a perverse vision of hope. . . .

But the spiritual battle extends well beyond Christianity or any other religion. There is a strange secular version of it involving technocratic nuclear strategists. Some of those strategists combine the ideology I call "nuclearism" (exaggerated embrace and even near-worship of the weaponry . . .) with polarized imagery of Soviet evil and American virtue. They can then experience a secular version of the lure of Armageddon. . . . That secular lure could come close to the theological longing. . . .

There is, then, a real sense in which we can speak of "secular Armageddonists," who, like their religious counterparts, renounce responsibility for the holocaust they anticipate and, in some cases, press toward bringing about. They may view that holocaust as an inevitable outcome of our time and technology, or they may consider it preferable to an assumed alternative of "giving in" or of "surrendering to the Russians." . . .

It would be no exaggeration to view the struggle as one between love of this life and hatred for it—between responsibility toward the lives of others as opposed to vitriolic renunciation of the "other" as a carrier of evil. . . . There is a disturbing parallel here between Armageddonism in general and the Nazi vision of killing in the name of healing.[84]

In our nuclear policies we have flirted with a total surrender to death as if it can be our salvation. Whether in a religious or in a secular guise, our public policies are ruled by the myth of life through death, of killing in order to heal. We live in a MAD world, a world of mutually assured destruction. A fundamental assumption of narrative ethics, that rationality is determined by the story you understand yourself to be in, is well illustrated by contemporary nuclear policy. Once you accept the apocalyptic "master story," with its central mythic theme of life through death, that divides the world into the sacred and the profane (i.e., into communities of unambiguous good and evil), then MAD-ness becomes perfectly rational. Under these circumstances, MAD-ness assumes the cosmological language of realism, the hard rationality, of acting on the basis of the way things really are, and anyone who suggests otherwise is dismissed as a hopeless utopian romantic. Although, with the dissolution of the Soviet Union in December 1991, psychological tensions have eased between the United States and Russia, continuing regional/ethnic conflicts demonstrate that this demonic logic is still rampant both within the various (nuclear) countries that made up the Soviet Union and elsewhere in the world.

The policy of mutually assured destruction is a psychologically demonic game that forces nuclear powers into developing stockpiles of weapons at levels far in excess of anything required to destroy each other. The idea is to convince one's enemy that there is no hope of surviving an assault on one's own nation and so prevent this enemy from even trying. "The paradoxical idea, enchanting to foreign policy specialists and former national security advisers, [is] that peace is most effectively pursued by preparing for war."[85] Even if we assume that no one is mad enough to start a nuclear war under these conditions, the risk that such preparation increases our chances of war by accident or misunderstanding cannot be eliminated and therefore is accepted as a rational and realistic risk under these supposedly unchangeable conditions. These risks are rendered even greater by a long history of subtle threats to use nuclear weapons to protect our national interests.

The changing international situation encourages those policy makers who have urged that we move away from an explicit public policy of MAD-ness to NUTs, or strategic nuclear utilization theory, which argues that, given the precision and control we now have over nuclear weapons, limited nuclear war is possible without risking total nuclear Armageddon. This approach, however, is not really new. From the beginning the United States has used the bomb politically as if it could be a strategic weapon.

> Every president going back to Truman and up through Nixon has actually threatened, usually in a secret communication, the use of nuclear weapons so as to control the behavior of adversaries. A partial list of instances includes Truman's threats to use nuclear weapons in Iran (1946) and Korea (1950); Eisenhower's nuclear threats or preparations in Korea and China (1953), offering the French three atomic bombs for use in Indochina (1954), preparation and threats in relation to the landing of marines in Lebanon (1958), and the defense of the off-shore Chinese islands of Quemoy/Matsu (1958); Kennedy's consideration and threat of nuclear weapons in relation to Laos (1961), Berlin (1961), and Cuba (1962); Johnson's consideration at the time of the Khe Sanh

siege in Vietnam (1968); and Nixon's repeated threats to Vietnamese negotiators (1969–1972). Some of these threats were more serious than others, but throughout this whole period, behind the backs of the American people, our leaders were secretly contemplating the use of nuclear weapons, and, in each instance, for rather restricted foreign policy goals.[86]

This history was further exacerbated by Star Wars proposals that seek to totally automate the process of detecting a nuclear attack and responding to it, through an elaborate link up of computers and defense technology that at its logical end would virtually eliminate the human element from the decision-making process and place us completely at the mercy of our autonomous technology.[87]

The massive reality of contemporary nuclear policy structured by apocalyptic and mystical mythologies, both sacred and profane, of life through death, makes it seem as if "there is a logic in our MAD-ness," a logic that makes us bold enough unashamedly to choose acronyms such as MAD and NUTS to name these policies. And this reality has forced on us a doubling as pervasive as any that typified the Nazi era in Germany. We live, says Jonathan Schell in "two worlds," one nuclear and the other pre-nuclear. It is painfully obvious that the word *nuclear* renders the word *war* an oxymoron. War is something human beings once engaged in, in which one side could win and the other side could loose. In a nuclear age, war is rendered impossible. And yet we plan our public policies, "as if" we still lived in a pre-nuclear world where the political and military use of nuclear weaponry still offered the possibility of winning instead of collective suicide. To live in these two worlds, says Schell, requires a "double vision." Like Himmler's SS, he tells us, contemporary nuclear strategists are given to understand that "it is not obedience to our moral feelings but resistance to those feelings that is presented as our obligation. . . . Once the 'strategic necessity' of planning the deaths of hundreds of millions of people is accepted, we begin to live in a world in which morality and action inhabit two separate, closed realms.[88] All strategic sense becomes moral nonsense and vice versa, and we are left with the choice of seeming to be either strategic or moral idiots."[89]

Accepting the logic of MAD-ness, the entire population of the world (at least all who are aware of the nuclear situation) was forced into doubling, with one self living day to day as if everything were perfectly normal, while all along one's other self is perfectly aware that at any moment everything and everyone we love may all be destroyed. This second self accepts the logic of MAD-ness as the price it must pay to keep the first self living in a "normal world." Through a process that Lifton refers to as *psychic numbing* we compartmentalize these two selves so as to block our capacity to feel and imagine our true situation. Most of the time we manage to force this second self completely out of consciousness. This very compartmentalization is what prevents us from imagining our situation accurately and taking action. The problem is, says Jonathan Schell, "that we do not have two earths, one to blow up experimentally and the other to live on; nor do we have two souls, one for reacting to daily life and the other for reacting to the peril to all life. But neither do we have two wills, one with which we can intend to destroy our species and the other with which we can intend to save ourselves. Ultimately, we must all live together with one soul and one will on our one earth."⁹⁰

We have been in the process of surrendering ourselves to a new and final apocalyptic "Manhattan Project" through which increasing numbers of bigger and better bombs have been built with the assurance that the power to totally destroy life is what will make it possible for us to have new life and a future. The apocalyptic path, we have been told, is really the path to utopia. Through our surrender to the myth of life through death we have allowed our mythic consciousness, West or East, Christian or Hindu, Muslim or Buddhist, religious or secular a-theist, to shape our public policies along paths that lead not from the dark night of despair to new life and light but rather to the total darkness of planetary suicide.

After Auschwitz and Hiroshima: Utopian Ethics for an Apocalyptic Age

Theology unmasks the tyranny of false assurances and deceptive hopes nourished by religion. It denounces the despotisms underlying all disfugurations of man. Indeed, to the extent that it speaks of God, theology sides with man—by taking sides for his future.

—Gabriel Vahanian, *God and Utopia*

God is not the answer to our humanity but the question. . . . God is a God who speaks to us, allowing himself to be put in question, less by nature and its catastrophes or history and its tragedies than by language.

—Gabriel Vahanian, *Dieu anonyme*

In the biblical view, the world in itself is neither sacred nor profane: it is an instrument of the holiness of God.

—Gabriel Vahanian, *God and Utopia*

The word does not seek totality or universality. It does not seek to restore the other to itself. Nor others to themselves. Or God to humanity. It implies a relation of which the word is at the same time both the condition and testimony. . . . It attests to an irreducible otherness. An otherness without which there is neither communion nor communication. . . . Language presupposes the Other.

—Gabriel Vahanian, *Dieu anonyme*

God is not sacred: God is holy, radically other.

—Gabriel Vahanian, *L'utopie chrétienne*

I have no other God than the God of others.

—Gabriel Vahanian, *Dieu anonyme*

The Ethical Challenge of Auschwitz and Hiroshima to Technological Utopianism

Ethics: From Sacred Narratives to Utopian Critique

As far back as we can see into the misty recesses of time and the human adventure, human beings have told stories. Human beings are not just storytellers, they are story dwellers. Stories structure our sense of who we are and what kind of world we dwell in. The choices we make, even the options we think we have, are governed by the kind of story we think we are in and the role we see ourselves playing in it. It is significant that, prior to the modern period, all peoples everywhere conveyed their stories in song, drama, and dance, that is, in mythic and ritual enactment. Their stories coursed through their veins and sinews and lived in their every gesture and movement. By dwelling in the story, by living *through* the narrative, one became human. To be human was to be like the gods or God or to do as the sacred ancestors did. That is why, in primal (oral) cultures the right way to do anything is the ritual way. For ritual is the archetypal repetition of those actions through which the right order of the world was created. It is significant that both the words *right* and *rite* are derived from the Sanscrit term (*rita*) for sacred cosmic order. Mythic narrative and its ritual enactment creates a public sense of order, conforming human action to the cosmic order of things—*the way things are* as established *in the beginning.*

In premodern societies religious narrative communicated what was most public and most certain—the commonly shared truth of the sacred cosmic order. Secularization, it is often observed, privatizes religious experience. Religious narrative is reduced from the most public of all narrative forms to the one of the most private. In a pluralistic world permeated with a sense of cultural relativism, religious truth is reduced to a matter of personal opinion. However, it is a mistake to see this as the complete picture. Some religious narratives may be privatized but only to be replaced by other quite public narratives. Why might this be so? Because religion is about power, and power is an inherently social and public phenomenon. If some forms of religious experience have been privatized it is only because the public, commonly shared order of society is now responding to a new sense of the sacred, one that, both Jacques Ellul and Gabriel Vahanian argued, has shifted from nature to technology. In this sense, our secular technological civilization manifests a religiously sanctioned public order just as surely as any premodern society.

Although our age has been dominated by secular stories it would be a mistake to assume that our age and its stories are any less religious than those of previous ages. The word *religion* most likely comes from the Latin *religare,* which means "to tie or bind," even as *myth* comes from the Greek *mythos,* which means story. Myth, we could say, is a symbolic story about the origins and destiny of human beings and their world that relates them to whatever power(s) they believe ultimately governs their destiny. The force of such stories lies in their capacity to tie or bind the life of the individual into some cosmic and social drama of meaning and purpose and to whatever form of power their story identifies as governing their life and death, fortune and misfortune in this drama. However such power is understood, as one or many, personal or impersonal, spiritual or material—if it is believed to govern one's destiny it will evoke a sense of the sacred; that is, *fascination* and *dread* and motivate one to conform to its demands. And as Jacques Ellul's sociological work suggests, this remains true even in our secular civilization where technical bureaucracy ritually structures public order.

To say that something is *sacred* for someone is to say that it is what *matters most* to that person, it is what that person values most highly. What typically matters most to people is living and dying and the quality of one's life. Therefore what is sacred to a person or a community is whatever form of power that person or community believes governs these aspects of one's destiny. The religious experience of sacredness provides the ground for the moral experience of value. Whatever is *sacred* or *valued most* provides a measuring rod for a hierarchy of values that will govern human action. The blueprint for the parameters of action will be expressed in the myth and ritual, that is, symbolic story and action, which embody and communicate these values through the traditions of a society or a community. The central function of such myth and ritual is to unite one with the ultimate power(s) that governs human destiny and bring one into conformity with its sacred order.

The great French sociologist Durkheim saw the role of religion as the essential force for social integration and the legitimation of the order of society. For Emile Durkheim of course that was a necessary and a positive function. For Karl Marx, however, this legitimating function was viewed as an expression of a class-bound ideology that oppressed the many to benefit the few. Jacques Ellul, however, like Max Weber, holds that religion serves not only the *routine* function of legitimation but also the *charismatic* function of delegitimation and social transformation.

The distinction Weber and Ellul make, and Durkheim and Marx do not, highlights the distinction between sacred order and transcendence—between the sacred and the holy. To the degree that religion is about being tied or bound, through myth and ritual, to a sacred order defined by whatever powers are believed to govern human destiny, religion is the opposite of transcendence. This would help to explain why for Weber and Ellul secularization and the experience of transcendence go hand in hand. Transcendence can manifest itself in society only by desacralizing or secularizing sacred order. Whether we speak of transcendence in opposition to religion (as sacred order) or of two types of religious experience (being bound to sacred order as opposed to being bound to transcendence) is a matter of preference. Karl Barth preferred the former, Paul Tillich the latter. Barth's approach has the advantage of highlighting the affinity between transcendence and secularization. However, Tillich, in his own way, also took account of this affinity (as we shall see).

Transcendence, as the literal meaning of the word suggests, means to "go beyond." Transcendence is the uniquely utopian capacity of human beings to go be beyond what they are to become what they are not, as a society and as individuals. Although other dimensions may be relevant to individual religious traditions, for the purposes of theology of culture or social ethics, transcendence is to be understood not in terms of either spatial metaphors (e.g., above and below) or metaphysical categories (e.g., being and nonbeing) but rather in temporal, historical and sociological terms. Indeed, theology of culture, as I imagine it in the tradition of Paul Tillich, is an empirical discipline similar to history or sociology.[1] Transcendence is to be recognized through the identification of the ability of certain forms of human community to go beyond their original social, cultural, and historical contexts to profoundly influence other times and places.

At the individual level transcendence expresses itself in the utopian capacity to become other than what one is through a surrender to the inner demand to be open to the infinite. *The infinite* need not be hypostatized into "being" or "a being." It is simply a way of naming a category of experiences whose primary characteristic is just this radical openness to the possible that cannot be limited or defined. The most ordinary form of this openness is the experience of doubt and questioning, for although our life span is finite our questions themselves have no finite limit. Doubt is an experience that opens the self to the infinite by putting the self in question. Doubt releases the self from every given social order and social role and opens the abyss of infinite possibilities. As such, it is a radical experience of transcendence, an erotic experience of seduction by otherness. For by putting ourselves and our culture in question, doubt relativizes both and opens us up to seduction by our utopian possibilities, our infinite possibilities to become other than what we are.

Morality is a term which refers to the "customs" of the people. These customs are the normative patterns of social interaction, the way we have always done things. But why this way and not some other? Because these patterns are sacred, established by the gods or sacred ancestors "in the beginning." The Sanskrit term *rita,* which is the root for both our words *right* and *rite,* suggests this meaning. It reflects a time when in primal or tribal societies the right thing to do was the ritual thing to do. Why? Because "in the beginning" when the gods and sacred ancestors created the heavens and the earth they established the correct pattern for doing all things. These sacred patterns reflect the power of myth and ritual to transform chaos into cosmos and provide an ordered world in which human beings can dwell. The primal ritual of retelling and reenacting the stories of creation was at once both a moral and a technological act. It was an act that created a human order in which to dwell and at the same time sacralized that order by *cosmicizing* it, to make it appear as if the contingent humanly created social order was actually part of an essentially unchanging cosmic order created by sacred powers. Cosmicization makes it seem as if the way things (in origin or in essence) are is the way they ought to be. Myth and ritual exemplify the power of religion to structure public order by tying and binding the individual to his or her place and duties in this sacred sociocosmic order.

In tribal cultures human identity is collective and undifferentiated. The tribe lives in each individual and each individual is an embodiment of the tribe. The mythic symbols of such cultures do not clearly differentiate between self, society, and nature. The social order is experienced as an extension of the cosmic rhythms of nature, and the individual is not really an individual but a microcosmic embodiment of the sociocosmic order, expressed through the rhythms of nature, the cyclical rhythms of death and rebirth. Mircea Eliade classified the diverse mythic narratives of such cultures under the heading of *myths of eternal return*,[2] for despite their diversity of detail they share the common theme that all life is cyclical and eternal. Time is a circle that returns to its own origin, like day and night or the seasons of the year. Myth and ritual in such cultures centers on fertility, on eternal rebirth. The order of nature is what lasts. It is neverending, as is the tribal society as a part of the cosmic order. In such a society death is not a personal problem because identity is not yet personal, individuated, and mortal but collective, cosmic, and eternal.

Urbanization represents a shift from collective tribal identity to individuated urban identity or individual egoconsciousness. As society grows more complex and differentiated, the continual encounter within this environment with others who are different from oneself promotes a fundamental alteration of human identity. Human beings begin to experience themselves as separate from each other, their communities, and the cosmic order of nature. Writing further heightens this process of individuation. Writing allows one to preserve and interiorize unique individual details that would otherwise be lost to memory in oral traditions. With the formation of the differentiated self emerges self-consciousness as *interior* consciousness. Mythological consciousness does not differentiate inner and outer experience and thus projects *inner* experience on the *outer* world. The differentiation between the two seems to occur in all urban cultures, but the way in which it is evaluated tends to distinguish cultures. In India, for example, it was decided that the truly real was *within* whereas the more illusory or playful dimensions of reality (*Maya*) were *out there*. In Mediterranean-European cultures virtually the opposite evaluation came to be made. In either case, this differentiation results in the construction of the symbolic or metaphorical *inner space* required for the emergence of consciousness of self.

The Epic of Gilgamesh represents the situation of the newly individuated person of the ancient urbanized world, a self no longer clothed in collective *myth of eternal return* but stripped naked and exposed to his mortality as an individual. Enkidu who is both like Gilgamesh and yet slightly different (slightly shorter), represents the differentiated other who is the mirror for Gilgamesh's own self. Enkidu becomes the symbol of Gilgamesh's self-consciousness: his ability to imagine himself through the eyes of his friend and to imagine his own personal destiny through the mortality of his friend. Enkidu, as the bearer of Gilgamesh's ego, symbolizes the emergence of the urban self from the collective myths and rhythms of nature. No longer participating in the eternal rhythms of nature Gilgamesh can no longer find comfort in them. Having become a self, the myths of collective participatory tribal identity no longer speak to him. He is left with the burden of his own mortality, death as the anticipated loss of self. That is the situation symbolized by his failed quest for immortality. Primal animism and polytheism have no answer to the problem of death as the loss of one's own self, except the answer of collective consciousness to which Gilgamesh, having fallen into individuated selfconsciousness, can never return.

Gilgamesh represents a transitional type. He represents the urban self that has been stripped naked—stripped of its collective identity while not yet having developed the capacity to articulate its own inwardness. Therefore Gilgamesh can seek an answer to old age, sickness, and death only outwardly, in a plant at the bottom of the sea. He has not yet found a language through which to glimpse the dizzying depths of inwardness as an openness to the infinite. If we can place Gilgamesh in the early stages of the urbanization process, somewhere between 2000 and 1500 B.C.E., Siddhartha Gautama (563–483 B.C.E.), the Buddha or *enlightened one,* appears a millennium later in India, where urbanization was intensifying at a pace that parallels that of the Mediterranean. Like the story of Gilgamesh, his is also a story of *loss of innocence* and the quest to find an answer to the problem of death. But unlike Gilgamesh, who dove deep into the watery depths of the outer world in search of an answer, only to end up empty handed, Siddhartha is said to have turned inward, dove deep into the murky depths of the self, penetrated its illusoriness, and returned enlightened—grasping the emptiness of the self and the interdependent becoming of all things. In dissolving the illusion of self, Siddhartha robbed death of a self to take, and hence, of its sting.

Eric Voegelin calls this new *inner space* the *sensorium of transcendence.* It is a metaphorical space, one that Plato viewed as an *inner city* in which the diverse emotions and desires once mythologically projected onto nature are now heard, as if they were the distinct voices of its diverse citizens. It is as if these inner citizens were demanding to be heard and each given his or her due. In this inner *agora,* or public square, the otherness of transcendence makes itself heard as the voice of an eros that seeks to order the desires of its citizens according to the unseen measure of the Good. Through this eros, justice is established as the right order of the inner polis, which then serves as the model for the right order of a just society.[3] The Socratic-Platonic language of inwardness is just one of several languages that were invented for the inner public square of the urbanized self. The poetic language of the Hebrew psalms is another. Christianity drew on both traditions for its language of the soul. And the Buddhist Abidharma literature and the Hindu Upanishads represent yet other vocabularies of inwardness.

Urbanization, we could say, shattered the collective sense of tribal identity and individuated human identity opening up the potential for inward reflectiveness. Alienated from the collective myths of its tribal past the urban self develops a reflective self-awareness. Through various poetical and philosophical languages the self discovered itself as capable of doubling or standing back from itself to observe itself. This experience of alienation, of becoming a stranger to oneself, gave the self the psychological distance or self-transcendence it needed to observe and judge its own actions.

By alienating the self from its primal stories, urbanization pulls the rug out from beneath the self. Urbanization, if left unchecked, desacralizes or secularizes the self. It unclothes the self, it strips it of its collective identity and leaves a naked self to quest for a sense of identity adequate to its new social and historical situation. This secularization process prepares the way for opening the self to the holy, that is, the wholly other dimension of the infinite encountered within the metaphorical space of inwardness. Where before the self had stable foundations in an established and sacred cosmological order, once the language of inwardness emerges, the abyss that underlies the self's nakedness will emerge into consciousness. Now the self discovers itself to be not only naked (i.e., without collective mythic identity) but also empty. The abyss of infinity opens beneath the self and leaves the new urban self swimming over Kierkegaard's 60,000 fathoms.

This new urban self that emerged in the ancient world was then faced with two options, either to attempt to recosmiscize its existence as ancient Hinduism did or else to plunge into the abyss in the hope of discovering the path of transcendence through the inward encounter with the infinite, as both ancient Judaism and Buddhism did.[4] In other words, either the self can be resacralized, that is, tied and bound once more to its cosmological role or identity as it is in ancient Brahmanic Hinduism, or it can be the secularizing instrument of a transcendence that calls the sacred order of all social roles into question in the name of an unseen (un-image-able) measure of transcendence—the measure of an unbounded openness to the infinite (as the Buddha did ontologically and the prophet Jeremiah did eschatologically).

Under the impact of such experiences of transcendence, ethics came to mean something more than simply affirming the rightness of the way we customarily do things. Once a language of inwardness was created a whole new realm of experience was opened, which stood in sharp contrast to the experience of the external world. The realm of inwardness opened up various types of experiences of transcendence as experiences of the holy in the sense of the Hebrew term *qadosh;* that is, as a *separate* or wholly other reality. These experiences of the infinite, by sheer contrast with the finite, call into question the way things are. Our answers always belong to the finite order of things but our questions keep us open to the infinite and the utopian possibility of a new world.

Ethical consciousness emerged with such diverse experiences of transcendence because they forced a differentiation of human experience into the two realms of *Is* and *Ought*. Ethics in the Greek tradition (and elsewhere) became a questioning of sacred order. On the basis of an inward experience of a wholly other reality (the "unseen measure" of the Good, as Socrates called it) the present order came to be called into question. The question became, "Is what people say is good, really the good?" The way things are (the Is of the sacred order of society) was called into question in the name of an "otherworldly" Ought.

The reality of *Ought* transcends the reality of *Is*, even as the infinite transcends the finite and the holy transcends the sacred. In a manner consistent with our distinction between the sacred and the holy as antonyms rather than synonyms, we can distinguish between morality and ethics. *Morality* (from the Latin *mores* meaning customs), as I will use the term, is the unquestionable, taken-for-granted patterns of value built into the sacred structure of every society. *Ethics* (from the Greek *ethos* originally also meaning customs) by contrast, is the calling into question of every sacred moral order on the basis of experiences of the holy or transcendence.

Whether theistic or nontheistic, whether understood as sacred or secular, morality, as a society's pattern of sacred custom or routine, is by definition religious. Ethics, as the rational critique of morality, is an inherently secularizing philosophical activity, for the task of philosophy is precisely to rationally critique what we hold as sacred. All philosophy is, in turn, inherently theological in the sense that philosophical reflection always begins with the experience of transcendence, an experience of transcendence as the capacity to doubt and question.

For the polytheistic civilization in which Socrates grew up society was viewed as "the cosmos writ small," and humanity's task was to conform to the divinely sanctioned order of nature. But, as Eric Voegelin argued, Socrates introduced a new *anthropological ethic,* a humanistic ethic in which society is understood as "man [or, the human] writ large." In this view, society is to be more than simply the cosmos in miniature (i.e., a sacred cosmic order). It should rather make the human the measure of a right and just social order so long as (unlike the Sophists) the measure of the human is the unseen measure of the Good. This is the measure that transcends the cosmos and yet reveals itself experientially within the inward realm of the soul as the *sensorium of transcendence.*[5] An anthropological ethic is grounded in an inner experience of that which is Wholly Other than this cosmos. Whereas polytheism was monistic (i.e., the humans and the gods were part of the one cosmic order), the monotheistic propensity of the Greek Socratic philosophers tended toward a dualism of this world and the other world. The ethical importance of such mythological and metaphysical dualisms is that they introduce an element of negation or doubt that can relativize the status quo. In so doing, for instance, Socrates separated the Is from the Ought and brought an otherworldly Ought to bare in judgment of the existing social order. And so Socrates was executed for impiety toward the gods (and hence toward the sacred order of society) and corrupting the youth (i.e., seducing them into asking the critical question, "Is what society defines as the good, really the good?"). An anthropological ethic grounded on the otherworldly unseen measure (i.e., the infinite) has the unique capacity to transcend the order of society and call it into question.

For Socrates, the fictional reality of the Ought is more real than reality. As Plato's account of his death in the Apology suggests, he would rather die for the sake of the Ought than reduce the Ought to the way things are in Athenian society. To those whose experience of reality is totally structured by a cosmological morality of sacred order, the choice Socrates made must seem like madness. Socrates apparently refused to face reality and chose to live in a world of fiction. In their view, morality is about being realistic. It is about living in the real world and accepting the way things are instead of being hopelessly idealistic. For Socrates the Ought may be fictional, a utopian fiction that is nowhere perfectly realized in this world (as in the case of justice, for example), but the erotic power of this utopian fiction is stronger than that of reality. Ethics shares with aesthetics the experi-

ence of aesthetic distance that releases the imagination from conformity with reality. But unlike the pure aesthetic experience, the experience of Ought demands that the imagination transform reality.

It is inherent in the very nature of ethics that it always appears
hopelessly utopian to the realist. The very nature of the experience of
Ought as an inner demand is utopian; namely, a demand to transform
reality so as to conform to fiction. This conflict between reality (Is)
and utopian fiction (Ought) forces all ethical reflection to be reflection
on the relation between two realms; for example, this world versus
the other world (or "world to come" or "Kingdom of God"; or the
wheel of Samsara versus the Wheel of Dharma; or Utilitarian consequentialism versus Kantian deontology, and so forth).

Alongside the Socratic philosopher, another figure who was
overwhelmed by the fictional reality of the Ought and so introduced
such an ethic into the West was the biblical prophet. His parallel in
Asia was the Buddhist sage. The prophets from Amos to Isaiah,
through their intense personal religious experience of the One God
who acts in history and yet remains the unseen Wholly Other who
transcends the cosmos, attempted to break apart the cosmological
identification of the Is and the Ought. They demanded that human
society be ordered to a world-transcending ideal of justice, through
which one strove to become like the God in whose image one was
created; namely, the God without image (Gen. 1:26 & Duet. 4:15). In
Asia, a parallel phenomenon emerged in India with the appearance of
the Buddha, who called the sacred order of the caste system into
question on the basis of an experience of enlightenment that revealed
all selves to be empty or void. As in Socratic philosophy so in both
Judaism and Buddhism we have the emergence of a humanistic non-
anthropocentric anthropological ethic, that is, one in which the human is the measure of a just society but only when the measure of the
human is transcendence as the unseen measure of an infinite that
cannot be grasped by the imagination.[6]

If ethics involves a mode of consciousness that embraces a utopian or fictional view of what human life could be, as if it were more
real than reality itself, then it would seem that the utopianism of
modern technological consciousness, with its drive to transform reality into something as yet only imagined, should lend itself well to the
ethical mode of consciousness. That, however, is not the case. This is
because modern technological utopianism tends to produce a mode of
false consciousness that renders it unable to see the narrative structure that it expresses. As a result the distinction between fiction and
reality, so essential to ethics, disappears.

If modern human beings, no longer understand themselves as living in a normative cosmos, it is because they know that such cosmic stories are cultural fictions. Human beings are now historically self-conscious and enlightened creatures who can do without such stories—or so the story goes. Such stories, it is thought, belong to the childhood and adolescence of the human race. Having reached the enlightened adulthood of the modern situation, contemporary individuals have put aside these childish stories. But, as Stanley Hauerwas has observed, the modern person is still living out a story, one that is meant to put an end to all stories.[7] The form of the story is one we have already encountered, one modeled on the vision of Joachim of Fiore's three ages. As a result of this self-negating narrative, the capacity to distinguish between the way things are and the way things ought to be disappears. Consequently, the way things are is equated with the way things ought to be.

A significant difference must be noted in the way Is and Ought are equated in modern societies as compared to premodern societies. In premodern societies utopia lay in the past. In modern societies utopia becomes identified with the present. Both are expressions of a religious consciousness that sacralizes the social order. However, although sacred power in premodern societies sacralized a conservative social order modeled on a past ideal Is (i.e., the "time of origins"), in a modern storyless technological society the sacred sacralizes the empirical Is of current technological order and its imperative—it can be done it must be done. Nothing is more sacred than technical efficiency, not even human life. A sacralized technological utopianism inevitably unleashes an acpocalyptic dynamic that drives toward the sacrifice of human beings on the altar of MAD-ness, the madness of technological self-annihilation. In a technological society, the sacralization of the current finite order tends to be unambiguous and uncompromising, undermining ethical consciousness and promoting the possibility of the demonic. A genuinely utopian ethic would have the power to secularize and humanize this order, opening the past and present to the utopian possibilities of the future.

In premodern societies there always remained some ethical tension between the way things are empirically as opposed to how they are "in the beginning" (or "in essence"), which provides the leverage for a conserving criticism (i.e., being faithful to the ideal past). That tension disappears in the ideological utopianism of modern society, which refuses to accept the authority of either the utopian narratives of the ideal past nor those of a radically different future. Convinced that utopia has already arrived, modern sacral consciousness sees no need for utopian stories (or any other narratives): the future should only be more of the same. A genuine technological utopianism, by contrast, would be heir to the ancient traditions of transcendence or the holy. That is, a utopian narrative ethic would require that we desacralize modern consciousness to place human existence once more within an unfinished story in which a new future is really possible.

Theology of Culture as the Utopian Critique
of Technical Civilization

An enormous gulf separates modern culture from all premodern cultures, a gulf with far-reaching consequences for human self-understanding and conduct—consequences that have profound implications for the way in which we engage in philosophy, theology and ethics in our contemporary situation. I am speaking of the gulf between nature and culture that has emerged with the technological understanding of self and society. In premodern cultures human nature and society were seen as part of a sacred natural order. Only the tools, crafts and other artifacts made by humans were understood as being artificial. In the modern world both the self and society are now included in the realm of artifacts, both are now seen as human creations. Modern culture, says Bernard Lonergan, "is not normative but empirical. . . . so it is that modern culture is the culture that knows about other cultures, that relates them to one another genetically, that knows all of them to be man-made."[8]

The word *culture* comes from the Latin *cultura* and originally referred to the cultivation of the earth. This origin suggests the modern meaning succinctly; namely, that "culture" is nature rearranged by human intention and action. As such, culture is artificial—that which is made by human design. The artificial is not, as commonly supposed, wholly other than the natural but nature rearranged to express distinctively human purposes and meanings. The very word *culture* as a part of our modern vocabulary and awareness implies a technological understanding of human existence, that is, of culture as our "second nature," our humanly constructed identity.

Our world, says Peter Berger, is socially constructed through conversation, through which "man not only produces a world, but he also. . . . produces himself in a world." Indeed, "what appears at any particular historical moment as 'human nature' is itself a product of man's world-building activity."[9] The modern self, therefore, is existential or technological. As Gabriel Vahanian has argued, the technological self "far from being a robot . . . is the man who makes himself."[10] And the modern managerial understanding of society is its sociological correlate.

To live self-consciously in the world of culture is to realize that the primary milieu in which we dwell is not nature but language, the world of mediated meaning.[11] Our capacity for language, for culture, and for technology is one and the same. For through language humans alter the world of nature. "Poetically dwells man upon this earth," says Holderlin. Indeed, the Greek root of *poeisis* suggests the power "to make, or do, or bring forth," which expresses the skill or *techne* of the human.[12] The ritual tellings and enactings of the earliest creation myths are poetic acts of primal technological skill— transforming chaos into cosmos. The metatechnological act, which provides the foundation for all other techniques, is the creation of a symbolic universe in which to dwell, a cultural world of mediated meaning. In the very mythological mimesis of nature, human beings were unconsciously creating an artificial world in which to dwell. "Myth has not brought man back to nature," says Gabriel Vahanian, "so much as it has sought to settle him in culture. . . . The mythique of man has always included a technique of the human."[13]

The gulf that separates modernity from previous worlds, as Harvey Cox insisted, is one of historical self-consciousness or self-understanding. Unlike premodern persons, we know that we create the world in which we dwell. Modern sociohistorical consciousness generates a technological or managerial understanding of society. The historically grounded social sciences have generated three uniquely modern disciplines: management in the economic realm, social policy in the political realm, and social ethics in the cultural realm.[14]

In the modern world, for the first time in history, we ask not only that individuals be just, but also that society be rationally organized for the maximization of social justice. When managerial consciousness is generalized to embrace society as a whole we find ourselves debating questions of social policy; namely, what specific values and techniques should govern the shaping of our future. Once such questions emerge, it is necessary to invent a new discipline to deal with them, namely, social ethics, whose function is to evaluate those norms and procedures through which we seek to change our social order.

There is no such thing as social ethics, in this sense, in premodern cultures, not even in the biblical tradition. One can clearly find a concern for social justice in such societies. Nevertheless, not even the ancient prophets of Israel call for the replacing of kingship with some other form of government, nor do they call for a change in economic systems. Rather they demand, in the name of God, that both king and merchant be just and generous. Ethics remains the province of individuals not institutions. Nor does Paul of Tarsus call for the abolition of slavery, but rather a new attitude between slaves and masters. Among the ancient Greeks you do get the emergence of debate about differing orders of society, but even they attempt to settle the question by an appeal to a metaphysical order of nature as normative.[15] The narratives that governed the human ethical imagination in the ancient world were, for the most part, cosmological narratives that obscured the role of human agency (and hence responsibility) in shaping the structure of society.

As long as the social order was believed to have "sacred origins" established "in the beginning," its order was the unchangeable fate of humanity. Once that order was desacralized, society was open to being shaped and changed. But to the degree that the values which shaped public order were understood to be part of the sacred normative order of nature, secularization destroyed the normative horizon of order and left human beings naked and adrift in Nietzsche's horizonless world where only a demonic and unchecked will to power reigns.

The task of social ethics today is to discover those norms that transcend any given culture, in order to critique the present order of society and imagine and outline a new world in which the human is realizable through its utopian capacity for self-transcendence. And the effecting of social ethics today is the personal, political and managerial task of a shaping a public policy capable of sustaining the utopian order of an open society where, in the face of finitude and tragedy, we can remain willing and able to make new beginnings.

To accomplish this task requires that we replace the traditional approaches of natural theology and natural law with theology of culture. Modern theology is of necessity theology of culture. To speak of theology of culture immediately brings to mind the work of Paul Tillich. If the twentieth century is peculiarly the century of the technological society and the nineteenth century can be said to have really come to an end only with World War I, then it is of considerable significance that Paul Tillich's first published lecture, "On the Idea of a Theology of Culture" appeared immediately after that war.[16] The question preoccupying him in that essay was the function of theology in a modern secularized scientific and technological culture, and the place of theology among the faculties of the modern university.

In that lecture he argued that "once a secular culture has been recognized in principle by the church there is no longer any question of a theological system of ethics—nor of a theological system of logic, aesthetics, and sociology. . . . What was essentially intended in the theological system of ethics can only be realized by means of a theology of culture applying not only to ethics but to all the functions of culture. Not a theological system of ethics, but a theology of culture."[17]

Theology of culture replaces traditional theological ethics because once we understand culture to be a human creation ethics can no longer be restricted to reflection on individual behavior. Now humans are understood to also be responsible for the shape of society. Thus one cannot raise the question of ethical actions without raising the question of the morality of society and culture (of institutions and the symbolic meanings that legitimate them) as a whole. Today, Jacques Ellul has suggested, we must choose our institutions and our identities together. We cannot chose one without the other.[18] The emergence of a technological civilization represents a quantum leap in the task of ethical reflection, in which all ethical reflection must necessarily be social ethics and all social ethics a fundamental critique of culture and its institutions, as the basis for social policy.

The foundational insight of Tillich's theology of culture is that every culture has an inherent religious dimension, even as every religion is shaped by the culture in which it emerges. Every culture is driven by its religious "substance," which is the human need for meaning expressed and embodied in its religious, that is, its "ultimate concerns." The way in which the need for meaning is expressed is shaped by the symbolic forms available in that culture. Neither *substance* nor *form* should be confused with the *content* of culture. The religious dimension is revealed not by the content in itself, but rather by the meaning (i.e., substance) attributed to the content through symbolic forms of expression. This relationship between religion as the drive for meaning and culture as the expressed patterns or forms of meaning is summed up in his formula that, in every age, *religion is the substance of culture and culture is the form of religion.* This way of approaching the question of the relationship of religion and culture therefore does not see religion as a separate sphere within culture but rather as a religious depth dimension that underlies all cultural activities, attributing to them a sense of meaning, value, and purpose. In an age in which we have become aware of culture as the artificial or linguistic realm in which we dwell and through which nature is transformed, we are forced to recognize that culture and technology are one and the same reality. It follows that Tillich's formula, religion is the substance (i.e., meaning) of culture and culture is the form of religion, can be translated (in accord with Jacques Ellul's analysis of technological religiosity)—religion is the substance of technology (i.e., technique) and technology is the form of religion.

At the same time, at the level of surface structure, religion as an institutional function of society plays a restricted role in the social order. This is because in a modern society every sphere of human activity is differentiated from every other, and each has its own auton- omy (e.g., the differentiation of disciplines in the university and the differentiation of institutional functions in society). That any of these activities should fall directly under the heteronomous authority of the church (or any other single institution) would be alien and unaccept- able. And yet the religious dimension remains pervasive because each differentiated realm, whether ideational or institutional, is a human activity. This means that each is rooted in an unconditional drive toward meaning, the religious substance of all cultural activities. Inso- far as each is faithful to this religious dimension or drive for meaning, its *autonomy* may become *theonomy.* Religious substance, said Tillich, has the power to transform cultural form in every sphere of human activity.

In a secular technological culture it is no longer acceptable for a theologian on a university faculty to define his or her role confession- ally. Nor is it acceptable for theology to be the intellectual arm of a church that dictates the normative order of society. This would threat- en the autonomy characteristic of modern intellectual disciplines: the freedom to evolve their own self-definition in terms of the data, the questions and publicly verifiable criteria of judgment. Therefore the Medieval role of theology as queen of the sciences is relativized by the intellectual and institutional differentiation of an emerging tech- nological civilization.

Thus Tillich argued that only when theology is understood as a "normative branch of knowledge concerned with religion" can it find its place in the secular university.[19] The theologian of culture is not a church theologian, bound by a confessional stance but rather "a free agent," open to exploring the import of religious and cultural phe- nomenon in all their diversity. "As a theologian of culture, he has no interest in ecclesiastical continuity and this of course puts him . . . in danger of becoming a fashionable religious prophet."[20] As a human being, he or she needs to responsibly assume a concrete standpoint. Theology of culture, Tillich insisted, is like all other cultural sciences. For "every universal concept in cultural science is either useless or a normative concept in disguise; it is either an alleged description of something that does not exist or an expression of a standpoint."[21] The concrete standpoint of the theologian should therefore be explicit and acknowledged in his or her work rather than implicit and un-acknowledged. This standpoint may be within a particular confessional community. Thus a theologian of culture may also be a church theologian, but the two roles must be kept in a precarious dialectical balance. A normative theology of culture, then, is an attempt to "draw up a normative system of religion based on the categories of philosophy of religion, with the individual standpoint being related to the standpoint of the respective confession, the universal history of religion, and the cultural-historical standpoint in general."[22] In this process, one identifies normative experiences of transcendence and then proceeds to make a case for their distinctive status by making a case that they have in fact played a culturally self-transcending role in the history of religions and cultures.

The theologian of culture, operating as an interdisciplinary scholar within the secular university, sets about this task in a manner which sets him or her apart from the confessional theologian. Theology is "brought . . . down from heaven to earth."[23] Theology of culture, as Gabriel Vahanian's work suggests, is an iconoclastic way of speaking about the human.[24] It is not so much reflection on "God" as it is the critical appropriation of the language of transcendence (theistic or nontheistic) for the utopian critique of culture. Theology of culture defines its subject matter, not as God or revelation or even "dogma," but rather as the study of human religious experience and behavior as a social and public phenomenon in all its diversity. Moreover, theology of culture stands in relation to the descriptive study of religion, said Tillich, in the same way normative ethics stands in relation to metaethics. As an ethical discipline, it is concerned to do more than describe religious experience. It is especially concerned to identify the norms for the critique of both religion and culture.

Given Tillich's insistence that the religious drive for meaning is the dynamic substance of every culture, even as culture provides the symbolic forms for the expression of this dynamism, theology is not restricted in its reflections to some narrow religious sphere but rather is a critique of the religious dynamic at work in the diverse autonomous spheres of human endeavor that typify modern culture. Tillich viewed the task of the theologian of culture as identifying and critiquing the religious dimension implicit in all culture, including secular culture. This critique draws on a typology of possible relations between religious meaning and cultural form as one of three possible types: heteronomous, autonomous, or theonomous.

Secular Enlightenment culture is seen, for example, as an autonomous rebellion against the heteronomy of an earlier church dominated culture. Heteronomy is the temptation to identify ultimate or religious meaning with some particular institution, which then is experienced as having the authority to impose a normative order on the self (and society) as if from the outside. Autonomy correctly understands that authority imposed from the outside is always an arbitrary and authoritarian *law from without*, but makes the mistake of substituting its own vision of order, which is an equally arbitrary expression in which one becomes *a law unto oneself*. Between these extremes there is the possibility of "theonomous culture," which occurs whenever there is a surrender to the dynamic drive toward ultimacy at work in every sphere of human activity. Heteronomy and autonomy end up by freezing cultural development in a given finite form. They absolutize the finite either in the form of a demonic Procrustian totalitarianism or a demonic Protean anarchism. The demonic manifests itself whenever the finite is arbitrarily elevated to the category of the ultimate. Theonomy is born out of the inner dynamic of the drive toward ultimacy that brings every finite form under the criticism of the experience of the infinite embodied in our doubts and questions. *Theonomy* is Tillich's name for the experience of transcendence as self-transcendence. It is the question put to every answer, the utopian inner drive for meaning that can break through any given form and transform any and every sphere of cultural activity. Thus the task of theology of culture as social ethics is not to impose some arbitrary religious vision on culture but to release the inner drive toward self-transcendence already at work in every sphere of culture. Tillich's theology of culture reflects the transforming impact of modern consciousness on the traditional discipline of theology, extending its scope beyond reflection on theism to include reflection on *transcendence* in whatever form it is discovered. Theonomy, in this context, must be understood to refer to all authentic experiences of transcendence, whether theistic or nontheistic.

Given that the data of theology is the religious dimension manifested in *all* realms of human activity, such a theology becomes a "theological questioning of all cultural values."[25] Thus, although theology is relativized as a discipline, it retains a kind of universal relevance to all disciplines and all realms of human experience and interest. This questioning of all cultural values presupposes that the theologian of culture has identified theonomous or culturally self-transcending norms for the critique of culture. Based on such norms, he or she then constructs a utopian critique of culture. This critique

"produces a general religious analysis of all cultural creations; it provides a historical-philosophical and typological classification of the
great cultural creations according to the religious substance realized
in them; and it produces from its own concrete religious standpoint
the ideal [i.e., utopian] outline of a culture penetrated by religion".[26]

The Dialectics of the Critique of Culture: From the Sacred and Profane to the Holy and Secular

The critique of culture as a whole can be accomplished only if in
fact there are normative values that are capable of promoting human
individual and sociocultural self-transcendence. These norms cannot
come from nature because our conceptions of nature are themselves
cultural. Tillich suggested that norms for the critique of culture must
come from the history of religions. Nevertheless, one might legitimately ask why religions should be thought of as providing criteria
for normative judgments of culture. It could be readily argued that
religion is just one more expression of culture—no better and no
worse than any other. And in some respects, of course, this is true.
And yet the contemporary theologian John Dunne, for one, has
pointed out that some religions seem to be capable of transcending
historical epochs and cultural boundaries in which they originated to
profoundly influence other cultures and epochs. Some religions have
proven themselves capable of outliving the cultures of their origin in
this fashion. One might think, for example, of the centuries and
countless cultures that Judaism has outlived. Dunne suggests that the
reason for this transcendence (i.e., going beyond) of any given culture is that such religions engage the whole self, whereas any particular culture addresses only part of the self.[27]
    Any appeal to the whole self however is unnecessarily problem-
atic. How could we know what the whole of the self is? But to understand transcendence we do not need to answer that question. If the
uniquely human reveals itself through our continuing openness to
the infinite (our capacity to transcend what we have been and become
what we are not) then whatever religious communities and narrative
traditions have historically demonstrated an ability to promote self-
transcendence will serve the normative role we are seeking to sustain
both self and society as self-transcending. Everything hinges on the
way the religious symbols of a narrative tradition relate the self to its
sociocultural world. If the only way in which religions have related
self to culture is by providing a sacred canopy for the legitimation of
society as a sacred natural order, then they will not be able to provide

culturally transcendent norms. Anthropologists and sociologist have generally been inclined to see religion in this way. They have been inclined to see religion as a dependent rather than an independent variable, as an expression or extension of culture rather than an independent social force.

Religious narratives and their social embodiments, however, really fall into two distinct categories: the narratives of sacred order and narratives of self-transcendence. In the first case, the symbols of the narrative express a sacralization or cosmicization of a particular cultural order, thus legitimating the status quo. These religious symbols tie or bind the self to the social order. In this case there is no real difference between the religious symbol and the cultural symbol, religion and society are one. In such cases when the culture dies so does its religion. Various forms of animism and polytheism fit this category. In the second case, the religious symbol ties or binds the self not to the social order but to self-transcendence. In such cases the self is understood not as a mirror of the sociocosmic order but as reality radically open to the infinite. In the first case the possibilities of the self are tied to its social role, which defines its destiny. In the second case, the self as radically open to the infinite can never be reduced to its social role or definitively integrated into the sociocosmic order. In this second option, there is something irreducibly self-transcending about the self, it cannot be fully measured but rather reflects an unseen measure—unseen and unimaginable. It is this openness to the infinite, the capacity for self-transcendence, that gives an inherent inalienable dignity to the self.

Cultural symbols express the need to actualize our humanity through some actual range of limited possibilities. All actual cultural worlds are limited because not all possibilities are compatible. Sacred narratives legitimate (in the sociological sense) such actual worlds. However, although the limited possibilities of cultural symbols eventually exhaust themselves, so that cultures eventually die to be replaced by other cultures or cultural epochs, symbols of transcendence, by contrast, have the capacity to draw the self beyond the world as given, precisely because they evoke the human openness to the infinite. Unlike cultural and sacred narratives that identify the self with the parameters of the world as given, narratives of transcendence or the holy keep the self open to its inexhaustible possibilities.

The distinction I have been making between the sacred and transcendence is the distinction that Eric Voegelin makes between cosmological and anthropological social orders and both Gabriel Vahanian and Jacques Ellul make between the sacred and the holy.

They confound ordinary usage by treating the terms *sacred* and *holy* as antonyms rather than synonyms. Indeed, for Ellul, the sacred is the opposite of the holy, "no longer close to God, it is part of this world."[28] The sacred, he argued, performs the sociological function of integration and legitimation. Its positive function is to create a sense of order within which human existence can be carried on. But its *demonic* propensity is to create an absolute or closed order that sacralizes the way things are (i.e., Is = Ought), preventing the continuing transformation of self and society. And without a self-transcending openness to the future, life ceases to be either human or free.

Therefore for human life to be creative the claims of the social order to be sacred and unalterable must be relativized by that which is its opposite—the holy. The holy is that which is Wholly Other than society. Where the sacred demands integration and closure, the holy (as the Hebrew word *qadosh* indicates) demands separation and openness to transformation. A consciousness of the holy, creates a feeling of tension and separateness between self and society (i.e., between self and social role). And that very tension prevents the social order (as a complex structure of sacralized social roles) from becoming absolute because it prevents the total integration of the self into society. This, in turn, forces the institutional structures of society to remain fluid and open to further development.

The experience of transcendence always forces a symbolic differentiation of human experience into two realms or two kingdoms (e.g., Is versus Ought, or this world and the other world, or this present age and the age to come). If this otherworldliness takes a nondialectical dualistic form it will result in either a Gnostic (i.e., Manichaean) or a chiliastic attempt to break with (or sometimes simply ignore) the sociocosmic world altogether. If it takes the form of a dialectical dualism it will assume the utopian form of an alternate community oriented to at least partially transforming the larger society. It is the inexhaustible capacity to draw the self and the holy community into new worlds that makes certain religious narratives possible norms for the critique of culture.

Narratives that structure the order of society can be sacred even if that society assumes a secular guise. It is not the content (e.g., talk about gods or spirits) that makes a narrative sacred but its sociological function of *cosmicizing* or legitimating the order of society. Likewise it is not the content but the function of certain narratives that differentiates them as narratives of the holy rather than the sacred—the iconoclastic function of keeping both self and society open to the infinite. Narratives of transcendence are embodied in the myths and rituals of *holy communities.* A holy community is a community set apart from the larger society. These separated communities are in fact the social carriers that enable these narrative traditions to transcend the boundaries of their time and place in ways that remain inexhaustibly relevant to other historical periods and other cultures. This capacity to "go beyond" the culture and historical period of origin is what gives narratives of transcendence their otherworldly quality.

Although there are a plurality of possible norms for the critique of culture, as more than one religion has evidenced this capacity for the transcendence of culture, nevertheless the number of such norms, I suspect, is extremely limited. Two types of experience of transcendence have given rise to narrative traditions that appear to offer the most promising models for a technological civilization: (1) the Jewish affirmation that we are created in the image of a God without Image, (and its equivalent in the Christian tradition, the doctrine of Trinity and Incarnation), and (2) the Buddhist affirmation that both the ultimate (i.e., nirvana) and the self are "empty" (*sunyata*).

Each tradition sustains a form of self-transcending consciousness through the formation of institutionally differentiated holy communities (e.g., the synagogue, the church and the sangha) that embody this culturally self-transcending mode of consciousness in a way that *separates* them (*qadosh*) from the larger society and places them in tension with it (i.e., being *in* but not *of* the world). The holy community is the social carrier of a symbolic religious vision, a utopian vision that can neither be exhausted by, nor identified with, any particular cultural vision of reality. Such utopian communities provide an alien space within the larger order of society, a social space that fosters a consciousness of the openness of the human to the infinite as the basis for a critique of culture.

Although Jewish, Christian, and Buddhist experiences of transcendence should not be equated, they do share family resemblances. Each manifests a similar pattern of response—a consciousness of a radically other unimaginable order of value (of Ought rather than Is). What marks these experiences as authentic is (1) an understanding of transcendence as unimaginable rather than merely ineffable, that is, as Wholly Other, so that it produces a radical break with the cosmological imagination of the surrounding society; (2) this break, of necessity, requires the creation of an alternate community, a utopian community oriented toward realizing a radically other Ought that stands in an ethical tension to the Is of the encompassing society; (3) the tension between these two ethical orders creates the need for a two-realm or two-kingdom ethic and; (4) the measure of the authenticity of this ethic is its requirement to welcome those who are social analogues of the Wholly Other, namely, the alien, stranger, or outcast. Both Judaism and Buddhism introduce a radical anthropological ethic into the world, in which human dignity rather than sacred order is the primary measure of a just and good society, provided that the measure of human dignity is understood to be the *unseen measure* of the infinite.

In positing these similarities between Judaism and Buddhism, I am not claiming that Judaism and Buddhism share the same experience of the infinite. That cannot be assumed. The "infinite" as I use the term is a formal category, which can have more than one type of experiential content. The infinite refers to that category of experiences which suggests an understanding of our humanness as radically open to *becoming*, such that every attempt to enforce a fixed identity on human beings amounts to an act of oppression that violates the essence of what it means to be human. In Buddhism this openness is ontological. In Judaism it is eschatological. Nor am I claiming that Buddhism and Judaism do not have cosmologies. They certainly do. But there is a decisive gap between cosmology and transcendence. This gap is one of imagination not experience. Both transcendence and cosmological order are copresent in experience but in the mode of tension and conflict between the Is and the Ought, which gives rise to the need to symbolize ethical experience as a dialectic of two realms or kingdoms or modes of being in the world. The otherness of transcendence may have metaphysical dimensions but it is its purely experiential, historical, and sociological parameters, as the capacity to go beyond, which are relevant here. Transcendence as otherness expresses the utopianism of the human, our ability to transcend our past to become something new. This experience of transcendence as otherness defies being tied and bound (*religare*) to some cosmological order by the imagination. Yet, having a body that mediates our ecological interdependence with all beings, we cannot live outside this cosmological order. So we must find an ethical position that can mediate between these two orders to render our humanity, not a reality entirely separate from nature and society (as in Manichaean types of Gnosticism) but rather dialectically related to both nature and society, expressing a utopianism of the body.

Mediating between these two orders is the ethical task of a holy community. Such alternate communities act on the larger society as a desacralizing force, calling into question the present order of sacred caste or class structured existence which claims to be normative for human thought and action. At the same time they attempt to embody in their internal organization and interpersonal relations a utopian ideal of what society ought to be like. For example, contra the ancient Hindu claim that enlightenment reveals an eternal self (Brahman-Purusa) that can be imagined to pervade all things, the Buddha insisted that nirvana is beyond imagination. Rather than putting the emphasis on the language of imagination (analogy, metaphor) Buddhism emphasizes the language of negation (*anatta* or no-self); saying what nirvana is *not* rather than what it is.[29] This experience of emptiness or no-self has sociological implications. If everything is impermanent and interdependent and all selves are empty of all eternal self, then there is no Brahman reality that legitimates the hierarchical cosmological social order of the caste system. Hence all selves are equal by virtue of their emptiness. The radical break with the Hindu religious imagination is at once both a religious and a political act with direct sociological consequences. It gave rise to an alternate or separate community, the sangha, as the utopian community of those who were aware of their equality and interdependence. The sangha created that alternate social space within the cosmological order of Upanishadic society from which the Is could be confronted by a transcendent Ought, calling into question and desacralizing the way things are (i.e., the caste system) in the name of transcendence.

Every holy community offers an anthropological ethic of negation and as such each exists in a symbiotic relationship with the society that surrounds it. An anthropological ethic can occur only in the context of a larger cosmological ethic of sacred order that it negates and relativizes. It expresses itself through a fundamental No to that sacred order as a normative order of absolute value for human existence. That No protects the self from being totally integrated into that order. It protects a sense of human dignity that reflects a non-anthropocentric understanding of the human self as the measure of a just and good society. That is, the human itself is understood to be uniquely irreducible because it reflects the unseen measure of transcendence. The self and its holy community must not be reduced or conformed to the order of society as contingently given. Order is made for humans not humans for some sacred order. The No that is said to society, however, must not be the absolute No of a sectarian community but rather the dialectical No of a utopian community. To say, as Eric Voegelin does, that the anthropological ethic of a holy community can exist only in a negative but symbiotic relationship with a larger sacred society is to see the need for a constant and precarious dialectical balance between these two orders.

As Voegelin argues, every society that wishes to maintain its

existence must maintain a paradoxical and precarious balance between the principle that society is the cosmos writ small and the
principle that society is the human writ large. On the one hand, the
cosmological principle is the principle of realism that forces us to deal
with the limitations placed on us by the ecology of our finite bodily
condition. On the other hand, the anthropological principle is the
principle of transcendence whereby we come to doubt the absolute-
ness of those limits and to, at least partially, transcend and transform
our human condition.

Problems emerge when the two orders are not kept in dialectical
balance, when one side is affirmed at the expense of the other. This
dialectic occurs between mass society and its subcultures or minority
communities. The mass patterns of routine give plausibility (in the
sociological sense) to the way of life of a society so as to make it seem
an unchangeable sacred expression of cosmic order. The alternate
patterns of value embodied in minority holy communities introduce
an alien presence into society that calls these sacred patterns into
question, delegitimating them (in the sociological sense) and introducing the possibility of transformative change. Without the cosmological principle a society would fail because it would fail to accommodate itself to its ecological context and the need every society has
for order. But without the anthropological principle, a society would
also fail through its inability to innovate and adapt to new situations.
When a dialectical balance is not achieved, these two principles succumb to the myths of Procrustes and Proteus, either conforming human possibilites to preconceived limits or else claiming that there are
no constraints on human possibilities at all. At the first extreme,
human existence is conformed to the ecological limits of the body
(i.e., nature). At the second extreme the requirements of the body are
ignored as human beings attempt to shape their existence without
regard to the necessities of their ecological-bodily condition. The first
is a Procrustean society incapable of novelty, a society that has suppressed individual creativity and much of what it means to be human
in favor of a collective conformity to the sacred order of nature. The
second is likely to be a Protean society, intent on social and political
transformation with an almost chiliastic disregard for the limitations
imposed on us by nature and history. Political wisdom would require
that we embrace both truths in a paradoxical dialectic. Individual and
social transcendence can occur only if there is a mutually limiting
dialectical tension between these the two principles. Authentic social
transcendence tempers realism with iconoclastic transformation.

This dialectic of order and transcendence reflects a differentiation of human experience into the two-realms or dimensions of Is and Ought. As Lewis Mumford once observed, the predisposition for the differentiation between order and transcendence is built into our very biological structure. These two realms reflect the distinction between the *autonomic* and the *sympathetic* nervous systems. The first system automatically regulates the biological functions of our body so that we can function successfully as organisms within the ecology of our environment without devoting deliberate conscious attention to these functions. The automatic, routine, and orderly functioning of our body both makes our consciousness possible and frees it from concerns with bodily functioning to express itself through the sympathetic nervous system in those acts that uniquely express human imagination, freedom, and creativity. Mumford made this point to argue that the structure of society should reflect this distinction so that we routinize only those aspects that sustain the order necessary for life and leave all other areas of life open to freedom and creative transformation.[30] My point in bringing this biological analogy up is not to argue for some kind of biological reductionism but rather to suggest that a human being as body-self is attuned to both the order of nature and to transcendence.

Because the anthropological order depends on a constant dialectical No to sacred order as the condition of its existence, it is in constant danger of collapsing back into the sacred cosmic order out of which it is differentiated, to the degree that this No is weakened or compromised. To critique one's culture requires one to be able to stand back from it. One must be able to psychologically and sociologically disengage oneself. One must experience oneself as *alienated* from one's own society, as an alien or stranger in an alien community. But the human hunger to belong and be secure makes sustaining the tension of alienation a great burden. A failure of nerve and insight is a constant threat. The individual and collective temptation of holy communities and their members is to reintegrate themselves into the larger social order. This is especially true when a holy community that begins as a separate community succeeds in converting virtually an entire society. At such a point the temptation is to believe that the values of society are identical to its anthropological values, failing to see the countless compromises every social order exacts from a successful anthropological ethic that inevitably transform it into a cosmological morality. An anthropological ethic is a constant utopian task and can never be a finished accomplishment.

The history of every religion in relation to its culture is a history of the conflict between its experiences of the sacred and experiences of the holy. In every religion and every culture we can find individuals who have wrestled with these contrasting experiences. And yet, sociologically speaking, the institutionalization of that contrast through the formation of a holy community is the exception rather than the rule. In most times and places throughout history, religion has typically manifested itself in the form of a sacred society. This is true of tribal religions and of early urban polytheistic civilizations. It also seems to be true of neo-Confucian, Hindu, and Islamic traditions—all of which tend to identify religion with a total sacred order for society. Only Judaism, Christianity, and Buddhism (and for a while Greek philosophical schools) originated as holy communities.

When I identify Buddhism, Judaism, and Christianity as anthropological traditions I mean that they have the distinction between these two orders built into their originating experiences, their narratives, their rituals, and their social structures. This makes a two-realm or two-kingdom ethic available to their traditions for potential actualization. It does not mean that they have always done so or will always do so. Both Buddhism and Christianity have often aspired to be religious civilizations and in the process collapsed back into cosmological modes of being. And to the degree that Judaism in the twentieth century has ceased to be an exclusively diaspora religion, it too now must deal with that constant temptation. To put it another way, a holy community can remain holy only by remaining separate. In the moment when a holy community trades its two-kingdom ethic for a single kingdom it has won the world and lost its soul, trading its utopian anthropological ethic for a cosmological morality. When this happens there is a tendency for such a society to become demonic; that is, to be prepared to sacrifice human dignity to ensure conformity to sacred order.

Islam is a perplexing case for this typology. Islam represents a one kingdom tradition that has at times shown itself capable of generating a two-kingdom model. Sharing much with the biblical traditions of Judaism and Christianity, including the ethic of welcoming the stranger, still Islam failed to develop an explicit ethic of two realms or kingdoms. As a result its symbolic self-interpretation continues to require a sacred society. And yet in practice, as it has struggled with the forces of modernization and secularization, it has shown itself capable of generating alternate communities that can act quite independent of the Islamic state.[31] However, I believe Islam remains especially politically volatile because it has not been able to provide a narrative (symbolic) justification for these alternate communities, and hence religious reform has the propensity to be fundamentalist and conservative, continually moving in the direction of reestablishing a one-kingdom model. If I do not say more than this about Islam in this book, it is because I am still uncertain what account to give of it.

Drawing its norms from the experiences of transcendence found in holy communities, theology of culture will always take the form of an ethic of two realms or kingdoms. To speak of a *two-kingdom ethic* is to use the terminology of the Christian tradition, but the reality to which it refers is not uniquely Christian. An ethic of two realms or two kingdoms is characteristic of all forms of anthropological religious experience. The experience of *radical otherness* or transcendence generates a holy community and an other way of life that automatically separates itself from the larger society. The experience of holy creates communities of aliens, those who become strangers to their own culture. But there is more than one mode of separation or alienation that a holy community can opt for, and each option has its own socioethical implications. H. Richard Niebuhr's *Christ and Culture*[32] outlined five such options with respect to the Christian tradition. However, we can also take these options as valid for other two-kingdom traditions such as we find in Judaism and Buddhism. The five types are (1) Christ *against* culture, (2) Christ *of* culture, (3) Christ *transforming* culture, (4) Christ and culture in *paradox,* and (5) Christ *above* culture.

To construct a general theory of the ethical options available for relating religion and society all we need to do is substitute the word *religion* for Niebuhr's *Christ.* Niebuhr viewed two of these types as extremes, with *religion of culture* (i.e., the sacred society) at one end of the spectrum and *religion against culture* (i.e.,the millenial sectarian community) at the other end. These two would correspond to our extreme nondialectical types of Procrustean cosmological and Protean anthropological religion. In the first, Is equals Ought—the way things are is the way they ought to be and the need for a second kingdom is denied. It is essentially a one-kingdom ethic that allows no alien social space within the society from which to criticize its order. In the second, the Ought is asserted in defiance of what Is, as if society did not need so much to be criticized as defiantly ignored. The first identifies religion so completely with the cultural status quo that the ideals of the religion become confused with and reduced to the ideals of the culture. Because everything is as it should be and no social space is allowed for an alternate perspective, the possibilities for such options as development, reform, or revolution are not consciously allowed for. The second rejects society as totally corrupt and stands against culture, withdrawing to live behind sectarian walls. In its own odd way, it is also a kind of one-kingdom model as it refuses to compromise with the larger society in any way (although in practice this is virtually impossible).

In Voegelin's terms, the sectarian community has embraced the anthropological at the expense of the cosmological principle, and the sacred society has done just the opposite. Each has lost touch with one or the other pole of the basic paradox of human existence; namely, that human beings realize themselves through a combination of realism about the limits imposed by their ecological condition as finite bodily creatures (the cosmos writ small) and the iconoclastic freedom of transcendence (the human writ large) whereby such limits are strategically shattered and partially overcome, permitting the further development appropriate to creatures whose freedom is both real and yet finite.

Between these extremes however Niebuhr saw three mediating options that did assume a dialectical relation between these two orders. In each model the religious community understands itself as separate from society but also recognizes some kind of interdependence between the two orders. Each of these models sees the holy community as providing a necessary alien space within the larger society from which to exercise a certain ethical leverage for the critique of society. It is as if the holy community is a social analogue for a culturally transcendent perspective from which it attempts to speak and act. The first of these dialectical or mediating models is *religion and culture in paradox*. This model shares the pessimism of sectarian religion about reforming society but unlike sectarian religion does not believe you can successfully withdraw from society. As a result, one must learn to live in the world paradoxically, being in but not of it. One accepts certain compromises as necessary even if not measuring up to one's highest religious-ethical ideals. The second is *religion above culture*. This model offers a hierarchical society a transcendent ideal within the parameters of that type of society. It does not reduce religious values to cultural values but tries rather to raise human relationships to a new ethical level within the structures of society as given. Finally, the third is *religion transforming culture*. In this model the religious community assumes a utopian stance toward the world, with the goal of transforming society and its institutional order to reflect at least in some modest degree its ethical ideals. In its neosectarian form it sees itself as needing to provide a continuing leavening or fermenting presence in a society that will always fall short of the holy community's transcending ideals. In its more militant ideological form this model can assume the totalitarian program of an ideological utopianism that tries to impose its ideals on the whole of society. Ideological utopianism implicitly has already assumed the stance of religion of culture and if successful this model explicitly collapses into the religion of culture model.

Every theology of culture will draw upon one or more of these mediating or dialectical models but there is no mathematical precision that we can bring to the choice among them. The choice of a fundamental ethical stance toward society is an interpretive or hermeneutical task. One must assess the cultural situation and the impediments to transcendence within it. That assessment in turn depends on one's interpretation of the history of religions and cultures and the lessons to be learned from that history. Also, one's fundamental assumptions about the degree to which society and the self are really open to change, in part based on one's reading of history, will affect one's judgment. Those who are pessimistic, either about the general capacity of self and society to undergo change and transformation or their specific ability to do so under what are judged to be currently severe impediments, will be inclined to assume a stance of either sectarian rejection (the religion against culture model) or of paradoxical compromise (the religion and culture in paradox model). Those who are more optimistic about the general possibilities for change or transformation or the specifically weak impediments to transcendence in the current cultural situation will be inclined to assume a stance of either the religion above culture or religious transformation of culture models. It is possible and probable that one's stance will change under changing circumstances.

The appropriate stance has to be worked out again and again in constant dialogue with the witnesses to transcendence in other holy communities. The shaping of public policies occurs through the interplay of the stances that these alternate communities take in relation to the sacral public order of society. In the context of an emerging pluralistic global civilization, such as our own, the communities one needs to be in dialogue with will extend beyond one's own tradition to include communities of transcendence from diverse traditions. My own stance, as it is being worked out in this book, interprets our present situation as one on the verge of a new millennium, which will either be aborted by an apocalyptic war of total nuclear destruction (or less dramatic forms of technical destruction such as pollution) or brought to fruition in a new cosmopolitan world civilization in which we shall find unity-in-diversity around the common thread of utopian self-transcendence. I am attempting to work through our present options for the future in the light of the past failures of religions and cultures symbolized by Auschwitz and Hiroshima. My stance is that of an alienated Christian seeking to practice theology of culture as an academic form of inquiry and to understand his situation imaginatively through the eyes of the other communities of transcendence brought to mind by Auschwitz and Hiroshima, namely Judaism and Buddhism.

To understand the task of a religious two-kingdom ethic in a secular civilization presents a unique challenge. It requires clarity about the relationship of the secular to the religious. Voegelin's distinction between cosmological and anthropological order and Ellul's and Vahanian's parallel distinction between the sacred and the holy are helpful. Even more helpful is Paul Tillich's similar but more differentiated distinction between sacramental religion, on the one hand, and mystical-prophetic-secular forms of religion, on the other.

For Tillich, the theonomous experience of transcendence could take either secular or religious form. In his last public lecture, just before his death, "On the Significance of the History of Religions for the Systematic Theologian," he argued for the need for a theology of religions in an emerging world civilization and against the idea that any society could be entirely secular. Both of these points reaffirm the themes of his 1920 essay on theology of culture, but with an important shift of emphasis. In 1920 Tillich was concerned primarily about the dialogue with secularity. In 1965, Tillich was now most concerned about the dialogue with other great world religions and the possibility of other authentic forms of transcendence. Nevertheless both were persistent themes throughout his life work and integral to his conception of theology of culture.

The two themes which preoccupied Tillich, religious transcendence and secularization, are intimately related, as if two sides of the same coin. "The sacred," said Tillich, "does not lie beside the secular, but it is its depths. The sacred is the creative ground and at the same time a critical judgment of the secular. But the religious can be this only if it is at the same time a judgment on itself, a judgment which must use the secular as a tool of . . . religious self-criticism."[33] The human mind, however, can apprehend the secular as secular only by contrast with the sacred. Thus, as we have seen, Tillich understood religion to be operating at two different levels in modern culture. On the one hand, religion provides the depth dimension for all cultural phenomenon, on the other hand, at a surface level, so to speak, the differentiated social structures of religions, with their own myths and rituals, continue to be important. They are important because the differentiated social role that religion plays in a culture provides the

necessary contrast that enables the human mind to grasp the significance of the secular.

"The reformers were right," Tillich argued, "when they said that
everyday is the Lord's Day and, therefore, they devaluated the sacredness of the seventh day. But in order to say this, there must have
been a Lord's Day, and that not only once upon a time but continuously in counterbalance against the overwhelming weight of the secular."[34] The mistake of the secular theologians (here we might think of
both Harvey Cox, at the time of writing *The Secular City*, and also
Richard Rubenstein) was to think that desacralization or secularization was a one-way historical development in which the sacred becomes progressively more secular. Tillich viewed the sacred as a continuing dimension in all historical periods and desacralization as a
continuous task. It is a task that manifests the dynamics of transcendence as the capacity to criticize and go beyond the sacred order of
any given society.

This criticism takes three forms: mystical, prophetic, and secular. Each of these is a criticism of the religious in its sacramental form,
the form that expresses the powerful experience of *the holy within the
finite*. Although this is an authentic type of religious experience, when
it is left uncriticized it leads to the demonic identification of the holy
with the finite. Functionally, this situation is identical with what Ellul
called the sacralization of the secular. The mystical experience criticizes the sacramental or sacred in the name of the radical otherness of
the holy that cannot be identified ontologically with any finite thing.
Alongside of the mystical critique, the prophetic critique identifies the
ethical danger of elevating the finite to the status of the infinite for
this is equivalent to identifying what Is with what Ought to be. To
treat as ultimate that which is limited and less than ultimate is a
fundamental and dangerous category mistake equivalent to idolatry.
The prophet criticizes what Is in the name of the radical otherness of
what Ought to be—to open the present to its infinite (theonomous)
possibilities.

Finally, said Tillich, "secularization is the third and most radical
form of de-demonization. . . . The secular is the rational and the
rational must judge the irrationality of the holy. It must judge its
demonization."[35] The secular functions in an ethical-critical manner
that parallels that of the prophetic and the mystical criticisms. Indeed
the mystical and the prophetic paves the way for the secular. According to Tillich: "Both the prophets and the mystics were predecessors
of the secular. The holy became slowly the morally good, or the
philosophically true, and later the scientifically true, or the aesthet-

ically expressive. But then, a profound dialectic appears. The secular shows its inability to live by itself. The secular which is right in fighting against the domination by the holy, becomes empty and becomes victim of what I call 'quasi-religions.' And these 'quasi-religions' imply an oppressiveness like the demonic elements of the religions. But they are worse, as we have seen in our century."[36] They are worse because once the secular has sealed itself off absolutely and totally from the holy, it has sealed itself off from its infinite possibilities. The totally secular lacks the religious depths out of which to renew itself through self-criticism. In a word, it lacks the capacity for self-transcendence and is a prisoner of its own finitude. Or to put it in Ellul's terms, not being the holy, it seeks to infinitize its finitude (symbolically expressed as 666) by claiming for itself an absolute and unquestionable sacred order. When this occurs, the secular assumes a totalitarian posture that denies transcendence to either self or society. Such a posture leads inevitably to the apocalyptic incarnation of the demonic. The secular needs the experience of the holy (Wholly Other) to remain secular. In the absence of such experience the secular gravitates toward the sacred and the demonic.

Tillich's typological analysis bears directly on a central thesis that I am arguing in this book: that the secular is never neutral. The secular and the holy mutually require each other. It is the holy that keeps the secular secular. The absence of a dialectical relationship between secular and the holy results in a sacralization of the secular. The inevitable consequence of this is a set of secular categories that reflect a nondialectical demonic dualism of opposition—the sacred (those who are the same) and profane (those who are different). In contrast to such a sacral ethic, the dialectic of the secular and the holy opens up the possibility of constructing a social ethic of secular holiness that would be relevant to both those who think of themselves as religious and those who do not. In fact, the need for this dialectic may imply that religious and secular ethics are mutually required if an openness to transcendence is to be sustained in a society.

The Challenge of Auschwitz and Hiroshima: From Sacred Morality
to Alienation and Ethics

Although every culture is inherently utopian in its potentiality, the internal social dynamic through which its symbolic world-view is maintained as a sacred order has a tendency to transform it into a closed ideological universe (in Karl Mannheim's sense of the ideological; namely, a world-view that promises change while actually reinforcing the status quo) that tends to define human identity in terms advantageous to some and at the expense of others. Historically the process of dehumanization has typically begun by redefining the other as, *by nature*, less than human. So the Nazis did to the Jews, and European Americans did to the Native Americans, men have done to women, and whites to blacks. By relegating these social definitions to the realm of nature they are removed from the realm of choice and ethical reflection. Hence those in the superior categories need feel no responsibility toward those in the inferior categories. It is simply a matter of recognizing reality. Those who are the objects of such definitions find themselves robbed of their humanity. They are defined by and confined to the present horizon of culture and their place in it, which seeks to rob them of their utopian capacity for theonomous self-transcending self-definition.

The cosmicization of social identities is inevitably legitimated by sacred narratives, whether religious or secular-scientific (e.g., the Nazi biological myth of Aryan racial superiority), which dehumanize not only the victims but also the victors. For to create such a demonic social order the victors must deny not only the humanity of the other who is treated as totally alien but also their own humanity as well. That is, to imprison the alien in his or her enforced subhuman identity (an identity that attempts to deny the victim the possibility of self-transcendence) the victor must imprison himself or herself in this same world as it has been defined and deny his or her own self-transcendence as well. The bureaucratic process that appears historically with the advent of urbanization increases the demonic potential of this process, especially the modern state bureaucracy organized around the use of the most efficient techniques to control every area of human activity. The result is, as Rubenstein reminds us, the society of total domination in which virtually nothing is sacred, not even human life.

The heart of such a bureaucratic social order is the sacralization of professional roles within the bureaucratic structure such that technical experts completely identify themselves with their roles as experts in the use of techniques while totally surrendering the question of what those technical skills will be used for to the expertise of those above them in the bureaucratic hierarchy. It is no accident that the two cultures that drew the world into the cataclysm of World War II, Germany and Japan, were militaristic cultures, cultures that prized and valued the militaristic ideal of the unquestioningly obedient warrior. In these nations, the state and bureaucratic order became one and the same. As Lewis Mumford has argued, the army as an invention of urban civilization is a near-perfect social embodiment of the ideal of the machine.[37] The army brings mechanical order to near perfection in its bureaucratic structure, where human beings are stripped of their freedom to choose and question and where each individual soldier becomes an automaton carrying out orders always "from higher up" with *unquestioning obedience*. Bureaucracy dehumanizes because it separates means from ends. The self becomes an instrument or means for ends chosen by others. The self that is forbidden to choose its own ends is deprived of its utopian possibility of choosing to become other than what it is. In both Germany and Japan at the beginning of World War II we have cultures prepared by their tribal histories to be cultures of total domination. And in both the bureaucratic and the tribal elements converge with modern technology, while at the same time they paradoxically attempt to reject modernity, secularization, and the emergence of an international global order. Whatever else World War II was about, it was first and foremost a rejection of the possibility of a universal human community in favor of the superiority of one particular race, whether Aryan or Japanese, and the right of that race to the world as its "living space" (*lebensraum*).[38]

The task of theology of culture as social ethics is the critique of culture as the basis for social policy. It will be a critique of both the public narratives and public order that a given society holds as sacred. Today that means the ethical critique of the morality of our secular technological civilization. Viewing this civilization in the light of Auschwitz and Hiroshima, we must begin with a critique of the bureaucratic and technical tendencies of our social structures and the sacral legitimation of our cultural and professional identities. The purpose of this critique is to break open the ideology of our cultural universe and in the process reimagine, reconceive, and reorient our personal and societal self-understanding so as to promote those interpretations and actions that will enable us to shape and change our world. The goal is an open society in which utopian self-transcendence continually remains a possibility for all.

The best way to describe the style of the theology of culture proposed here is as "decentered" or "alienated theology." As I indicated in the Prologue, this is theology done "as if" one were a stranger to one's own tradition, interpreting one's tradition from the perspective of the stranger who may be affected by that tradition. As such, it is the inverse of apologetic theology. Its purpose is not defense of one's tradition but rather its ethical critique and transformation. Alienated theology is the appropriate mode for theology in an emerging world civilization, a civilization that lives in the shadow of Auschwitz and Hiroshima and totters in the balance between apocalypse and utopia. We can be dragged into world history through war or we can walk in by way of mutual understanding.[39] By the first path global civilization emerges as a totalitarian project of dominance that risks a global nuclear apocalypse. By the second path we prevent the first, creating global civilization through an expansion of our understanding of what it means to be human, which occurs when we welcome the stranger, that is, when we *pass over* to another's life, religion and culture and come back with new insight into our own.

I see alienated theology as standing in direct continuity with Tillich's theology of culture in its openness to transcendence wherever it can be found in the history of religions and cultures. In a certain sense alienated theology picks up where Tillich left off. In his first published paper, in 1920, Tillich put forward his vision of the theologian of culture as a *free agent,* not bound by the restrictions of the confessional theologian. Yet Tillich's own theology of culture, embodied in his systematic theology, was essentially a Christian apologetic theology. Tillich spoke of his own theological stance as being "on the boundary." In fact, he operated between the center of his own tradition and its boundary. However, in the last paper he delivered before his death he returned to his original larger vision of a theology of the history of religions and cultures, as if returning to unfinished business. Yet, even here he did not really pass over the boundary for he still offered a tentative Christological center to "The Religion of the Concrete Spirit" that he outlined.[40] Tillich never quite became the free agent he envisioned at the beginning of his career. The reason why, I think, is that he realized the danger of a free agent becoming "a fashionable religious prophet." He insisted that even the theologian of culture needed to speak from a concrete religious standpoint to avoid the irresponsible illusion that he or she could speak from some neutral vantage point. Tillich's dilemma was how to speak from a concrete standpoint and still be a free agent open to other experiences of transcendence.

Alienated theology is my attempt to answer that dilemma through a theology and an ethic of welcoming the stranger. Alienated theology understands openness to the stranger and his or her strange stories as the decisive test of the authenticity of one's own openness to transcendence within one's own tradition. The tradition of hospitality, which lies at the heart of not only Judaism and Christianity but also Buddhism, is a way of conceiving of my concrete standpoint that both acknowledges its particularity and yet requires me to pass over the boundary into the life, religion, and culture of the stranger and see my own tradition through the eyes of the other. Alienated theology is rooted in an openness to the stranger that requires a selfless compassion, a compassion or empathy that demands that I forget my own self and my own religion and culture for a brief time and, in so doing, come back to them transformed by new insight. Tillich's boundary problem can be overcome, because in a holy community the center lies not inside the boundary (as in a sacred society) but beyond it—in the holy other. For the Christian, for example, to welcome the stranger to is welcome Christ without knowing one is doing so (Matthew 25:31–46). The paradox of Christocentrism, as I imagine it, is that it requires Christians to decenter themselves from their own tradition and identity (i.e., the experience of alienation) to discover Christ in the stranger.

Alienated theology, rooted in passing over, keeps me honest by allowing me to acknowledge the particularity of my standpoint, and yet it does not so bind me to my horizon that I must somehow subordinate the stranger's world to my own in some abstract Christocentric theological formulation. Alienated theology forbids me the option of integrating the other into my world-view. It demands that I respect the other as a transcending presence within my world. I must welcome the stranger precisely in his or her *otherness*, not as a potential candidate for *sameness*. For only as I am open to the otherness of the stranger am I open to the otherness of transcendence. The openness to the one is identical with openness to the other. In the double gift of this otherness I am invited to discover the richness of my own humanity. A fundamental axiom of alienated theology is that the sacred closes me off from the stranger whereas the holy opens me to the stranger. The experience of the sacred defines the stranger as profane and so dehumanizes him or her. That is, the category humanity is defined to include all who are *the same* and exclude all who are *different*. By contrast the holy pluralizes and secularizes to embrace difference as a humanizing experience that finds its expression in welcoming the stranger. For me, alienated theology begins with the resources of the biblical tradition and finds its norm in the story of Jacob wrestling with the stranger, as well as the story of Babel as a description of our emerging global civilization as a land of promise where every stranger is an invitation to self-transcendence.

In the remaining chapters, I shall continue this experiment with theology of culture as alienated theology. I shall continue the attempt to see my own tradition through the eyes of the stranger and on that basis suggest a model for a transcultural and transreligious ethical coalition on behalf of human dignity, human rights, and human liberation amidst the pluralistic babbling of our modern technological civilization.

Utopian Ethics: From Human Dignity to Human Rights and Human Liberation

The Utopianism of Job: From the Ethics of Obedience to the
Ethics of Audacity

After Auschwitz, says Irving Greenberg, "Nothing dare evoke our absolute, unquestioning loyalty, not even our God, for this leads to possibilities of SS loyalties."[1] The path from Auschwitz to Hiroshima and nuclear MAD-ness only reinforces the truth of Greenberg's observation. Equating authentic religious self-transcendence with the total surrender of the self in unquestioning obedience is ethically and politically hazardous. Such an equation occurs within a narrative context that interprets life as warfare. The conditions of war are unique, in that during them we suspend ordinary ethical conventions and invert ordinary ethical norms to make a virtue out of killing in order to heal. Narratives of warfare invert the symbolism of the holy-infinite so as to sacralize some finite order, now rendered more sacred than the dignity of the stranger. Narratives of warfare inevitably cast an impending conflict in apocalyptic terms, seeing the struggle as a sacred task whose purpose is to eliminate the profane other (i.e., the stranger) who threatens the sacred order of the society of the elect (i.e., those who are the same).

However, an ethic of total self-surrender in unquestioning obedience is not the only option made available by the history of religions. For there are, in this history, not only narrative traditions of apocalyptic conflict but also narrative traditions of utopian audacity on behalf of the stranger—traditions as old as Abraham and Siddhartha and as recent as Gandhi and Martin Luther King Jr. If apocalyptic narratives require a demonic doubling to kill in order to heal, utopian narratives encourage one to welcome the stranger and act with audacity in defense of the stranger's dignity. Such narratives invert the meaning of sacred stories of war and transform them into stories that encourage a nonviolent struggle in defense of human dignity—even, and especially, if the stranger is one's enemy.

Perhaps the most ethically powerful such narrative tradition took shape within the history of Judaism. Although obedience to the God who commands plays a central role in Judaism, as it does in Christianity and Islam, argues Anson Laytner, "yet, on the other hand, [unlike Christianity and Islam] there has existed alongside this mainstream tradition another expression of the covenantal relationship. . . . According to this view of the Covenant, it is as though God and the Jewish people grew up together and so treat each other with the familiarity common to old friends or lovers."[2] This understanding of the divine-human relationship gives rise to the uniquely Jewish narrative tradition of chutzpah.

There is in the Jewish tradition, says Beldon Lane,

> an audacious faith, almost bordering on insolence, that stalks the high country of belief and disbelief. It seems especially prevalent in the rarefied air above Mt. Sinai. Rooted deeply in the human experience of adversity and anguish, it opens onto a landscape where God and human beings walk as friends. *'hutzpah k'lapei shamaya'* it is called in the Jewish tradition—a boldness with regard to heaven. From Moses, the Psalmist, and Jeremiah to such rabbinical figures as Honi the Circle Drawer in the first century B.C.E.—from Levi-Yitzhaq of Berditchev in the Hasidic world of Eastern Europe to the pain-soaked novels of Elie Wiesel—it echoes through the Jewish past with a stubborn insistence.[3]

There is in Judaism an understanding of *covenant* as a personal and communal relationship that is essentially a two-way street. It is a dialogue between God and God's people grounded in a set of mutual expectations. The formula "I will be your God and you will be my people" is understood as an ethical contract of love and commitment obligating *both* parties. Jews are obligated to live by the commandments, but God also has obligations: to be with the people of Israel, to guide them and protect them. Although the term *chutzpah* has rather lighthearted connotations in American Jewish culture, the Israeli scholar Mordechai Rotenberg argues that it has a weightier meaning in the talmudic tradition and is the most appropriate term for this contractual relationship "according to which God as a dynamic 'personality' allows man to influence him. . . .[Indeed, *chutzpah* is] a symbol for man's capacity to affect God and change his decrees and consequently man's future by his actions and justified 'complaints'."[4]

Standing behind this tradition is the great patriarchal figure of Abraham. Contrary to the typical Christian interpretation of Abraham, the Judaic model of Abraham as a man of faith balances the obedient Abraham of the *Akeda* (Genesis 22) with the Abraham who has the chutzpah to call God into question in the confrontation with God over the fate of Sodom and Gomorrah (Genesis 18:16–33). Faith, in Judaism, as exemplified in the stories of Abraham, is seen as a dialogical and dialectical tension of trust and questioning. Trust is not seen as precluding the challenging and questioning of God, trust is not an unquestioning obedience that authorizes a Kierkegaardian teleological suspension of the ethical, but rather a confidence that the two-way street of the covenant relationship both permits and demands this kind of honesty between God and the person of faith. The element of chutzpah in this dialogical covenant relationship is most prominent precisely when the tragedies of life seem to call into question the very justice of God. Perhaps no other book in the Tanakh (or its Christian parallel, the Old Testament) speaks to the theme of faith as chutzpah more profoundly than the Book of Job.

One of the most salient characteristics of the Job story is the dialectical reversal of the trial metaphor. In the framing story (1–2:10 and 42:10–17) Job is put on trial by God, but in the main body of the book, the dialogue with the comforters, the roles of God and Job are reversed and Job places God on trial. The comforters wish to make Job guilty so that God does not appear unjust for allowing the infliction of suffering upon Job. Job refuses to play that game. He steadfastly insists: "Till I die I will not renounce my integrity. My innocence I maintain, I will not relinquish it" (27:5–6).[5] So Job demands his day in court: "I will say to God: 'don't condemn me; let me know your case against me'" (10:2). Nevertheless he is skeptical that he will get a fair hearing: "But how can man be acquitted before God? . . . If I summoned and he answered, I do not believe he would heed me. He would crush me with a tempest" (9:2 and 9:16–17) Prophesying his own fate that will come true when God finally appears to him in the whirlwind, still Job persists in his challenge: "Let Shaddai answer me" (31:35).

Like Abraham—who argued with God over Sodom and Gomorrah and dared to ask, "Shall not the Judge of all the earth do what is just" (Genesis 18:25)?—Job is not afraid to put God in the judgment seat of the accused. But unlike Abraham, Job is not overconfident that God will answer "Yes" when the question of justice is raised. Job refuses to sacrifice his integrity just to make God appear just. Job, no doubt, expresses the spiritual situation which many Jews experience after the Holocaust.

The comforters are the prosecuting attorneys who seek to defend God's honor by making Job appear guilty. Eliphaz argues: "What innocent ever perished? (4:7). Bildad asks: "Does God pervert justice?" (8:3). And Zophar insists that although "these were your words, you say, 'My doctrine is pure.' You are clean in your own eyes. But would that God might speak, might open his lips against you. He would tell you what is hidden." (11:4–6) The logic of the comforters is clear—God is just, therefore, Job must be guilty; he deserves his suffering.

In Job's encounter with God in the whirlwind, everything Job had predicted about his inability to get a fair hearing from God seems to come true. He predicted that God would not listen to him but "crush him with a tempest"(9:17). And that is exactly what happens. Job is overwhelmed by the mighty power who ignores the question of his guilt and innocence and instead roars forth a challenge; "Where were you when I founded the earth?"(38:4). "Would you annul my judgment; condemn me that you may be justified, . . . can you thunder with a voice like his?" (39:8–9). And Job is forced to repent and recant through shear force of intimidation (42:6). God wins, but it is a hollow victory, for Job's prophecy is fulfilled and God's arbitrariness is unmasked.

But the story is not yet over. What of the comforters? Here we encounter a dialectical reversal. In the very last chapter, God says to Eliphaz the Teminite, "My anger burns against you and your two friends; for you have not spoken truth of me, as did Job, my servant. So now take yourselves seven bullocks and seven rams, and go to Job, my servant, and make a burnt offering for yourselves, and Job, my servant, will pray for you, for I will accept him, so that I may not do anything rash to you, for you have not told truth of me, as did Job, my servant"(42:7–8)

What we have here is the paradoxical vindication of Job in his court claim against God. The comforters have been saying, "if you suffer you deserve it, for God is just." Job has steadfastly insisted on his innocence and integrity and therefore questioned the justice of God. Now we find God confirming that Job told the truth and the comforters were lying. The paradox is that Job is vindicated in his audacity to call the justice of God into question even though God must find God's own self guilty. God chooses to be on the side of human dignity and integrity even if it means that God's own authority must be called into question.

This same audaciousness is also found in the talmudic tradition. For the Talmud, says Jacob Neusner, sanctifies the capacity to doubt and to criticize. "The wonder of the Talmud is its tough-minded claims on behalf of the intellect, not in search, but in the service, of God."[6] God is found in the "thrust and parry of argument." Talmudic debate is in fact a ritual for experiencing God through the questions. And yet, although the talmudic scholar is vigorous and bold in his questions, his questioning cannot be divorced from the mythic context in which it takes place. The Talmud is constructed on a dialectic of trust and questioning that is foundational to faith as an expression of chutzpah. According to one talmudic story, Rabbi Eliezer ben Hyrcanos began to prove his interpretations of the Talmud by working miracles. But other scholars challenged and chided him for such tactics and invited him instead to "wrestle with us over the text." Finally Rabbi Eliezer called on heaven to vindicate his interpretation and a heavenly voice responded: "What do you want already with Rabbi Eliezer? The Halakha is always as he says." However, Rabbi Joshua stood up and cried out, "'The Torah says not even to trust voices from heaven!' and Rabbi Yirma added, 'You, Yourself God, told us on Mt. Sinai to follow the community of those who agree on the truth.'" After this God was silent. Later the prophet Elijah was asked to interpret that silence and "he smiled . . . and said, 'My children have defeated me. My children have defeated me!'"[7] The meaning of the Halakha is not to be determined by miracles or even the voice of God. Even God is bound to accept the meaning the rabbis come to understand through wrestling with the Word. The talmudic way is the art of wrestling with God and human beings and winning. The essence of this understanding of the faith relationship is captured in the biblical story of Jacob's wrestling with a stranger who, although refusing to give his name, blesses Jacob and promptly changes his name to *Israel*; that is, one who wrestles with God and humans, and wins. (Genesis 32:23–32).

This powerful tradition of audacity in the face of unjust suffering is what enables Jews to find continuity with their tradition, even after Auschwitz. As a voice out of the Shoah itself, Elie Wiesel speaks with a unique authority. More than any other author, Wiesel deserves to be seen as the bearer of the tradition of chutzpah in our post-Shoah world. Wiesel tells us: "I . . . remember my Master . . . telling me, 'Only the Jew knows that he may oppose God as long as he does so in

defense of His creation."[8] To be a Jew "means to serve God by es-
pousing man's cause, to plead for man while recognizing his need of
God."[9] Or again, "Judaism teaches man to overcome despair. What is
Jewish history if not an endless quarrel with God?"[10]

Like Job, Wiesel chooses to put God on trial and call God to
account. This is a persistent theme throughout his writings, which
culminates in his play *The Trial of God*.[11] The play is set on the eve of
Purim in 1649, in a small town that has just been decimated by a
pogrom. The innkeeper Berish and his daughter Hanna survive to put
God on trial. But before the trial can be brought to conclusion it is
interrupted by an impending second pogrom. The village priest urges
them to flee or, if they wish, convert. But Berish responds: "My sons
and my fathers perished without betraying their faith; I can do no
less."[12] And yet, though he is prepared to die for his faith he is not
ready to forgive God and bring the trial to an end. "The trial will go
on. . . . [says Berish,] I lived as a Jew, and it is as a Jew that I shall
die—and it is as a Jew that, with my last breath, I shall shout my protest
to God! And because the end is near, I shall shout louder. Because the
end is near, I'll tell Him that He's more guilty than ever!"[13]

The Trial of God embodies the paradox of Jewish faith, the paradox of trust and audacity (chutzpah). But it is more than a work of the
imagination. It is based, Wiesel tells us, on an experience he had in
the death camps, where he witnessed three rabbis who "decided one
winter evening to indict God for allowing his children to be massa-
cred."[14] And when the trial was over and God was found guilty, the
rabbis realized it was time for prayers and so they began to pray.[15]
The dialectical and dialogical faith of trust and chutzpah is not the
fictive invention of post-Shoah theologians. It is a lived faith, a tradition of faith reaffirmed in the very bowels of the death camps.

Emil Fackenheim sums up this powerful tradition of audacity
when he says:

> There is a kind of faith which will accept all things and renounce
> every protest. There is also a kind of protest which has de-
> spaired of faith. In Judaism there has always been protest which
> stays *within* the sphere of faith. Abraham remonstrates with
> God. So do Jeremiah and Job. So does, in modern times, the
> Hasidic Rabbi Levi Yitzhak of Berdiczev. He once interrupted
> the sacred Yom Kippur service in order to protest that, whereas
> kings of flesh and blood protected their peoples, Israel was un-
> protected by her King in heaven. Yet having made his protest he
> recited the Kaddish, which begins with these words: "Extolled

and hallowed be the name of God throughout the world . . . ".
Can Jewish protest today remain within the sphere of faith? . . .
In faithfulness to the victims we must refuse comfort; and in
faithfulness to Judaism we must refuse to disconnect God from
the holocaust.[16]

After Auschwitz only an ethic of audacity is appropriate. The world
can no longer afford the luxury of unquestioning faith. Unquestioning faith is pagan faith—a faith that demands the sacrifice of life
(whether animal or human) in order to promote life. Unquestioning
faith is a nearly universal characteristic of religion throughout the
world. Virtually all forms of religion have asked followers to sacrifice
their will and surrender themselves to a higher reality. And all faith
that asks for a total surrender of will in unquestioning obedience is
finally not only pagan but demonic. For all such faith is a training
ground in fanaticism that blurs the distinction between God and the
state (or other finite authorities) and leads to the dehumanization of
the *chosen* victims of the state. The only authentic faith is a questioning faith, a faith prepared to call into question even God. The difference between God and an idol is that an idol will brook no dissent.
The test of authentic faith is the possibility of dissent against all authority in the name of a human dignity.

    In the biblical tradition, one encounters God, as Jacob did,
through the encounter with the *stranger*—the one who is alien or
wholly other than oneself and one's religion or culture. Biblical ethics
is grounded in the ability to identify with the stranger. The command
to welcome the stranger appears more often (some thirty-six times)
than any other command in the Tanakh (Old Testament). "You must
not oppress the stranger; you know how a stranger feels, for you
lived as strangers in the land of Egypt" (Exodus 23:9). Knowing how
the stranger feels one must "Love the stranger, then, for you were
strangers in the land of Egypt" (Deuteronomy 10:19). In encountering
the stranger, one encounters a witness to the transcendence of God,
one who, like God, cannot be domesticated to legitimate one's life or
religion or cultural-national identity. Thus compassion for the stranger is an implicit recognition of the transcendence of God in the transcendent dignity of all persons. Such compassion compels one to call
into question all authority, sacred (i.e.,the god of one's nation) or
secular (i.e., the state) that would abuse that transcendent dignity.

    In the post-Shoah world, provided one manages to avoid de-
spair, one seems to be forced either into a mystical silence or into a
utopian hope against hope. Sometimes, as in Elie Wiesel, one finds

both present. Wiesel, who so often turns toward the silence, can also find the voice to say to the God of Israel: "Either You are our partner in history or You are not. If You are, do Your share; if You are not we consider ourselves free of past commitments. Since you choose to break the Covenant, so be it. And yet, and yet . . . we went on believing, hoping, invoking His name. . . . In other words we did not give up on Him. . . . For it is the essence of being Jewish: never to give up—never to yield to despair. . . . When all hope is gone, Jews invent new hopes."[17] And in a mood that echoes Fackenheim and Wiesel, Greenberg argues that to succumb to despair is to grant Auschwitz the final word. To be a Jew is to engage in a hope that is "sober, and built on the sands of despair, free from illusions. Yet Jewish history affirms hope."[18]

For both Greenberg and Wiesel, everything depends on a willingness to live out of such an illusionless utopian hope in the midst of the unresolvable tension between the silence of God and the demonic realities of the modern world. It is precisely this willingness that prevents one from embracing a false hope in either the sacred or the profane. The sign above the gates that lead to the post-Auschwitz and post-Hiroshima world of modern civilization should read: "*Abandon all hope in both the sacred and the secular, ye who enter here.*" The reality of God or transcendence, if it is to be found anywhere, is not tied to either the sacred or the profane but, in the tradition of Job, to human dignity wherever it is affirmed. If God is to be God, it cannot be at the expense of human beings, rather it must be the God who says to all false *comforters:* "You have not spoken truth of me as did my servant Job." The utopian audacity of Job is precisely what is needed after Auschwitz and Hiroshima. For we must refuse to grant the final word on the future of humanity to the demonic. If the world were utopia, utopianism would be redundant, but in an apocalyptic world a utopian ethic is a necessity. Instead of a world headed for some apocalyptic, nuclear final solution to the ambiguity of the human existence we must choose to remain in an unfinished world, a utopian world where, like Job, we choose human dignity over all final answers and all final solutions.

After Auschwitz and Hiroshima, every narrative tradition, whether religious or secular, must be weighed against the measure of human dignity. And every narrative tradition must be prepared to be transformed by the eruption of the demonic that Auschwitz and Hiroshima represent. The survivors of Auschwitz and Hiroshima are the ultimate strangers of our world in that they have literally come from a world few have visited. To excavate the abyss of the demonic, as Arthur Cohen encourages us to do, requires a kind of identification with these ultimate strangers. Spiritually we must strive to descend into the abyss of their experience. Everyone who descends into this abyss to confront the magnitude of the demonic that erupted at Auschwitz and again at Hiroshima becomes, in some sense, a survivor. I do not mean to suggest that those of us who were not there dare think of ourselves as survivors in the same way as those who were. But each of us becomes a survivor in three senses. First, we become survivors through empathy. To descend into the abyss of the demonic for them was literal, for the rest of us it will be a spiritual journey that we make by welcoming these strangers and empathetically passing over into their lives and experiences to come back with new insight into our own. Second, when we engage in such passing over we are likely to come back alienated from our own history, religion, and culture insofar as these may have contributed to the eruption of the demonic. Therefore our spiritual descent into the abyss may make us survivors in relation to our own narrative traditions. For example, as a Christian, I can never in good conscience return to the faith of my ancestors as it has been passed on to me through the myth of supersession. I can embrace that tradition only if it can be purged and transformed. Buddhists, I should think, are faced with a similar challenge in the light of the tragic outcome of their own ethic of unquestioning obedience and its propensity to legitimate the demonic power of nationalism in pre-World War II Japan. Third, our world of nuclear MAD-ness so alters our consciousness, Robert Lifton suggests, that psychologically we all become survivors, trying to cope with life in an absurd post-Shoah and post-Hiroshima world where we could all be annhilated in a matter of a few minutes.

In such a world every sensitive person has moments of despair. Every person of faith who has descended into the abyss, whether literally or spiritually, undergoes a transforming experience. Such persons now live in a new time—the time After Auschwitz and Hiroshima. They know something of the meaning of unbelief, of the desolation that is a loss of faith and hope, a sense of abandonment.

Both Arthur Cohen and Richard Rubenstein remind us that we live in a world that is functionally Godless. "Indeed, Hiroshima and Auschwitz seem to have destroyed any kind of Providence," says Emil Fackenheim. "After these dread events, occurring in the heart of the modern enlightened, technological world, can one still believe in the God who is necessary Progress any more than in the God who manifests His Power in the form of a superintending Providence?"[19] It is not only belief in Providence that founders on the rocks of Auschwitz and Hiroshima. In some ways, the Asian narrative traditions of karma are even more seriously challenged by these eruptions of the demonic.

Recent reflections by the Zen Buddhist scholar, Masao Abe illustrate the radical challenge that Auschwitz and Hiroshima present to even a karmic world-view. Abe has sought to come to grips with Auschwitz and Hiroshima in a illuminating dialogue with both Jewish and Christian theologians. He begins by arguing that from a Buddhist perspective all things are "empty" (*Sunyata*) of "own being" (*Svabhava*) because all things arise in interdependence (*Paticca-Samuppada*) and therefore nothing has its being independent of all other things. It follows from this that karma itself is always more than personal: it is social and collective as well. Therefore, he argues:

> From the perspective of the Buddhist doctrine of karma, I am not free from responsibility for the Holocaust in Auschwitz. I must accept that "Auschwitz is a problem of my own karma. In the deepest sense I myself participated as well in the Holocaust." . . . The Holocaust is *ultimately* rooted in the fundamental ignorance (*avidya*) and the endless blind thirst to live inherent in human existence in which I am also deeply involved through my own individual karma. . . . I believe that only through . . . fundamental enlightenment as the realization of fundamental ignorance, can one properly and legitimately cope with such a historical evil as the Holocaust.[20]

Abe goes on to argue that an ethic of justice is not the right framework for dealing with the Holocaust, since judgments about justice and injustice lead to defensive counterjudgments on the part of those who are judged. This kind of dualistic thinking creates interminable conflicts which can only result in a further increase of negative karma.[21]

The Buddhist goal, as he interprets it, is to finally see the emptiness and relativity of the ethical dimension from a perspective that lies beyond it—the religious dimension of enlightenment.[22] Abe believes Christianity, to some degree, shares such a relativizing of the ethical. He sees *kenosis,* the "self-emptying" of Christ, as an analogue to the Buddhist experience of emptiness. He takes Paul's letter to the Philippians 2:5–8 as the key text, where Christ does not cling to equality with God but empties himself, taking on the form of a servant and "becoming obedient *even* unto death, yea, death on the cross."[23] Buddhism and Christianity find some of their deepest affinities, he perceptively suggests, in this ethic of obedience brought about by the realization that the total death of the self (e.g., the Great Death, Dying with Christ) leading precisely to a new level of consciousness (e.g., the Great Joy, Rising with Christ as a new creature). On this new plane of consciousness one engages in a kind of teleological suspension of the ethical, one goes beyond the sacred and the secular and all ethical judgments of good and evil. From his Buddhist perspective, says Abe, "there is no continuous path from ethics to religion. In order to enter the realm of religion, human ethics must . . . die."[24] At the level of enlightened consciousness there are no dualistic ethical distinctions or judgments (even as the Gospel narratives suggest that in Christ there is neither male nor female, free person nor slave, etc., and God's rain falls equally on the just and the unjust alike).[25] To respond constructively to the Holocaust, we are told, one must get beyond the dualism of love and hate and "realize its [i.e., the Holocaust's] relationality and nonsubstantiality."[26]

As Abe unfolds the full implications of karmic interdependence, this transmoral perspective that relativizes all ethical judgments leads to the problematic claim that somehow the victims of the demonic have in some way contributed to their own suffering. "In the ethical and relative dimension, responsibility for the Holocaust clearly resides in Nazi, not in Jewish, individuals. But the same Buddhist doctrine of karma teaches us that . . . . in an immeasurable way, even the uttermost evil of the Holocaust is related to the innumerable events in the past and present of human history in which all of us, assailants and victims alike, are involved. When we are victims of a horrible suffering such as what occurred in Auschwitz or Hiroshima, we tend to absolutize the evil involved as if it happened to us passively, unrelated to our own karma."[27] After Auschwitz and Hiroshima, the lines between sacred and profane, religious and nonreligious, believer and unbeliever, have become blurred—but not, I would argue, the line between good and evil. If anything that line must become clearer and no religious narrative vision must be exempted from that demand. At the moment when the bomb dropped on Hiroshima, said one survivor: "I thought, 'There is no God, no Buddha. . . . There is no God, no help.'"[28] This was not her last word, as time passed she was able express some faith and hope again. But whenever she recalled her experience of the demonic at Hiroshima, remembering those she was not able help or save, Robert Lifton reports, these reaffirmations would be overcome by her sense of death guilt—a phenomenon survivors of both Auschwitz and Hiroshima manifest. This is a profound feeling of guilt for having survived when so many others have not. The survivor vacillates between moments of faith and hope and moments overwhelmed by the hopeless abyss of the demonic. This vacillation reminds me of Irving Greenberg's description of Jewish faith after Auschwitz as "momentary faith" in which moments of renewed faith and hope alternate with moments of hopelessness and despair and neither can be definitively eliminated.[29] Indeed Lifton describes the psychological state of survivors in just this way. It is precisely this kind of experience that led Arthur Cohen to conclude that the wound of the demonic delivered at Auschwitz can never be fully healed over.

After Auschwitz and Hiroshima I do not believe the karmic narrative traditions of either Buddhism or Hinduism can survive intact any more than the biblical narratives of divine providence. All affirmations of meaning will have to stare meaninglessness in the face. We shall have to settle for, at best, a partially meaningful world. I suspect the extraordinary passion for justice and human dignity that is uniquely emphasized in the biblical tradition, giving us the prophets and the book of Job, has its roots in the fact that the biblical narrative traditions provide a much less adequate meaning system than that provided by the narrative traditions of karma found in Hinduism and Buddhism. The difference between the Asian narratives of karma and the Mediterranean narratives of providential history illustrates the profound difference narrative can make at the ethical level. Karmic narratives provide a vision of multiple lifetimes through which perfect justice is always done, for all always get exactly what they deserve. These who are poor or suffer injustice in this life, it is assumed, deserve it as a punishment for evil deeds done in a previous life. All suffering, therefore, is viewed as just. Such narratives undermine the possibility of experiencing suffering as unjust and therefore experiencing the moral outrage and indignation of an Abraham or a Job. By contrast, when you find yourself in a narrative that understands human existence as a single journey through time from birth to death, guided by a personal God, the level of unexplained suffering increases dramatically. Suffering becomes experienced, as in the book of Job, as an undeserved injustice. Job's audacity to question even God and demand justice is rooted in such an experience.[30] The Mediterranean traditions (Judaism, Christianity, and Islam) attempt to alleviate this threat to meaning by promising life beyond death. But, unlike the karmic vision of Asia, this promise is never able to adequately explain why suffering is necessary in the first place. The attempt to identify the cause of suffering as sin in these traditions is dashed on the rocks of Auschwitz and Hiroshima. It makes God appear a vindictive tyrant. Like Job, the survivors of

Auschwitz and Hiroshima have a right to take offense at such a cheap solution.

If Masao Abe found similarities between the Buddhist understanding of *Sunyata* (emptiness) and the Christian understanding of *kenosis* as the self-emptying of a Christ who is obedient even unto death on the cross (Philippians 2:1–11), his attempt to deal with the Holocaust forced him to acknowledge a profound dissimilarity between these two traditions and Judaism.[31] In response to a challenge from the Jewish theologian, Eugene Borowitz, concerning his transmoral interpretation of the Holocaust, Abe argued:

> It is also stated in Exodus that God told Moses he could not see his face without dying. We can encounter God not directly but only through death—a spiritual death. In Buddhism the great death—the death of the ego is emphasized as the necessary moment for awakening. In this regard, religion is not an extension of ethics. . . . As the key characteristics of Judaism, Borowitz emphasizes divine forgiveness, the responsibility and culpability of all people to turn from evil, and the creation of holiness through righteous living. Learning this, I have realized that in Judaism the relation between ethics and religion is not understood to be discontinuous but distinctively continuous. Judaism is clearly different from Buddhism, a tradition in which there is no continuous path from ethics to religion or from religion to ethics, for in Buddhism ethics and religion are dialectically connected through mutual negation. It is also significantly different from Christianity in which there is a continuous path from religion to ethics . . . but there is no continuous path from ethics to religion. . . . This characteristic of Judaism is all the more evident when Borowitz states that "because God is holy/good Jews are to be holy/good" (p. 82). This means that in Judaism the realization of spiritual death . . . and great death (the complete death of the human ego) are absent.[32]

Abe's observation confirms the argument I have been advancing; namely, that both Buddhists and Christians need to rethink the meaning of their own narrative traditions of death and rebirth in the light of the historical implications of the myths of life through death and their links to the ethics of obedience, the narratives of killing in order to heal and the public policies of nuclear MAD-ness. For those narrative traditions that lead to the teleological suspension of the ethical seem to have, historically speaking, been closely tied to the eruption of the demonic. Both Buddhist and Christian narrative traditions have lessons to learn from the narrative traditions of Judaism—lessons concerning wrestling with transcendence and audacity on behalf of the stranger.

As a religious narrative, the Book of Job is unusual in its courageous willingness to call into question the reality of cosmic justice. The hunger of human beings for meaning is so great that we would rather believe we deserve to suffer than to believe the world is meaningless and unjust. But Auschwitz and Hiroshima are events of such devastating proportions that not only the "suffering for our sins" apologetic of the biblical traditions, but even the "bad karma" apologetic of the Asian traditions seems an inadequate explanation. Such explanations are desperate attempts to retain a hope that our world is a meaningful world. But both providence (i.e., belief in a just and merciful guiding presence in history) and karma (i.e., belief in cosmic justice over many life times) as myths of cosmic meaning are shattered on the rocks of Auschwitz and Hiroshima. Like Job, something in us rebels at the suggestion that the men, women, and children who died in these places of desolation deserved their suffering and death, whether for deeds done in this life or in another. And like Job, we must refuse to make them guilty just so that life in this world (and therefore God or the cosmos) can seem just and meaningful. The experience of Job speaks profoundly to an apocalyptic age and its worlds of desolation.

Because of their unique narrative tradition of audacity, the post-Shoah Jewish theologians, it seems to me, have become spokespersons for the whole human race. So far as I am aware, there is no body of post-Hiroshima religious literature in Buddhism comparable to the Jobian literature of audacity or chutzpah in post-Auschwitz Judaism. What is striking about these Jewish theologians is their persistent linking of the particularity of the Jewish experience to the destiny of whole human race, persistently drawing a connection between Auschwitz and Hiroshima. Again and again I have found these authors linking Auschwitz to Hiroshima, not to draw exclusive attention to the plight of the Jews but, on the contrary, to interpret what happened to the Jews as a prophetic warning of the peril facing the whole human race.

It was Irving Greenberg, we can recall, who told us that: "The Holocaust was an advance warning of the demonic potential in modern culture. If one could conceive of Hitler coming to power not in 1933 but in 1963, after the invention of nuclear and hydrogen bombs, then the Holocaust would have been truly universal. It is a kind of last

warning that if man will perceive and overcome the demonism unleashed in modern culture, the world may survive. Otherwise the
next Holocaust will embrace the whole world." [33] "It was at Auschwitz," said Elie Wiesel, "that human beings underwent their first
mutations. Without Auschwitz there would be no Hiroshima. . . . or
attempts to dehumanize man by reducing him to a number, an object:
it was at Auschwitz that the methods to be used were conceived,
catalogued, and perfected. It was at Auschwitz that men mutilated
and gambled with the future. The despair begotten at Auschwitz will
linger for generations." [34] Or as Eliezer Berkovitz has put it:

> Auschwitz has tragically dramatized the meaning of the new era
> that has broken in upon mankind. In our days, man has concen-
> trated in his own hand adequate physical force to bring about
> the final solution to all of man's problems in one apocalyptic
> world conflagration. . . . For what was proved by the holocaust
> is not what man was capable of doing to the Jew, but what man
> is capable of doing to his fellow. The bomb has rendered the
> final solution on a universal scale a practical possibility; Ausch-
> witz has demonstrated it to be morally feasible. . . .
>   It is no mere coincidence that having countenanced the
> Final Solution to the Jewish problem, partly with glee and partly
> with equanimity, the world is now confronted with the serious
> possibility of a Final Solution to the entire problematic existence
> of man on this planet. . . . Had the nations and their churches
> not been silent and indifferent to what was recognizably afoot in
> the early days of nazism, world history would have taken an
> entirely different course and mankind would not now be balanc-
> ing on the very edge of the thermonuclear abyss. [35]

The fundamental problem as Richard Rubenstein viewed it is
how we treat the stranger. The problem is the human penchant for
creating "the self-defeating ethos of exclusivism and intolerance . . . derived from a religious tradition that insists upon the
dichotomous division of mankind into the elect and the reprobate." [36]
The logical outcome of such a civilization, Rubenstein argued, is nothing less than an apocalyptic "world-wide catastrophe in which hundreds of millions of human beings are destroyed and civilization as
we know it disappears. . . . [And] we have the weaponry to bring it
about." [37]
    The ethical task as Arthur Cohen conceived it is to excavate the
demonic, to descend into the abyss of the demonic. One must demy-

thologize its overwhelming reality and uncover the human roots of its inhumanity. One must come to understand the many faces and hidden depths of its manifestations so as to be able to build a wall of containment around it and a bridge capable of sustaining the traffic of human life over it. The challenge is to divert our present historical trajectory away from any possible apocalyptic outcome. "The task of excavating the demonic," said Cohen, "is no metaphor. How can we regard the atomic bomb, or Vietnam, or the revelations of Solzhenitzyn's *Gulag,* if not as modalities of the abyss, excavations and elaborations of the human penchant to self-infinity, to the ultimate *hubris* which brings not only Jews but all creatures to the borderlands from which there is return for none. It begins with the Jews and it may end with the habitable world."[38] This self-infinitizing sacralization (absolutizing) of some portion of the finite as a substitute for the infinite leads to a dualistic division of the world into the elect (sacred) and the reprobate (profane) and the demand for unquestioning obedience to the genocidal imperative—killing in order to heal.

Secular Holiness in Defense of Human Dignity: The Commanding Voice from Auschwitz and the UN Declaration of Human Rights

The Emergence of An Ethic of Secular Holiness

If the twentieth century is the age of the *apocalypse* (i.e., revelation) of the demonic, it is also the age of the birth of human rights. Emil Fackenheim has argued that the refusal of Jews to give up their Jewishness, despite the devastation of the Shoah, suggests that they have heard and responded to a silent yet commanding voice from Auschwitz, forbidding them to grant Hitler a posthumous victory. "They are commanded to survive as Jews, lest the Jewish people perish. They are commanded to remember the victims of Auschwitz lest their memory perish. They are forbidden to despair of man and his world, and to escape into either cynicism or otherworldliness, lest they cooperate in delivering the world over to the forces of Auschwitz. Finally, they are forbidden to despair of the God of Israel, lest Judaism perish."[39] In claiming that Jews had heard such a command, Fackenheim was not so much advancing a theological hypothesis as making an empirical observation. He was simply articulating and making conscious what, in fact, had already happened. For the audacious visceral response to the Shoah by Jews, both religious and non-religious, has been to continue to affirm their Jewishness.

It is not implausible to suggest that the call for an ethic of human rights is a similar response to a silent yet commanding voice from

Auschwitz—a voice directed, in this instance, to the whole human race. For the movement for human rights arose after World War II largely in response to the trauma of the Shoah and culminated in the formation of the United Nations in 1946 and the UN Declaration of Human Rights as well as the UN-backed founding of the state of Israel in 1948. The Preamble to the Declaration (See Appendix) recalls the "barbarous acts which have outraged the conscience of mankind" and prepares the way for a strong affirmation of the unity of humanity in the main body of the declaration. Consequently this document stands against all mythologies that would divide humanity, racially or otherwise, into superior and inferior groups to claim the world and its resources for the superior ones, as both the German and Japanese mythologies of the World War II period sought to do. The unity and sanctity of the human community, it declares, may not be violated by any political order. Human dignity transcends all social and political orders. It is the true measure of a just society, the limit that no political authority may transgress.

The power of the ethical vision of human rights expressed in the UN document lies in the fact that it too is rooted in an audacious visceral response, one that cuts across cultures and creeds. Unlike the language of most academic reflection on ethics, which remains technical and esoteric, human rights language is a language that has spontaneously taken root in cross-cultural public discourse. The language of human rights has become embedded in the language of politics and international relations. Even if in many cases the political use of this language is hypocritical, still that is *the homage that vice pays to virtue*, which means that this standard has taken root in public life and can be used as a measuring rod (canon) for social and political criticism. To a considerable degree the world has already embraced an ethic of human rights and now scholars are scurrying to see if it is a coherent and defensible ethic.

The emergence of a human rights ethic marks the emergence of an ethic of secular holiness. It parallels the convergence of the secular and the holy that Irving Greenberg has noted in the history of Judaism. Greenberg breaks down the history of Judaism into three stages, based on his own version of the three ages of history as a process of secularization, a version with implications for the gentile world as well. According to Greenberg, the first era of the Jewish covenant, the biblical, ended with the fall of the second temple, which in turn lead to the rabbinic era that lasted until the Shoah and the emergence of the modern state of Israel, which inaugurated yet a third era. The trend in this unfolding pattern is one of the increasing hiddenness of

God and the increasing responsibility that human beings must bear for the covenant. In the first age, God intervened directly in history and bore the primary responsibility for the covenant. In the second age God became more hidden. God went into exile and diaspora with God's people and placed more responsibility on the human side of the covenant, allowing the rabbis to determine the binding nature of covenant obligations. But now after the Shoah, the talmudic age has come to an end. "It is estimated that more than eighty percent of the Rabbis, Judaica scholars and full-time Talmud students alive in 1939 were dead by 1945. Ninety percent of Eastern European Jewry—the biological and cultural heartland of Jewry—was decimated."[40] "The Nazi assault shattered the covenant of redemption. Thus, the third era opens with a crisis of faith and meaning."[41] But even as the Shoah shattered faith, so the creation of the state of Israel stands on "a par with Exodus" as a miraculous event rekindling hope. Out of the contradiction of these two events, Shoah and Israel, neither of which is capable of canceling out the other, Greenberg argues, a new age of Judaism is being born. Living with these contradictory experiences— "there are moments when the Redeemer and the vision of redemption are present and moments when the flames and smoke of burning children blot out faith"—"faith reasserts itself" and yet "the smoke of Auschwitz obscures the presence of God." Hence the new era is even more secular than the rabbinic. In this new era God is not only more hidden but "religious activity itself must be profoundly immersed in the secular."[42]

"The old categories of secular and religious are undone."[43] If in the first era God was to be found in the temple in Jerusalem, and in the second era God was found in exile and diaspora with the people of Israel, then in the third era God is found hidden everywhere beneath the secular. In this third era, the primary responsibility for keeping the covenant has fallen on the human side of the covenant. In this era, Greenberg argues, the covenant is no longer binding on Jews. After the Shoah God cannot with justice require any Jew to keep the covenant. The covenant has become a voluntary covenant. And yet Jews are choosing to keep it of their own free will but in a radical variety of ways. In direct continuity with the rabbinic principle of pluralism in interpretation, but going beyond the principle of majority rule, the placing of the covenant more completely in human hands means there will be increasing diversity both in the interpretation and application of the covenant. There will legitimately be a plurality of Jewish covenantal life-styles. It is binding on Jews to accept each other in these plural ways of keeping the covenant. For any one Jewish community to reject other Jews because of the choice of how they will keep the covenant would be a betrayal of those Jews, both secular and religious, who died in the camps. Such a betrayal only furthers the possibility of a posthumous victory for Hitler. Indeed, it is the more secular institutions of Judaism and their lay leadership,(e.g., the state of Israel and the United Jewish Appeal), not the ultra orthodox (who would refuse some Jews admission to Israel), who are championing the dignity of *every* Jew as created in the image of God, against all future Hitlers. These secular institutions and lay leaders represent the emergence of a new era and a new ethic of *secular holiness* for Jews.

We can recall (from Chapter 2) that Harvey Cox once argued that the modern secular age, far from leading necessarily to nihilism, leads instead to a new conscious consensus on human values as exemplified in the UN Declaration on Human Rights. "It does not . . . rest on affirmations concerning the inalienable right with which men are 'endowed by their Creator.' . . . Nor is it based on some theory of natural law. It is the expression of a consensus which draws together several cultural and religious traditions including those which believe neither in a Creator nor in any form of natural law."[44] I think Cox was right to point to the human rights movement as a significant development but I think he is wrong to see it as rooted in a purely pragmatic consensus. Human rights claims suggest that we have a human dignity which must not be violated even if this consensus should change. Human rights claims are rooted in a uniquely modern understanding of the human self as making a moral claim on us by its very existence. Human rights claims are rooted in the spontaneous recognition of the transcendent dignity of the human self. The UN Declaration on human rights represents nothing less than a response of the human community to human dignity as an experience of transcendence that evokes a new international covenant community-of-communities.

I believe the international movement to embrace and defend an ethic of human rights, inaugurated by the UN Declaration in response to the Shoah, represents the emergence of a parallel new covenant with the whole of humanity—parallel to that of the renewed voluntary covenant of Judaism. The new Jewish covenant, as Greenberg interpreted it, really has two levels. On the one hand, the vocation to witness as a light to the nations, of whether and how to be Jewish, is now a matter of choice. But Jews do not have the option of not recognizing each other's diverse forms of Jewishness as authentic. The dignity of each Jew, as one created in the image of God, must be acknowledged. The new covenant with humanity represented by the

UN Declaration of Human Rights parallels the Jewish covenant only at the second level. This covenant is not experienced as voluntary but as an unconditional, nonnegotiable demand. It is as if a silent yet commanding voice was heard from Auschwitz demanding that the human dignity of every stranger, beginning with the Jews, be recognized and affirmed as of infinite value.

This covenant is at once both holy and secular. It cuts across the religious (sacred) and the secular (profane), winning adherents from both. It is unique in its ability to transcend the privatistic and relativistic attitudes of modern consciousness to elicit and create a public transcultural holy community-of-communities of all those *called out* to champion human dignity. It has created its own secular organizations to champion this dignity. Such organizations include the United Nations itself, especially its Commission on Human Rights and its various subcommissions, as well as the International Court of Justice and regional Conventions on Human Rights in Western Europe, America, and Africa. Then there are the governmental offices of individual nations that monitor each other for rights violations and use this information to political advantage. (Motivations of self-interest aside, this political game does keep the pressure on to observe human rights.) Finally, there are nongovernmental voluntary associations such as Amnesty International, the Anti-Slavery Society, and the International Committee of the Red Cross. Also in this category are religious communities (churches, synagogues, etc.), labor organizations, and professional associations. This community-of-communities represents a parallel to the secular holiness of which Greenberg speaks with reference to Judaism, in which the measure of holiness is not belief but action on behalf of human dignity. At the time of the Six Day War, Greenberg argues, it was the atheist philosopher, Jean Paul Sartre, and not Pope Paul VI, who spoke out on behalf of Jewish lives and thus Sartre and not the Pope who is the truly holy man. Likewise it is the secular Israelis who are truly holy and not the ultraorthodox, for it is they who insist on welcoming all Jews to Israel not the ultraorthodox who would turn their backs on nonorthodox Jews. The test is the deed. Anyone who protects human dignity and human life is a witness to its infinite value, to our being created in the image of the God without image.

As a universal response to Auschwitz and Hiroshima, and all the atrocities of World War II, the human rights movement appears through the eyes of the biblical narrative traditions as a renewal of God's original covenant with the whole human race, the covenant with Noah, signified by the placing of the rainbow in the sky. In that covenant, God promised: "I will never again curse the ground because of humankind . . . nor will I ever again destroy every living creature" (Genesis 8:21). But after Auschwitz and Hiroshima the responsibility for this covenant has shifted to the human side, and the human race must promise, "Never Again." Human rights is the fence around this new covenant, the fence that must be erected to protect the infinite dignity of every human being and the sanctity of all creation. An ethic of human dignity and human rights is the common response of Jews and gentiles to the silent yet commanding voice that came from Auschwitz and also from Hiroshima, the voice that commands "Never Again." Human rights is the name for a new covenant that has emerged through a wrestling with the stranger who comes from other cultures, other religions, other races. A human rights ethic is an ethic of audacity on behalf of the stranger. It's purpose is to protect the human dignity of strangers no matter what race, religion, or culture they come from. We must wrestle with the stranger as if with God—the God who remains hidden, who refuses to reveal his name, who remains transcendent yet immanent, *God with us*, the God who blesses us and offers us a new name and a new identity. The consensus of which Cox spoke is more than a rational consensus. It is a covenant response to the hiddenness of transcendence beneath the countenance of the stranger, a response which calls forth a secular holiness. This new identity and new covenant can be embraced only by embracing the stranger, by welcoming the stranger, and by the audacity to champion the dignity of the stranger against all the dark social, political, and religious forces of dehumanization.

Although this new covenant can be understood as a renewal of the Noachite covenant, it is one deeply influenced by the Mosaic and Christological covenants of Jews and Christians. For these traditions introduced an understanding of human beings as created in the image of the holy and then introduced the secularizing power of the holy into the world, fostering human freedom, dignity, and interdependence. And as we pass over into other religions and other cultures, we shall find kindred spirits for this new covenant of secular holiness among the members of the Buddhist sangha as well. If Auschwitz and Hiroshima are the expression of the dark and demonic side of urban secularization, the movement for human rights represents the positive side, the secularization of the anthropological ethical traditions of the holy communities. For the first time in history, the anthropological measure of human dignity is finding official embodiment in the secular political-institutional-cosmological order of society as the true measure of a just society.

From an Ethic of Honor to an Ethic of Dignity

"Human rights are rights that everyone has, and everyone equally, by virtue of their very humanity."[45] The call for human rights is both a uniquely modern ethical phenomenon and, at the same time, rooted not only in the historical process of urban secularization but also in the emergence of the holy communities such as the synagogue and the sangha. To fully appreciate both the ancient roots and the uniquely modern character of human rights, we need to understand the fundamental shift in ethical sensibilities that modernization has produced. As Peter Berger has argued, there is a fundamental difference in the ethical sensibility of the modern individual as compared to the individual in a premodern society. "The [modern] age that saw the decline of honor also saw the rise of new moralities and of a new humanism, and most specifically of a historically unprecedented concern for the dignity and the rights of the individual."[46] The modern person operates out of an ethic of dignity whereas the person from a premodern society is governed by a morality of honor. To fully understand the implications of, and reasons for, this shift we must understand the social and historical location of these contrasting ethics/moralities.

Honor and duty, says Berger, are concepts rooted in an understanding of self found in premodern hierarchical societies. These are precisely societies that understand both self and society as part of a sacred natural order. In such societies, the self is basically identified with or clothed in its social role, given as its destiny at birth into a particular place in the hierarchical stratification of society. One's identity is basically collective. Your family and your clan reside within you, so that if you are insulted not just you but your whole family or clan is insulted. Moreover, if you fail to live up to the obligations of your social status it is more than a personal failure. You bring dishonor on your whole family or clan and you may be expected to risk your life to reestablish this collective honor. An insult may require a duel or intertribal warfare. Individual failures entail a loss of face that may require reparations as drastic as suicide, as in the Japanese tradition of *hara kiri*.

It is very difficult for a modern person to understand this ethic because it is rooted in a sense of human identity totally at odds with the modern sensibility. Whereas the traditional self is from birth clothed in a culturally defined human nature (i.e., a fixed set of social roles), the modern self takes off and puts on social roles or identities as if they were different suits of clothes. For the modern person, the self is never identified with its social role. The modern self is a naked self that identifies itself not with its roles but rather with its capacity to choose its roles. The modern self is an existential self, free to choose who to become through its choice of roles. Because the naked self does not identify with its social role, it does not experience insult as a threat to its honor any more than it experiences failure as a loss of face or identity.

In a premodern society there is a hierarchical ordering of human selves in status and value. The hierarchical order is a normative order, reflecting the sacred order of the cosmos. Thus one's place in society determines not only who you are but what are your obligations or duties toward your peers as well as those above and below you in the hierarchy. Such a hierarchy implies levels of humanity. The operative value governing human relationships is not equality but rather "to each his due." Those in higher positions having been given more humanity also have greater obligations of duty than those who are lower in the hierarchy, having less humanity. A very clear example of such society would be the classic Brahmanic caste system in India or the classical familial-hierarchical ordering of human relations in neo-Confucian societies. In both, one of the greatest sins is to violate the sacred cosmic order of nature by the mixing of castes or roles, ignoring the proper ritual obligations of caste or social position. It is a great sin because it violates the sacred order that makes life possible, introducing disharmony into the universe and causing the disintegration of the cosmos into chaos. In all such societies myth and ritual legitimate the sacred order of society, reinforcing the obligation of everyone to perform his or her sacred duty.

By contrast, the naked self transcends it social roles. It is not that such a self is ever found without some social role or other but rather that the modern self views itself as prior to its roles, which are understood as diverse opportunities for self-expression. As a result all human selves are essentially equal, no matter what their social status because one's humanity resides not in a role but in an essential nakedness shared with all other selves. "Modern man is Don Quixote on his deathbed, denuded of the multicolored banners that previously enveloped the self and revealed to be *nothing but a man*."[47] This is the essence of the modern understanding of human dignity that has replaced the notion of honor. "It is precisely this solitary self that modern consciousness has perceived as the bearer of human dignity and of inalienable human rights." [48] All selves have an equal human dignity and equal human rights because all selves are equally naked.

This understanding of self, although typical of modern society, says Berger, has its origins in such ancient precursors as the Hebrew Bible, Sophocles, and Mencius.[49] Its modern manifestations appear in the "formulations of human rights, from the Preamble to the Declaration of Independence to the Declaration of Human Rights of the United Nations. These rights always pertain to the individual 'irrespective of race, color or creed'—or, indeed, of sex, age, physical condition or any conceivable social status. There is an implicit sociology and an implicit anthropology here. The implicit sociology views all biological and historical differentiations among men as either downright unreal or essentially irrelevant. The implicit anthropology locates the real self over and beyond all these differentiations."[50] The transition from an ethic of honor to an ethic of dignity, Berger suggests, can be viewed both positively and negatively. Conservatives view the decline of honor as a profound loss, whereas modernists see it as a "prelude to liberation." On the one hand, the naked self is in a situation of perpetual identity crisis, marked by excessive individualism and alienation from its social roles. On the other hand, this same deinstitutionalizing of the self makes possible "the specific modern discoveries of human dignity and human rights. . . . The new recognition of individual responsibility for all actions, even those assigned to the individual with specific institutional roles, a recognition that attained the force of law at Nuremberg—all these and others, are moral achievements that would be unthinkable without the peculiar constellations of the modern world."[51]

The gravest weakness of the naked self in comparison to the clothed self, Berger suggests, is that the former is ahistorical. Individuals participate in history through their social roles whereas the ethic of dignity emerges through an emancipation from social roles that are understood as a form of oppression from the past. In equating the ethic of honor with history, Berger seems to be identifying history with the valuing of the past and past traditions. But this is an inadequate notion of history, for history requires not only a past but a present and a future. As Eric Voegelin has amply demonstrated, hierarchical societies, operating out of ahistorical mythologies, discourage social change and openness to the future. By contrast, the desacralizing power of the biblical myth of history gave Western civilization its eschatological or utopian orientation toward the future. It is precisely a willingness to let go of one's institutional roles so as to transform one's relation to them that saves history from being simply an ahistorical repetition of the past. The naked self rather than the clothed self, once it experiences its openness to the infinite (especially within the context of the biblical narrative), becomes both historical and utopian.

I understand Berger's reaction, however. It is one he shares with Stanley Hauerwas and Alasdair MacIntyre. They are all reacting to the extremes of the modern Protean self who embraces *the new* and *the future*, with total disregard for the past. They are reacting to a Manichaean form of disembodied ahistorical existentialism that has ignored the importance of culture, community, and tradition. However, true historical existence lies between these extremes of Procrustean (cosmological) totalitarianism and Protean (anthropological) individualistic anarchism, in a communal utopianism that, in the *present*, opens the past to its future. The balance Berger seeks between individual freedom and societal responsibility will be achieved not when an ethic of human rights based on human dignity is balanced by an ethic of honor as Berger seems to suggest but when an ethic of rights is balanced by an ethic of obligation. I do not believe that the sociological context of modern consciousness will permit the recovery of an ethic of honor. What it does do is evoke a sense of personal obligation toward the other, a sense of obligation rooted in recognizing in the other the same dignity that one experiences as one's own. The modern social counterpart to dignity and rights is not honor and duty established through a sense of identity with one's social role but the experience of obligation to respect the human dignity that all share equally.

Berger's distinction between honor and dignity makes it possible to understand how both the desacralizing power of the holy and the desacralizing power of urbanization converge with modern consciousness to form an ethic of human rights as an ethic of secular holiness. Such an ethic, understood with the proper qualifications, might bridge the gap between religious and secular ethics. For the naked self is a product of the history of secularization both as a result of urbanization and as a result of the emergence of holy communities. These two processes converge to remove the self from the sacred cosmic and hierarchical order of nature, where identity is fixed and given, in order to place this self in the new secular world of the naked public square.

Transcendence and Human Dignity

The origins of human rights thought is controversial. I do not think it is either possible or desirable to trace a human rights ethic to a single source. Human rights emerge as a distinct theme of modern ethical consciousness as the result of the influences of a variety of sources both ancient and modern, both secular and religious. Most typically humans rights have been associated with natural law theories and the emergence of the idea of natural rights. But natural rights theory is ultimately unsatisfactory as a primary source for human rights. Historically, the language of nature is primarily associated with the language of sacred order and duty that legitimates the identification of self and social role and produces an ethic of honor. With the important exception of the Stoics, the language of nature has been used to legitimate not the unity and equality of all persons but natural differences, the natural inferiority and superiority between sexes, races, social class, and nations. The language of nature has been used almost exclusively to impose fixed identities on both self and society, domesticating the language of transcendence and using it to legitimate the status quo. Stoicism, the exception, did offer a kind of transcendence of social differences. It was the outgrowth of a new cosmopolitanism created by urbanization in the ancient world. As such it is a precursor of the modern naked self.

The modern naked self, which experiences itself as having an inherent human dignity no matter what its race, or religion, or social and economic class, must be seen as drawing on human experiences both universal and particular—as universal as civilization itself and as particular as individual narrative-communal traditions within civilization. The universal root is urbanization. Urbanization is a secularizing process that alienates the self from the sacred mythological order of nature, stripping the self of its collective identity and leaving it naked in its new urban world. Urban individuation creates the burden of self-consciousness. The pluralistic and institutionally complex urban environment individuates human identity and fosters the "doubling" of reflective self-consciousness. This process heightens our sense of human individuality and uniqueness but also our sense of human alienation and meaninglessness. Thus when human beings first underwent the urbanization experience, they rapidly sought new ways to recosmicize the self and reintegrate it into a sacred meaningful cosmic order. In China, where urbanization began much later (and individuation was much less intense) than in the Mediterranean world and in India, ancient animism, polytheism, and ancestral worship were reanimated in Taoism and Confucianism. Taoism and Confucianism minimize doubling by keeping the self assimilated to the collective cosmological rhythms and collective identity of a sacred natural order. In India, where urbanization was more intense and individuation more advanced, Brahmanic Hinduism offered a way for the individual to minimize the effects of doubling, in the long run, by treating individuality as an illusion that can be transcended through the four yogas. Because of the importance of Karma yoga (caste duty), however, this path continued to clothe the self in its role identity by tying the realization of one's true self (Atman as Brahman) to the selfless performance of one's caste duty. In the Mediterranean world, the Greek philosophers Plato and Aristotle flirted with genuine transcendence rooted in the Socratic experience of the inner world of the soul and its "unseen measure." But, as in Hinduism, the Greek language of transcendence never made a decisive break with the cosmological imagination, and therefore the early Greeks were never able to conceive of a genuine equality among human beings. Aristotle suggested that some men are born to be slaves and friendship was impossible between a master and a slave because friendship is possible only between equals.[52]

In the ancient world, friendship between persons who were socially unequal was rare, but it was viewed as a possibility within the holy communities of Buddhists and Jews, and later in Christianity. What these holy communities offered, which was unavailable to either the early urbanized naked self (e.g., Gilgamesh) or the clothed self (as found in the sacred societies shaped by Taoism, Confucianism, and Hinduism), was the development of a language of inwardness that breaks with the cosmological imagination—a language for exploring the openness of the naked self to the infinite. In the traditions of the holy communities, the naked self created by urban secularization is not clothed in some new cosmological myth but rather discovers its emptiness. The consciousness of the equality of selves within holy communities is rooted in an awareness of the openness of the self to the infinite. The self is understood not as created in the image of nature (with a natural caste or class identity) but in the image of the wholly other (e.g., God or Nirvana), a transcendence that is unimaginable (i.e., un-image-able) and hence can never be fully integrated into the cosmological-social order. The self, stripped of its natural identity, turns inward to discover that its nakedness is not the equivalent of an eternal self. There is no floor of Tao or Brahman beneath the self, only an emptiness that is a radical openness to the infinite. In this respect, the Buddhist speaks of the self as void or empty. Jews and Christians speak of the self as created in the image of a God who is without image.[53]

In addition to urban alienation and the experience of the holy, the modern naked self has roots in the emergence of modern so-

ciohistorical or technological consciousness. Much of the ethical power of the human rights movement comes from a secular experience of
transcendence that, in some respects, parallels the religious insight
into the emptiness and imagelessness of the self. That is, once modern sociohistorical consciousness emerged with the appearance of the
social sciences in the nineteenth century, the inalienable or transcendent quality of our humanity became visible not only to the religious
eye but also to the secular eye. Once the distinction between the self
and its social roles is made and the processes by which we become
acculturated and socialized can be studied, it becomes manifestly apparent to us that no culture or society has ever succeeded in totally
socializing the self. There always remains some part of the self that
escapes being encapsulated by society and reduced to its social roles.
As every parent knows from practical experience, no child can ever be
totally socialized. Some part of the child always remains holy (that is,
"set apart"). It is that aspect of the experience of self which makes
every human being a perpetual alien or stranger, both in relation to
society and to itself. And it is that experience of alienation or being set
apart which enables us to doubt, question, and rebel.

The modern sense of human dignity is directly rooted in these
experiences of the irreducible inalienable transcendence of the self to
its social identity that are now embedded in the urban consciousness
of the naked self. Paralleling the experience of the holy, the modern
naked (existential) self now experiences itself as radically other—as
that which cannot be captured by the sociocosmic or bureaucratic
imagination and hence cannot be reduced to its social role in some
sacred cosmic order. Every ideology begins by defining the human in
a language of natural differences so as to separate the superior from
the inferior, whether by race or sex or class. Defining the human
inevitably occurs only for the purpose of violating someone's human
dignity. But the human cannot be defined. To put it another way, the
human can be defined only by its undefinability. Our inalienable
dignity is rooted in our undefinability.

However, without the transformative experience of the emptiness or imagelessness of the self found in holy communities, the
existential self-transcendence of the modern urban self is liable to find
itself in the situation of Nietzsche's *Übermensch*, who takes self-
transcendence to be an act of self-creation in which the self can never
allow itself to be put in question or open to the infinite. The plunge of
the Nietzchean self or *Übermensch* into the abyss of inwardness, because it will never allow itself to be put in question, replaces a genuine
openness to the infinite with the infinitizing of the self—the will to

power. The *Übermensch* is a naked self that will not allow itself to discover its own emptiness, its own openness to the infinite, but rather remains imprisoned in the icy light of its own "solar will." Apart from the transforming experiences of openness to the infinite nurtured through prayer-meditation and through the alternative myths and rituals of holy communities (or its secular philosophical equivalent of surrendering to the questions) the modern self-transcending self ends up trapped in the egoistic individualism of the *will to power,* which reduces rights claims to the struggle of all against all.

What the experience of the emptiness or imagelessness of the holy-infinite does is to transform the anarchic individualism of the urban self into an authentic experience of the interdependence of the utopian becoming of all things, an experience of interdependence whose authenticity is measured by the readiness to welcome the stranger. When the Platform Sutra tells us that in the Buddha nature "there is neither north nor south"[54] (*north* and *south* representing class differences in China) it is making an affirmation that parallels the statement of Paul of Tarsus, that "there is no longer Jew or Greek, there is no longer slave or free, there is no longer male and female; for all of you are one in Christ Jesus" (Galatians 3:28). In both cases what is being affirmed is that the experience of the self as empty, as being without image, leads to a realization that all selves are equal and interdependent. But neither of these affirmations of the inherent transcendence and equality of all selves is as radical as the Jewish affirmation that the test of faith lies in welcoming the stranger.

The statements "in Christ there is neither male nor female" or "in the Buddha nature there is neither north nor south" are expressions of states of consciousness in which the self experiences itself as either mystically or eschatologically equal and interrelated with all others. But the temptation, obvious in the history of both Christianity and Buddhism, has been to restrict that interrelatedness and equality to those who belong to the holy community (i.e., those who are the same),—those who are "*in* Christ" or "*in* the Buddha nature." I can think of good exegetical reasons why neither of these statements should be interpreted that way. Both ought to give rise to an ethic of welcoming the stranger and the outcast. But as a matter of historical fact the phrasing lends itself to such an interpretation and partially explains the tendency of both Buddhism and Christianity to merge with the larger society in which they find themselves so as to legitimate racial and national identities. Both Nazi Germany and Meiji Japan illustrate this tendency. Only the Jewish formula of welcoming the stranger forces us to acknowledge the humanity of those selves who are *different* (who are outside our community) as also created in the image of the God who is without image. Thus, I would argue that experiences of the empty self in all three holy communities are direct precedents for the modern notion of the inherent inalienable dignity and equality of the naked self, but insofar as the modern ethic of human rights is to be a cross-cultural ethic that demands we recognize the dignity precisely of the one who is different, its greatest legacy can be found in the contribution of the Jewish holy community.

Phenomenologically, the secular analog of these experiences of openness to the infinite occur through experiences of doubt. Doubt and emptiness-imagelessness belong to the same category of experiences—the experiences of our radical openness to the infinite that creates the gap between the self as self-transcending subject and the self as cultural-institutional role. The abyss of the self, its emptiness, can never be filled or encapsulated by one's culture or society. Something of the self always escapes definition and encapusulation. The Upanishads ask, "How can the knower be known?" as a way of pointing out the impossibility of the reflecting self ever being so encapsulated even by its own reflection. The thinker always transcends that which is being thought about, especially when what is being thought is one's self. The mistake is to clothe the thinker in an eternal self. Augustine of Hippo came on this same reflective paradox. Like the Buddha and other forest dwellers he turned inward, traveling through the "caverns" of memory of past life events (more than one life in the Buddha's case) and concluded on exploring these caverns of his own inwardness that the mind is so vast it cannot contain itself and hence is un-image-able and radically open to the infinite as wholly other. Hence the mind discovers its own contingency, its own emptiness or openness to the infinite. In Augustine's case that lead him to the conclusion that God is not the mind but "the lord God of the mind" (*Confessions*, X, 25),[55] even as the Buddha came to insist that the experience of nirvana is not an experience of an eternal self but radically other than all self; namely, *anatta* (no-self).[56] In both cases the self is left swimming over the abyss of the infinite.

Doubt emerges out of the experienced gap between the self and its social world. Doubt is the secular experience of transcendence, whose religious correlate is the experience of the holy (i.e., the experience of emptiness or imagelessness). Doubt and emptiness give birth to the utopian rebel who calls the sacred order of society into question to bring about a new order of things, open to the infinite. At the reflective level, the experience of doubt gives birth to the philosopher even as the experience of imagelessness gives birth to the prophet and the experience of emptiness to the sage. And at the everyday level of common sense, doubt gives birth to the unreflective rebel, who, although he or she cannot say why, feels the need refuse the demand of the religious, political, technological, economic, or social order for total conformity. The rebel in the street is born in response to the violation of human dignity, out of indignation as an intuitive visceral awareness of the silent yet commanding voice that witnesses to the irreducible dignity all selves have in common. The movement for human rights is rooted experientially in both the secular and the religious forms of the experience of the holy as irreducible experiences of openness to the infinite. For as I have argued (in Chapter 4) the secular and the holy are not alien to each other. On the contrary, they are dialectically united in their power to alienate the self from all sacred order in the name of a hidden transcendence we call *human dignity*. And the demand that the human dignity of all persons be respected and protected is in fact the basis for an ethic of secular holiness, an ethic that theists and a-theists (whether Buddhist or secular) ought to be able to construct cooperatively. For unlike the experience of the sacred that treats reason as the enemy of both religion and politics (demanding instead an unquestioning obedience), the experiences of the holy gives rise to critical reason, manifest through both the experience of doubt and the experience of emptiness. Secular holiness unites religion and reason in the common task of creating a public world respectful of the "unseen measure" of human dignity.

Human Rights and Narrative Diversity

An ethic of human rights cannot be substantiated by empirically surveying the diversity of cultures. By definition ethics reflects on what Ought to be. And what ought to be can never be determined by what Is, by the way things are. Ethics always inserts a utopian narrative of the way things ought to be into a world defined by realistic narratives of the way things are. Therefore, one of the major challenges to a human rights ethic misses the mark. It is often argued that human rights are fictitious because we have no clear and unambiguous international consensus on what they are. Some have pointed out that in fact three successive generations of human rights claims have emerged: "The first generation of 'negative ' rights that were concerned with non-interference with individual liberties, and a second generation of 'positive' rights that dealt with social, economic and cultural rights. The third generation was composed of 'rights of solidarity', including the right to development, the right to a healthy and ecologically balanced environment, the right to peace and the right to ownership of the common heritage of mankind."[57] As the list of rights continues to grow, the legitimacy and universality of human rights, some suggest, becomes more and more doubtful. First World countries seem to prefer to limit rights to first generation rights. Second World countries prefer second generation rights and tend to ignore first generation rights. And Third World countries have a special interest in third generation rights even as their citizens often find themselves in a situation where none of these rights (first, second or third generation) are respected. Observing the way different rights claims seem to reflect the special interests of different societies, some have suggested that at least some human rights claims mask a new form of Western cultural imperialism, seeking to impose Western values on Second and Third World countries.

These challenges, however, are not fatal to the case for human rights. For I think it is possible to concede that to some degree human rights must be defined contextually without falling into an ethical relativism. The heart of an ethic of human rights is the recognition of human dignity. Human dignity is primary. Human rights are derivative and secondary. Human rights are the rational fence we build around human dignity to protect it under various circumstances. *In a sense there is only one universal human right—the right to have our human dignity respected*. Rights multiply as we try to respond to the various ways in which human dignity is threatened. Therefore rights can be as many and as diverse as there are threats to human dignity. The number and validity of these rights depend on our ability to make a case for them with respect to these perceived threats. Some will be more obvious (for example, the right to life) and less disputable than others (for example, the right to holidays with pay).

Narrative ethicists, such as Stanley Hauerwas and Alasdair MacIntyre, raise a related form of the charge of imperialism, namely, that a human rights ethic is a form of Western Enlightenment imperialism that seeks to impose a universal, rational, storyless ethic on the whole human race. And because all rationality, they argue, is contingent on story and there is no single universal story, such an ethic is impossible. The case I have been making for the emergence of a human rights ethic in this chapter should make it possible to answer these objections. First, human rights have universal roots in the transformations of human consciousness brought about by urban secularization and in universal experiences of doubt and self-questioning. Second, human rights have particular roots the emergence of sociohistorical consciousness that began in the West and is now being globalized.

Third, rights have cross-cultural roots in experiences of transcendence that gave rise to the formation of holy communities in diverse cultures, East and West. Fourth, what needs to be agreed on in a human rights ethic is the inalienability of human dignity, an experience available cross-culturally in both secular (e.g., the experience of doubt) and religious (e.g., the experience of the holy as emptiness or imagelessness) forms. Fifth, disagreements between First, Second, and Third World countries, or between various religious traditions, about the number and types of human rights should be seen as the occasion for the global discussion and working out of a human rights ethic, without which human rights would indeed be a form of cultural imperialism. Sixth, therefore, a human rights ethic must not be built on a single narrative tradition but rather needs to be constructed within a pluralistic ecology of complementary narrative traditions. The only common requirement of such narratives is that they promote an ethic of welcoming strangers and their stories. Those narrative traditions that require one to welcome the stranger implicitly testify that it is not so much participating in one particular story that makes us human but rather participating in a story that enables us to recognize the humanity of the one who does not participate in our particular story. To welcome the stranger is to recognize that, as with the divine (or transcendence), human dignity cannot be confined to any one particular culture or story.

A universal human rights ethic expressed in a single story would be a contradiction in terms. That is, such an anthropological ethic would be transformed by its very universality into the cosmological ethic of a sacred society—an ethic that has no place for the stranger. The fear of cultural and religious imperialism is a legitimate one. The answer lies in the development of a complex, pluralistic, global social ecology in which diverse holy communities, by virtue of their critical separateness, keep an ethic of human rights centered in self-transcendence. By virtue of a focus on welcoming the stranger or the outcast, the center of each holy community lies beyond itself in the person and community of the other. Holy communities (Jewish, Christian and Buddhist, for example) play a special role in this ecology because their alternate myths and ritual traditions enable them to sustain their sense of separateness (although clearly they have not always been faithful to this call to holiness). This is much more difficult for secular proponents of human rights. The philosopher and secular humanist, lacking communities structured around an alternate myth and ritual, are much more vulnerable to integration into the stories and rituals of the larger political-social-cosmic order. On the other hand, secular philosophers and humanists, by virtue of their surrender to the questions and by virtue of being aliens or strangers who stand outside all holy communities, are in a position to perform a prophetic function, forcing holy communities to face their own inconsistencies and self-contradictions honestly. Paul Tillich was right to see critical secular reason (e.g., critical philosophical humanism), radical mystical consciousness (e.g., Buddhism), and prophetic consciousness (e.g., Judaism) as parallel and dialectically related phenomenon. All three are expressions of the holy (i.e., modes of openness to the infinite) that break with the sacramental imagination which sacralizes the finite.

The holy community that rejects critical reason is in danger of collapsing into a demonic form of sacred unquestionable order. Secular critical reason, when rooted in a surrender to the questions, is a theonomous phenomenon, capable of calling religious communities to be faithful to the rational implications of their own deepest experiences of the holy. For example, it is only with the secularization of society that religious communities claiming that all are equal in the image of God or in the emptiness of the Buddha-nature have had to face their own biased treatment of women (and, in the ancient world, slaves). Judaism, Christianity, and Buddhism have all been guilty of a male chauvinism, which is fundamentally inconsistent with their own central religious insights. Buddhists accepted women into the sangha, which was a breakthrough. But at the same time, the Pali canon suggests that allowing women into the order polluted it to such a degree that the length of its future vitality as a movement in society would be halved because of their presence.[58] The records of Judaism and Christianity on the treatment of women are even worse. And while masters and slaves could be friends in ancient Judaism and Christianity, the social position of slaves and women in both was not significantly changed. In the ancient world, neither Jews nor Christians were forbidden by their traditions from having slaves. Moreover, neither Buddhists, nor Jews, nor Christians, expected the larger society, beyond the holy community to approximate the sense of equality and dignity to which they aspired within the community.

As I have already argued, in the ancient world there really is no such thing as social ethics in the modern sense I have been proposing (Chapter 4). Whether the world was viewed as defined by nature as one's unchangeable fate, or by sin, or as a world of samsara-illusion— it was viewed as a world that could not be altered significantly by human intention. It is only when the peculiarly modern notion of society as artificial and managerial emerged in the nineteenth and twentieth centuries that social ethics was born. This is the unique contribution of the West to the emergence of human rights. And this new sociohistorical or technological-managerial consciousness radically alters the situation for all religious and philosophical traditions, East or West, virtually forcing the anthropological traditions of both to develop a new dimension—social ethics as the ethics of human liberation.

The conjunction of holiness, secular rationality, and modern sociohistorical or technological consciousness is hermeneutically and sociopolitically explosive. It forces human communities to move from the conviction of the *dignity of the self* to an affirmation of *human rights* and finally to audacious acts of *human liberation*. For example, in the first century, Paul could say that in Christ there is neither male nor female. Nevertheless, Pauline communities, and Christians in general, continued to subordinate women to men in hierarchical social roles. Why? Because the order of society was seen as an unchangeable sacred order and therefore the statement of equality was taken as an eschatological statement of spiritual equality to be realized in the flesh only at the end of time. Or again, the peasants took Luther's preaching about the freedom and dignity of the Christian to heart and were inspired to revolt against oppression. But Luther, still sharing the conviction that society is part of a sacred cosmic order, explained to them that in this world all must know and keep to their place, only in the world to come will they be actually equal. But today, when a believing community reads Paul's statement in the light of modern managerial consciousness, that is, with the knowledge that the social order is not sacred and unchangeable but secular and artificial, these believers are suddenly confronted with a new level of ethical obligation, the demand that society be transformed so as to allow for freedom and equality between the sexes and social classes here and now. The combination of consciousness of the holy and managerial consciousness is at one and the same time both radically apocalyptic and utopian, for it leads to an ethic of human liberation that brings our old world to an end even as it calls for a new society.

Human Rights and Western Individualism

Some have feared however that this liberation is just another disguised form of Western cultural imperialism seeking to impose an excessive Western individualism on Second and Third World countries. There is some legitimacy to the charge of overemphasis on the individual in Western culture. As we have argued, human rights have

their roots, in part, in the sociological process of secularization introduced by urbanization, which individuates the self. Left unchecked
this process produces individualism as an extreme condition of alienation both from nature and society, which leaves the newly created
individual feeling totally separate and disconnected. During the period of intense population growth and renewed urbanization in Europe
beginning in the late Middle Ages, urban individualism succeeded in
breaking the spell of premodern collectivism. Sociologically, this occurred through the process of creating new communities in which
individuals were offered the possibility of making their individuality
felt through the incorporation of free cities, professional guilds, and
so on. (This social process of incorporation was a direct outgrowth of
the traditions of the holy communities, the synagogue and church,
and will be addressed in Chapter 7.) Ideologically, this took the form
of a nominalism that argued that only individuals are real. Nominalism, rebelling against the tyranny of collective experience, down-
played an important truth of social experience: that individuality
emerges within community.

This nominalist sense of the real as the individual delegitimated
the Medieval hierarchical notion of society and its metaphysical counterparts in Aristotelianism and neo-Platonism. In the Medieval view,
reality (metaphysical and social) emanated from the top down by
hierarchical degrees, in a kind of pyramid fashion, with God and the
Emperor at the pinnacle of the divine and human hierarchies. Individuals were real only as they participated in the universal or in the
whole. In the nominalist view, which underlies the Renaissance,
these relationships were inverted. Now universals were considered
purely mental abstractions, even as society was considered no more
than the sum of its individual parts. In this new view, society was not
an eternal hierarchical order imposing a set of roles upon individuals
but rather was viewed as a social contract between individuals. Within this contract, social and political authority emerged from, and was
answerable to, the people who are all radically equal in their individuality.

The human rights tradition as it emerged in the West clearly has
important roots in this individualism. The Western rights traditions,
especially as embodied in the French Declaration of the Rights of Man
and the American Declaration of Independence and Bill of Rights,
have deep roots in Renaissance and Enlightenment individualism that
emphasized individual freedom and autonomy. These traditions
clearly played a dominant role in the formation of the UN Declaration. But it is a mistake to read either these traditions or the UN

Declaration in purely individualistic terms. What is really championed is the right to create self-governing communities that foster individual autonomy and responsibility. The UN Declaration reflects this concern with its insistence that the protection of individual freedom and dignity requires protection of the rights needed to form communities—the rights of freedom of assembly for both religious and secular purposes and freedom of speech (Articles 18, 19, and 20). Historically, the model behind this claim to the right to form autonomous, self-governing communities, not under direct centralized control (whether sacred or secular, religious or political), is the model of the holy community (with its two-kingdom ethic).

To define the issue of human rights as a conflict between East and West or communalism and individualism essentially misses the mark. Nathan Katz argues that "a religious tradition has essentially two options regarding the nature and status of the person. Either one accepts an isolated, individualistic conception, or one holds to a communalistic or network notion of the person. I don't see how it is really possible for a religion . . . to balance between both; somehow a choice is made and, given such a choice, Judaism would certainly opt for the latter framework. This communal view of the person is accepted by all truly ancient religions, and one finds very similar conceptions in Hinduism and Confucianism as well."[59] Katz is right to challenge individualism but he is wrong in seeing collectivism as his only other option. There are really three: a *radical individualism*, partially characteristic of secular societies (which he rightly rejects), a collective communalism which is characteristic of cosmological societies such as Brahmanic Hinduism and Confucianism (which he too quickly accepts as his only remaining option); and *individuated communalism*, which stands in between. The choice is not limited to the extremes of secular Western individualism (which asserts the equality of individuals but destroys the fabric of community) and cosmological societies, like Brahmanic Hinduism and Confucianism (which subordinate the individual to the sacred hierarchical order of society). For there is a middle path between these extremes, the path of the anthropological traditions of holy communities, separated from the larger hierarchical order of society, calling such sacred orders into question in the name of an understanding of the human selves as both equal and interdependent.

The appropriate analogy is not between Judaism, on the one hand, and Hinduism and Confucianism, on the other. The obvious analogy to be drawn is between Judaism and Buddhism as holy communities—the two great originating traditions of anthropological ethics, both of which affirm that all selves are equal by virtue of being both empty and interrelated. It is precisely in Judaism and Buddhism that we find the mediating models of a third option, one that offers a balance between the extremes of individualism and collectivism.

Unlike metaphysical notions of equality such as that found in Brahmanic Hinduism (e.g., that all beings share one eternal Brahman self), which are purely ideational and do not translate into social equality, Buddhism's radical denial of the metaphysical imagination originally led directly to the social embodiment of human equality. That is, all selves are equal by virtue of being empty of "own being," which translates directly into social life in terms of an the interrelatedness of all beings as manifest in the equality of the holy community or sangha. This interrelatedness is profoundly different from the interrelatedness of selves in a cosmological society. In a Confucian society, says Henry Rosemont, Jr., "I am the totality of roles I live in relation to specific others. I do not *play* or *perform* these roles; I *am* these roles. . . . with no remainder with which to piece together a free autonomous self."[60] Relationality is defined at the ontic level of obvious natural distinctions, of color, of class, of family and status, but treated as if such relations had ontological status, that is, as if they were built into the order of reality. In the traditional Confucian or Brahmanic Hindu cosmological order of society, the self is either identified with (Confucian) or irrevocably subordinated to (Brahmanic Hinduism) its social roles. Both Buddhism and Judaism, however, force the insight of relationality to a deeper ontological level that breaks with the sociocosmic imagination (e.g., the no-self or the self created in the image of the imageless God) and transcends these distinctions so as to discover a deeper relational equality. As W. Theodore de Bary, points out, for neo-Confucians the principles of relationality (e.g., father-son, emperor-subject) are " 'real,' 'substantial,' or 'solid, (*shih*)', in contrast to the Buddhist view of things as 'empty' (*k'ung*), that is, insubstantial, having no nature of their own, no 'own nature.'[61] Therefore, we should look especially to the traditions of such holy communities for models of human rights as grounded in a self-transcending relational equality, which establishes an ecological balance between the individual and communal dimensions of our humanity.

Christianity, as it first emerged out of Judaism, once understood this balance, even though, especially since the Reformation, it has perhaps gone too far toward accommodating itself to urban individualism. But the emphasis on individualism goes back even further. I suspect it began when Christianity sought to downplay its roots in

Judaism and Jewish eschatology and began to promote itself instead as a sacramental mystery religion of a dying and rising god. Jewish messianic eschatology was about the transformation of creation. The pagan mystery cults, on the other hand, were concerned with individual immortality. When Jesus failed to quickly return as the victorious Messiah, bringing a new heaven and a new earth, Christians deferred the messianic hope to the distant future and found consolation in the hope of individual salvation instead. But something is morally unsatisfying about a vision of salvation that, in shifting the focus from the objective power of God to make all things new to the subjective disposition of faith as the means of personal salvation, allows one to envision oneself as saved while many of one's friends and relatives, as well as strangers, are eternally condemned for their lack of faith. I find myself viewing Christianity as if I were a stranger to it, as if I were seeing it with Buddhist eyes—applying the ethical ideal of the Bodhisattva tradition to the Christian understanding of salvation. The Mahayana Buddhists criticized Theravadins as ethically deficient in compassion for teaching that one could be enlightened and enter nirvana by oneself. Whether they were fair in the characterization of Theravadins is an open question. Nevertheless the argument is persuasive as an argument opposed to a certain understanding of liberation-salvation. Any individual who made a claim to individual liberation, it was argued, cannot be truly enlightened, for such an individual is still under the illusion of having his or her "own being" (*svabhava*). But enlightenment is precisely the realization of the interdependence of all beings so that one could never imagine entering nirvana until all beings are free of illusion and suffering. Thus the Bodhisattva vows to remain on the wheel of suffering out of compassion for all others until the last blade of grass is enlightened. By that act of compassion, the Bodhisattva is said to show himself or herself to be truly enlightened.

The Buddhist Mahayana-Theravada argument makes a point by analogy that is perhaps easier for Christians to see, because it is indirect, than the similar point Judaism has often made about the Christian view of salvation; namely, the odd way in which Christians are able to view their eternal destiny as a private affair. The Israeli scholar Mordechai Rotenberg has argued that the Protestant doctrine of individual salvation (and we should also add Catholic[62]) is fundamentally ego centered in a way quite alien to the Jewish "alter-centered"or "other-centered" understanding of salvation, especially as it is mediated by the Hasidic tradition. In this tradition you cannot even talk of salvation in individualistic terms. You cannot save yourself. You can only save another and must depend on the other to save you. Such a view is rooted in an understanding of God as found in the Cabalistic tradition with its view of divine *contraction* (*tsimtsum*) as the model for social relationships. God , it is said, relates to humans through a process of self-contraction of divine power so as to create a space for the other. This contraction process enables the covenant to be a two-way street in which God withdraws himself "so that the weaker interaction partner may have space to grow by affecting or influencing the stronger side."[63] The talmudic idea of chutzpah or audacity has its roots precisely in such an understanding of the divine-human relationship. God does not simply command and human beings obey. Rather God contracts God's very being and makes human beings partners in a mutual process. God and human beings, dare we say it, work out their salvation mutually, and each is responsible for the other. And even as with the divine-human relation, so it should be among human selves, who must learn to create a space for the other, especially the stranger and the alien.

According to Gershom Scholem, says Rotenberg: "Christianity conceives of redemption as an event . . . in the private world of each individual, . . . which effects an inner transformation." By contrast, the Jewish category of redemption is community.[64] According to Talmud: "One who solicits mercy for his fellow while he himself is in need of the same thing will be answered first" (Talmud, Baba Kama 92) for " all Israel are sureties one for another" (Talmud, Shevuot 39a).[65] Rotenberg goes on to make a favorable comparison of this view with the other-centered view of salvation in the Bodhisattva ideal of Buddhism. However, he notes the ways in which Judaism differs. In the case of Buddhism "there is only one salvation goal, and altercentrism does not lead to an interactive this-world activism."[66] Rotenberg's judgments of Buddhism are too much influenced by the now outdated and inaccurate views of Max Weber. Contrary to Weber's stereotype of Buddhism as otherworldly and asocial, its sangha tradition, as Trevor Ling has pointed out, began as a holy community responding to the social and spiritual ills of urban society. Its two-kingdom ethic parallel's that of Christianity.[67] In any case, Judaism, Rotenberg insists, is not a monolithic salvation system. Monolithic systems that offer only one path to salvation, he argues, inevitably promote inequality as all will not equally exhibit the required talents for salvation however defined. Some will always have more faith, or do more good deeds than others. Only a multicentered community and a multicentered view of many paths to salvation allows people to be both different (strange or alien) and yet equal.

An analogous sense of other-centeredness can be found within Christianity although it has been largely buried under historical layers of Western individualism. We have to look only to the writings of Paul, writings that express the consciousness of one who is still too steeped in, and part of, the Jewish tradition to imagine salvation in individualistic terms. Paul's understanding of a saving remnant is the Judaic (other-centered) understanding of the *tzedakkhim* or "righteous ones" for whose sake the world is spared. The remnant saves not itself but the whole of which it is a part (see Chapter 1 of my book *Narrative Theology After Auschwitz* for a fuller discussion).

Another dimension of this alter-centered relationality is revealed in Paul's understanding of the new self or new Adam. If the illusion of having one's "own being" so that one can pursue one's own good apart from that of others is alien to Buddhists and Jews, it is equally alien to the vision Paul offers for Christians. Only the old Adam, the fallen self held in bondage by sin and death can believe such illusions. But the new self, the new Adam who has died and risen with Christ can speak of self only by saying "we are members one of another" (Romans 12:5) such that " if one member suffers, all suffer together . . . if one member is honored, all rejoice together" (1 Corinthians, 12:26). Like the Buddhist notion of interdependence or the Jewish notion of mutual contraction, the new self raised up in Christ has died to its individualistic "own being" to become one body—a differentiated unity of interdependent parts.

Individualism, the illusion of the independent self (i.e., own being), is the social correlate of modern nominalistic collectivism. Modern collectivism parallels premodern collectivism in affirming the primacy of the group and the need to sacrifice the individual to the group. Modern collectivism differs in that premodern collectivism preceded the emergence of individuated consciousness, whereas modern collectivism can exist only by repressing individuality, robbing individuals of their individuality and reducing them to interchangeable parts. This interchangeable individualism is the expression of the naked self created by urban secularization and alienation in so far as it is unmitigated by the discovery of inward depths of transcendence and the interrelatedness that belongs to the self in its emptiness or imagelessness.

National communities as entities unto themselves are so large and abstract that they can produce only individualism and collectivism. Individuation, by contrast, is produced in smaller intermediate or mediating communities. These alternate or holy communities bring to the larger society their unique stories and traditions of transcendence. Such communities produce ethically autonomous (or rather theonomous) selves through a nurturing process of interdependence. Only a national community willing to promote a rich pluralistic ecology of mediating alternate communities will be able to produce a nation ethically sensitive to human dignity—and only if those communities are other-centered communities prepared to welcome the stranger and the outcast. If there is to be an international ethic of human rights it must not and cannot be constructed by one religion and culture and imposed on another. Rather it must be constructed through an other-centered passing over into another's religion and culture and then a coming back to discover in and through the other what is missing, neglected, or atrophied in oneself and one's own community.

The Convergence of Utopian Narratives: From Abraham and Siddhartha to Gandhi and Martin Luther King, Jr.

Passing over and Coming back: The Spiritual Adventure of Our Time

The tale of our time is a tale of two cities. It is the best of times, it is the worst of times—a time of Apocalypse or Utopia. It is no accident that the modern age is both the age of genocide and the age of human dignity. As Richard Rubenstein has reminded us: "It is an error to imagine that civilization and savage cruelty are antitheses. On the contrary . . . . mankind moved from one type of civilization involving its distinctive modes of both sanctity and inhumanity to another."[68] Rubenstein has complained that the Shoah proves that human rights are not inalienable and that therefore we must protect ourselves with whatever civil rights our political communities are willing to enforce. But Rubenstein is wrong. The Shoah does not disprove the inalienability of human rights. On the contrary, it is what proves the inalienability of the human dignity in which our rights reside. As we have seen, inherent in modern consciousness is the consciousness of a dignity inseparable from our humanity, no matter what our station in life. It is precisely because our dignity cannot be separated from our humanity that genocide occurs. For if it is true that the experience of our irreducible human dignity is empirically evidenced in the truth that no person can ever be totally socialized and conformed to the sacred order of society; and if the experience of doubt and its questions reveals the irreducible priority of the self to the social order, then we can understand why every dictator and totalitarian regime lives in terror of doubt and its questions. And we can understand why every such regime restricts the freedom to gather in community and to speak, lest such doubts and questions be spoken aloud and acted on. And we can understand that the only way to guarantee that these doubts and these questions are not raised is to eliminate all doubters and questioners. It is precisely because of the irreducible and inalienable transcendent dignity of the self that the only way to eliminate human dignity is to eliminate human beings. Reinhold Niebuhr once argued that the only empirically provable doctrine in Christianity was *original sin*. But Niebuhr was wrong. For there is another; namely, that every human being is created in the image of a God without image (or its Buddhist parallel, all selves are empty).

Genocide is the secular equivalent of deicide. For when transcendence is experienced as embodied in the secularity of human dignity it inspires a murderous rage against that dignity on the part of every unmitigated sacred order that has no place for the stranger. It is a rage in which genocide is the equivalent of deicide, a deicide that can be complete only when all transcendence (and hence all who are capable of questioning) has disappeared from the face of the earth. That ineluctable and demonic logic rooted in a fear of the stranger has placed us under the dark and threatening cloud of a nuclear holocaust, a holocaust that threatens to escalate the genocidal impulse into the equivalent of omnicide—the murder of the whole human race and, indeed, all living things. The ultimate irony is that to eliminate all who are capable of doubt and questioning, logically entails not only annhilation of the other but of one's self as well.

If fear of the stranger has created our MAD world, audacity on behalf of the stranger can transform our apocalyptic age into a utopian age. Although some of the boldest formulations of utopian narratives of audacity on behalf of human dignity come from the Jewish tradition, the ethic of human dignity, human rights, and human liberation, which is emerging in our time and is associated with such names as Gandhi and Martin Luther King, Jr., has deep cross-cultural roots in diverse religious narratives. The amazing religious history behind these figures is one that has taken up and transformed the sacral morality of obedience into a utopian ethic of audacity. The cross-cultural ethic of human dignity, human rights, and human liberation coming to birth in our time is the product of a spiritual adventure that is the unique task of our time—the time of the coming of the third millennium and the emergence of a global civilization.

The age in which a new world religion can emerge seems to have passed, suggests John Dunne in *The Way of All the Earth*. "The holy man of our time, it seems, is not a figure like Gotama or Jesus or Mohammed, a man who could found a world religion but a figure like Gandhi [or Martin Luther King, Jr.], a man who passes over by sympathetic understanding from his own religion to other religions and comes back again with new insight to his own. Passing over and coming back is, it seems, the spiritual adventure of our time."[69] The goal of such an adventure is neither converting the other nor being converted by the other. It is rather a wrestling with the stranger as if with God.

To welcome the stranger as other is to share the other's story, not for the purpose of either totally embracing it or totally rejecting it, but rather for the purpose of greater understanding of the other and of oneself as well. In this odyssey into the world of the stranger, says Dunne, Gandhi began as a Hindu, passed over into Christianity "but . . . always came back again to Hinduism. A Christian, in accordance with this, would begin and end with Christianity, a Jew with Judaism, a Muslim with Islam, a Buddhist with Buddhism. If we examine the matter more deeply, though, we find that there is a more ultimate starting and ending point, and that is the person's own life. . . . From this point of view all the religions, even one's own, became part of the wonderland in this odyssey. One's own life is finally the homeland."[70] This adventure is possible because all religions address the common experiences and problems of human existence—birth and death, power and sexuality, individuality and community, and so forth. What is often unique and uncommon are the questions and insights each bring to these common experiences.

In passing over into the life of another we not only discover our common experiences but glimpse the abyss of the infinite. For "there is a depth which can appear in the most common human experiences. It is an abyss which opens up like a narrow and bottomless crevice at crucial points in a human life. A man leaps over it when he goes from one stage of life to another, from childhood to youth, from youth to manhood, from manhood to age. He crosses it in passing over by sympathetic understanding to another human being and crosses it again in coming back to himself. He goes down into it when he withdraws from the cares of his existence and comes back out of it again when he returns to them once more."[71]

The abyss of the infinite and the abyss of the demonic are one and the same abyss—the abyss of inwardness through which the self can discover its own openness to the infinite. This does not imply, however, that transcendence and the demonic have the same source. The demonic emerges when the self, in its descent into the abyss of its own inwardness, like Nietzsche's *Übermensch*, fails to poetically penetrate the depths of its own nakedness and so fails to discover its emptiness or unbounded openness to the infinite. In such a situation the self tries to recover by transforming its own finitude into the infinite by absolutizing its own will to power in some sacred social order. In passing over and coming back we excavate the abyss of inwardness and its demonic distortions. In discovering the diverse modes of the demonic we discover our own capacity for self-deception and evil and are offered the possibility of taking responsibility for it. In discovering the diverse authentic modes of openness to the infinite we discover the modes of our capacity for compassion and self-transcendence. In every case we come to expand and enrich our understanding of ourselves through our understanding of the alien and the stranger. If, as Dunne suggests, there are indeed two ways in which to enter world history—to walk in or to be dragged into it—then "passing over" represents the first and "MAD" represents the second.

The task of excavating the demonic *tremendum*, Arthur Cohen reminded us (Chp. 2), binds us together across religions and cultures.

> Auschwitz or Hiroshima or Vietnam or Cambodia or Uganda— what does it matter as long as each person knows the *tremendum* that bears his name; and it is one name only, for the rest what endures beyond the name and binds each human being in abjectness and torment to the other is that the configurations overlay, the *tremendum* of the Jews becomes the *tremendum* of the nations. Over the abyss which each hollows out of history, human beings renew their sense of themselves as creatures beleaguered by their destinies as Jews or Christians or Africans or Buddhists or whatever name is called victim and murderer.[72]

But if the various configurations of the demonic overlay, perhaps this is also the case for the configurations of the holy with their diverse narratives of welcoming the stranger. That is the hypothesis underlying my proposal for an interreligious cross-cultural ethic of human rights sustained by a social ecology of narrative diversity.

The Convergence of Utopian Narratives

When one thinks of nonviolence one thinks first of all of Mahatma Gandhi. It is no secret that Gandhi's encounter with Jesus' Sermon on the Mount was a major factor motivating him to turn to the great Hindu narrative from the Mahabharata, the Bhagavad Gita, to find the message of nonviolence within his own religion and culture. But people do not always recall that it was Gandhi's encounter with the writings of the great Russian novelist Tolstoy that especially drew his attention to the power of the Sermon on the Mount.

Tolstoy came from the wealthy classes of landed gentry in Russia, and his novels brought him not only fame but fortune. And yet in the middle years of his life he underwent a conversion. As a result he freed his serfs, gave away all his wealth and spent the rest of his life serving the poor and attempting to live by the Sermon on the Mount. Whereas Gandhi's Hinduism was clearly influenced by Tolstoy's Christianity, it is equally important to note that Tolstoy's Christianity, in turn, was deeply indebted to Buddhism. For Tolstoy's conversion was brought about in large part by reading a story from the lives of the saints about a monk named Barlaam who brought about the conversion of a young Indian prince named Josaphat. The historian of religions, Wilfred Cantwell Smith has traced the history of this story. He notes that Tolstoy was converted to the Christian life as spelled out in the Sermon on the Mount on hearing a thinly disguised version of the life of the Buddha that had made its way into the lives of the saints.[73]

The story is that of Josaphat, a wealthy young Indian prince who gave up wealth, power, and family to seek an answer to the problems of old age, sickness, and death. In the midst of his urgent quest he met a Syrian monk, Barlaam, who told him a parable about a man who fell into a well and was hanging on for dear life to two vines. Along came two mice, one white and one black, and began to chew on the vines, so that before long the vines will be severed and the man will plunge to his death. This parable depicts the man's spiritual situation in which the mice represent night and day, the forces of time eroding his life and bringing him surely to his death. The paradox, spiritually speaking, is that instead of waiting for death to come he must learn to let go now, for if he no longer clings to his life but totally surrenders it to God, his spiritual death will lead to new life.

A century before Tolstoy, in Japan the great Zen master Hakuin (1685–1768) told a similar story (related in chapter 3) about a man who clung to the side of a cliff and had to learn to let go so as to experience the "Great Death" of enlightenment or nonattachment, a Great Death that paradoxically gives way to the "Great Joy" of achieving "No-Self."[74] The parallel between these two stories is no accident for the same story and the same parable made its way not only from India into China and Japan but also from India through Persia into the Mediterranean world and eventually into Northern Europe. Versions of the story can be found in Greek, Latin, Czech, and Polish, in Italian, Spanish, French, German, Swedish, Norwegian, and Icelandic, as well as Arabic, Hebrew, and Yiddish. The story seems to have made its way into virtually all the world's religions. The Greek version came into Christianity from an Islamic (Arabic) version, which is how it passed into Judaism as well. The Muslims, in turn, got it from the Manichees in Persia, who got it from the Buddhists in India. The Latin *Josaphat* is a translation of the Greek *Loasaf*, which is a translation of the Arabic *Yudasaf*, which is a translation of the Persian *Bodisaf*, which is a translation of the Sanskrit *Bodhisattva*, which is, of course, a title for the Buddha. The parable of the man clinging to a vine appears to be even older than the story of the Buddha and may go back to Hindu, Jain, and even pre-Aryan sources.

The story of the prince who renounces the world and of the accompanying parable allow us to see the profound ways in which the narrative traditions of the world's religions can be interdependent. For if Gandhi came to appreciate the message of nonviolence through exposure to the life and teachings of Tolstoy, it turns out that Tolstoy's conversion itself represents a convergence of the life stories of two of the greatest teachers of nonviolence in the history of religions, Siddhartha Gautama and Jesus of Nazareth. But what Gandhi found lacking in Tolstoy's understanding of the Sermon on the Mount he found present in the Bhagavad Gita; namely, the notion of nonviolence as an active rather than a passive virtue, that is, as capable of producing an active resistance to evil. The spiritual genius of Gandhi was to transform the metaphor of warfare in the Bhagavad Gita from one that authorized killing in order to heal into one that authorized and demanded an audacity on behalf of the stranger. In so doing, Gandhi transformed the Gita into a story of nonviolence on a par with the story of Jacob wrestling with the stranger and Jesus' Sermon on the Mount. Wrestling with the stranger does not have to lead to conquest any more than turning the other cheek has to lead to cooperation with evil. Both can be combined in an audacity on behalf of the stranger which is expressed in an active civil disobedience against unjust laws and on behalf of human dignity.

When Martin Luther King, Jr., embraced Gandhi's teachings on nonviolence he was in fact drawing on the mystical and ethical insight of at least four great religious traditions—Hinduism, Buddhism, Christianity, and also Judaism (for the Sermon on the Mount is rooted in the Jewish ethic of welcoming the stranger and audacity on behalf of the stranger, even if the stranger is one's enemy). Both Gandhi and King also explicitly drew on the Socratic witness to civil disobedience.

What Gandhi's and King's ethic of nonviolence illustrates is that narrative traditions are not mutually exclusive worlds. Moreover, it illustrates that even a cosmological tradition such as Hinduism is open to radical transformation through the process of passing over and coming back. It illustrates that such transformations can awaken even a sacred society to the need to welcome the stranger and the outcast and to back up that awakening with the audacity of civil disobedience if necessary. Most impressively, it suggests that even the narrative traditions of total surrender and unquestioning obedience can be rehabilitated and transformed into traditions of audacity the way Gandhi transformed the Bhagavad Gita from a story authorizing killing in order to heal into a story of radical nonviolent resistance to evil. The spiritual adventure of passing over into the life of the stranger and coming back with new insight into our own is not a parlor game for dilettantes; it is a world-transforming process whose results have been keenly felt in the emergence of a global ethic of nonviolent resistance to all incursions on the sanctity of human dignity.

After Auschwitz and Hiroshima, speaking from a biblical perspective, we live in a time of a new covenant with the whole of humanity, a covenant whose saving remnant is composed of holy communities such as those found within the narrative traditions of Judaism, Christianity, and Buddhism. These communities, in response to the silent yet commanding voice heard from Auschwitz and Hiroshima, are called to a covenant with transcendence that renews the covenant of Noah. These are the communities that have separated themselves from the sacred order of society to embrace a two-kingdom ethic that measures justice by the measure of human dignity, where the measure of human dignity is the unseen (and un-imageable) measure of emptiness. These are the communities that sustain human dignity and equality through an ethic of audacity on behalf of the stranger. In the global ecology of an emerging world civilization it is the unity-in-diversity of these (and other kindred) traditions that promises to form the creative leaven for the emergence of a human rights ethic.

The ethic they can inspire, however, is not limited to members of these communities. The impact of Gandhi on India is dramatic evidence that the witness of holy communities can have a profound transforming effect on cosmological traditions, such as Hinduism, as well. However, although Gandhi relativized the importance of caste in India, insisting that even the low caste and outcast should be treated with equal dignity, for some he did not go far enough. For he continued to believe one could have both a caste system and a respect for the dignity of all. He did not fully appreciate the power of social hierarchy to undermine respect for human dignity. He did not fully appreciate that the recognition of human dignity requires profound sociological changes in the social order. Thus Gandhi's movement left a residual tension in the culture of India. This is a tension between the two kingdoms, that is, between the anthropological and cosmological order, expressed in the tension between the traditional caste social structure of India and its modern constitution. As a sacred society, India's caste system is deeply rooted in narratives of cosmological order and yet its constitution begins: "We, the People of India, having solemnly resolved to constitute India into a Sovereign Democratic Republic and to secure to all its citizens: justice, social, economic, and political; Liberty of thought, expression, belief, faith, and worship; Equality of status and of opportunity; and to promote among them all Fraternity assuring the dignity of the individual and the unity of the Nation; In our Constituent Assembly this twenty-sixth day of November, 1949, do hereby Adopt, Enact, and Give to Ourselves this Constitution."[75] That constitution is the result not only of the influence of the Western anthropological ethical tradition (through the influence of the British) but, perhaps more important, was largely written by one who had been an outcast from Hindu society and who led his people in a movement to embrace Buddhism—Dr. B. R. Ambedkar.

Ambedkar recognized in Buddhism the indigenous tradition appropriate for sustaining human dignity and human rights in India (and indeed for all of Asia). As Hindu scholar John Carman has pointed out.

The language of *dharma* is strangely absent from the Indian constitution. One reason . . . is that the chief framer of the constitution, the Minister of Law in Nehru's first cabinet in independent India, was sharply opposed to the structure of Hindu *dharma*. He came from the untouchable community of Mahars and had worked with Gandhi and Nehru in the struggle for independence. But he made a very emotional break with Gandhi because of what he considered Gandhi's very halfhearted support of the effort to get rid of untouchability. In 1935 the Mahars renounced their membership in Hindu society and gave Dr. B. R. Ambedkar the task of choosing a new religious alliance. He had talks with Muslims, Sikhs, and Christians before deciding that the Mahars should become Buddhists. The formal accession to Buddhism came twenty-one years later, in 1956, six years after the new Indian constitution came into force, and only a few months before Dr. Ambedkar's death. He deliberately chose 1956 as the 2500th year of the Buddhist era, and chose the date of October 14 on which the Emperor Ashoka had embraced Buddhism. It is no wonder, then, that universal rights of equality, the special rights of minorities and the outlawing of untouchability should loom so large in the constitution's statement on fundamental rights.[76]

In arguing for the capacity of holy communities to at least partially transform sacred societies, we must also recognize the continuing value of these sacred societies. Such societies remind holy communities and modern societies of the importance of living in harmony with the ecological complexity of the cosmos. When an anthropological tradition collapses into individualism it tends to abuse the natural ecology necessary to sustain human dignity. Traditional hierarchical societies should also remind modern democratic societies just how difficult it is to be rid of human hierarchies. They remind democracies that they too have biased class structures—ones created by economic forces that generate their own outcasts of the homeless and poverty stricken.

The ethical commitment to human dignity and secular holiness I am espousing is one that best thrives in the context of multiple communities and diverse stories, religious and nonreligious, theistic and a-theistic. It is precisely the diversity of holy communities, in story and community (mythos and ethos), that can make a universal ethic of human rights possible as an ethic of human liberation, one capable of shaping public policy on a global scale. If a human rights ethic were to be rooted in any one communal narrative alone, the danger of a religious and cultural imperialism would be grave. But the diversity of communal narrative traditions, overlapping in their common commitment to welcoming the stranger, makes it possible for them to create a mutually correcting, mutually balancing, ethical ecology for an emerging global civilization.

Alfred North Whitehead once estimated that approximately 10 percent of the European population participated in the Renaissance and yet the Renaissance transformed Europe. The ethics of the holy that I am advocating does not envision itself as a totalitarian ethic in which everyone must adhere to the same story. Ten percent of the world's population working through the presence of holy communities—Buddhist, Jewish, and Christian (and other kindred religious and secular communities)—can be a saving remnant, a remnant sufficient to create the public order necessary for the unity-in-diversity of a global civilization; that is, a public order that answers to the measure of human dignity, protects human rights, and brings about human liberation.

Beyond Technopolis: The Utopian Promise of Babel

The story of Babel (Genesis 11:1–9) as I have already suggested, seems uniquely suited to illuminating the ethical challenge of our time. According to that story the citizens of Babel sought to grasp transcendence through a common language and a common technological project—building a tower to heaven. Transcendence was equated with the technical and social power that can be martialed by a society unified in its language, meaning, and values. By sharing a common story, they seemed to believe, transcendence could be domesticated and made subservient to human desires. But God, seeing the idolatry in what the citizens of Babel had in mind, confused their tongues so that they no longer were able to understand each other. They became strangers to each other and so had to abandon the dream of technical control over their destiny. A great deal of Babel's spiritual pathology is present in our own MAD apocalyptic world. We also are caught up in such technological fantasies. Much in us still longs to return to the imagined days before Babel's disintegration, when everyone in the public square had a sense of belonging to the same sacred society, speaking the same language, and sharing the same values.

In our pluralistic world we long for the common morality of a sacred society and lament our fragmented ethical diversity and the confusion it seems to bring. We wish for everything to be once more clear and unambiguous. From such a perspective the actions of a God who would deliberately make a sacred community into a society of strangers seems at best a perverse judgment on human effort. But for a God who is Wholly Other, whose ways are not our ways, such an act might seem to be not a curse but a blessing. For it is through the stranger or holy other that the infinite enters the finite and closed world of a sacred society, calling it into question and opening it up to its genuinely utopian possibilities. For those who have the ears to hear and the eyes to see, Babel may not be so much a curse as a gracious opportunity filled with utopian promise. If we are to realize this promise, however, we must be prepared to break with those fantasies of a linguistically and technologically unified world that typified Babel before its fall. We must shatter the linguistic imperialism of secularism and technobureaucratic rationality to make a place for human dignity and human rights, especially those of the stranger.

The Linguistic and Narrative Poverty of Secularism

What is liberating about technopolis, the modern secular city, it is often assumed, is that we are no longer forced to conform to a single story. For in fact we have arrived at a point in history where the public square has been freed from all normative stories. In our private lives we may wish to occasionally indulge in fanciful stories, but certainly the public square must be guided by a sober, secular rationality. The paradox of the view that we now live in a public square free of dominance by any story is that it is communicated through a mythic story that tells us that we have no story. According to this story, although humans once lived within sacred stories, gradually we have been liberated from those stories by a process of secularization that has culminated in our own uniquely rational age of science and technology. In such an age, we are told, religious stories are nothing more than anachronisms from the past clung to by those who are unwilling to live in the present. Our task as responsible modern human beings is to sweep the public square clean of all such remnants.

What this story, which is meant to put an end to all stories, reveals is that there is in the history of Western civilization not only a religious myth of supersession wherein Christianity claims to replace Judaism and Islam claims to supersede both, but also an intellectual myth of supersession—the story of secularization as a three-stage process. Both Harvey Cox's *Secular City* and Richard Rubenstein's *The Cunning of History,* for instance, embraced this view of history. Despite their dramatic differences, they shared the Comtean version of Joachim of Fiore's vision of the three ages of the human race, in which the religious age of myth is replaced by the metaphysical age of philosophy, which is finally replaced by the secular age of scientific-technical rationality. This supersessionist narrative tradition views modern science and technology as having demythologized and replaced both myth and metaphysics so that we are now able to abandon such irrational world-views and deliberately construct our world through the use of mature technical rationality and scientific realism. Thus the story of our storylessness, it turns out, has a long narrative history. Unlike "secularity," which as the dialectical expression of the desacralizing power of the holy remains continually open to the infinite, "secularism" is a closed and sacral world-view that would exclude as profane all who do not wholeheartedly surrender themselves to it. To the degree that we live in a society that seeks to impose this storyless story as the common framework for our public life, we ought to recognize that secularism is itself a sacred narrative. Our secular society is in fact, as Jacques Ellul contends, the most recent guise of a sacred society.

There is, however, another nonsupersessionistic way of reading this same history of secular rationalization, one advanced by Bernard Lonergan. In this view, there are indeed three ages but what is going forward through these historical periods is not a supersession but a complex differentiation of language, a refinement and coordination of control over linguistic meaning. In the earliest stage of meaning, the highly imaginative imagery of myth tried to answer all questions: questions of meaning and purpose (religious-symbolic), theoretical questions about how the world works (philosophical-scientific), and pragmatic questions about how to get on with our work in the world (common sense).

If the first stage language was dominated by a mixture of myth and common sense, the emergence of philosophy produced a second stage in the linguistic mediation of meaning. Questions of theory were differentiated from the compact symbolism of myth, giving rise to metaphysics. Then as the questions about being became more precise and empirical, the sciences were differentiated out of philosophy and both the language of theory and the language of common sense came to be distinguished from the language of symbolic meaning. Historically, the human surrender to the questions, pursuing them wherever they lead, has resulted in the differentiation of mediated meaning into these three realms: common sense, theory, and transcendence.

Common sense seeks to understand, for pragmatic and practical purposes, the relation of things to persons. Hence, it is dominated by the sensual imagination (i.e., how things appear to the perceiver as when I say "the sun rises"). The realm of theory emerges from common sense when the question arises of how things are related to each other, independent of how they appear to me (e.g., as when we account for the sun "rising" in terms of the rotation of the earth on its axis as it circumnavigates the sun). These two realms, Lonergan insists, are complementary. "The sciences need methods to reach their abstract and universal objects; but scientists need common sense to apply methods properly in executing the concrete tasks of particular investigations."[1] Yet neither is capable of addressing the questions of meaning and purpose. Even if we could exhaustively explain how the world works and how to work in the world, we would still be left with the question of what the world and our work in it means. If pragmatic language is that literal language which permits me to work in the world, and theoretical language is that relational language (e.g., mathematics) which explains how the world works, religious language is that symbolic language which communicates what the world means (as when Christians speak of the sun rising in symbolic terms, as for instance in the Christian Easter liturgy's declaration: "Rejoice for Christ our Light has risen on us").

Like ancient myth, modern secularism tries to return to a pre-Babel condition in which these differentiated linguistic worlds are confusedly reduced to one single language. But whereas ancient myth confused the realms of transcendence and common sense while having no place for theory, our modern myth tends to confuse common sense and theory and allows no place for transcendence. However, a fully differentiated consciousness would recognize that none of these languages is reducible to the other and all are essential to the successful functioning of the human community. It is not a matter of one superseding the other but of an ever-increasingly differentiated coordination and control over our modes of linguistic expression to meet the ever more precise demands of these three realms of meaning. Theory can no more replace the pragmatic language of common sense than either can replace the symbolic language of meaning. A differentiated consciousness is one that can move comfortably between these three levels of meaning and in each case know what one is doing when one is knowing, that is, fully conscious of the different but complementary demands for truth required by each.

These three realms of meaning should not be thought of as mutually exclusive circles but rather as overlapping circles, mutually interdependent and mutually conditioning each other. What these three realms share is the task of promoting the utopian possibilities of our humanity by keeping the human adventure eschatologically open to the infinite through a surrender to the questions.

The dimension of transcendence is revealed through our experiences of doubt and the questions that follow from them. Such experiences guide the unfolding dynamic of intentional (i.e., questioning) consciousness. It is the seductive power of the questions, our unending questioning, that drives us beyond each finite horizon and on to the next, on a path of successively higher viewpoints, until we have asked the question of the ultimate horizon of meaning and value for every experience—the religious question that opens us to the infinite. Our unending questions reveal the fundamental ontological and eschatological openness of our finitude to the infinite. Death may stop us from questioning but not because there are no more questions. This openness is the foundation of the utopian capacity of the human, of the unrelenting need to transcend the given horizon of experience and realize new worlds. "It is," says Lonergan, "what Paul Tillich named a being grasped by ultimate concern."[2] This is Tillich's theonomous dimension present in every human activity that keeps the finite open to the infinite and self-transcendence.

In the first and second stages of control over linguistic differentiation, meaning was thought of as normative, given (either mythically or metaphysically) with the sacred and fixed horizon of the natural order that subsumed culture. But in the third stage, culture is differentiated from nature and viewed empirically and descriptively rather than normatively. In this stage meanings are understood as expressions of human consciousness tied to the continually receding temporal (or eschatological) horizon of human sociohistorical existence.

In this third stage, Lonergan suggests, it is possible for us to become aware that there is an invariant set of operations that belong to the experience of knowing. The intentionality of consciousness oriented by a surrender to the questions and pursued toward the horizon opened by specific questions, operates dynamically, moving from *experience* (attending to the data) to *insight* (understanding the data) to *judgment* (raising all the relevant objections in order to determine whether the insight is an error) to *decision* (appropriating the insight as a guide to further action). There is a spontaneous dynamic of self-transcendence in such a process of inquiry. Once we have experienced the data brought into focus by our questions, we then experience an inner need or demand to understand what we have experienced. We search for an intelligible pattern. And once we have an insight, that moment of "aha!" when we think we have discovered such a pattern, we immediately find ourselves faced with an inner demand to raise all the relevant objections we can think of that would show us to be mistaken. But if all such objections can be met, then the moral quality of the noetic act comes to light, for if all relevant objections are met, the judgment "it is so" becomes inescapable. The subject has no choice but to make such an assent or fall into self-deception or self-contradiction. And of course, to make that assent if all relevant objections are not overcome would be equally self-deceptive.

Lonergan's phenomenological analysis of the quest of the questioning self reveals that, at least for finite minds, truth must be viewed as an eschatological process, continually open to the future, rather than a final point of arrival. Authentic understanding in every realm is guided by an open-ended process of truthfulness. Every question leading to an insight opens up yet further questions, which come to us as we seek to imagine the various possible oversights that would prove to us we are in error. The questions themselves suggest techniques to test the validity of the insights we come to. The overcoming of all objections to the insight, ending in assent, leads us to "virtually unconditioned" truths—not "absolute truths," but finite truths that are contextually true and will suggest to us yet further questions that will leads us beyond our present horizon of understanding toward the promise of ever receding horizons. Thus the process of inquiry is continuous and eschatologically open-ended. And yet it is not an arbitrary, for it is guided by the passion for insight and the ethical quality of the questioning process.[3]

In the third stage of differentiated meaning, then, truth is not so much a fixed quantity as a self-authenticating process leading to yet further insights. Given the sociohistorical self-consciousness of the modern technological self, when theories do emerge from meta-methodical questioning in this stage, they no longer function as *descriptions* of reality, as if knowing were "taking a look," but rather as heuristic notions. We expect from them, not so much pictures of reality as procedures for arriving at virtually unconditioned truths. By virtually unconditioned truths we mean affirmations that have met the test of all relevant objections and whose confirmation leads us on to yet further fruitful questions.

In this context, theology becomes a theology of culture, "left with the enormous and quite new task of mediating the significance of Christian faith [and other experiences of transcendence] with ongoing and changing sets of cultural meanings and values."[4] If there is to be a normativity that can authenticate the mediation of meaning in this third stage, therefore, it will not be discovered in theories, whether metaphysical or scientific, but in the process by which theories are generated. Normativity will be found, not in theory but in method, specifically in the metamethod of a linguistically differentiated consciousness guided by a surrender to the questions—the metamethodical surrender that underlies the discovery of all particular methods.

Culture has come to be viewed as "a function of the development of human consciousness," argues Robert Doran, one of Lonergan's most able interpreters. Culture is understood empirically as
the operative meanings and values of a society that shape and legitimate its way of life. Every culture embodies a quest for human meaning. Thus we can say that every culture exemplifies the universal
human "search for direction in the movement of life."[5] But while the
quest is universal its symbolization has, as Eric Voegelin has argued,
undergone degrees of differentiation out of the original compactness
of early cosmological civilizations. Cultures emerge as linguistic uni-
verses out of the convergence and divergence of different narrative
traditions. In this process, our Western cultural heritage has been
decisively shaped by certain epochal cultural breakthroughs, each of
which represents a "leap in being." (1) The anthropological-noetic
differentiation that emerged out of the Greek philosophical critique of
its narrative traditions—a critique grounded in the experience of the
soul as the inner "sensorium of transcendence" through which "the
human is the measure of all things" so long as the measure of the human is the world transcending "unseen measure." (2) The historical
eschatological-soteriological order of existence differentiated by the
prophetic critique of Near Eastern narrative traditions in the history
of Israel and witnessed to in Jewish and Christian scriptures, in which
the Greek eros from below upward is met by the agapic movement of
the "unseen measure" from above downward. For Voegelin the classic integration and expression of these differentiations occurred in the
theology of Augustine.[6] (3) In Asia we can find parallels to the above
differentiations in the Buddhist critique of the narrative traditions of
India on the basis of the experience of turning inward to discover the
emptiness of the self.[7]

In Robert Doran's view, the third stage in the differentiation of
linguistic meaning (i.e., the modern) brought a further "leap in being" when the control over meaning shifted from theory to self-
conscious method. This shift was forced upon us by the emergence of
sociohistorical or technological consciousness. For this consciousness
made us aware of the degree to which the presuppositions, questions, and methods of the inquirer are conditioned by time and place,
and finally influence the kind of theoretical answers we arrive at. In a
world of pluralism and relativity we are aware that our perspectives
are colored by our cultural frames of reference, and we no longer look
for a normative frame of reference from some metaphysical order of
nature or human nature. Therefore Doran's work suggests that in our
time culturally normative theories of human nature have to give way

to the task of integrating all the relevant cross-cultural normative differentiations of human experience, which have emerged
through the critique of sacred narratives on the basis of diverse secularizing (or desacralizing) experiences of the holy. Through this new
quest we will find orientations of self-transcendence for the human
community and a constructive new direction for the movement of
life.[8]

Such a quest will require passing over into other religions and
cultures and their normative stories and coming back to our own with
new insights and further questions. This quest cannot begin with
theory, as if we could have the answers before we have formulated
the questions; on the contrary, the questions must be prior to both
our answers and our particular methods. Lonergan's phenomenology
of *questioning* illuminates the dynamic open-ended structure of
the process of inquiry disclosing a normative metamethod of theonomous self-transcendence (i.e., surrender to the questions) that
underlies every particular theory and method and every field of inquiry.

Welcoming the Stranger as the Utopian Norm of Secular Reason

Transcendence manifests itself in human experience through
the self-transcendence made possible by the unrestricted otherworldly passion revealed in our doubts and our questions, which lure
the self beyond itself toward the ever receding horizon of what is true
and worthwhile. *Otherworldly* must not be taken here as a spatial
metaphor but rather a temporal, eschatological, or utopian metaphor.
This infinite passion is *not of this world*, precisely because it drives the
self beyond itself and its every finite horizon and is presupposed in
every horizon through which we grasp and transform this world.
Self-transcendence is the fruit of a surrender to the infinite through a
surrender to doubt and its questions. Transcendence manifests itself
methodologically in that conjunction of logical and nonlogical operations wherein the "logical tend to consolidate what has been
achieved. The non-logical keep all achievement open to further advance."[9]

Once the self-transcendence of the questioning self is recognized as normative, it is possible to define the nature of ideology and
with it the criterion for identifying progress and decline in the history
of culture. Ideology is rooted in a form of double alienation (i.e.,
alienation from alienetion) whereby we seek to escape alienation's
liberating possibilities of self-transcendence through a leap into a

fixed and unambiguous world of meaning. Ideology is rooted in "man's disregard of the transcendental precepts [i.e., the inner demands upon consciousness to attend, to understand, to judge, and to act in accordance with one's knowledge]. . . . The basic form of ideology is a doctrine that justifies such [double] alienation. From these basic forms, all others can be derived. For the basic forms corrupt the social good. As self-transcendence promotes progress, so the refusal of self-transcendence turns progress into cumulative decline."[10] Ideology then is the refusal of self-transcendence, a refusal most likely to emerge when what is to be affirmed as true or good would be inconvenient or unfavorable to the individual or group interests involved. The root of ideology, in the Marxist sense of the term, is individual and group bias that corrupts the integrity of the questioning self.

Culture is the product of our technological or utopian (i.e., linguistic) capacity to define a world of mediated meaning rather than be confined to the world as a given. Ideology is a linguistic illusion created by a refusal of self-transcendence, which makes the world as artifact appear as if it were fixed and given with the order of nature. Ideology is the excuse we create to explain why we cannot engage in self-transcendence—why we must be realistic. Ideology cosmicizes the human world and says "that's simply the way things are." As such ideology brings transformation to a halt. There is change but nothing really changes, everything becomes repetition: "The more things change the more they remain the same."[11] Ideology is a generalized cultural pattern of refusal to meet the metamethodical demands of human consciousness for integrity (honesty and ethical courage) that are forced on us by our questions. Ideology introduces stasis and decline into a society. Whether there is progress or decline within any society depends on whether this humanly created cultural world of mediated meaning is mediated ideologically or methodologically.

The metamethodical mediation of linguistic meaning opens up a path of self-transcendence that grounds a normative scale of values. Such a scale is possible because there are degrees of self-transcendence. This scale begins with the cosmological, that is, with the body and its ecology, giving rise to the *vital values* of health and well-being. These in turn make possible the emergence of *social value*, that is, the sacred patterns of social routine that provide the good of order required by any society. The good of order, in turn makes possible the pursuit of *cultural values*, which embody "the meanings and orientations that inform human living." Finally, within the cultural sphere, anthropological order differentiates itself from cosmologi-

values that open us to the infinite, drawing us beyond our every finite horizon.

Although it is clear that in this scale the lower values precede and make possible the higher ones, it is also true, as Robert Doran suggests, that the continued existence of the lower values can be promoted only by the successful operation of the higher values. That is, when self-transcending anthropological values disappear in a society, the culture's narrative traditions no longer champion human dignity but are reduced to the legitimation of the good of order—the present biased order of society. And when there is no social carrier of the symbolism of transcendence (i.e., a holy community) in the infrastructure, the institutions of that social order go unchallenged and the human dignity of the stranger and the outcast is neglected in favor of the ruling elites. And when the human dignity of significant portions of the population of a society is neglected, their subsistence needs are neglected as well and go unmet. And when the needs of these persons go unmet there is fear and social unrest. In response, the tendency to totalitarian rule increases, which in turn increases the odds of revolution and social anarchy. And when social anarchy sets in, subsistence needs for food, shelter, and clothing become a daily challenge, freedom and justice disappear, and the social landscape of one's society begins to look more and more like contemporary Lebanon.

What ideology does is truncate the scale of values so that, although promising change and transformation, it actually limits the scale of values to the biased patterns of distribution that already exist, as if they were fixed and given with the order of reality. Ideology affirms the good of the existing order, that is, *the way things are*, and denies there is any higher Ought to be brought to bear on the issue.

Unlike premodern societies, modern societies tend to be institutionally pluralistic. Modern societies tend to be differentiated into semiautonomous systems. Daniel Bell divides these into three: (1) the techno-economic, (2) the political, and (3) the cultural.[12] Doran, however, differentiates them into five by separating technology and economics and adding a "primordial base" of "intersubjective spontaneity"; that is, the sense of belonging embodied in family, kinship, and the spontaneous sense of group loyalty to *one's own* (i.e., those who are the same) that precedes the development of every complex society and to which such societies revert if they begin to disintegrate.[13]

A society extends its order beyond such primal loyalty groups, through the social patterns of an infrastructure made up of technological, economic, and political institutions. Such institutions are intended to extend both the responsibilities and the goods of society, and hence the realm of justice, beyond one's primal loyalty groups to embrace those who are strangers. Under the influence of ideology, the role of cultural values is usurped by technological, economic, and political institutions dominated by personal and group bias and limited in vision to the good of an existing order that serves the special interests of those who are the same. Under the dominance of ideology, the higher values are rendered marginal. Personal values that emerge in response to the experience of the holy (e.g., alienation) and the presence of the stranger (and to the doubts, questions, and unconditional demands for self-transcendence such a presence evokes) are dismissed as fictitious or irrelevant and "rendered inefficacious in the structuring of the cultural and social order. And religious [anthropological] values are either explicitly denied and even forbidden in the public cultural domain, or they are twisted into perverse supports for the distorted culture and society."[14]

When holy communities emerge in such a society, a critical point of dialectical tension is created between the cosmological and anthropological orders leading to the emergence of two realms or two kingdoms. Values introduced into society by individuals within alternate communities create demands for self-transcendence or openness to the infinite. The communally nurtured experiences of *anthropological-religious values* (whether they assume the guise of the holy or the secular) lure the self beyond itself into self-transcendence and confrontation with the larger society. These values, Doran argues, are those anthropological values that

> lie beyond the three levels of value that constitute the public formation of the superstructure and infrastructure of the society [i.e., vital values, the good of order and cultural goods], in the realm of personal decision and orientation. As Voegelin said . . . there are problems of order that extend beyond the existence of a concrete society and its institutions. But these values do not constitute a merely private realm of existence without relevance to the cultural superstructure and the social and vital infrastructure of the society. Quite to the contrary, they are the ultimate determinants of cultural integrity, or social progress, of the appropriate relation among the five elements that constitute society, and so of the equitable distribution of vital goods.[15]

As Lonergan envisioned it, there are two cycles of decline in society, the shorter cycle and the longer cycle, both of which truncate a culture's scale of values. The shorter cycle is governed precisely by the conflicts of individual and group bias. But the causes of the ideological truncation of value in society cannot be reduced to class conflict alone. In attempting to do so, Marx himself, says Doran "has fallen victim to general bias" that governs the longer cycle.[16] The shorter cycles of decline can be reversed so long as the commitment to the meta-methodical pursuit of self-transcendence is operative in society. The longer cycle of decline is much harder to reverse for it is governed by a subtler form of ideology—the shortsighted "general bias" of common sense that infiltrates the very process of knowing, quite apart from our self-interest, making it seem unnecessary to raise further questions because reality can be taken at face value. This leads us to abandon critical self-transcending reflection in favor getting on with the prag- matic affairs at hand, governed by "what everybody knows."[17] The bias of group interests will be practiced by only some groups within society, whereas general bias can infiltrate virtually all groups, substi- tuting a world of positivist facts and established orthodox procedures for the process of self-questioning and self-transcendence.

In the longer cycle of decline, "corruption spreads from the harsh sphere of material advantage and power to the mass media, the stylish journals, the literary movements, the educational process, the reigning philosophies. A civilization in decline digs its own grave with a relentless consistency. It cannot be argued out of its self- destructive ways."[18] For intelligence becomes defined as appealing to the facts "and the facts in the situation produced by decline more and more are the absurdities that proceed from inattention, oversight, unreasonableness and irresponsibility."[19]

How does one turn around a civilization that "cannot be argued out of its self-destructive ways"? How can the unwilling become will- ing? When you have a whole civilization engaged in the longer cycle of decline, when virtually all social groups are engaged in embracing a technological order as if it were a cosmological reality (i.e., part of the natural order of things) whose very patterns of "legitimate thought" are refusals of self-transcendence, it is hard to imagine a way out.

The kind of change required is nothing less than a cultural con- version. A civilization's decline, one must hope, can be reversed by a saving remnant; that is, through the fermenting presence of minority communities who are founded on a conversion to self-transcendence. To be a member of a holy community is to have undergone a conversion that reorients the self toward the infinite. Such reoriented selves keep their respective communities oriented to self-transcendence. Moreover the surrender to transcendence by some can seduce others to engage in this surrender, either consciously and unconsciously. This is possible because there is the transformation we call love in all its varieties, from love of family through love of country and humanity on to the all inclusive love of the divine (i.e., of transcendence itself), that orients humanity in the cosmos. And "where hatred reinforces bias, love dissolves it, whether it be the bias of unconscious motivation, the bias of individual or group egoism, or the bias of omnicompetent shortsighted common sense. . . . Love breaks the bonds of psychological and social determinisms with the conviction of faith and the power of hope."[20] And where love fails to bring about conversion, it turns the other cheek, it prefers the nonviolent role of the Suffering Servant to that of the vengeful agent. Thus even when it fails, love reduces the level of absurdity in the world.

As a reorienting conversion of the self, falling in love is a surrender to the infinite. Through such "falling" the self experiences itself as an unbounded openness to the infinite. For Doran conversion is a fourfold process—beginning in *religious conversion,* leading to *ethical* and *intellectual conversion,* and culminating in *psychic conversion.* Conversion implies a transformation of the whole personality whereby authentic or self-transcending existence is embraced successively by the religious, moral, and intellectual and psychological dimensions of personality.

The core of conversion is understood as religious. A falling in love or total surrender of the self to the inner yet otherworldly demand for self-transcendence lures the self beyond itself and its every finite horizon. It exemplifies itself noetically in a surrender to the infinite passion to know what is *ultimately* true and worthwhile. When this conversion penetrates the ethical dimensions of personality, it manifests itself as a surrender to the inner demand for integrity between one's knowing and doing, even if that requires the sacrifice of personal satisfactions in order to actualize what one knows to be true or valuable.

Finally, when conversion penetrates the intellect, one understands that knowing is more than simply "taking a look." Looking or attending is but the first step in knowing. "For the word spoken and heard, proceeds from and penetrates to all four levels of intentional consciousness. Its content is not just a content of experience but a content of *experience,* and *understanding* and *judging* and *deciding* [italics added]. The analogy of sight yields the cognitional myth [i.e., that knowing is taking a look]. But fidelity to the word engages the whole man."[21] Thus when conversion penetrates to the depths of one's personhood, what one sees must be critically mediated by the word so that one understands what one sees and critically judges one's understanding, leaving one finally with the task of bringing one's doing into congruence with one's knowing. In so doing, the self is carried beyond itself and into an eschatological openness to the infinite.

But for conversion to fully open the self to the infinite, Robert Doran argues, it must penetrate not only the conscious dimensions of one's personality but the unconscious as well. This requires what he calls *psychic conversion.* Doran forms his concept of psychic conversion in continuity with the evolution of Lonergan's understanding of the differentiation of consciousness. He points out that "in *Insight,* existential or deliberative consciousness is collapsed into intelligent and reasonable consciousness. As a result . . . the good is identified with the intelligent and the reasonable."[22] By the time that Lonergan wrote *Method in Theology,* however, he had differentiated the notion of value.[23]

What was missing from *Insight* was a fully differentiated account of the possibility that emotions can be orienting rather than disorienting to the processes of intellectual and ethical reflection. In *Insight* Lonergan was still suffering from a Kantian bias against the emotions.[24] But in *Method* "instead of bypassing human feelings, the account of the good . . . begins with them."[25] Hence *Method in Theology* "heuristically opens the possibility of what Eric Voegelin has called a psychology of orientation, in contrast to a psychology of passional motivation."[26] There is, as Fred Crowe suggests, a movement in Lonergan's thought between *Insight* and *Method in Theology* that could be characterized as a movement from the Thomist phase to the Augustinian phase of his work.[27] This movement opens up the possibility of a psychology of orientation.

Such a psychology has deep roots in the theology of Augustine. For, as I have argued elsewhere (in *Narrative Theology After Auschwitz*), the decisive turning point of authentic conversion in Augustine occurred not at age 32 but at age 19, when he read the *Hortensius* by Cicero. This book set him on fire with a new kind of desire, the desire for wisdom. "I was not encouraged by this work of Cicero's," said Augustine, "to join this or that sect; instead I was urged on and inflamed with a passionate zeal to love and seek and obtain and embrace and hold fast wisdom itself, whatever it might be" (III, 4).

The awakening of the desire for wisdom represented the appearance of a new kind of seductive power in Augustine's life. That it is a seduction is evident in the way he speaks of this event. He does not say that the *Hortensius* changed his *thinking* but rather that it *"altered my way of feeling . . . and gave me different ambitions and desires"* (III, 4). For more than a decade, from the time of his reading of the *Hortensius* until his conversion to Christian faith, Augustine experienced his life as a war between two selves grounded in opposing patterns of emotion. One self, present since birth, was driven by *cupiditas* or self-love and was constellated by the seductive power of the world with its offers of fame, power, and pleasure. Then the reading of the *Hortensius* evoked a second self driven by a new emotion, *caritas* or the surrender of selfless love constellated by seductive but hidden power of the infinite manifest through the passion for wisdom. The worldly emotions that constellated the first self seduced him away from self-transcendence leaving him wandering and disoriented. But not all emotion was disorienting. The reading of the *Hortensius* set him ablaze with the desire for wisdom and sent him "panting" after truth, causing him to surrender himself to the questions no matter where they led. This new passion for wisdom carried him beyond himself and, though he was not fully aware of it at the time, was seducing him into an openness to the infinite. As I read the *Confessions*, this experience provides the guiding norm as Augustine goes from story to story in search of a true story. That is, a truthful story is one that welcomes questions and encourages us to follow them wherever they lead. A false or disorienting story is one that either avoids or forbids the raising of such questions.[28]

Lonergan's understanding of faith and reason stands directly in the Augustinian tradition of faith as a surrender to doubt and to its questions, in which reason and emotion unite to promote self-transcendence. In *Method in Theology* intentional consciousness is recognized as rooted in intentional feelings. Contrary to his position in *Insight* Lonergan now recognized that the *affective* can promote rather than retard the *effective* orientation of human agency in the world. Now feelings are said to give "intentional consciousness its mass, momentum, drive [and] power" by which we are "oriented massively and dynamically in a world mediated by meaning."[29]

Feelings themselves then can be differentiated into those that simply promote personal and group satisfactions and those that move the individual to self-transcending affirmations of the truly worthwhile. "Thus, social values call for a more self-transcending response than do vital values."[30] And cultural values likewise sublate [sacred] social values, personal values sublate cultural and religious [holy] values sublate personal values—to orient one's self and one's community toward self-transcendence. For as religious conversion indicates, "there is in full consciousness feelings so deep and strong, especially when deliberately reinforced, that they channel attention, shape one's horizon, direct one's life."[31]

The implication Doran draws from Lonergan's new emphasis on the importance of feeling is that there is an aesthetic base to ethical insight that makes psychic conversion itself an ethical demand. "Psychic conversion" says Doran, "consists in the development of the capacity for internal communication in the subject among spirit (intellectual, rational, deliberative and religious consciousness), psyche (sensitive consciousness), and organism (the unconscious), by means of the attentive, intelligent, rational, and existentially responsible and decisive negotiation of one's imaginal, affective and intersubjective spontaneity."[32] Psychic conversion is the last step in the differentiation of consciousness because it requires the application of all previous differentiations of consciousness to the sensitive psyche so as to disengage the aesthetic images that emerge in dream and fantasy and gain insight into them as a guide for self-transcendence.

Psychic conversion, in Doran's view, brings Lonergan's quest for the self-conscious self-appropriation of the questioning self full circle. For the massive feelings that evoke the surrender to the questions unfold the operations of the questioning self and shape a fully differentiated consciousness. This differentiated consciousness is then brought to bear on those feelings, as mediated through aesthetic images cast up by the psyche, for the purpose of acquiring self-knowledge. That is, one attends to, understands, judges, and decides on the meaning of one's own psychological imagery as a way of coming to understand oneself.

Influenced by C. G. Jung's theory that dreams and other images cast up by the psyche have a teleological function, Doran suggests that such images try to bring to consciousness a compensating function.[33] They compensate for the narrow focus of our ego-centered consciousness that neglects both the needs of the world beyond our egos and our own need for self-transcendence and transformation. The image brought up by the dream makes our ego consciousness aware of its neglect and so reorients our deficient or dysfunctional modes of consciousness toward self-transcendence.[34] Such images therefore promote transcendence of the limitations of our biased consciousness.

The existential drama of our lives, Doran insists, has a social and historical context. We shape our lives "in the presence of others, who also are actors in life's drama."[35] The shaping of our identity occurs within the context of a community in the process of historical becoming. "What images we admit into consciousness will be a function of our antecedent willingness or unwillingness to accept the insights that are needed if we are authentically to constitute the human world and ourselves within the parameters set by the historical process."[36] And thus when the social context of the drama of life is governed by the ideological bias of one's family, class, religion, race, or nation, the needed images will not be available.

Just as the existential formation of our identity, when dominated by ideology, blocks access to the imagery of the psyche, so the existential reorientation of the self brought about by conversion reaches down into the unconscious to release those images. "One must locate a domain of imaginal production where images are released unhindered by the guardianship of waking consciousness under the dominance of the biases" of current ideologies.[37] "This domain is the dream." It is, he says, "the key to psychic conversion."[38] *Psychic conversion* is the name Doran applies to the conscious attempt to question our dreams so as to elicit ethical insight into our lives and bring about the necessary emotional or empathic transformation of our selves that will release us from all inhibitions to ethical action.

The dream is a kind of barometer for measuring the degree of one's self-transcendence. It "displays the current linkage of image and affect. If one's subterranean life has been made the unwilling victim of one's own repression of conscious insight, the dream will display the plight, the crippled condition, the anger, the violence, the perversion, the helplessness of the oppressed."[39] The dream accuses one for one's refusal to heed the call for self-transcendence and seeks to awaken one's compassion for the stranger. The crippled and disfigured images in one's dreams are the inner victims of one's own self-deception (i.e., the violence one is doing to oneself) that permits one to neglect the inner demands for truth, justice, and compassion and that therefore allow one to act toward others in the world without truth, justice, or compassion. Thus the dream suggests the degree to which the subject is resisting or cooperating in the promotion of his or her own self-transcendence. The bizarre and crippled images of one's psyche are meant as a compensating corrective to one's conscious orientation. They warn of the distance between one's conscious attitude and the inner demand for self-transcendence or selfless compassion. Given that the drama of one's own life is embedded in the sociohistorical drama of one's time, the dream is also of "historical and political significance. . . . The dreams of an existentially capable adult are a cipher precisely of one's existential participation in the promotion, obstruction, or decline of the human good."[40]

Robert Lifton, in *The Nazi Doctors*,[41] provides a dramatic example. A Nazi physician, Ernst B., who was assigned to the death camps, thought he recognized a Jewish friend from his youth among the camp inmates. But when he later sought to find him he had no success. Then he began to have recurrent dreams about this friend— Simon Cohen: "He was always a very attractive young man. And now [in the dream] he had really deteriorated. . . . And he looked at me with a reproachful, beseeching expression . . . sort of [saying], 'It can't be possible that you stand there and I am . . . [like this] . . . ' or more like a disappointed expression: 'How can you belong to those people? That can't be you.' . . ."[42] Lifton commented on these experiences: "We can say that the illusion [of seeing his friend in the camp] (as it probably was) and the dream were insistent assertions of Ernst B.'s humanity, and of his discomfort and guilt at being part of the Auschwitz machine. *In their questioning* of his personal camp reality . . . they expressed his resistance to succumbing, or at least succumbing completely, to the very 'Auschwitz mentality' he was in the process of discovering" [emphasis added].[43] It is significant too that this physician who had never fully confronted his culpability in the perpetration of Auschwitz continued to have this dream in the decades after the war, right up to the time of the interview in the 1980s.

There is a correlation between the strangers and aliens, the poor and the oppressed, of one's psyche and one's society. The latter are the product of the former and both demand the *preferential option* of one's attention. The poor and the oppressed are the victims of "social and economic systems [which] are nothing other than the intrasubjective neglect of the movement of [psychic] life writ large and, as it were, 'projected' into the dialectic of history."[44]

Initiated by religious conversion, psychic conversion sensitizes the self to its own inner demands for self-transcendence and promotes the surrender of the self to its questions (i.e., to the infinite) and as a result opens the self to its social analogue—the stranger who comes to us both inwardly and outwardly, unsettling us, provoking us to surrender to our doubts and to engage in imaginative self-questioning. Psychic conversion "reaches into and transforms the unconscious itself, " opening it to the infinite and to the stranger,[45] for "spontaneous psychic images function in human consciousness in a manner analogous to the role that questions play in intelligence, reflection and deliberation."[46] This convergence of image and question renews both imagination and intellect, uniting emotion and intelligence to release the self's ethical impulse in self-transcending actions on behalf of the stranger.[47]

Technobureaucratic Rationality and the "Myth" of Human Rights

The naked public square of the modern technological city, as Harvey Cox envisioned it over a quarter of a century ago, seemed to promise a secular city where strangers are welcome. His vision promised a pluralistic world of tolerance and humanizing technological innovation. But that utopian hope seems to have been an illusion. The naked public square that appeared to offer the cosmopolitan possibility of a new international human community, a unity-in-diversity, seems instead to be producing a global Disneyland.[48] The modern secular world is turning out to be, not a community but its antithesis—scarcely more than a collection of privatized fantasylands held together by a hidden technobureaucratic structure. It is a compartmentalized world ideally designed to subvert not only communion between strangers but also conscience, replacing both with a Manichaean demonic doubling—a multiplication of compartmentalized and privatized selves. As a result, public policy in the naked public square of technopolis is virtually impossible, for we scarcely have a public world, only the bureaucratic world of technical experts on the one hand and our private disconnected worlds (our own diverse fantasylands) on the other hand.

When Nietzsche's madman entered the *naked public square* to announce the death of God and the coming of a new secular order governed by a "will to power," he was prophesying the birth of a MAD world without ethical horizons. He was anticipating a world held together not by the bonds of human self-transcendence and compassion for the stranger but by bureaucratic technicism and technological dread. Public policy in such a MAD world assumes a Star Wars (SDI) mentality, treating the world of technology as if it were an autonomous reality entirely disconnected from all things human. When technology is separated from the human in this way, it inevitably becomes demonic and dehumanizing. Rather than a human world served by a humanizing technology we end up careening toward a desolate inhuman world, a global death camp.

The vulnerability of democracy to totalitarianism in a technological civilization lies within rather than without. As Neuhaus has argued, "the prelude to . . . totalitarian monism is the notion that society can be ordered according to secular technological reason without reference to religious[ly] grounded meaning."[49] The fall of democracy will not be due to outside influences. On the contrary, as John Courtney Murray has argued, it will be because, "it will have undertaken to establish a technological order of most marvelous intricacy, which will have been constructed and will operate without relations to true political ends: and this technological order will hang, as it were, suspended over a moral confusion; and this moral confusion will itself be suspended over a spiritual vacuum."[50] The naked public square, says Richard John Neuhaus, is an "impossible project" that cannot sustain itself. The climate of relativity and the spiritual vacuum it creates will inevitably be filled by some new absolute. In our modern secular society, dominated by technology, where religious symbols of transcendence are systematically excluded from the public square, technology, or more precisely the bureaucratic technological nation-state, assumes the status of the absolute arbiter of life and death. To champion the naked public square, in this view, is to champion the ethical relativism of the technological barbarians—a relativism that tends to overcome its own ambiguity by a leap into some new absolutism.

These technological barbarians, says Neuhaus, "are composed of the most sophisticated and educated elites of our society, . . . those who in principle refuse to recognize a normative ethic or the reality of public virtue."[51] In a technological civilization public issues tend to be reduced to political issues and political issues to technical issues. Instead of public policy we get Disneyland, a world held together by technical and bureaucratic procedures that so skillfully pander to our hidden desires and private fantasies that, in our distraction, we scarcely notice the disappearance of either our common political life or our common public life. In a world where all important decisions are deferred to those with the proper technical expertise, neither political nor public decisions are possible. Nowhere is this more apparent than in the conduct of nuclear policy. For, as Richard Falk has pointed out, the history of nuclear policy from the Manhattan Project until the present has been cloaked in a technicality and secrecy that is antidemocratic and undermines the democratic procedures of society. This antidemocratic political strategy is given legitimacy by an appeal to being in a permanent state of (cold) war.[52] The rhetoric of war legitimizes the necessity for realism. And realism requires secrecy "in the national interest," lest our enemies (who are viewed as the embodiment of evil) acquire our technical knowledge. Hence it is not realistic to expect to conduct nuclear policy through normal democratic processes. Realism under conditions of war requires that we exempt our policies from both the political and ethical-questioning so essential to democratic process to do what we must do to survive. As Robert Lifton's work indicates, these are the ideal conditions for the emergence of demonic doubling that renders MADness logical, convincing us that preparation for total annihilation is the only thing that makes the future possible (i.e., "slaying to make alive"). The only way to be in charge of our destiny, we are told, is to place our unquestioning trust in the very technology that is threatening to annihilate us, even as the only way to protect democracy requires that we subvert it.

The modern secular world of technopolis has been an experiment in substituting technical knowledge for public narrative and technical bureaucratic procedures for public ritual. Auschwitz and Hiroshima represent the triumph of the technical and the bureaucratic, of the demonic and inhuman over human self-transcendence and compassion for the stranger. In the last chapter I argued that the appropriate response to the demonic is an ethic of human rights sustained by a global ecology of those holy communities whose narrative traditions focus on welcoming the stranger. The antidote to bureaucratic compartmentalization is an ethic that requires us to assume responsibility for our multiple selves (i.e., our double) even as it requires us to recognize the primacy of human dignity and human rights, especially those of the stranger, as an absolute limit to which all sacred orders must be subordinated.

From the perspective of Alasdair MacIntyre, however, techno-bureaucratic managerial efficiency and the claims for human rights are equally illusions or "myths" (in the pejorative sense) fostered by our technical civilization. On the one hand, managerial expertise is a fiction based on the illusion that social science can produce law-like generalizations which can be the basis for rationally controlling institutions. But "the salient fact about those [social] sciences is the absence of the discovery of any law-like generalizations whatsoever."[53] Managerial expertise (i.e., the claim to maximize efficiency and effectiveness), therefore, is nothing more than a social-scientific myth used to legitimate the managerial will to power—a will to power which fills the vacuum created by an ethical relativism which is itself a product of the impact of the social sciences. On the other hand, human rights as the proposed cure for the ethical relativism of the techno-bureaucratic order, MacIntyre argues, is really just a further manifestation of the disease of modern bureaucratic individualism. Rather than being an authentic ethical language, the language of human rights is simply an emotional individualistic response to the emergence of the normless world governed by technical bureaucracy and the will to power. "Each of us," says MacIntyre, " is taught to see himself or herself as an autonomous moral agent; but each of us also becomes engaged . . . in manipulative relationships [aesthetic or bureaucratic] with others." Like Nietzsche's *Übermensch,* "seeking to protect the autonomy [of self-creation] that we have learned to prize, we aspire ourselves *not* to be manipulated by others; seeking to incarnate our own principles and stand-point in the world of practice, we find no way open to us to do so except by directing towards others those very manipulative modes of relationship which each of us aspires to resist in our own case."[54]

The language of rights, MacIntyre argues, is a modern invention, beginning with the notion of natural rights in the late Middle Ages and ending with the modern concept of human rights that "are supposed to attach equally to all individuals, whatever their sex, race, religion, talents or deserts."[55] "The truth is," says MacIntyre, that "there are no such rights, and belief in them is one with belief in witches and in unicorns. . . . Every attempt to give good reasons for believing that there *are* such rights has failed."[56] Instead we appeal to intuitions of *self-evident truths,* "but we know that there are no self evident truths . . . . [and] the introduction of the word 'intuition' by a moral philosopher is always a signal that something has gone wrong with an argument."[57]

In MacIntyre's view, *rights* are moral fictions invented by a culture of bureaucratic individualism to protect the emotivist individual from the incursion of managerial values of utility. The result is the clash of incommensurate ethical languages in which a protest "occurs as a reaction to the alleged invasion of someone's *rights* in the name of someone else's *utility.*"[58] Such language, he argues, emerges when people are removed from traditional societies that provide role-defined functionally normative notions of what it means to be human, in which the virtues enabled a person to make the transition from who he or she Is to what he or she Ought to do. In such a society one knows what a good soldier or citizen is and ethical disputes can be settled by an appeal to the facts. "It is only when man is thought of as an individual prior to and apart from all roles that 'man' ceases to be a functional concept."[59] The modern *naked self* that refuses to be defined by its social roles, in MacIntyre's view, is functionally normless. As such the modern self is reduced to ethical emotivism in which all ethical choices are assumed to be nothing more than personal preferences. Such emotivism, we are told, is nothing but a form of individualistic egoism that expresses its displeasure at violations of its individual freedom by inventing the language of rights.

Although our discussion of technology after Auschwitz and Hiroshima, based on the work of such social critics as Jacques Ellul and Richard Rubenstein, suggests that MacIntyre is right to bring the bureaucratic-manipulative dimension of the modern social order under ethical critique, his dismissal of human rights as pure emotivism and his reduction of rights to sociologically conditioned responses is extremely problematic. The arguments I have constructed (especially in the last chapter) would suggest that there is more to human rights claims than MacIntyre allows.

I find four major problems with MacIntyre's thesis in *After Virtue*. First: Although MacIntyre is partially right, he is also wrong in important ways. Modern technical bureaucratic expertise and modern claims to human dignity and human rights are a two-edged sword. Both bureaucracy and consciousness of human dignity are historical outcomes of a process of urban secularization whose apocalyptic dark side is exactly as MacIntyre describes it. Secularization demythologizes institutions (i.e., removes them from the sacred canopy of fixed cosmological values) and leaves us with a normless manipulative view of institutional management justified by utilitarian pragmatism. And urbanization along with secularization does produce a radically individualized naked self whose only norm is the will to power. This self views others as objects to be manipulated and itself as having sacred human rights that must not be violated. The result is an egoistic, compartmentalized, technobureaucratic society. But that is only half the story—the dark half. For when the naked self is transformed into the empty self, through a conversion to self-transcendence, then the apocalypticism of the naked public square can give way to the utopianism of human dignity, human rights and human liberation.

Although it is true that modern sociohistorical consciousness has not produced lawlike generalizations that would justify manipulative models of managerial expertise, MacIntyre himself admits that the social sciences are capable of producing usable wisdom.[60] Not even MacIntyre thinks we could eliminate sociohistorical consciousness. Indeed his reconstruction of the Aristotelian tradition systematically replaces nature with historical consciousness. We are irrevocably aware that the world we live in is shaped by human values and commitments. Thus, although scientific manipulative management may be based on a fiction, it does not follow that management as such is. Rather we are forced to rethink our understanding of management. We are forced to abandon those cosmological models of the social sciences and management theory rooted in the paradigms of the natural sciences. For such paradigms obscure the fact that the social and technical world is a product of human decisions and commitments. It is necessary to reintroduce the human dimension into our social science and management models. The kind of social science we need is one that enables us to understand how human decisions and value commitments both shape the world we live in and are shaped by the worlds we enter (i.e., the interaction between self, institutional social roles, and social structures) so as to provide our ethical imagination with the insights necessary to act within the world we have created.

Modern sociohistorical consciousness with its accompanying claims for human rights does originate within a specific cultural and religious context as MacIntyre suggests, but it does not follow that the truth claims for human rights are necessarily culturally dependent variables. On the contrary modern sociohistorical consciousness produces an awareness of the irreducible transcendence of the self to any given culture (i.e., our inability to be totally socialized) which does in fact give us a direct intuition (i.e., a direct insight) into the irreducible dignity of the self. This consciousness is spread by modern technological urbanization patterns that awaken this awareness of the irreducible transcendence or inalienable dignity of the self wherever modern technological consciousness is integrated into urban patterns.

The experiences of the holy in traditions such as Judaism, Christianity and Buddhism add an important dimension to this modern consciousness. These narrative traditions have the capacity to transform the individualistic egoism of the technological self, offering the possibility of saving modern consciousness from manipulative individualism by evoking a consciousness of the socioecological interdependence that makes human dignity or self-transcendence possible. Modern sociohistorical consciousness has the potential to work cooperatively in tandem with the anthropological religious traditions that prepared the way for this consciousness. The social and historical conditions which make awareness of human dignity possible do not create a moral fiction but rather disclose an ethical and spiritual truth in such a way as to make what was once a rare insight intuitively available to large numbers of people.

Second: Although emotions can be ethically vacuous and disorienting, not all emotions function in this way. As the work of Lonergan and Doran, in the tradition of Augustine, suggests, some emotions actually orient the self toward self-transcendence to guide the human capacity for critical rationality. Conversion as a surrender to the utopianism of doubt is in fact such an emotional transformation, which orients the self toward the holy (i.e., the infinite). This transformation not only orients the questioning mind toward transcendence but also extends empathy beyond one's family, friends and compatriots to include the stranger in a normative hierarchy of values that promote self-transcendence. In this sense, the modern self-transcending self is not inherently normless, as MacIntyre suggests, but operates under an imperative of self-transcendence expressed in an openness to the infinite and to the stranger. Thus not all ethical emotion fits MacIntyre's emotivist category or succumbs to his critique of emotivism as normless.

Third: MacIntyre's supposition that the problem of incommensurate first principles (e.g., rights versus utility, or deontology versus teleology/consequentialism) is a uniquely modern problem is likewise problematic. The modern ethical tension between deontology and consequentialism (e.g., utilitarianism) corresponds directly the distinction between anthropological ethics (the holy) and cosmological ethics (the sacred) that appeared in the ancient world with the emergence of Judaism (and later Christianity) and Buddhism. Each of these traditions recognized that a single story ethic is impossible. Ethics requires at least two stories. And each therefore developed a *two realm* or *two kingdom ethic.* But that development did not necessarily entail an ethical relativism between totally incommensurate first principles. The problem with philosophical ethical theories, whether deontological or consequentialist, is that each tries to cover the full range of ethical experience with a single theory, when in fact each type is applicable only in dialectical tension with the other. Therefore, consequentialist theories represent appropriate cosmological-societal concerns for the collective good, even as Kantian style deontological theories point out an inviolable core of human transcendence or dignity that must not be violated by pragmatic or utilitarian concerns for order. The tradition of the virtues has a place in each type of story (cosmological and anthropological), provided the cosmological (i.e., the good of order) is subordinated to the anthropological (the "unseen measure" of human dignity) in much the way the four cardinal virtues of Greek philosophy were once subordinated to the three theological virtues.

Fourth: the irony is that MacIntyre, who ostensibly seeks to preserve the value of the biblical tradition for ethics, develops a position that systematically exhibits a nostalgia for pre-Biblical cosmological forms of moral order. He seems to long for a single-story ethic despite the fact the biblical tradition requires at least a two-story ethic (e.g., Augustine's two cities.)[61] Indeed, even as he decries the universal pretensions of the Enlightenment ethical (storyless) story, he seems to long for a world in which everyone does in fact share one story and therefore the same first principles.

From Narrative Diversity to the Utopian Promise of Babel

There is a significant difference in the way MacIntyre and Hauerwas approach narrative ethics within our modern technological city of Babel with its ethical pluralism and narrative diversity. For it seems to me that MacIntyre bewails this diversity and prepares us for a new "dark ages" by *settling* into the one story which he wishes were universal, whereas Hauerwas does not *retreat* into the particularity of his Christian narrative tradition but rather embraces its particularity while insisting that other narrative traditions may have something to teach us as well. The difference in attitude to the narrative pluralism of our world can be traced to Hauerwas's strong emphasis on the biblical ethic of welcoming the stranger. For how can you welcome strangers without being interested in their stories? To welcome strangers entails an ethical encounter in which one must inevitably be open to their stories and traditions apart from which they would not be who they are. To welcome the stranger inevitably involves one in a sympathetic passing over into the other's life and stories and a coming back into one's own life and stories enriched with new insight. To welcome the stranger requires seeing Babel not as a curse but a blessing. Indeed, the story of Babel offers us a clue not only to the relation of transcendence to the stranger but also how that relation can alter the technobureaucratic ideology that threatens to submerge us in the suicidal abyss of the demonic.

Let us recall once more the story with which we began in the Prologue. According to the book of Genesis:

> Now the whole earth had one language and the same words. . . . Then they said, "Come, let us build ourselves a city, and a tower with its top in the heavens, and let us make a name for ourselves; otherwise we shall be scattered abroad upon the face of the whole earth." The Lord came down to see the city and the tower which mortals had built. And the Lord said, "Look, they are one people, and they have all one language; and this is only the beginning of what they will do; nothing that they

propose to do will now be impossible for them. Come, let us go down, and confuse their language there, so that they will not understand one another's speech." So the Lord scattered them abroad from there over the face of all the earth, and they left off building the city. Therefore it was called Babel, because there the Lord confused the language of all the earth; and from there the Lord scattered them abroad over the face of all the earth. (Genesis 11:1, 4–9)

The story of Babel is especially interesting for what it suggests about the linkage of language, technology and the quest for self-transcendence. Technology is viewed as the mediator of the human quest for transcendence. That is, technology is thought to enable humans to reach heaven and be like God—as they imagine God, that is, in total control. And even as technology is viewed, within the story, as mediating transcendence, language is viewed as mediating technology. It is by virtue of sharing one language, one world-view, that this transcendence or total control is viewed as possible. God's intervention, confusing their language so that the building project is interrupted, is usually interpreted as a curse or punishment for the sin of pride.

Perhaps that was the meaning of this ancient story before it was incorporated into the biblical narrative traditions. However, in the Torah the command to welcome the stranger occurs more often than any other command—some thirty six times.[62] In the light of this emphasis I think another conclusion must be drawn. God's confusion of human language must be understood not as a punishment but as a blessing. Humans, unable to imagine the infinite as anything other than the infinitizing of their own finitude, seek to appropriate transcendence through the linguistic ideology of a single world-view as the precondition for total technical control of their lives. But rather than punishing them for seeking transcendence, God intervenes to redirect them toward authentic self-transcendence, which can occur only when there are strangers to be welcomed into one's society. For strangers, speaking different tongues, telling different stories, and communicating different values, are an invitation to self-transcendence, opening our closed world to the infinite and the possibility of utopian transformation. In place of the totalitarian language of one world-view, Babel offers us a plurality of languages and world-views, each offering the possibility of a finite insight into the infinite—insights that might be mutually enriching. Such a plurality of insights is appropriate to our finite condition. What is inappropriate is the pretension to omniscience. Rather than making ethics impossible, because the definitive (omniscient) answer cannot be given, it renders ethics a human task of questioning and questing for insight and the sharing of that insight. Ethics, so conceived, is a common quest to understand what is truly good, in which the good manifests itself not so much through absolutely *right* answers as through a shared commitment to be *responsible* for each other. As such, Babel redefines our relation to technique. Rather than a managerial public policy ideology of total control over society, it suggests the more modest goal of a society of pluralistic institutions, each with a limited area of authority and each exercising responsible self-control. Babel replaces the closed totalitarian world of *sameness* (i.e., of the false infinite) with the unfinished world of human finitude and human diversity—a world that is utopian because it is unfinished. A world in which the finite, without ceasing to be finite, is open to the infinite and hence further transformation.

Like Jeffrey Stout, I would argue that,

> our problems do not result from the confusion of tongues in a society that has fallen from the coherence and community of an earlier age. The plurality of moral languages in our society is closely related to the plurality of social practices and institutions we have reason to affirm. Our moral languages exhibit a division of conceptual labor, each doing its own kind of work. But they also sometimes get in each other's way. Some languages, in particular those of the marketplace and the bureaucracies, creep into areas of life where they can only do harm. They tend to engulf or corrupt habits of thought and patterns of interaction that we desperately need. Protecting them is a grave problem, worthy of the best social criticism and political experimentation we can muster.[63]

The problem then is not the pluralism of languages but the imperialism of some institutional languages, especially technobureaucratic and economic languages. For the imperialism of these languages tends to destroy the complex sociolinguistic ecology that sustains human dignity by reducing the individual to a component in a complex bureaucracy to be manipulated for the achievement of maximum efficiency at a minimum cost. The problem is, as Peter Berger suggests, that technical bureaucracy has replaced the sacred canopy as the organizing principle of modern social life because it is experienced as the power that transforms chaos into cosmos.

As we have seen, both Ellul and Rubenstein suggest that the demonic power of a technological civilization lies in creating a bureaucratic society of total domination. Such a society is a total reversion to that mythic time before Babel when society was governed by one language and one technology which absolutizes its finite social order as sacred and unquestionable and seeks to eliminate all self-transcendence by substituting sameness for diversity. The question remains, however, whether a technological civilization must necessarily result in the bureaucratization of human life. The Bergers (Peter and Brigitte) and Kellner argue that, although bureaucracy and technology are the primary social carriers of modernization, they are not the same, nor are they inextricably linked. Bureaucracy and technology are as old as urbanization itself. But the modern "technological phenomenon," as Jacques Ellul describes it, with its emphasis on efficiency and the managerial restructuring of society to promote maximum efficiency, is a distinctively a modern phenomenon. When technological efficiency becomes linked to the bureaucratic domination of life its impact on society and personal life becomes totalitarian.

The heart of the problem lies in the transformation that ccurs when modern technological consciousness is subsumed by bureaucratic consciousness and generalized to the whole of society. For inherent limits in technological consciousness are removed when it enters the bureaucratic environment. In areas of genuine technological production, the materials one is working with and the objectives one is trying to realize are specific. They impose discipline, limits, and measurable goals on the technological process. All of these are absent when technical attitudes are carried over into bureaucratic processes. "In political bureaucracy there is less pressure from the logic of technology and therefore more of a chance for the peculiar 'genius' of bureaucracy to unfold."[64]

As bureaucracy overtakes technology and engulfs society, the means are no longer related to and disciplined by ends beyond themselves. The whole of society becomes divided into areas of bureaucratic expertise to be regulated by the appropriate experts according to established anonymous and impartial procedures. Organization and orderliness become ends in themselves.

Bureaucracy is not only orderly but orderly in an imperialistic mode. There is a bureaucratic demiurge who views the universe as dumb chaos waiting to be brought into the redeeming order of bureaucratic administration. . . . The engineer puts phenomena into little categorial boxes in order to take them apart further

or to put them together in larger wholes. By contrast, the bureaucrat is typically satisfied once everything has been put in its
proper box. Thus bureaucracy leads to a type of problem-solving
different from that for technological production. It is less condu-
cive to creative fantasy, and it is fixating rather than innovat-
ing. . . . In the technological sphere, social organization is largely heteronomous, that is , it must be so shaped as to conform to
the non-bureaucratic requirements of production. This imposes
certain limits on organization. . . . In the political sphere, which
is the bureaucratic sphere par excellence, these limits are much
less in evidence. Here, organization can be set up autono-
mously, that is, as following no logic but its own. . . . Paper
does not resist the bureaucrat in the way that steel parts resist
the engineer. Thus there is nothing that intrinsically prohibits
the passport agency from deciding that ten rather than three
bureaucrats must approve every passport application.[65]

In a technobureaucrat society all of life is compartmentalized and
individuals are expected to unquestioningly follow procedures without necessarily understanding the larger goals to which their actions
contribute. For, on the one hand, the intelligibility of required procedures is opaque because the problem it solves is not a genuine technical problem. On the other hand, one is expected to abide by regulations and procedures that are "too technical" for the average person
to understand, on the assumption that the appropriate experts understand and legitimate these ends, providing the reasons why things
must be done in a certain way.

Albert Speer, reflecting on how he came to be involved in
Hitler's Third Reich emphasizes just these tendencies of technobureaucratic order. Thus, he tells us:

The ordinary party member was being taught that grand-policy
was much too complex for him to judge it. Consequently, one
felt one was being represented, never called upon to take personal responsibility. The whole structure of the system was
aimed at preventing conflicts of conscience from even arising. . . . Worse still was the restriction of responsibility to one's
own field. . . . Everyone kept to his own group—of architects,
physicians, jurists, technicians, soldiers, or farmers. The professional organizations to which everyone had to belong were
called chambers . . . and this term aptly described the way people were immured in isolated, closed-off areas of life. The longer

Hitler's system lasted, the more people's minds moved within such isolated chambers. . . . What eventually developed was a society of totally isolated individuals.[66]

Such a technobureaucratic society forces a doubling and quadrupling of selves. It forces individuals to generate a plurality of selves appropriate to each compartmentalized area of human life, selves that are, at best, amoral, having surrendered the option of ethical reflection and judgment to the experts. These selves, denuded of everything that makes them truly individuals (i.e., their personal and communal histories and values) become finally dehumanized interchangeable and replaceable parts in a vast bureaucratic machine. Thus whereas technological production gives persons a sense of creativity and potency and even self-transcendence as one overcomes obstacles and realizes a goal, bureaucracy creates just the opposite; namely, a sense of impotency, helplessness, and the necessity to conform to a reality so real, massive, and all pervasive that "nothing can be changed." The result is a social structure that separates ends from means and deciders from actors, relegating all decisions to "higher levels." Such a social structure prepares the way for the demonic, preventing ethical questions from ever arising even as it creates bureaucratic individuals who feel no personal responsibility for their actions.

The presence of theonomous (i.e., self-transcending) holy communities (both religious and secular), including technical and professional societies, who surrender to the genuine questions of their discipline and resist the monolithic incursion of the technobureaucratic political mythos, is absolutely essential to the sustaining the dignity of human life. Most important is the presence of religious holy communities that serve as a fence around human dignity. For these communities prevent the usurpation of human dignity by bureaucratic expediency, especially by forcing the naked self to recognize its emptiness or essential interdependence with all other beings. Such communities undermine demonic forms of doubling by fostering a sense of self that breaks down the compartmentalized walls between its various role-defined selves (all of whom speak only one language, "bureaucratese"), encouraging the reflective self to assume responsibility for all its selves.

Our capacity for ethics is rooted in our imaginative capacity assume the place of the other who will be affected by our actions. This capacity is fostered by the experience of alienation that makes it possible for us to assume different roles in different social contexts. The capacity to assume diverse roles is precisely what prepares us to identify with the stranger. The ethical dimension of every institutonal role we assume is rooted in a feeling of obligation toward the dignity of the persons whose needs we meet through that social context. However, the tendency of virtually every social institution is to consider its purposes as sacred or ultimate. So each demands a total unquestioning commitment of the self to its goals and values at the expense of all others. To acquiesce in that demand would require a demonic doubling. By contrast, the holy community, when it is faithful to its calling, is not just one more institution competing for the self but the one community that raises the question of justice. It is the one community that raises those questions that force the reflecting self to weigh and balance all the demands placed on it by its diverse roles so as to recognize and embrace that socioecological balance that will best allow it to respect the human dignity of others in every social context of its life. This it does by weighing and balancing its diverse roles to promote a complex moral balance in its sociolinguistic ecology that does justice to human dignity in all its social contexts.

Contrary to MacIntyre, human rights claims cannot simply be dismissed as fictions invented to counter bureaucratic imperialism. On the contrary they are an expression of our deepest religious and ethical insights concerning the status of the stranger. Our problem is not, as MacIntyre appears to suggest, that we no longer all share the same story as in the days before Babel. A human rights ethic does not require narrative uniformity. It requires only that our diverse stories make a place for the stranger. Indeed, as I have been arguing, human rights ethics are best promoted not by narrative uniformity but narrative diversity. The diversity of Babel is not a curse but a promise: a promise that can be realized through a process Jeffrey Stout calls *moral bricolage*. A *bricoleur* is one who creatively makes use of what ever is at hand. "All great works of creative ethical thought . . . involve moral *bricolage*. . . . Take Aquinas, . . . his real accomplishment was to bring together into a single whole a wide assortment of fragments— Platonic, Stoic, Pauline, Jewish, Islamic, Augustinian, and Aristotelian."[67] Although I think there could be more theoretical clarity to this process of *bricolage* than Stout's pragmatism offers, I do not find myself in disagreement with his basic premise: The secularization of language in the naked public square enables individuals using a variety of religious and non-religious ethical languages, drawn from diverse layers of our historical heritage (e.g., the Reformation, Renaissance, Enlightenment and Romantic periods), to forge a public order where persuasion and compromise replace warfare as a way of dealing with differences.

When it comes to discussing ethics and human rights in the naked public square, he suggests, *bricolage* can produce a very creative and functional linguistic *creole*.

> Our secularized language of human rights seems in fact to have begun as what the linguist call *pidgin*—a sparse dialect used entirely for communicating with members of other groups, nobody's native tongue or first language of deliberation but a handy mode of discourse with strangers. But what used to be a pidgin can undergo further development, catch on as a language to be learned in infancy, and function as a subtle medium for deliberation and discourse with friends and family. Linguists call such a language a *creole*. A creole can become, over time, as rich a moral language as one could want—drawing vocabularies from diverse sources and weaving them together, if all goes well, into a tapestry well-suited to the needs of a time and place. Need we reduce our moral discourse to Esperanto or confine ourselves to the scant conceptual resources of a pidgin to make the language of human rights our own? Not if we can give it a place within a language sufficiently rich and coherent to meet our needs.[68]

The language and ethic of human rights that I have been envisioning approximates Stout's proposal. But the creole that I imagine would continue to be viable only if it acted as a bridge between particular traditions and their stories and not as a replacement for them. To Stout's credit he recognizes the ethical discourse of the naked public square must have a place within it for religious dialects as well as secular. "If we want to understand our fellow citizens," he says (speaking for the "secularist" perspective), "—whether they be Dorothy Day, Martin Luther King, Jr., Jerry Falwell, the Roman Catholic Bishops, Mario Cuomo, or Elie Wiesel—we had better develop the means for understanding the moral languages, including the theological ones, in which they occasionally address us and in which their deliberation is couched."[69] One might add that the reverse is true also. Those who speak out of religious narrative traditions need to be able to hear and understand those who speak out of secular stories as well. For this to happen, the religious fundamentalism that characterizes many religious communities and the secular fundamentalism that pervades the naked public square will both have to be desacralized and replaced with a secular holiness that welcomes strangers and the diversity of story and tradition they bring with them. The utopian promise of Babel lies neither in a secular uniformity nor a sacred uniformity but in the possibilities for self-transcendence that occur when we welcome strangers into the public square even though welcoming them is likely to change and transform us.

The kind of creole Stout seems to have in mind is well illustrated by the cross-cultural human rights ethic whose emergence we reviewed in the last chapter. This ethic, symbolized by the convergence we found in the ethics of Gandhi and Martin Luther King, Jr., is the product of a long history of interaction between narrative traditions, East and West, that has resulted in a powerful ethic of audacity on behalf of the stranger. Indeed, I believe the ethical creole emerging out of this multicultural and multireligious narrative history is capable of embracing both religious and secular ethics to reveal the utopian promise of Babel in a unified yet pluralistic response to the silent voice that commands from Auschwitz and Hiroshima—Never Again.

A Utopian Vision: Narrative Ethics in a MAD World

Beyond the Naked Public Square

The Paradox of Relativism and Absolutism

Lewis Mumford began his book *The City in History* by observing that urbanization began with "a city which was symbolically a world" and seems to have culminated, in our time, in "a world that has become, in many practical aspects, a city."[1] The modern cosmopolitan city of an emerging world culture, I have argued, is uniquely characterized by the *naked public square*, which Richard Neuhaus defines as "that public space which is free of any direct control or influence by religious belief and authority." Neuhaus's definition brings to mind Harvey Cox's vision of *The Secular City*. In premodern societies, a single commonly shared (although typically syncretistic) sacred canopy of myth and ritual created a common public world and shaped public order. In such societies heresy was a public crime because it was destructive of public order. Harvey Cox once argued that the secularizing power of the biblical tradition shattered the absolute religious beliefs that generated intolerance in premodern societies, giving rise to a liberating secular pluralism. The shattering of these absolutes, he argued, was a humanizing process that relativized and privatized religious beliefs and created a new spirit of unity-in-diversity, of community and pragmatic cooperation in the secular city. To others, however, the unity of the premodern world, now broken and shattered by modern technology and urbanization, seems like a tragic loss. Richard Neuhaus, like Alasdair MacIntyre, appears to mourn the coming of Babel and the passing of a world governed by a commonly shared story.

"The naked public square," says Neuhaus, " is the result of political doctrine and practice that would exclude religion and religiously grounded values from the conduct of public business. The doctrine is that America is a secular society. It finds dogmatic expression in the ideology of secularism. . . . The doctrine is demonstrably false and the dogma exceedingly dangerous."[2] The privatization Cox once applauded as making unity-in-diversity possible Neuhaus condemns as an illusory pluralism created at the expense of removing religion and all religious diversity from the public realm. Whereas separation of religion and politics (or church and state) is as ancient as the prophets, the naked public square is a modern invention created to deal with religious diversity (i.e., the problem of many churches-religions within one state). It emerged largely as a result of hard lessons learned from the religious wars fought in Europe as a consequence of the religious pluralism created by the Protestant Reformation. Religious intolerance and religious fanaticism forced the emergence of the secular state to create a neutral framework for peaceful coexistence among diverse religious communities. Radical religious-political fanaticism, Neuhaus conceded, leaves little space for the rational argumentation and compromise necessary for self-governing communities. Nevertheless, "the case can be made that the great social and political devastations of our century have been perpetrated by regimes of militant secularism, notably those of Hitler, Stalin, and Mao. That is true, and it suggests that the naked public square is a dangerous place. When religious transcendence is excluded, when the public square has been swept clean of divisive sectarianisms, the space is opened to seven demons aspiring to transcendent authority. As with a person so also with a society, the last condition is worse than the first."[3] The paradox, as Neuhaus sees it, is that the naked public square as a purely secular sociopolitical form of social order creates a moral and spiritual vacuum, whose pluralistic relativism invites new and more viciously totalitarian types of secular-religious absolutism. In the modern period, we are told, the most powerful example of a "consistently denuded public square" has been, "Red Square in Moscow. . . . Because the naked square cannot remain naked, the direction is toward the state-as-church, toward totalitarianisms."[4]

It is impossible to keep religion and politics from mixing, argues Neuhaus, therefore "the question is whether we can devise forms for that interaction which can revive rather than destroy the liberal democracy that is required by a society that would be pluralistic and free."[5] The liberal and mainline Christian churches, he suggests, have gone too far toward accommodating themselves to the secular order by privatizing their religious and moral convictions in the name of tolerance and public order. As a result they remove the public dimension from the Gospel story and render it irrelevant to public life. Whatever the criticisms one might wish to level against the Evangelical and Fundamentalist churches and their insistence on a "Christian America," he argues, still one must give them credit for not surrendering to the privatization of the Gospel story. For them the Gospel remains a public story capable of shaping public order. The problem with the "religious Right" is not that it wishes to see a public role for religion, specifically Christianity, but that its understanding of religious truth is authoritarian and arbitrary and cannot be held accountable to public reason. Much of the rhetoric coming from this direction reduces religious-ethical injunctions to irrational taboos.

In *After Virtue*, Alasdair MacIntyre suggests that the reduction of morality to taboos is a sign of our immersion in a sea of ethical relativism. In *Ethics After Babel*, Jeffrey Stout tries to understand and recover the moral logic of taboos.[6] Once one understands the difference between experiences of the sacred and experiences of the holy, however, it becomes clear that the morality of irrational taboos is a direct expression of the sacred. For, although the holy unites faith and reason through its surrender to doubt and the questions, the sacred is fiercely antirational, declaring its truths as divinely given and unquestionable. When the sacral imagination shapes the public witness of religious communities the results can be both comic and tragic. Neuhaus sums up the typical outcome well: "The stature of 'prophetic' leaders [of the religious Right], magnified by communications technology of all kinds, is not unlike that of those who in other cultures forecast future events by reading the entrails of doves and rats. Bible study is reduced to a kind of reading of entrails."[7]

But having said this does not eliminate the challenge which the Evangelical and Fundamentalist churches represent to the mainline and ecumenical traditions.

> By asserting the public nature of its truth claims, however, fundamentalism serves notice that it is not content to confine itself to the privatized sphere of religion. Those of us in the ecumenical churches who have traditionally railed against the bifurcation of the sacred from the secular and who have insisted that religion cannot remain captive to the personal or private sphere should not now reverse field and charge that fundamentalism's public assertiveness is an assault upon democratic pluralism. Such a reversal would put us in subordinate alliance with secularist proponents of the very privatization of religion that we have rightly criticized. Our quarrel with politicized fundamen-

talism is not that it has broken the rules of the game by "going public" with Christian truth claims. Christian truth, if it is true, is public truth. It is accessible to public reason. It impinges upon public space. At some critical points of morality and ethics it speaks to public policy. [8]

The quarrel then should not be about the public nature of religious claims but about the relation between faith and reason.

Neuhaus put the quarrel between religious advocates of public policy and their secular opponents in terms of Tillich's contrast between religious *heteronomy* and secular Enlightenment *autonomy*. The goal should be to move the discussion beyond these opposites and into the realm of *theonomy*. Beyond the dichotomy of "authoritarian" and "autonomous," says Neuhaus, is the "authoritative," which is, "the free acknowledgment of that by which we are bound."[9] In a relativistic world of autonomous reasoning (where every thinker is a law unto himself or herself) the resulting uncertainty tempts us to seek for certainty and create that certainty, if necessary, by an arbitrary leap that makes some relative position absolute. Only a recognition of the authoritative can undermine that outcome by demonstrating that there is, what I would call, a *provisional* or *utopian* public order of truth as an unfolding process that calls us to a self-transcendence that can carry us beyond "the authoritarian claims of both fundamentalist religion and secular culture."[10] What is needed is a theonomous or authoritative public ethic.

The answer, for Neuhaus, is the reconstruction of a

"sacred canopy" for the American experiment. Such a moral legitimation does not mean declaring that the way things are is legitimate. . . . Moral legitimation means providing a meaning and a purpose, and therefore a framework within which the violation of that meaning and purpose can be criticized. The vision that is required cannot be produced by the political process itself. Politics derives its directions from the ethos, from the cultural sensibilities that are the context of political action. The cultural context is shaped by our moral judgments and intuitions about how the world is and how it ought to be. Again, for the great majority of Americans such moral judgments and intuitions are inseparable from religious belief. Perhaps this is true not just of the majority but of all of us, whether or not we call our ultimate values religious. In any event, whether it is called the Judeo-Christian ethic, or Christianity, or the operative social values, or a civil religion, it is the dynamic of religion that holds the promise of binding together (*religare*) a nation in a way that may more nearly approximate *civitas*.[11]

Neuhaus's terminology here, which alludes to Peter Berger's characterization of traditional societies as legitimated by a religious narrative or *sacred canopy*, suggests a desire to return to a premodern sacred cosmological social order. And yet that is not quite what he has in mind. For he is advocating neither a legitimation of "the way things are" nor the elimination of pluralism.

Neuhaus, it seems, is arguing that our choices are not restricted to the collectivist sacred canopy of traditional cosmological societies and the individualist naked public square of modern secular society. Both, he suggests, lead to a totalitarianism that cannot tolerate pluralism and the questioning of its political order. It seems as if these options confront us with either a totalitarianism of the sacred or a totalitarianism of the secular. In both cases we are offered a false pluralism, either of *religious syncretism* (so long as each conforms to the overarching sacred cosmology and negates the secular) or of *secular syncretism* (so long as each conforms to secular values by either negating or privatizing the religious). Our situation being the latter, we are confronted by a religious and moral vacuum created by the relativism of the naked public square. This vacuum destabilizes democracy, creating the hunger for absolutes that makes the religious and political Right seem attractive.

"Fearing a religiously oppressive public square," Neuhaus argues that Americans who react to the religious Right "find themselves supporting a naked public square, when what they really want is a theonomous public square."[12] Theonomy presents us with a third option, one that transcends both absolutism (heteronomy) and relativism (autonomy). A theonomous culture, Neuhaus suggests, provides a "sacred canopy" that legitimates a social order without legitimating either a sacred totalitarian society or a profane public square. Because, as he argues, no society can exist without a sacred canopy, our best option is to choose to be guided by a sacred canopy that values both pluralism and the self-questioning made possible through the theonomous conjunction of faith and reason. The kind of religious vision of public order needed is one that both allows for a genuine pluralism (including both the religious and non-religious) and at the same time gives provisional legitimacy to the social order even as it continuously calls it into question. Neuhaus calls on ecumenical Christianity to respond to the challenge of both secularism and the religious Right and construct the middle path of authoritative (i.e., theonomous) religion as the sacred canopy of the modern public square.

Neuhaus rightly distrusts the sacred aura of unquestionability that attaches itself to the values of a secular society. "In the naked public square there is no agreed-upon authority that is higher than the community itself. There is no publicly recognizable source for . . . criticism nor check upon . . . patriotism. Therefore criticism becomes impossible and patriotism unsafe."[13] Thus, he argued, rather than remove all reference to religion from the public square, we would do better to affirm that we are "One nation under God"— meaning, "under the judgment of God." To make such an affirmation means that we acknowledge "that there is a transcendent point of reference to which we as a people are accountable. . . . We can consent to the finite claims made upon us . . . because we have first consented to a claim that is infinite. We can consent to the *civitas* because we know it is not our ultimate home."[14]

Effective opposition to totalitarianism, Neuhaus argues, requires institutional pluralism. This argument has merit, provided that the institutional pluralism advocated is not a pure egoistic, interest-group pluralism. For that kind of pluralism can be as destructive and dehumanizing as totalitarianism. For pluralism to protect human dignity each institution must be rooted in the theonomous surrender to the questions and openness to the stranger that gives rise to an ethic of audacity. Both secular theonomous institutions and religious holy communities must demand that we weigh and balance all the institutional demands that structure our life to find that balance of justice which permits us (as individuals and as a society) to remain open to the questions and the stranger. Such a complex institutional ecology checks the power of the state and protects human freedom and dignity. Theonomous pluralism is the context for the nurturance of conscience and the creation of a public order that transcends techno-bureaucratic political order and establishes the parameters of public policy. Private conscience, says Neuhaus, "is communal ." "As for 'the public conscience,' it is a categorical fallacy. . . . 'The Public' does not have a conscience. 'The People' does not have a conscience. Only persons and persons-in-community have consciences. . . . There is a growing awareness of the limits of the political, a recognition that most of the things that matter most are attended to in communities that are not government and should not be governmentalized. . . . Far from this being a process of reprivatization, it is an expansion of our understanding of what is public. We are no longer content to let 'public' be synonymous with 'government.'"[15] The kind of religion we need in charge of the public square is the kind that neither legitimates nor delegitimates the political order as such but rather claims public space for the nongovernmental and refuses to allow public policy to be reduced to political bureaucratic policy.

In arguing for institutional pluralism, Neuhaus is appealing to the two-kingdom tradition of Christian ethics, especially those versions that have promoted the rich institutional pluralism which has undergirded the democratic experiment. However, he hedges this affirmation of pluralism with a certain nostalgia for the sacred canopy of the Christendom of an earlier day. He affirms pluralism but seems to continue to wish to see the Christian churches as somehow the first among equals. "The church is the particular society within society that bears institutional witness to the transcendent purpose to which society is held accountable."[16] The pluralism of the churches in American culture, Neuhaus argues, is itself a safeguard against the identification of church and state—an identification that would only result in the collapse of Christianity back into the cosmological mode of religion. Nevertheless, he is still offering us a vision of Christian hegemony, in which Christianity is to again provide the sacred canopy for the public square.

Neuhaus is aware that this might justifiably make non-Christians nervous. In his own way he argues against a sacral ethic and for something approximating an ethic of the holy—an ethic of audacity on behalf of strangers. Thus he argues that the Christian two-kingdom tradition must face up to the history of Christian anti-Judaism. When Jews hear the words "Christian America" or "Christian Civilization," he says, they cannot help but see visions of "barbed wire." If a Christian sacred canopy is to be viable in America, Neuhaus argues, Jews are going to have to be reassured that it will be a different sacred canopy than that of previous generations. The ultimate barrier to the temptation of the church to monopolize power, he argues, must be "a thoroughly internalized Christian understanding of the continuing importance and theological status of living Judaism."[17] If a trusting cooperative link with Judaism can be achieved, then "the religious freedom of those outside the Judeo-Christian consensus is best protected by grounding such freedom in that consensus. . . . Terms such as 'minorities,' and 'the marginal' have a high moral status in our society. Ironically, this too is deeply rooted in the Judeo-Christian tradition. Biblical justice is obsessively concerned with . . . the 'orphans and widows and fatherless children.' Special attention must be paid to 'the stranger within thy gates.'"[18]

Although Neuhaus's suggestions are useful, the centrality he wishes to give to the role of the Christian story for the public square, given the past history of Christian imperialism, is not likely to put non-Christians at ease. Although they are not far apart in their positions, non-Christian's I think would rightfully prefer Michael Novak's position to that of Neuhaus. For unlike Neuhaus, Novak argues that there must always be "a 'reverential emptiness' at the heart of the social order."[19] In his view there should be no overarching sacred canopy in American society, only a plurality of smaller canopies. For him, this is as it should be. "Many regard the emptiness at the heart of pluralism as a flaw," he argues. "Its consequences among individuals are looked upon as illnesses: anomie, alienation, loneliness, despair, loss of meaning, etc. But all this is an attempt to judge pluralism by a standard appropriate to a traditional sense of order."[20] By the standard of the cosmological order of pre-modern societies that offered people a secure sense of identity, purpose, and meaning, modern society may seem a poor trade. The anomie, the alienation, the crisis of meaning to which Novak refers are the consequences of urban individuation, which make possible the self-transcendence through which individuals are able to call themselves and their cultures into question. Hence, these experiences, Novak argues, "may be regarded from a quite different point of view. . . as the necessary other side of any genuine experience of liberty. For if in relationship to the values and symbols of my family, my church, and my culture, I am free to ask such radical questions as 'alienate' me from them, it does not follow that I am ill, misused, or deranged. The human capacity to raise questions is testimony to our capacities for the more than finite. . . . The human spirit is not imprisoned by the realities of its culture."[21]

Novak rightly views the desire to reconstruct a sacred canopy over American society as a kind of nostalgia for prebiblical cosmological forms of order. The role of the biblical tradition in creating the modern secular pluralistic society, however, makes it entirely appropriate that the center of society be empty of all idols, that is, of all legitimating images. He argues,

> In a genuinely pluralistic society, there is no one sacred canopy. *By intention* there is not. At its spiritual core, there is an empty shrine. That shrine is left empty in the knowledge that no one word, image, or symbol is worthy of what all seek there. Its emptiness, therefore, represents the transcendence which is approached by free consciences from a virtually infinite number of

directions. (Aquinas once wrote that humans are made in the image of God but that since God is infinite He may be mirrored only through a virtually infinite number of humans. No concept of Him is adequate.) Believer and unbeliever, selfless and selfish, frightened and bold, naive and jaded, all participate in an order whose *center* is not socially imposed.[22]

In Novak's view, "God" functions as an "empty" but important symbol in the American political and cultural tradition. Our constitution says that human beings are endowed by their creator with inalienable rights. But such official statements are not intended to "embarrass or to compromise those who do not believe in God. They have a pluralistic content."[23] No group or person or institution can enforce their understanding on all others. In terms of the argument I have been formulating, we could say the Declaration of Independence exhibits a type of secular holiness. By tying or binding (*religare*) human dignity and the infinite (i.e., the imageless God in whose image we are created) together, it opens up the opportunity to affirm a singular truth in either secular terms (i.e., human dignity) or in religious terms (endowed by our Creator).

> These words [God, Creator, etc.,] are like pointers, which each person must define for himself. Their function is to protect the liberty of conscience of all, by using a symbol which transcends the power of the state and any other earthly power. Such symbols are not quite blank; one may not fill them in with any content at all. They point beyond worldly power. Doing so, they guard the human openness to transcendence. . . . The values and habits required to maintain this transcendent center, however, entail a spirit of cooperation, mutuality, and common striving. A "sacred canopy" of this sort—practical rather than creedal—allows for unity in practice, diversity in belief. . . . Like the dark night of the soul . . . this desert [the emptiness of the naked public square] has an indispensable purpose. It is maintained out of respect for the diversity of human consciences, perceptions and intentions. It is swept clean out of reverence for the sphere of the transcendent, to which the individual has access through the self, beyond the mediations of social institutions. The domain of the transcendent, of course, is mediated by literature, religion, family, and fellows. But it is finally centered in the silence in each person. . . . Humans are not . . . fully plumbed by the institutions in which they dwell.

> Each experiences a solitariness and personal responsibility which renders him (or her) oddly alone in the midst of solidarity. . . . It is because individuals are capable of the experience of nothingness—that is, able to raise questions about all schemes of community, order, purpose, and meaning, and able to choose in darkness—that individuals have inalienable rights.[24]

Although this statement affirms individual conscience, it is not a statement that supports an unadulterated individualism but rather insists on a communal pluralism. Like Neuhaus, Novak also argues for the importance of institutional pluralism as a limit on political authority and as essential for the protection of human dignity. The freedom to create communities and thus institutional diversity, especially through voluntary associations, is understood to limit the authority of the state by refusing to surrender all public space to political authority. Public space is claimed for the life of communities—space that is largely free of direct political intervention.

Both Neuhaus and Novak agree that, far from individualistic freedom, we are talking about the freedom for community—communities in which individuality, interdependence, and ethical conscience are shaped by unique narrative traditions. The reclaiming of public order as a reality that transcends political authority and to which political authority is answerable is what makes institutional pluralism a fence about the secular holiness of human dignity, especially in a technological civilization. Still, it would be wrong to gloss over the difference between Neuhaus and Novak. As Neuhaus puts it:

> While agreeing with much of Novak's argument, one must raise a serious question about the "emptiness" at the heart of the public order. Such emptiness is very close to the idea of the naked public square. Novak speaks of virtue being "socially imposed," of its "public enforcement." But the democratic interplay of substantive moral discourse need not be coercive. . . . Democratic persuasion, not emptiness is the alternative to coercion. The sense of transcendence that in its beginning and to this day marks the American experiment in democracy is not contentless. Both historically and in present sociological fact, it is religiously specific, it refers to the Judeo-Christian tradition. The acknowledgement of this reality is in the most particular interest of the considerable number of Americans who do not

subscribe to that tradition in any conscious manner. And that is because it is precisely by the authority of that tradition that the rights to dissent are protected.[25]

Despite this statement, Neuhaus and Novak are not as far apart as Neuhaus makes it seem. I think Novak is right to see the emptiness of the naked public square as the appropriate social symbol for the human dignity of beings created in the image of an imageless God. But I do not think we are forced to make the choice Neuhaus offers between dialogue and emptiness. In the biblical tradition the God who is without image is precisely the God who can be encountered only through the word. Emptiness or imagelessness and the word belong together. Through their conjunction human community emerges as a unity-in-diversity that respects the dignity of the other as other, that is, as a stranger who represents the transcendence of the Wholly Other (whether that be the Imageless God of Jews and Christians or the Emptiness of Buddhists). Novak's emptiness at the heart of the naked public square, it is clear, is not a vacuous emptiness. It is a symbolic emptiness, a witness to transcendence. As such it is a canopy. Yet it is not a canopy of the sacred but of the holy—open to both the Wholly Other and the holy other.

As an expression of the holy, this canopy places sacred public order under the judgment of a transcendent Ought as the "unseen measure" of human dignity—a measure that forces the recognition that the social order is made for humans and not humans for the social order. This is precisely the kind of canopy Neuhaus is calling for, one capable of both allowing for pluralism and continually calling the present order of society into question in the name of human dignity and human rights. But for it to be a holy canopy, it must remain far more empty than Neuhaus seems prepared to grant. The symbolic power of the emptiness of the naked public square as a possible model for a global civilization lies in the overlapping narratives of holy communities, East and West. Although this emptiness draws directly upon biblical symbolism, it is not alien to the Buddhist sangha traditions of Asia. What Sinai and the Bo Tree have in common, for all the diversity of their stories, is the insistence on the *imagelessness* and *emptiness* as the appropriate symbols evoking at one and the same time both ultimate transcendence and human interdependence. Likewise, the Christian understanding of God as trinity, like a Zen *koan*, defeats the imagination and reaffirms that God is without image, even as it concurs with Sinai and the Bo Tree in affirming that transcendence occurs not through individualism but through interdependence (i.e., the unity-in-diversity of three persons in one).

The Empty Square as a Global Model for Unity-in-Diversity

The purpose of reviewing this debate between Neuhaus and Novak on the role of religion in public policy in a secular society has not been specifically to address the problem of religion and public policy in America, but to see its import for the larger question of religion and public policy in an emerging global civilization. And that is precisely the focus that Max Stackhouse gives these issues in *Creeds, Society and Human Rights*. There he also argues that institutional pluralism provides the social ecology necessary for the protection of human dignity against all encroachments of sacred order. While admitting that Christendom as a whole was more often than not an oppressor rather than protector of human freedom and dignity, still, he suggests, there is an important exception—a minority free-church tradition, persecuted in Europe, which fled to the New World in defense of its freedom and dignity. This tradition, and its secular analogue, the liberal tradition spearheaded by John Locke (himself a child of the Puritan tradition), has championed human freedom and dignity. This tradition, he suggests, gave rise to the rights tradition that underlies the American Declaration of Independence which was in turn a powerful model for the UN Declaration.

At the end of a detailed historical and sociological cross-cultural comparative analysis of America, India, and East Germany, Stackhouse concludes that, although a human rights ethic must be formulated cross-culturally and interreligiously, still, the Christian minority tradition he has identified, and its model of the holy community, provides a better model of creed and social order for the protection of human rights than either the Hindu caste system or the Marxist social order under single-party rule. Stackhouse uses the term *holy community* to describe any social order and its legitimating myth or public narrative. But if we analyze his conclusions in terms of our distinction between a sacred society and a holy community the force of his argument becomes clearer. In effect what Stackhouse is saying is that a cosmological social order with its single-kingdom ethic is not adequate for the protection of human dignity. A two-kingdom ethic is required, one that introduces an anthropological desacralizing ethic of the holy and places it in dialectical tension with the sacred social order. Of the three societies, only the American model is structured to permit and even encourage the presence of autonomous alternate communities within its boundaries. The Christian free-church tradition's creed and ecclesiology, he argues, provided the model for an institutionally pluralistic democratic society based on the right of free association in such alternate communities, and this best provides the institutional structures necessary to safeguard human freedom and dignity.

> The social space defended by the church over the centuries has now broadened to allow a wider range of "voluntary associations," interested groups, dissenting committees, experimental associations, opposition parties, and "private assemblies." This is of considerable importance in human rights discussions, for it is precisely in these organizations that the competing doctrines of human rights are hammered out, and it is from these centers that governmental policies, economic structures, and familial and personal understandings are influenced. Where the space for these organizations is constricted, torture, political imprisonment, economic deprivation, intellectual and cultural constraint, and religious repression dominate and dehumanize life. . . . In . . . [Marxist and Hindu] societies, to live outside a prescribed family pattern or beyond the prescriptions of the political party is to live a very precarious existence. There is little "social space" for membership and communal life beyond kinship and *polis*.[26]

The key question for human rights, says Stackhouse, is "What *social* relationships are constitutive of *individual* dignity."[27] Both the hierarchical order of the caste system and the totalitarian order of the Communist party severely restrict this freedom to form alternate communities, and as a result both tend to prefer the language of duty to the language of rights, for the language of duty, contrary to the rights tradition, provides the legitimation for sacrificing the individual to the good of social order.

Stackhouse has touched on a crucial dimension of the human rights issue—the sociological. We can recall Richard Rubenstein's pessimistic challenge to human rights. Human rights claims, he argued, seem to make no practical difference. Even if all religions could agree in championing human rights, who would enforce them? He seemed to suggest that a right which cannot be enforced is no right at all. For Rubenstein, the only rights that matter are civil rights. "To the extent that men have rights, they have them only as members of the polis" he argued; and no commonwealth of nations functions as a political equivalent to protect human dignity.[28] The argument Stackhouse is making, and with which I concur, is that the championing of human rights cannot be safely left to nations. Rubenstein would agree but sees no practical alternative. Stackhouse rightly sees that the alternative is a complex social ecology of autonomous alternate communities.

A complex social ecology is the foundation for an effective ethical ecology. This ecology, however, is no panacea. Hitler's first act on taking power was his policy of *Gleichschaltung*, which was precisely the destruction of the autonomy of all such communities and associations and their integration into a unified Nazi polity. This, however, only teaches us the importance of such communities and the need (learning from hindsight) to see that under no conditions should a political community grant such sweeping powers to its leaders. And it is important to remember that Hitler was *granted* the emergency powers to make these "temporary" changes. Although I think Stackhouse is correct in his emphasis on the importance of institutional pluralism as guaranteed by the rights of free assembly and free speech, he does not give sufficient due to the importance of the synagogue as a model of the holy community and also downplays the problem that the history of Christian anti-Judaism presents for his thesis that the Christian *ecclesia* is the best model for institutional pluralism. Had the church historically affirmed the presence of the synagogue as an alternate holy community within the society of Christendom, that would have been decisive proof of Stackhouse's thesis. But not even the free church tradition provides such an inspiring record with regard to the Jews. In retrospect, one would have to say that the true holy community of Christendom was not the church but the synagogue. The synagogue provided the social space in which the witness to transcendence as other could occur. Were it not for the synagogue, Medieval Europe would have been a completely closed society. Stackhouse also argues that the appropriate model of the holy community that protects human dignity would be one that is self-critical and that Christianity provides a better model for this than either the Hindu caste system or the Communist party. Given this comparison, he is probably correct. However, I have argued that the Jewish narrative tradition of audacity (chutzpah) provides a much stronger ethic for questioning sacred authority, whether human or divine.

Given his choice of comparisons, Buddhism does not come up for discussion in *Creeds, Society and Human Rights*. Clearly the sangha also provides a model of a self-questioning holy community that values institutional pluralism. Elsewhere, Stackhouse does discuss Buddhism and dismisses it as otherworldly, asocial, and individualistic and thus utterly incapable of generating a social ethic.[29] He seems to be a victim of Weber's stereotypical view of Buddhism. The creation of the sangha as an alternate community is as important to the history of religions in Asia as the creation of the synagogue (and the church modeled on the synagogue) is to Mediterranean-European culture. In each case the holy community introduced a dimension of transcendence into the larger society through the creation of a two-realm ethic. Unlike the early Hindu tradition of the forest dwellers out of which it emerged, the Buddhist tradition rapidly abandoned the individualistic pattern of the lonely seeker and developed a communal life. Whereas the Hindu tradition allowed for the shramanic path, which permitted the solitary figure to break free of the caste order by leaving society to enter the forest, this option did not in any way call the social order into question. It was rather a safety valve, the permitted exception that reinforced the normativity of the caste order of society. The Buddhist sangha, however, was a public and forceful presence, an alternate community living an alternate way of life in the world, one that called the Brahmanic vision of Hindu society into question.

The sangha, as Trevor Ling, has pointed out,[30] was a unique social invention probably modeled on the tribal republican political structures of the clans in Northern India, including the Shakya clan of Siddhartha. These tribal republics or sanghas, which were gradually being replaced by larger monarchical political systems, were self-governing bodies. The internal structure of the monastic community, following this model, took the form of a democratic republic or representative democracy, in which each monk had an equal vote. This inner structure expressed the Buddhist consciousness of the equality of all selves and stood in stark contrast to hierarchical and monarchical structure of the larger caste-structured society of India.

The force of the Buddha's teaching was to call into question all claims to authority, whether sacred or profane. "'Go ye forth,' said the Buddha to his disciples, 'I am delivered from all fetters, human and divine [i.e., profane and sacred]. Ye are also delivered from all fetters human and divine. Go ye now and wander for the gain of the many . . . out of compassion for the world."[31] According to the Buddhist logician Dharmakirti (seventh century C.E.) the cultural climate of India in the time of the Buddha was characterized by "the unquestioned authority of the Vedas" and the "arrogant division into castes." In response, the Buddha taught the questioning of all authority, including his own: "Just as the experts test gold by burning it, cutting it and applying it on a touchstone, my statements should be accepted only after critical examination and not out of respect for me."[32]

As with the Buddha's teachings, so the community was rooted in a radical questioning of all belief systems and all authority. As Ling points out, the Buddha refused to leave definitive instructions for the order, only the command "be ye lamps unto yourselves."[33] The Buddhist Vinaya, in the canonical literature of the Tripitaka, contains the laws and regulations for self-governance of the community. These laws provide a kind of anarchistic principle of schism in Buddhist self-rule, whereby if a sangha divides into factions that cannot agree, they are to separate and start separate sanghas.

As Ling describes it, the sangha would qualify as a kind of utopian community for, he says, "the Buddhist sangha might be seen, . . . in the context of the fifth century B.C., as the prototype social organization of the future," whose purpose was to reverse the rampant individualism of the new urbanized self.[34] The Buddha, says Robert Thurman, "led a nonviolent revolution by founding his 'Holy Community' (*Aryasamgha*) as a distinct social world within the larger society. . . . So the Buddhist community and the larger society were always in tension."[35] The separation of Buddhists into an alternate community meant that Buddhists were forced to work out an ethic for two realms, that is, a two-kingdom ethic through which to understand the relation of the sangha to the larger society.

Although Stackhouse seems to overlook the social dimension of Buddhism, I would concede part of his point; namely, that unlike the synagogue and the church, the Buddhist sangha does not seem to have functioned as a model for the incorporation of secular institutions and the development of institutional pluralism the way the traditions of the holy community have in Western civilization. However, even here the credit should be given more to Judaism than to Christianity.

The singleminded persistence of the Jews in remaining a *separate* or *holy* community marks the inauguration of a process of institutional pluralism that has fostered human rights in Western culture. The synagogue is the first holy community to achieve legal incorporation. Incorporation is a social invention whereby communities of individuals claimed autonomous control over aspects of their own lives (political, economic, educational, religious, etc.) vis-à-vis the state. Incorporation not only increases human productivity but human autonomy as well, by limiting the role of the state in social life and partitioning up areas of human need to be addressed by self-governing commu-

nities (professional, religious, civic, etc.). Incorporation is the fundamental social invention needed for the generation of the institutional
pluralism and citizen autonomy that makes democratic forms of government possible. Incorporation is a uniquely Western social invention, which by the late Medieval period included not only the professional guilds, but also free cities, the universities, and the churches.
Corporate charters were granted by political authority (e.g., nobles,
kings, the state) usually as a device for raising revenue (i.e., taxes).[36]
Thus corporations came to be legally defined as "artificial persons";
that is, as an artificial social body organized by permission of the state
for the accomplishment of a public purpose (good or service) through
the pursuit of private interest. Incorporation, therefore, is the means
whereby "private" and "public" realms were created, with their justification resting in the moral balance that was to be sustained between
private and public good.

   This history of incorporation as a limiting principle on the state,
which protects and promotes human autonomy and dignity within
alternate communities, has its origins in the legal autonomy achieved
by the Jewish community under the Romans. The legal agreement
between the Roman empire as an embodiment of cosmological order
and the Jewish community as an embodiment of anthropological
transcendence provides the prototype for the legal process of incorporation. Incorporation is a direct outgrowth of the distinction between synagogue and state that first emerged in the West in the
Roman empire with the privileged legal status allowed to the Jewish
community. Its further evolution can be traced through the continuing history of the synagogue and its refusal to be integrated into
Christendom, as well as through early apocalyptic Christianity as an
outgrowth of Judaism, which found its continuity in Benedictine monasticism.

   By the fourth century, Catholicism had emerged out of the peculiar conjunction of the church with Roman institutional structures
rooted in the cosmological-bureaucratic order. The result was
Christendom. The compromise of the church with the world became
the object of protest, giving rise to the eremetic and then monastic
tradition. In the West, the Benedictine communities were an attempt
within Christianity to embody the synagogal tradition of holiness or
separateness as a vehicle for the eschatological sanctification of the
world. It was this monastic tradition that served as the social carrier of
the tradition of incorporation out of Italy and into Northern Europe.

   In Benedictine monasticism we see the emergence of the prototype of the modern corporation. Here we find an artificial social body

(i.e., created by voluntary association rather than kinship) set apart from society and pursuing its private interests, which are understood to be for the public good. Rooted in an apocalyptic tradition of future-oriented hope for a new heaven and a new earth, the monastic community embodied a utopian understanding of itself as a prototype of things to come (i.e., the way society ought to be and would be in the Kingdom of God) and hence a model the rest of society should strive to emulate even in the present. In attempting to live out that vocational vision, the monks utilized Roman organizational techniques and linked them with the unique preoccupation of the Jewish and Christian traditions with time and the future, to form the first future-oriented institutions deliberately organized around the efficient use of time. In this they were motivated to create a productive society so as to permit the leisure to pray. With the organization of the day into the "hours," the Rule of Benedict may well be the prototype of the operations manual of the modern corporation. There are significant links between the Benedictine preoccupation with time, the invention of the mechanical clock (c. thirteenth century) to announce the hours for prayer in the monasteries and the cathedrals of Europe, and the modern time and motion studies of Frederick Taylor, which laid the foundations for contemporary management theory.

The monasteries, in pursuit of their "private interests" (i.e., interests not directly under the control of the state) as separated communities, ended up serving the public good, civilizing and transforming Europe with their agriculture and technology as well as their literate arts. In fact the decay that periodically occurred in the monastic movements was to a large degree the result of the very productivity and wealth their ascetic self-discipline created. Max Weber traced the heritage of this monastic paradox through the Calvinist wing of the Protestant Reformation, which secularized the monastic spirit, transforming it into the "spirit of capitalism."

Not only business corporations but also free cities, religious communities, educational societies, and professional societies, have their roots in this tradition of incorporation. The process that generated the modern corporation, the profession of management and our concept of the managerial society and public policy emerged out of the histories of the synagogue and the monastery through a process of secularization. This process included the fostering of a democratic ethos through the promotion of institutional pluralism and individual dignity and autonomy. And yet in saying this, we have to note an important difference between the monastery and the synagogue. Unlike the rabbinic tradition (or for that matter the Buddhist sangha) the monastic tradition and Christianity in general did not prize pluralism and autonomy. *Benedictine monasticism stands out in contrast by its emphasis on centralized authority and unquestioning obedience to the abbot.*[37]

Unlike monasticism in the Greek church, which generated its monastic converts from the lower classes, Benedictine monasticism attracted its converts largely from the Roman upper-class bureaucracy. With the collapse of the institutional order of Rome, these Roman managers found in the monastery (and in the Roman church at large) a new arena for their administrative talents. They seem to have introduced Roman authoritarian habits, which merged only too comfortably with the Christian understanding of faith as unquestioning obedience. The Cluniac reforms of the later Middle Ages (tenth century C.E.) stressed unconditional obedience to the abbot in an international model of centralized authority. The Cluniac model in turn became the model for the papacy in its successful efforts to centralize authority for the whole church in an unquestioning obedience to the Bishop of Rome. It is out of these reforms that the papacy reached the height of its power in the twelfth and thirteenth centuries, a period that saw the invention and growth of the Inquisition to suppress all dissidents, aliens, and heretics.

In this respect both the Buddhist sangha and the Jewish synagogue handled the question of authority and obedience more democratically than the Benedictine tradition and the Christian church. As Trevor Ling has argued, the early Buddhist sangha preferred diversity to ideological uniformity. Through its law of schism the sangha

> surrendered . . . ideological solidarity. Other political and religious institutions . . . have sometimes chosen the totalitarian way: formal organizational unity has been maintained at the expense of the rights of self-expression on the part of minority groups. . . . Any group which threatens the formal unity of the total organization has to be regarded as something alien. . . . In the Buddhist case, the inevitability of sectarian differences has been acknowledged, with the result that Buddhism has not experienced the internecine wars of religion that have characterized some other traditions where dissent or "heresy" has been something to be stamped out.[38]

In a manner similar to the Buddhist law of schism, the synagogue tradition of the rabbis affirmed human freedom, dignity, and autonomy by permitting, even authorizing human disagreement concerning Torah. As Irving Greenberg points out:

The prophets gave clear, unambiguous instruction from God. If two prophets disagreed about the divine mandate, one of the two was a false prophet. But if human judgment is the new source of understanding, then two Rabbis can come to different conclusions. The Talmud captures the uneasiness caused by this departure from the old certainty by stating that when the students of Hillel and Shammai did not serve their teachers properly, disagreements as to the law multiplied. People feared that the two school's opposing views could not coexist and therefore, one school's view must be false. After three years of anxiety, prayer and seeking divine guidance, a heavenly voice told them that "both views are the words of the living God." Since humans are being given more responsibility for leading Israel on its redemptive way, then it is right that there be more than one path to follow. For practical reasons, the majority decides which of the two paths shall be followed but the views of the minority are *not* wrong.[39]

Like the Buddhist sangha tradition, the rabbinic synagogue tradition values pluralism, freedom, and dignity both within and beyond the community. The synagogue tradition, however, offers a model more applicable to the democratic tradition of the West. The Buddhist principle of schism can work for religious communities in a way that is not practical for political communities. In the political realm a way must be found to incorporate both unity and diversity as in the rabbinic principal of rule by consensus while respecting the minority points of view. In the end the democratic tradition was more fully embodied within the rabbinic synagogue tradition than it was in Christendom.

The unique pattern of institutional history in the West helps to explain its imperialism and authoritarianism (which are hardly unique when compared the histories of other great civilizations such as India, China, and Japan) and also its counterhistory of institutional pluralism that made it an initiator in the proliferation (and secularization) of institutions protecting human dignity and human rights. Fortunately by the time the church had succeeded in institutionalizing the Cluniac model of unquestioning obedience to Rome in the thirteenth century c.e., the secularizing of power of institutional autonomy and diversity through the process of incorporation was well underway. Thus, the institutional pluralism of the newly incorporated free cities and universities, for example, was already undermining the papal claims to absolute authority. The seeds of institutional pluralism unleashed by the process of incorporation were decisive in creating the ethical ecology of institutional checks and balances necessary for sustaining the sense of human dignity, freedom, and autonomy typical of Western civilization.

To my knowledge, there is no Asian parallel to the history of incorporation in the West. In the West, rooted in the synagogue tradition, the priority of the lay over the monastic form of the holy community may partially explain the proliferation of communities of free association, but clearly external sociological forces of secularization also played a role. But it would be a missed opportunity to fail to see the potential ally these traditions have in the Buddhist sangha tradition. As Robert Thurman argues, "the principles of human rights were all there in the Buddha's earliest teachings, and he embodied them in the constitution of his *Aryasamgha* 'Holy Community' within the society. These principles often influenced the good among monarchs . . . but they never led to any sort of institutional democracy until modern times, which only happened then with outside help."[40] But then this is true of Christianity as well. Although Christian religious experience, through the "cunning of history," promoted secularization and institutional pluralism, the church did not welcome either of these developments. "Outside forces" were required. The Renaissance return to pre-Christian sources and the autonomy of new corporate institutions forced the church to accept this new order after a long and sometimes bloody struggle.

The Socio-Ecology of Emptiness

While I have serious reservations regarding Max Stackhouse's suggestion that Christianity offers the best model for a sacred canopy to sustain international human rights, I thoroughly concur with his insistence on the critical importance of institutional pluralism for the creation of a social ecology protective of human dignity. To illustrate his argument Stackhouse develops a chart of the diverse human needs that complex urban societies must meet through a process of institutional differentiation (see Figure 1). It is a model of the complex ethical ecology necessary for the protection of human rights which he uses to measure and compare civilizations.

Stackhouse's grid identifies nine areas of human need that a complex civilization must meet to protect human dignity. The argument here is not the one sometimes offered—that rights are based in needs. Just the opposite. Because of our inalienable human dignity,

FIGURE 1

A Map of Institutional Sectors of Society Based on Universal Human Needs

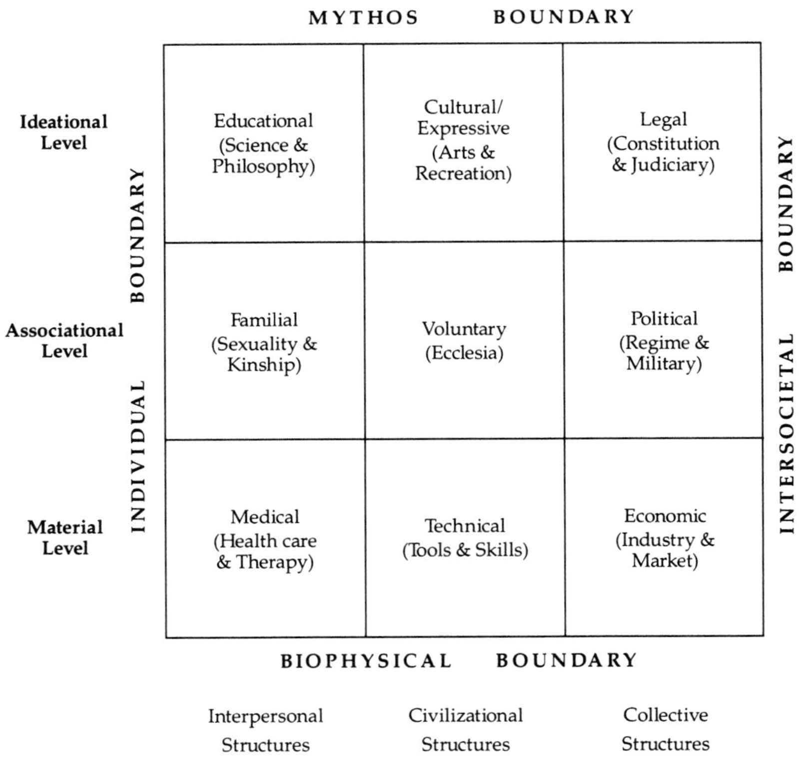
MYTHOS BOUNDARY
Ideational Level
Associational Level
Material Level
INDIVIDUAL BOUNDARY
Educational (Science & Philosophy)
Cultural/ Expressive (Arts & Recreation)
Legal (Constitution & Judiciary)
Familial (Sexuality & Kinship)
Voluntary (Ecclesia)
Political (Regime & Military)
Medical (Health care & Therapy)
Technical (Tools & Skills)
Economic (Industry & Market)
INTERSOCIETAL BOUNDARY
BIOPHYSICAL BOUNDARY
Interpersonal Structures
Civilizational Structures
Collective Structures

From *Creeds, Society and Human Rights: A Study in Three Cultures* by Max L. Stackhouse, © 1984 by William B. Eerdmans Publishing Co., Grand Rapids, Michigan, p. 18. Used by permisssion of the publisher.

these needs must be met. The nine areas are grouped into categories labeled *interpersonal, civilizational* and *collective,* respectively. Human needs in these three areas have to be met at three levels: *material, associational,* and *ideational*. The material level contains health needs, needs for technical skill, and economic needs. The next level up, the associational level, contains familial needs, needs for voluntary association, and political needs. Finally, the top level, the ideational, contains educational needs, cultural-expressive needs, and legal needs. The grid represents the social ecology of any complex urban society. As it is diagramed, the grid suggests that every society has four crucial boundaries: the biophysical, the mythological, the individual, and other societies.

This grid vividly depicts the ecology within which the dialectical tensions between the anthropological and the cosmological orders occur. Stackhouse notes that religion does not seem to fit into any particular category but rather is related to all and has had its primary location in different categories in different societies. I would argue that its location depends on whether we are focusing on a sacred society or holy community. In an urban cosmological society, religion provides an all-encompassing sacred canopy whose primary center of authority will be in the political category (e.g., sacred kingship, often in association with a sacred temple or priesthood). In such societies there may be a progressive bureaucratic differentiation of institutions, but they will not be autonomous. On the contrary, all will be integrated into, and answerable to, a sacred political authority that is heteronomous. The one category that will be absent in such societies will be the one at the very center of the grid, voluntary associations. But once an anthropological order is differentiated from the cosmological and socially embodied in a holy community, then a whole new category of voluntary associations made up of holy communities (both religious and secular) is created and with it a two-realm or two-kingdom ethic.

Once that differentiation occurs, a model is established that can be emulated within the other categories on the grid. When that happens, to put it in Tillich's terms, each activity moves beyond heteronomy to become theonomous, that is, open to self-transcendence. If this occurs, then the legal category moves beyond bureaucratic differentiation to become the locus of a community of professionals who answer not to the dictates of the state and its ruling elites but to the transcendent ideals of justice. Similarly, the political authority can be forced to decentralize its bureaucratic control by the formation of incorporated self-governing free cities, professional societies, citizens groups, and so on, guided by the transcendent ideals of freedom and justice. Education and the arts, in such a society, would be guided by a surrender to the questions rather than the dictates of sacred heteronomous authority (which would result only in propaganda). Families would provide the interpersonal ecology for the nurturance of human dignity and integrity. In such a society, health care would be not only for the elite, but for all who are in need. Technology and the economy would be similarly held accountable and guided by the demands of human dignity.

The final outcome of this type of differentiation is a complex social ecology of semiautonomous yet interdependent social spaces. Each of these spaces is devoted to ensuring the social embodiment of the measure of the human good as the measure of a good society, in which the good is measured by the implicit notion of transcendence contained in the modern consciousness of human dignity. These alternate communities are semiautonomous in that they are self governing and each one presents a partial limit to the state even as each interacts constructively with the state. They are interdependent in that each is oriented to ensuring that one particular area of human need is met, and therefore each depends on the others for the remaining human needs. And these associations are theonomous in their differentiated secularity to the degree that they remain faithful to the transcendent measure of human dignity, by keeping society open to the stranger. To the degree that these associations respond to the measure of human dignity, they represent what Irving Greenberg calls a holy secularity.

Modern society, with its plurality of institutions generates a plurality of selves (i.e., doubling). Every institutional context we step into demands that we generate a self (i.e., social role) to meet its demands. As a result modern individuals juggle a plurality of identities so that each one of us has an inner community of selves that mirrors the pluralism of the outer community in which we dwell. The demonic, as I have argued, emerges when these selves are bureaucratically compartmentalized so that the right hand pretends not to know what the left hand is doing. If we are to establish justice in the "outer" world we must find a way to establish justice in our "inner" world, where we struggle to balance our multiple role identities. The holy community promotes justice and compassion through the affirmation of otherness. It calls us to establish that ecological balance in our individual lives and in our communities that affirms our pluralistic interdependence so as to protect the human dignity of those we serve through every one of our role identities.

The other-centered questioning (i.e., questioning from the perspective of the stranger) of all our role-defined value commitments in the name of human dignity forces a differentiation in the public mythic narratives of a society, so that they no longer reflect only the values of the sacred narratives of cosmological order. The narratives of transcendence are placed in dialectical tension with the sacred order of society and break with the cosmological imagination by insisting that our humanity can never be captured or defined by (and reduced to) our socially defined roles. Our inalienable human dignity resides in the imagelessness or emptiness of the self. The holy community champions that transcendent dignity within the social order. The symbolic tension between cosmological and anthropological narratives in the symbolic realm of culture (i.e., the superstructure) is mirrored in a correlated social tension (in the infrastructure) between the sacred society and the holy community. This tension is created by the fact that the alternate mythos and ethos of the holy community forces a recognition of human dignity as the "unseen measure" of a just society. The reality of this "unseen measure" is manifest through openness to self-transcendence (i.e., to doubt and its questions) at the symbolic level and openness to the alien or stranger at the sociological level. A society into which this kind of tension is inserted will henceforth be forced to strike a balance between two alternate symbolic interpretations of itself. It will no longer be able to think of itself as only the sacred *cosmos writ small*. It will also be forced to recognize that the just society must also reflect *the human writ large*, where the measure of the human is the secular holiness of human dignity.

America as a nation made up of many nations represents a prototype of the problem of religion and political order in a cosmopolitan global civilization. It is not inappropriate that a country which had its beginning as a haven from totalitarian oppression and the violation of individual conscience and gained a reputation as a country that welcomes the stranger (the tired, the poor, the hungry, the oppressed) should provide a prototype for an emerging unity-in-diversity. One must hasten to add, however, that Americans have often betrayed that heritage, allowing their theonomous unity-in-diversity to collapse into egoistic interest group politics shaped by religious and racial prejudice. The ability to make that observation, however, means there is still ethical power in that tradition—the Ought has not been entirely reduced to the Is. America provides a flawed prototype that needs to live up to its own ideals even as it has much to learn from its diverse partners in an emerging global civilization.

What saves the secularization process from ending in total individualism is the presence of holy communities and their awareness of the naked self as empty. What such communities introduce into society is an understanding of imagelessness of human dignity as an expression of interdependence and therefore of the importance of alternate communities within society as essential for the social and ethical ecology of human dignity. Thus *emptiness* transforms urban individualism by tying and binding (*religare*) persons into ethically enabling (nongovernmental) alternate communities of self-transcendence. These communities claim a public space for a human dignity and human diversity that is not per se political even as they are iconoclastic of any governmental attempt to assume a sacred status. By that very fact they limit political authority and shape political order to protect human dignity. Such an empty public square provides a model for the promotion of a cross cultural ethic of human rights and human liberation.

Neuhaus worries about the similarity between the naked public square and the empty public square. Nevertheless, they are not the same. Apart from the experience of the emptiness or imagelessness of the holy, the naked square produced by urbanization and modernization will result in the emergence of an apocalyptic society of Nietzschean MAD-men who seek to rule by the will to power, that is, as those who kill in order to heal. The naked square unmodified by the presence of alternate communities becomes the Red Square of a Stalin or a Hitler, a square red with the blood of those sacrificed on the altars of a sacred order constructed by the will to power. Both Neuhaus and Stackhouse are right to insist that religion must play a role in shaping our public world. But contrary to their desire to reconstruct the sacred canopy, Novak was right to suggest that the religious symbolism at the center will be, appropriately, a negative symbolism. The holy manifests itself not by filling the center but by emptying it, that is, by secularizing the sacred. The shaping presence of religion would come, not from a center defined by an official state religion but from the plurality of holy communities surrounding the center, which by their very presence as communities of self-transcendence create a public space that is not subordinate to a political center and which, by their very existence, forces the center to remain empty.

This emptiness is not a vacuous emptiness but a relational emptiness, an emptiness at once both holy and secular. The difference between a vacuous or profane emptiness and a holy-secular emptiness is that, whereas a profane emptiness seeks to drive all diversity out of the public square and reduce the secular to sameness, a holy emptiness fills the secular public square with diversity by welcoming the stranger. These strangers are not stripped naked as a condition of entry, but rather are clothed in their communities, stories, and traditions. When the secular public square is structured by an unacknowledged or implicit sense of sacred order it can imagine the public square only as naked and uniform. In this situation "public" is equated with political and both are identified with "naked" and the diversity with which we cloth ourselves is privatized. But when holy communities insert their presence into the naked public square they reclaim public space as the arena of human dignity and human diversity to which the political must be subordinate.

A naked or secular public square, structured by the experience of the sacred, views pluralism in terms of bureaucratic individualism and raises *tolerance* as the essential democratic virtue. But a secular public square structured by the experience of the holy sees tolerance as an ideology whose purpose is to privatize and compartmentalize our differences to render them irrelevant to public life. A secular public square structured by holiness as emptiness replaces tolerance with the ethical obligation to pass over into the life, religion and community of the stranger and come back to one's own life, religion, and community with new insight. Unlike tolerance, passing over deprivatizes religious experience. Instead of living in our own private "fantasylands" and "doing our own thing," we are forced to welcome the stranger, to involve ourselves in the lives of others and their communities; and we can expect to be profoundly changed by this involvement.

Passing over could forge our private worlds into a new public world of shared experience, not by making everybody the same but by discovering a unity-in-diversity. Passing over or welcoming the stranger reclaims the public square as the arena of life in common. This arena is larger and more inclusive than the political arena as bureaucratically conceived. As such, it subordinates political order to the unseen measure of human dignity. Passing over offers the possibility of creating a global empty public square sustained by a complex socioecological diversity and interdependence that forms a protective fence around the sanctity of human dignity. An ethic of human rights cannot be created de novo by one person, it must emerge cross culturally and dialogically. An ethic of human rights derived from such a rich ecology will be rooted in stories that will be diverse, yet complementary and mutually correcting. *Ethical consensus will emerge not primarily by reconciling positions we already hold but through the transformation of our understanding of the Good that emerges in the very process of passing over and coming back.*

The ethical order of the empty public square I am envisaging is rooted in the utopian promise of Babel. Christians are fond of interpreting Pentecost (i.e., Acts 2:1–13: the descent of the Holy Spirit upon the apostles at the founding of the church) as a reversal of Babel. But it is not so much a reversal (i.e., a return to one language or world-view) as it is a confirmation of the utopian possibilities of

Babel—the possibilities for unity-in-diversity in which each speaks his or her own language and yet each is understood by all. For when the Spirit descended upon the public square where individuals "from every nation under heaven . . . [were] all assembled, each one [was] bewildered to hear these men [i.e., Apostles] speaking his own language" (2:5–6).

"Our only hope," says Stanley Hauerwas, "is the presence of the other, through which God makes present the kingdom in which we are invited to find our lives."[41] In welcoming the stranger, we are welcoming God, "the ultimate stranger," into our lives. "God is such a stranger to us because we have chosen to live as if we were our own masters. God thus comes challenging our fears of the other by forcing us to patiently wait while others tell us their story."[42] This encounter with the stranger as with God is a wrestling in which one can be expected to be wounded and yet blessed with a new understanding of oneself and what it means to be human. "Our friendships," says Hauerwas, "change us in ways we seldom anticipate."[43] Because of this, through one's encounter with the stranger, what at first may have seemed impossible, may yet be possible; that is, one may find a unity-in-diversity. In this wrestling, we are both wounded (i.e., changed) and yet blessed (given a new identity), for no one is defeated and human dignity is the victor.

After Auschwitz and Hiroshima, speaking from a biblical perspective, we live in a time of a new covenant with the whole of humanity, a covenant whose saving remnant is composed of holy communities such as those found within the narrative traditions of Judaism, Christianity and Buddhism. These communities, in response to the silent yet commanding voice heard from Auschwitz and Hiroshima, are called to a covenant with transcendence that renews the covenant of Noah. These are the communities that have separated themselves from the sacred order of society to embrace a two-kingdom ethic that measures justice by the measure of human dignity, where the measure of human dignity is the unseen (and un-imageable) measure of emptiness. These are the communities that sustain human dignity and equality through an ethic of audacity on behalf of the stranger. In the global ecology of an emerging world civilization the unity-in-diversity of these three (and other kindred) traditions promises to form the creative leavening for the emergence of a human rights ethic.

It is precisely the diversity of holy communities, in story and community (mythos and ethos), that can make a universal ethic of human rights possible as an ethic of human liberation capable of shaping public policy on a global level. For their very diversity, over-lapping only in their common commitment to welcoming the strang-er, makes it possible for them to create a mutually correcting, mutu-ally balancing, ethical ecology for an emerging global civilization. This ecology requires a dialectic of the holy and the secular; for the holy and the secular are two sides of the same coin. There is a place in this ecology not only for the witness from the side of the holy but also from the side of the secular. In the mutually correcting dialogue be-tween the communities of transcendence there is a place for the voice of the secular a-theist.

The ethical ecology necessary for globally sustaining human dig-nity is not one that pits the religious against the secular but rather the sacred-profane against the holy-secular. Sacred social orders, espe-cially in their modern secular forms, tend to deny the primacy of human dignity and dangerously simplify the ecology of social, politi-cal, ethical, and religious diversity. The insertion of holy communities into a sacred order can tip the balance in favor of the primacy of human dignity and the ecological complexity of human diversity (i.e., the value of difference over sameness). Without the opposing witness of the holy, the secular becomes sacred and the stranger becomes profane. Just as society cannot remain secular without the dialectical presence of holy (wholly other) communities, so holy communities cannot remain holy without the dialectical presence of those who are wholly other—those who are welcomed as strangers. A holy commu-nity cannot be a holy community without the stranger who comes from and is sustained by some other community. The very nature of a holy community both requires and supports the socioecological com-plexity of diversity.

The complex diversity of a public order shaped by the presence of holy communities finds its strength in the alliance and mutual critique sustained not only between holy communities as such but between these and a nondogmatic secular humanism that shares their theonomous concerns for the critique of sacred authority in the name of human dignity. As with theism, so with atheism, there are two kinds. There is a theism and an atheism structured by the experience of the sacred, and there is a theism and an a-theism structured by the experience of the holy. On the one hand, an implicit orientation to the sacred produces not only a fundamentalistic theism but also a funda-mentalistic atheism. Both are authoritarian (forbidding all questioning of its own authority) with totalitarian propensities. Both seek to recre-ate the world in its own image; that is, both promote uniformity or sameness and seek the elimination of all differences. On the other hand, there is also such a thing as a theism and a-theism implicitly oriented to the holy. The a-theism of the holy, moreover, can be subdivided into two types, religious (e.g., Therevada Buddhism) and secular (e.g., critical secular humanism). Both are characterized by their surrender to doubt (questioning all authority as a form of openness to the infinite) and by their eagerness to welcome the stranger (i.e., difference rather than sameness).

The struggle is between a sacralized (profane) secularism and a holy secularity. A sacral world, whether it assumes a religious or a secular guise, attempts to impose a single sacred story (even if only the storyless story of Enlightenment culture) on all humankind. It works outward from a sacred center, seeking to bring the whole world into conformity. Thus, whether in a sacred or secular guise, it politicizes the entire social order and equates public order with bureaucratically administered political order. It views its sacred world as complete, lacking nothing and therefore needing nothing beyond itself. Secular holiness, by contrast, is rooted in a recognition of human finitude and the utopian incompleteness of everything human. This incompleteness keeps the holy community open to the infinite and is inherently pluralizing. The center of every holy community lies not in itself but in the stranger beyond its own borders. By welcoming strangers, their stories and the questions they raise for one's own story, holy communities remain open to the infinite even as they affirm the infinite value or dignity of the other whose very difference is an invitation to self-transcendence. And by affirming the necessity of a plurality of holy communities they create a public order that transcends and limits political-technical-bureaucratic ordering, recovering the political as a dialogical process of finding and creating unity-in-diversity—a human world of interdependence in which to dwell.

The Utopian Quest in an Age of Apocalyptic Darkness

At first glance Alasdair MacIntyre seems to offer little help for imagining a relationship between religion, ethics, and public policy in the naked public square. He views the Babel of pluralism in this square as a sign that we have entered a "new dark ages." We have entered an age, it would appear, that lacks a story that could provide the common premises required for a public understanding of the good and the practice of virtue. The best we may be able to do, he tells us, is retire to small private communities where virtue might still be practiced and await the coming of a new St. Benedict.[44] And yet it struck me upon first reading *After Virtue* that MacIntyre seems to speak with two different voices in the first and second halves of this book. In the first half we are presented with an analysis of our situation as seemingly hopeless. The incommensurate first principles of our ethical pluralism, we are told, makes ethical agreement impossible. As a result we are reduced to the babbling of ethical emotivism. And yet in the second half of the book we are presented with an understanding of virtue that does not require us to agree on the good as a precondition of cooperation. We are thus in a situation in which, while rejecting MacIntyre's rejection of Babel, we can still find much of value in MacIntyre that will be of use in imagining how ethical cooperation in the pluralistic environment of the empty public square might proceed.

If at the opening of *After Virtue*, it seemed like an ethical society required a common conception of the good embedded in a common story, in the second half of the book we learn this is not really the case. Here MacIntyre tells us that "good life for man is the life spent in seeking for the good life for man, and the virtues necessary for the seeking are those which will enable us to understand what more and what else the good life for man is."[45] The good, it turns out, is an eschatological goal toward which we move by living a certain kind of life, structured by the virtues in relation to a variety of social practices. Through the virtues, the good we are seeking is at least partially realized even before we know what that good is and that partial realization continuously leads us on to yet further and fuller realizations of the good we are seeking. The good is a utopian reality that is realized as we move from horizon to horizon, as if on a journey.

Moreover, where before it seemed as if we needed consensus to pursue the good, now we are told that the good is realized within particular traditions and that "when a tradition is in good order it is always partially constituted by an argument about the goods the pursuit of which gives to that tradition its particular point and purpose. . . . A living tradition then is an historically extended, socially embodied argument and an argument precisely in part about the goods which constitute that tradition."[46] Traditions then are socially embodied in historical communities that either make the pursuit of the good possible or else inhibit that pursuit. Everything depends on sharing an appropriate narrative and the appropriate virtues. For these two things make this ongoing argument about the good possible.

At this point one might be tempted to say, "Aha, so there is some one story we have to share after all." But I think not. What is required is not one particular narrative but a certain type of narrative. What is required is an unfinished or incomplete narrative, that is a utopian narrative. "The unity of a human life," MacIntyre argues, "is the unity of a narrative quest. . . . Looking for a conception of *the* good . . . will enable us to order other goods. . . . It is in the course of the quest and only through encountering and coping with the various particular harms, dangers, temptations and distractions which provide any quest with its episodes and incidents that the goal of the quest is finally to be understood. A quest is always an education both as to the character of that which is sought and in self-knowledge."[47]

"The Quest" as a narrative form, far from being the property of any one tradition, has to be one of the most universal types of story in the history of the human race. All we need do is recall the quest narrative that Wilfred Cantwell Smith traced from the Indus River valley through Hinduism and Buddhism into Persian Manichaeanism and then onto Islam, Judaism, and Christianity, culminating in the audacious ethics of Gandhi and Martin Luther King, Jr. This is the story of the young prince on a quest to find an answer to the problems of old age, sickness, and death, who ended up suspended over an abyss. The power of this narrative lies precisely in its appeal to the universal human quest to find meaning in life in the face of death. As we saw, this narrative showed itself capable of being adapted into a wide variety of narrative traditions.

In addition to the quest narrative, says MacIntyre, there must be an associated tradition of virtues that make the quest possible. Like the quest narrative, these virtues must also have a utopian character, that is, they must make it possible to live life with an openness to the future. The "lack of justice, lack of truthfulness, lack of courage, lack of relevant intellectual virtues—these corrupt traditions, just as they do those institutions and practices which derive their life from the traditions of which they are the contemporary embodiments. . . . An adequate sense of tradition manifests itself in a grasp of those future possibilities which the past has made available to the present. Living traditions, just because they continue a not-yet-completed narrative, confront a future whose determinate and determinable character, so far as it possesses any, derives from the past."[48] The kind of virtues that MacIntyre requires for the narrative quest, I would argue, are precisely those required of holy communities founded on the "unseen measure" of human dignity; namely, openness to the infinite and its social analogue, openness to the stranger.

It is just such narrative traditions socially embodied in holy communities (both secular and religious) that I have had in mind in arguing for the importance of institutional pluralism in the creation of a public space that transcends and limits political technobureaucratic order. Such narrative traditions create a public space capable of sustaining the complex ecology of institutions and social practices in which the virtues, as MacIntyre understands them, can thrive. Social practices are, for MacIntyre, the immediate environment of the virtues. When Aristotle speaks of "virtue" or "excellence," says MacIntyre, he often refers to "practices" such as "flute playing, or war, or geometry."[49] This suggests to MacIntyre a notion of *practice* as a key to understanding what a virtue is. By *practice* he means,

> any coherent and complex form of socially established cooperative human activity through which goods internal to that form of activity are realized in the course of trying to achieve those standards of excellence which are appropriate to, and partially definitive of, that form of activity, with the result that human powers to achieve excellence, and human conceptions of the ends and goods involved, are systematically extended. Tic-tac-toe is not an example of a practice in this sense, nor is throwing a football with skill; but the game of football is, and so is chess. Bricklaying is not a practice, architecture is. Planting turnips is not a practice; farming is. So are the enquiries of physics, chemistry and biology, and so is the work of the historian, and so are painting and music. In the ancient and medieval worlds the creation and sustaining of human communities—of households, cities, nations—is generally taken to be a practice in the sense in which I have defined it. [50]

Virtue, as excellence, has to do precisely with extending the goods of a socially embodied practice. This notion of practice serves for MacIntyre as a substitute for Aristotle's metaphysics of human nature as the source of the *telos* of the human. It is his way of introducing sociohistorical consciousness into the discussion of virtue. It amounts to removing Aristotle from a cosmological frame of reference and inserting him into an anthropological-eschatological frame of reference. Excellence, says MacIntyre, as the verb *excel* suggests,

> has to be understood historically. . . . [as] progress towards and beyond a variety of types and modes of excellence. A practice involves standards of excellence and obedience to rules as well

as the achievement of goods. . . . The standards are not them-selves immune from criticism, but nonetheless we cannot be initiated into a practice without accepting the authority of the best standards realized so far. . . . If, on starting to play base-ball, I do not accept that others know better than I when to throw a fast ball and when not, I will never learn to appreciate good pitching let alone to pitch. In the realm of practices the authority of both goods and standards operates in such a way as to rule out all subjectivist and emotivist analyses of judgment."[51]

Excellence or virtue itself has an eschatological or utopian character that involves one in a quest for self-transcendence toward ever-receding horizons of excellence. Essential to this understanding of virtue is the realization that the goods one strives for are *internal* to the practice. *"A virtue is an acquired human quality the possession and exercise of which tends to enable us to achieve those goods which are internal to practices and the lack of which effectively prevents us from achieving any such goods."*[52] If a child learns chess purely because she is promised a reward, such as an ice cream cone, the good offered is external to the practice. On the other hand, once this child begins to learn the game and gets caught up in the challenge and takes delight in the skill involved, then the child is realizing goods internal to the practice. One can cheat to bring the game quickly to an end to achieve the external good. But once one embraces the internal good of the prac-tice, to cheat would be for the child to rob herself of the very good she is seeking. Internal goods are goods realized in the process itself and not just in reaching the goal. The virtues are acquired skills through which one realizes just such internal goods.

MacIntyre's account of virtue as self-transcending offers an alter-native model to the model of self-transcendence offered by Nietz-sche's autonomous self-creating individual. MacIntyre replaces auton-omous individualism with a theonomous communal model. Because virtues are realized through socially embodied practices, they are in-herently social. Moreover, because you submit yourself to a standard of excellence that calls you into question and involves you in an open-ended self-transcendence, these practices are also inherently the-onomous. The goods of virtues can only be achieved by subordinat-ing ourselves to the best standard so far achieved and entails

subordinating ourselves within the practice in our relationship to other practitioners. We have to learn to recognize what is due to whom; we have to be prepared to take whatever self-endangering risks are demanded along the way; and we have to listen carefully to what we are told about our own inadequacies and to reply with the same carefulness for the facts. In other words, we have to accept as necessary components of any practice with internal goods and standards of excellence the virtues of justice, courage and honesty. For not to accept these, to be willing to cheat as our imagined child was willing to cheat in his or her early days at chess, so far bars us from achieving the standards of excellence or the goods internal to the practice that it renders the practice pointless except as a device for achieving external goods.[53]

When you enter a practice you enter what Neuhaus would call the theonomous realm of authoritative value, a realm where you submit yourself to a community of practitioners, the long historical tradition of that community, the narratives which sustain that tradition, and the arguments of its best practitioners concerning the goods of that tradition. But most important, what makes this submission theonomous is that you are submitting yourself to the same inner demand for self-transcendence that sustains the quest of even its best practitioners. That is, you are driven neither by an arbitrary self-rule (autonomy) nor an authoritarian rule by others (heteronomy) but by an inner demand that is radically other. Practices are by definition rooted in experiences of transcendence that demand self-transcendence. Practices, however, are to be distinguished from *institutions*. Where practices are organized around internal goods, institutions, says MacIntyre, are organized around external goods as rewards, such as money, power, and status.

Nor could they do otherwise if they are to sustain not only themselves, but also the practices of which they are the bearers. For no practices can survive for any length of time unsustained by institutions. Indeed so intimate is the relationship of practices to institutions—and consequently of the goods external to the goods internal to the practices in question—that institutions and practices characteristically form a single causal order in which the ideals and the creativity of the practice are always vulnerable to the acquisitiveness of the institution, in which the cooperative care for common goods of the practice is always vulnerable to the competitiveness of the institution. In this context the essential function of the virtues is clear. Without them, without justice, courage and truthfulness, practices could not resist the cor-

rupting power of institutions. Yet if institutions do have corrupting power, the making and sustaining of forms of human
community—and therefore of institutions—itself has all the
characteristics of a practice.[54]

Contained in this distinction between practices and institutions is our
distinction between the anthropological ethics of holy communities
and the cosmological order of sacred societies. Anthropological communities of practitioners are the mediators of a transcendence that
can be actuated only in dialectical tension with the cosmological institutional orders that sustain them. One can discern here, an alternative model of management to the one MacIntyre debunked, the one
organized around the myth of scientific effectiveness and efficiency,
which is essentially driven by external goods. Institutions are structured around those external goods (food, clothing, shelter, etc.) necessary for survival. They are concerned to ensure the vital goods and
the good of order. Nevertheless they can ensure the good of order
only if they are subordinated to the higher good of self-transcendence
manifested in the pursuit of those goods that are internal to the practices sustained within institutions. We find ourselves returning here
to the hierarchy of values that promote self-transcendence outlined
by Lonergan and Doran, in which the good of order makes possible
the higher goods on the one hand and on the other the good of order
itself is dependent for its continued functioning on the effective presence of the higher goods manifested in the cultural realm through
personal commitments to self-transcending values operative within
holy communities.

A life guided by the virtues, says MacIntyre, is "apt to require a
highly determinate attitude to social and political issues; and it is
always within some particular community with its own specific institutional forms that we learn or fail to learn to exercise the virtues."[55]
MacIntyre's call for a return to Benedictine-type communities is a call
for a retreat from the new "dark ages" of our naked public square into
some sectarian haven where the virtues might still be practiced. But,
despite the apocalyptic tone of this call, it can be construed to have
quite the opposite implications. For the strength of the Benedictine
tradition over that of the radically sectarian traditions, which have
periodically rejected the world and retreated to await the coming end,
is that while the Benedictine monastic communities separated themselves from the larger church and society they (like the Buddhist
sanghas) never cut their ties to either. As a result these communities

were profoundly influential in reforming and reshaping both church and society in Medieval Europe. The Benedictine communities were a utopian transforming presence within the social order of Medieval Europe. The society of pluralistic (incorporated) institutions in which we now dwell is largely a product of the Benedictine tradition's transformation of feudal society. Western pluralistic societies are a far cry from feudal society and probably more hospitable to the virtues. The Medieval feudal world was certainly no more hospitable to the virtuous life than our own. The call for virtue would be redundant in a virtuous world. Society is always, more or less, in a "dark age."

What makes the virtues a utopian force for the transformation of society is their presence in society through alternate and holy communities. To the degree professional communities, for instance, remain true to the practice of their profession (including the ongoing arguments about the internal goods of that practice), they will not be conformed to the larger society and the lure of external goods but will introduce theonomous transforming values into society itself. And to the degree that holy communities resist conformity to the external goods of the larger society and remain communities "set apart," who question the sacred order of society and demand the weighing and balancing of all our goods, internal and external, against the unseen measure of human dignity, they have the power to create a public order in which the virtues can find at least partial realization. Hence, despite MacIntyre's hostility to the pluralistic Babel of the naked public square and despite his seemingly pessimistic and apocalyptic conclusion about a new dark ages, it appears that MacIntyre stands substantially in the utopian tradition I have been arguing for and offers us a suggestive model of how a public ethic might take shape within the empty public square.

MacIntyre is pessimistic about the virtues shaping the public life of the naked public square because, while the ancient Socratic view envisioned the political community as properly inculcating virtue, "for liberal individualism a community is simply an arena in which individuals each pursue their own self-chosen conception of the good life, and political institutions exist to provide that degree of order which makes such self-determined activity possible. . . ."[56]

The model of the empty public square I am suggesting, however, advocates neither a continuation of liberal individualism nor a return to ancient and classical models. It moves beyond liberal individualism by going beyond its way of dealing with pluralism through the virtue of tolerance—a way that simply legitimizes the privatization and hence removal of differences from the public square. If the chief virtue of naked public square is tolerance, the chief virtue of the empty public square is hospitality to the stranger. Unlike tolerance, passing over and coming back mutually involves strangers in the private lives and world-views of each other's communities and, by that very act, transforms these private worlds into a new public world of commonly shared experience.

Therefore, welcoming the stranger is the utopian virtue par excellence of public policy in a technobureaucratic world, for it creates a public world where none existed. Passing over liberates us from the technobureaucratic illusions of Disneyland, from our private fantasylands, into a new common public world. The creation of this new public order occurs outside the sphere of government and functions to limit and subordinate technobureaucratic political order to a public realm where human dignity is the measure of every political and technical order. As such, it places the life of the virtues in the public realm but outside the control of government and hence does not return to the ancient model of government either. It separates politics from government and technics and returns it to the realm of public dialogue and persuasion in a common utopian quest to discover the good of the polis. Passing over into the communal lives and stories of others is in essence the foundational public policy necessary for public life in the coming millennium, one that provides a rich and complex nongovernmental ecology for the life of the virtues.

When this model is taken as a model for public policy in an emerging global civilization, passing over between religions and cultures promises to create a new global public order. This order is the precondition for a new order of global politics that can relativize the technobureaucratic nation-state and subordinate it to a new global standard of human dignity, human rights, and human liberation sustained by a rich and complex transcultural socioecology of unity-in-diversity. Passing over is more than an individual activity, it occurs between communal individuals and builds bridges of interdependence between communities. Passing over, so understood, builds a bridge that could span the abyss of the demonic through the utopian audacity to champion the human dignity of the stranger, replacing the dualism of sacred and profane (i.e., the sacred *Volk* and the demonic enemy) with the pluralistic interdependence fostered by the experience of the holy and so make the total annihilation of the other unthinkable.

Utopian Technopoesis and the Limits of Political Realism

Modern society differs from premodern societies, we have noted, by differentiating itself into at least three semi-autonomous systems: political, technoeconomic, and cultural. We are quite conscious of the limitations that the separation of the economic from the political sphere places on politics. Economies have lives of their own that can easily undo the best laid plans of politicians. The bias of social science models, whether Marxist or non-Marxist, has been inclined to presuppose that culture is almost exclusively a dependent variable shaped by the economic and political realms. However, to deny that culture also can function as an independent variable is ethically paralyzing. For by the *cultural sphere* we mean the sphere of symbolic expression and intentional human action, the sphere of values, the sphere that uniquely expresses the ethical dimension of our humanity. To deny the potency of culture is to render ourselves ethically impotent. If nothing else proves the capacity of culture (expressed through symbolic narratives of mythic proportions) to act as an independent variable shaping political and economic policies, the history of anti-Judaism and anti-Semitism should be sufficient to settle the issue. Although often exacerbated by political and economic factors, the persistence of anti-Judaism over two millennia can only be explained by the continuity of one factor, anti-Judaic myth. As Nazi policy of diverting trains from the front to send Jews to the gas chambers during the final months of World War II illustrates, myth has the power to override political and economic reality and lead "intelligent" human beings to persist in self-destructive policies. Our brief survey of the MAD-ness of nuclear policy could be said to provide another cogent example.

If such is the symbolic power of demonic narratives, I am convinced that the narrative traditions of the holy are equally potent. I am not speaking of mythic narratives in the abstract but socially embodied myth. There is no form of consciousness, whether of the sacred or of the holy, except as socially embodied in some community. And in addition to the social and material conditions of existence, human life is conditioned by religious conversion, whether divine and demonic, which has the power to alter the social and material conditions of existence by reorienting human communities toward either good or evil. If mythic narratives have the power to kill, they also has the power to give life. We can no longer afford to accept the demonic myth that says we must *slay* in order *to make alive*. The myth of life through death must give way to those desacralizing narratives that have given rise to audacity on behalf of the stranger, from Abraham and Siddhartha to Gandhi and Martin Luther King, Jr. Most eloquent among these is the story of Job, a story that speaks to the experiences of desolation—whether of Auschwitz or of Hiroshima.

Human rights and human liberation depend on a fundamental reversal and transformation of the dominant family of mythological narratives that have shaped human existence—the myths of life through death. No authority can any longer be accepted as sacred and unquestionable which asks that we kill in order to heal and slay to make alive. What we need in our MAD world is not an ethic of life through death but an uncompromising ethic of life against death. The only authoritative ethic possible to guide public policy in a MAD world is one rooted in the traditions of the holy that defend human dignity. In the passing over and coming back through which an ethic of human rights and human liberation will emerge, the story of Job can play a central role. Its potential power to speak cross-culturally is rooted in the *kairos* of our time, a *kairos* created by the events of Auschwitz and Hiroshima which have placed us in a world of tragedy and unjust suffering of potentially global proportions. Job's story expresses a human response that spans cultures and religions—a visceral audacious indignation. As the UN Declaration on Human Rights indicates, Auschwitz and Hiroshima have awakened an awareness of our human dignity that will not go unheard, that demands a hearing, that demands justice. Job's world has become our world, and Job's irreverent experience of transcendence as irrevocably tied to human dignity has likewise become our own.

Thus Job's story is uniquely a story for our time. Seeing our world from within the narrative horizon of the biblical tradition it seems as if the silent yet commanding voice heard from Auschwitz and again from Hiroshima calls the whole human race to a new secular covenant that renews the covenant with Noah. That commanding voice is unmistakably the voice of the God of Job, the God who is Emmanuel, that is "God with us,"[57] the God who takes the side of human dignity against all sacred stories and all sacred authorities which seek to justify that suffering, indeed against all ultimate authority including God's own.

If the passing over and coming back to which we are invited in the empty public square is to support an ethic of human rights and human liberation, Buddhists, Christians, and others will need to immerse themselves in these Judaic stories, not to become Jews but to return to their own traditions and recall their own abandoned heritages. For although each lives through different stories, like Jews, both Christians and Buddhists belong to iconoclastic holy communities whose narrative traditions witness a transcendence that cannot be imaged and that demands of them that they question all authority and welcome the stranger and the outcast. Somehow the myths of East and West, of enlightenment and conversion (i.e., of life through death), became severed from these two normative criteria of self-transcendence (hospitality or "welcoming the stranger" and chutzpah or "questioning all sacred authority"), and their respective anthropological ethics were reduced to a cosmological morality in which the self is expected to surrender not to the holy but to sacred authority.

In the Christian case, as I argued in *Narrative Theology after Auschwitz*, these norms were severed by the myth of supersession that cut them off from this iconoclastic heritage. It is no accident that the paganization of Christianity is accompanied by a Marcionite (Gnostic-Manichaean) attempt to build Christian faith on the New Testament alone or in its less radical but almost as damaging forms, on a selective reading of the Tanakh (claimed as the Christian Old Testament), in which the New Testament becomes the criterion for what is valid in the Old. As a result, refusing to accept that their story grafts them into that of the Jews, Christians tried to invert the order and graft the Jewish story into their own. The result was a new demonic story, which divided them from Jews, as sacred is divided from profane, instead of grafting them into the pluralism fostered by the traditions of the holy. Thinking themselves better than the Jews, Christians cut themselves off from the covenant and began thinking like pagans, substituting narratives of unquestioning obedience to the sacred authority of the state (as the guarantor of sameness, i.e., Christendom) for the Jewish narrative traditions of audacity on behalf of the stranger.[58] In Japan, Buddhist ethics underwent a similar distortion. Its ethic of dependent co-arising of all things was reduced to the horizon of Shinto nationalism and a Confucian ethic of familial and political relations within this horizon. The result was the inversion of the Buddhist ethic of welcoming the outcast that resulted in an attempt, not unlike that of medieval Christendom, to remove all strangers from Japanese society. By such ethnocentric paths was the world dragged into the war that led to Auschwitz and Hiroshima.

"There is an ethical paradox in patriotism," says Reinhold Niebuhr, "which defies every but the most astute and sophisticated analysis. The paradox is that patriotism transmutes individual unselfishness into national egoism. . . . The unqualified character of this devotion is the very basis of the nation's power and of the freedom to use the power without moral restraint. Thus the unselfishness of individuals makes for the selfishness of nations. That is why the hope of solving the larger social problems of mankind, merely by extending the social sympathies of individuals, is so vain."[59] The moral paradox is that "the very extension of human sympathies has therefore resulted in the creation of larger units of conflict without abolishing conflict. So civilization has become a device for delegating the voices of individuals to larger and larger communities. The device gives men the illusion that they are moral. . . . A technological civilisation has created an international community, so interdependent as to require . . . ultimate social harmony. [But] modern man has progressed only a little beyond his fathers in extending his ethical attitudes beyond the group to which he is organic and which possesses symbols, vivid enough to excite his social sympathies."[60]

Nations seem to be the largest social unit whose symbolic narratives have been able to evoke a sense of common identity sufficient to motivate persons to sacrifice themselves for the good of others, and even nations seem to need the threat of war to stir up such fervor. Because the capacity to identify with others seems unable to transcend national boundaries, at these boundaries authentic self-transcendence is usually replaced by a surrender to some finite sacred order. Where the holy-infinite provokes questions; the sacred forbids them. Thus, instead of openness to the stranger, surrender to national identity generates an absolute unquestioning loyalty to the sacred order of one's society and its way of life. This transfer and diminishing of authentic religious self-transcendence is accomplished, Niebuhr suggested, by identifying the universal with the particular. Citizens are encouraged to believe their particular way of life and the values embodied in it are universal. As such their way of life ought to be universally accepted or at the very least it ought to be recognized that their way is the most fully human. Hence the stranger and his or her community, who live by some other standard, represent a threat to those who embody "true humanity."[61] Once one enters into such a story, its inner logic leads to the ideal of killing in order to heal. To destroy the stranger and the stranger's alternate way of life becomes a necessary moral obligation justified by the goal of "saving humanity."

Like Niebhur, Stanley Hauerwas argues that ethical reflection on war must begin with the recognition that war is based not so much on egoism as altruism. There are, he says, ethical reasons why nations engage in war. "War . . . teaches us to preserve the common life, even to kill for it, precisely because the common life transcends the life of the individual." Nations fight wars, he suggests, not just to protect their territory but their stories, "not just their existence but their interpretation of their existence."[62] War is viewed as a moral necessity. "We fear we will lose the ability to locate ourselves in a worthy story" if the option of war is not available to us.[63] So we give to the state the right to protect those "patterns of cooperation achieved by our society to preserve our particular shared goods. To preserve that cooperation and relative peace the state must be prepared to wage war. . . . That is the 'justice' that war protects."[64] The stories we seek to protect are the stories that give us our identity, stories that span the generations, tying us to our ancestors and to the generations to come. Such stories inevitably involve war as a major character in a drama in which our ancestors, by sacrificing themselves for us, obligate us to sacrifice ourselves for future generations, thus ensuring the immortality of our story.

The task of the church as a holy community, Hauerwas suggests, is to offer the world an alternate story. "Christians believe," he says, "that the true history of the world, that history that determines our destiny, is not carried by the nation state. In spite of its powerful moral appeal, this history is the history of godlessness. . . . For what is war but the desire to be rid of God, to claim for ourselves the power to determine our meaning and destiny? Our desire to protect ourselves from our enemies, to eliminate our enemies in the name of protecting the common history we share with our friends, is but the manifestation of our hatred of God."[65] Every national story left uncriticized is finally demonic, including the democratic liberalism of the United States. "No state will keep itself limited, no constitution or ideology is sufficient to that task, unless there is a body of people separated from the nation that is willing to say 'No' to the state's claims on their loyalties."[66] Institutional pluralism by itself is no final guarantee of freedom and human dignity unless those alternate communities are theonomous communities, committed to questioning of all authority, including the state. The fact that a state allows freedom of religion is no automatic guarantee of the virtue of that state. Hitler, Hauerwas reminds us, "never prevented the church from worshiping freely," because the church represented no threat to his authority.[67]

Everything depends on what kind of holy communities flourish in a pluralist society. What separates the story of a holy community from the stories of a sacred society is its ethic of hospitality and audacity on behalf of the stranger. This is as true of secular holy communities, such as professional societies, as it is of explicitly "religious" holy communities. As the history of Nazi Germany amply illustrates, when scientific, professional, or religious communities no longer welcome strangers and the questions they raise, then science, law, medicine, philosophy, and theology are reduced to nationalist racist ideology and cease to have anything to do with truth, justice, healing, or transcendence. To speak for the stranger is to speak for self-transcendence in the realms of both theory and practice. It is to embrace the holy in opposition to the sacred. Speaking for the Christian community, Hauerwas makes a point that is valid for all holy communities. In the holy community "we discover our particularity is not destroyed but enhanced by the coming of the stranger. In the church we find an alternative to war exactly because there we learn to make others' histories part of our own."[68] Because, the holy community, unlike the sacred society, has its center not in itself but in the stranger, Hauerwas can say, "our only hope is the presence of the other, through which God makes present the kingdom in which we are invited to find our lives."[69] The kingdom of God, we might say, reigns wherever the stranger is welcomed, for there we are open to the infinite—to self-transcendence and the utopian possibilities of the human.

The most important thing both Buddhists and Christians can learn from the Jewish narrative traditions of chutzpah is the audacity to question all authority in the name of human dignity and in defense of the stranger. Both Buddhism and Christianity have exhibited a disturbing propensity to reduce their anthropological visions to cosmological visions for the legitimation of nationalisms—nationalisms that inspire an ethic of unquestioning obedience whose logic culminates in obligation to kill in order to heal. The utopianism of an ethic of audacity on behalf of the stranger lies in its capacity to create a new public order that relativizes nationalism and subordinates it to human dignity and human interdependence.

For almost two millennia, Jews have been a holy community of strangers within societies ruled by others. As such the Jewish people have been a unique witness to the transcendence of the holy. Now, after the Shoah, the nation of Israel faces the challenge of the dialectic between the sacred and the holy, the cosmological and the anthropological. Israelis too have an obligation to transcend their nationalism and recognize the stranger in their midst—the Palestinian. But this obligation is tragically complicated by the double bind of political complexity in the Middle East. For although Palestinians represent the stranger, the minority in the midst of the Israeli nation, the Jews remain the stranger, the minority in the midst of the Christian and Muslim Arabs of the Middle East. The paradox is that the Israelis as

Jews and the Palestinians as Arabs are both minorities and majorities at the same time. For the Israeli to welcome the Palestinian it is necessary for the Arab (at the same time) to welcome the Jew, anything less would be suicidal. Christians have all too typically been more than willing to express "compassion for the Palestinians" (who do deserve our compassion) while supporting policies that amount to advocating that Israelis commit suicide. Christians have generally thought that Jews should be the ones to carry the cross rather than themselves. Every Christian who thinks that the problem of the Middle East is between Muslims and Jews and does not directly involve Christians is a Christian who has not confronted the history of anti-Judaism that made (and continues to make) Jewish life precarious. Neither Christians nor Muslims are in a position to makes ethical demands on Jews in general and the Israelis in particular without first finding a way to make Jewish existence secure. For it is Christians and Muslims who are historically responsible for creating a world in which the Shoah was possible and in which no Jew has ever felt secure. We must hope that Christians, Muslims, and Jews will find ways to be ethically audacious on behalf of the strangers in their midst and break this impasse.

Israel as a people, says Eliezer Berkovitz, has always existed in faith history rather than the power history that has governed the interplay of nations. Even as a nation, Israel exists, by comparison with other nations, without power. After Auschwitz and Hiroshima, "the inescapable demand of the historic moment requires the honest renunciation of material force in the dealings of the nations and power blocks with each other. . . . Today the very immensity of power gathered in human hands compels man to surrender its use against his fellow man. Power has overreached itself and, thus, it has defeated itself."[70] What is required is "a genuine embracing of ethical and moral principles for the ordering of the life of all mankind. This . . . has become the 'iron law' in this new phase of global history. Be decent or perish!"[71] Berkovitz believes in the capacity of Israel to introduce into power history the way of powerlessness, the way of nonviolence. As (in all likelihood) one of the nuclear powers of the world, one must hope that Berkovitz is right. In any case, Berkovitz's invitation to an ethic of nonviolence is one that both Christians and Buddhists ought to be able to affirm. And it is a challenge that stretches the anthropological heritage of each of these traditions to the uttermost limits of self-transcendence. The religious and political violence that emerged with the Protestant Reformation led to the naked public square. If religion is to have a future role in the public

square without returning to that pattern it is essential that holy communities seeking to call the nations to a standard of nonviolent coexistence be committed to nonviolence themselves. Violence, says Gandhi, can never be undone. Religious conviction combined with
violence leads to absolute and irreversible actions. Nonviolent resistence, by contrast, takes into account our finitude and fallibility. Unlike violent resistence, "if this kind of [nonviolent] force is used in a
cause that is unjust," says Gandhi, "only the person using it suffers.
He does not make others suffer for his mistakes."[72]

Berkovitz's talk of the rule of ethics between nations replacing
the rule of the will to power must seem to all "realists" to be hopelessly utopian. Realism is the apocalyptic language of death that masquerades as the language of survival. It is the language of cosmological sacred societies with their propensity to divide the human
community into the sacred and the profane. Realism is the language
of the demonic that "makes rational sense" out of the moral imperative to kill in order to heal. *The language of realism is the language of
MAD-ness that masquerades as sanity.* From the perspective of realism,
the commitment of holy communities to welcome the stranger, even
one's enemy, is "hopelessly utopian." To create a new world, a new
global public realm of unity-in-diversity between strangers and their
communities with ties so deep as to make the destruction of the other
unthinkable, especially through so simple, so unpolitical (in the bureaucratic sense) and untechnological a process as passing over and
coming back seems to the realist to be the ultimate utopian madness.

Utopians seem to offer vague hopes for some unrealizable future. Realists want to know where they are going. Realists like to be in
control of their destiny and thus prefer clear strategies, unambiguous
goals and "final solutions." But after Auschwitz and Hiroshima we
can no longer afford such final solutions. When the end is too clearly
defined it too easily justifies the means. Utopians prefer to live in an
unfinished world of proximate goals and partial solutions. Utopians
prefer to keep the future ambiguously open to transcendence. The
maxim of a utopian ethic could well be Ellul's, "think globally but act
locally." When it comes to action, one must not be distracted by the
global orientation of mass media. The place where the world can be
transformed is precisely where it intersects with the experience of
actual individuals and their particular communities. Utopians prefer
to love their neighbor rather than "the world," understanding that
the neighbor is, as the story of the good Samaritan (Luke 10:25ff)
suggests, primarily the stranger, even the enemy, who by chance
crosses our path. Utopians prefer an antibureaucratic ethic in which

every means is measured by the unseen measure of human dignity. They are convinced that the utopian good is a good internal to the practice of creating community. If the means do not respect human dignity neither will the end.

To the realist, all of this remains hopelessly utopian. Such utopianism has absolutely no chance of being effective or successful. And yet, even were that true, we ought to welcome the stranger. For being human is more important than exercising a will to power to be in control. We ought to act without clinging to the dharmas, a Buddhist might say, for we cannot stop time and control the destiny of the universe. Or to put it in the language of Paul, we ought to live every day as if our time was short, thus "buyers should conduct themselves as though they owned nothing, and those who make use of the world as though they were not using it, for the world as we know it is passing away" (1 Corinthians 7:30–31).

Realists are so committed to a view of the world as cosmological and hence unchangeable that they are always and inevitably unprepared for the possibility of utopian transformation. What realist would have predicted at the end of World War II, that Japan and Germany, then in utter defeat, would within a generation be two of our strongest economic partners and competitors. Who in the middle of the cold war could have imagined that within a generation Russia would be experimenting with open markets and a more open society. What realist at the time of the 1967 war of Egypt with Israel could have predicted the ascendancy of Anwar Sadat and his audacious and unexpected openness to Israel that, through the mediation of President Carter, lead to peace between the two countries within a decade. Realists are utterly unprepared to deal with the utopian dimension of history. The realists who plan the military strategies of NATO were utterly unprepared for the fall of the Berlin Wall and the Iron Curtain and the loss of hegemony by the Communist party all across Eastern Europe in the fall of 1989. As one news commentator put it, NATO had an endless variety of plans in place for war but it had not even one plan for peace. The "real" is always distorted by the sacred order through which it is perceived. Only when the limits of the "real" are desacralized or secularized by our experiences of the holy do our utopian possibilities for the future become visible. The utopianism of which we speak is not a naive utopianism, out of touch with reality, but the utopianism exemplified by those who have been the victims of the realists throughout history—the Jews. The utopianism of Jews is the utopianism of those who know the reality of exile but also of return, of those who have the utopian audacity or chutzpah to, as Elie

Wiesel says, refuse to give up hope and succumb to despair but are always ready to begin anew, taking a stand against all authority, even God if necessary, on behalf of human dignity.

Societies or whole communities, unlike individuals, says Reinhold Niebuhr (a realist) are incapable of moral feeling for the stranger because they are incapable of generating "symbols, vivid enough to excite . . . [their] social sympathies," to cause them to identify with the stranger. Our failure is a failure of ethical imagination. Our hope lies in good part in the poetic imagination that underlies passing over and coming back. Practicing the virtue of hospitality is a poetic task. It is a recovery of both politics and technology as human tasks rooted in our capacity for language and symbol rather than a techno-bureaucratic task reserved for experts. For politics is rooted in the art of dialogue and persuasion. And poetry, as its root meaning in Greek (i.e., "to make or to do") suggests, is the technological or utopian art of making new symbolic worlds in which to dwell. Passing over, says John Dunne, liberates one from one's private world by creating a larger common world of compassion. "The sympathetic understanding into which he must enter in order to pass over to another man's life is itself compassion, for it involves a sharing of feelings and images as well as insight into the images and feelings."[73] Passing over, he tells us, is rooted in our capacity for "eliciting images from one's feelings, attaining insight into the images, and turning insight into a guide of life. What one does in passing over is try to enter sympathetically into the feelings of another person, become receptive to the images which give expression to his feelings, attain insight into those images, and then come back enriched by this insight to an understanding of one's own life which can guide one into the future."[74]

The process Dunne describes is remarkably similar to that of psychic conversion as described by Robert Doran in his application of Lonergan's phenomenology of inquiry to the symbolism that emerges from the unconscious, especially the dream. The parallel is more than accidental, because both explore the interface between Lonergan and Jung. Our interest in Doran's work had to do precisely with the fact that he saw a significant relationship between our ability or inability to welcome the stranger and the strangers who enter our dreams. The point is, whether we are dealing with the stranger within or without, the stranger is a poetic invitation to self-transcendence and compassion. Passing over, whether within or without, is an occasion to enter into the story of the stranger and come back with new insight that can enrich and transform one's understanding of the story of one's own community and tradition and finally one's own life story.

In the beginning, new worlds were created by the poetic visions of religious seers and their communities who performed the techno-poetic act of creating new worlds in which to dwell. Only some of these worlds were visions open to the infinite. Especially influential was the technopoetic vision of Judaism that desacralized nature and opened the path to sociohistorical consciousness. The techniques-technologies of the human that emerged from these technopoetic visions generated their own histories, which have catapulted us into an emerging global civilization. These various technologies, liberated from their diverse sacral social orders by the dialectic of the secular and the holy, seem to have brought us full circle back to Babel. For our technologies are creating a global technological and economic infrastructure, forcing us once more to choose between technolinguistic uniformity and utopian diversity. After Auschwitz and Hiroshima, we are being given a second chance to welcome the stranger and realize the utopian possibilities of Babel. The price of rejecting the stranger at this point in history will be collective suicide for the whole human race.

Fortunately, the dialectic of the secular and the holy has the capacity to make strangers of us all, desacralizing our stories and alienating all of us from our own traditions. In a sacral world where all know who they are and what they ought to do, reconciliation with the stranger seems like MAD-ness and Babel becomes headed for some literal apocalyptic destiny. In such a world the promise of Babel is a world of desolation (Shoah). The utopian promise of Babel lies in the secularizing power of the holy. For the power of the holy relativizes all sacred absolutes, whether religious or secular, and discovers utopian possibilities in the emptiness that is our openness to the infinite. The power of the holy opens us to the possibilities of discovering anew who we are through the utopian process of passing over and coming back. Now the technopoetic task is no longer the task of creating a human city with one language and one story, but of realizing the utopian promise of Babel in an apocalyptic world. It is a task worthy of the human, one that calls us to build a bridge over the abyss of the demonic in order to encounter the infinite in the human dignity of the stranger who resides on the other side.

Technologically and economically the emergence of a global infrastructure makes this task the *kairos* of our time. Auschwitz and Hiroshima make it the ethical imperative of our time. If the nation has proven to be the largest community for which human beings can be moved to compassion, that need not remain an insurmountable limit. The sacred divides the world into universal abstractions that are analogues of the sacred and profane (i.e., the *Übermensch* against the *Üntermensch* or the truly superior human beings against the subhumans), which cannot be bridged. The encounter with the holy through human dignity of the stranger builds bridges of interdependence. Passing over and coming back builds such bridges not by passing over into universal abstractions such as "humanity" but by passing over into particular lives and particular communities with particular histories. Passing over builds a much more complex and stable socioecology within which humans may dwell. An ecology in which, rather than defining and confining the human to some cultural ideology, defines the human through its dignity; that is, its undefinability, emptiness, or un-imageableness—its utopian openness to the infinite.

From Apocalyptic MAD-ness to Utopian Madness: Public Policy Ethics as Critique of the Narrative Imagination

The alternatives for the coming millennium are between a sacral ethic of *apocalyptic MAD-ness* or an ethic of secular holiness, of *utopian madness*. The world of the Shoah, says Richard Rubenstein, was the product of *The Cunning of History* rooted in a mythology that produced a "self-defeating ethos of exclusivism and intolerance . . . derived from a religious tradition that insists upon the dichotomous division of mankind into the elect and the reprobate."[75] To quote a popular maxim: "There are two kinds of people in the world—those who divide the world into two kinds of people and those who do not." The real dividing line is not between religious and secular, nor between saved and damned, but between those whose narrative imagination is shaped by the experience of the sacred and those whose narrative imagination is shaped by the experience of the holy. The former see the world divided into two separate camps, the latter see a pluralistic world in interdependence. The way we imagine our destiny, whether in terms of "apocalypse" or "utopia," is decisively colored by these options, giving rise to alternative modes of "madness."

Two Kinds of Apocalyptic MAD-ness

Apocalyptic MAD-ness can take either a "realistic" or a "literalistic" form. Dean Curry offers a good example of the former and Hal

Lindsey of the latter. Both Curry and Lindsey are Christians who identify themselves as "Evangelicals." But Curry offers a form of apocalyptic MAD-ness that permits him to align himself with his secular counterparts, whereas Lindsey's MAD-ness is intelligible only to "true believers."

Curry's strategy is one which he shares with many theological minds in the mainline churches, such as Michael Novak or Richard Neuhaus, who would consider themselves "realists." This realism is premised on a version of a two-kingdom ethic that emphasizes the difference between the "already" and the "not yet" of biblical eschatology and the fact that the biblical message of peace found in the Sermon on the Mount belongs to a time that is "not yet," a time beyond the end of history when sin will be conquered. But here and now, the Gospel that makes present the "already" of the beginning of the end, must be "realistically" adjusted to deal with the continuing reality of sin. Therefore Curry tells us that,

> the Christian view of peace is one that can be characterized by its realism, in the sense of not being utopian. . . . The all-pervasive nature of human sin precludes the achievement of the kingdom of God within history. The fullness of the kingdom of God— shalom—awaits the final work of God. . . . Activist pacifism and some forms of nuclear pacifism, ignore the already-but-not-yet dimension of God's kingdom. . . . As Christians we distinguish between the "politics of eternity" and the "politics of this world." . . . Our faithfulness to kingdom values must be balanced alongside of our earthly responsibilities. Problems arise when we confuse these two ethics; specifically, when we attempt to apply the ethics of eternity to the politics of this world. . . . [when] the absolute ethic of Christ is viewed as not only normative but also as the appropriate guide for making public policy choices."[76]

To illustrate his point, Curry brings up an example especially relevant to our present topic. What "if the allies had disarmed or had refused to take arms against Hitler?" It is unlikely, he concludes, that even Gandhi's tactics of nonviolent resistance could have stopped Hitler. Pacifism would have lead to the extermination of the Jews. This, he argues, points out "the moral bankruptcy of attempting to apply the ethics of eternity to the politics of this world."[77]

There are of course serious problems with Curry's view. First, he seems to assume that *Christians* and *allies* are interchangeable terms and therefore Christians must take charge and slay the enemies of civilization. Second, he is absolutely right to suggest that nonviolent resistance probably would not have stopped Hitler *once the war was under way*. But that begs the question of the real failure of the church; namely, to publicly resist Hitler and the Nazi racist myth *as it was emerging in Germany*. Then it most certainly could have been stopped by a nonviolent public witness of the church, which should have come to the defense of the human dignity of Jews. But of course, the church did not make that defense because its own anti-Judaic narratives predisposed it to being coopted by the Nazis who were able to use Christian anti-Judaism as a springboard to achieve popular support. Third, the Papal decision to sign a concordat with Hitler was ethically disastrous. Pope Pius XI made that decision no doubt in agony over the consequences of not signing it; namely, for fear of what Hitler might do to Christians throughout Europe if he did not. But in making it he was thinking like a political and secular ruler and not the leader of a Christian community. A compassionate secular ruler would naturally have to weigh the potential amount of suffering and death against the possible success of refusal and resistance, feeling no right to risk the lives of others even if willing to risk his or her own. But the leader of a Christian community is freed from that kind of utilitarian cost-benefit analysis by the knowledge that every confessing Christian by virtue of that confession has already declared himself or herself ready for martyrdom. A church prepared from the beginning for public resistance and martyrdom, I am convinced, would have stopped Hitler with far fewer deaths than actually occurred on the battlefield and in the death camps. As it was, the allies did very little to save the Jews of Europe until the very end, when millions were already dead. It has often been observed, for instance, that the railroad lines to the death camps were never bombed. And of course most countries were reluctant to take in Jewish refugees. The United States did not even take in enough to fill its legally established quotas. So let us not pretend that the allies were preserving noble Christian values in defense of human dignity. Jews died in the camps and soldiers died on the battlefield because Christians reneged on their baptismal and confirmation vows and only too readily prepared the way for the Nazi hatred of the Jews. But even if Christian martyrdom would not have stopped Hitler, it is still what Christians ought to have done in witness to their own faith, in which there is no greater love than to give up your life for another.

It is no accident that Curry proceeds from an argument that our world is dominated by sin, to a justification, not just of the possession but also the use of nuclear weapons. By making "sin" the dominant feature of the Christian story, he can appeal to the need for "realism" as the appropriate strategy for Christian ethics. Once "realism," has been established, the arguments that follow to justify NUTS or nuclear utilization theory need not be distinctively Christian at all. The Sermon on the Mount can be safely dismissed and one's faith can be used to legitimate one's patriotism. Therefore, Curry argues: "God intends that I fulfill all my responsibilities to his kingdom just as he intends that I fulfill all of my responsibilities to my family. The same is true of my national identity."[78] Next we are told, "Government is an institution ordained of God to guarantee peace and justice."[79] And then: "In a very literal way, my heavenly citizenship may require that I embrace the specific earthly politics of the nation to which I am also a citizen."[80] Finally, we are told that the fixation on nuclear weapons as an expression of the demonic autonomy of technology is misplaced and "obscures the fundamental reality that the differences which exist between the United States and the Soviet Union do not represent misunderstandings or misperceptions. . . . In short, the problem of war and peace in our time is not of one of technology, it is not one of arms races, it is one of politics and ideology."[81]

The challenge of peace, we are told, is to resist all totalitarianism, especially that of the Soviet Union, while seeking to avoid nuclear conflagration. To do this we require a policy that goes beyond MAD-ness, beyond the threat of mutually assured destruction to embrace NUTs, a willingness to engage in a strategic use of nuclear weapons to wage limited nuclear war. "If a nation seeks peace, it must prepare for war," says Curry. The values of democracy are such that one must be prepared to kill in order to heal; even if, in the process, the whole human race is put at risk. Indeed, with the dissolution of the Soviet Union in December 1991, the greatest risks now appear to come from the use of tactical nuclear weapons. These weapons seem to have fallen through the cracks in nuclear negotiations. They are now in danger of being recklessly used to settle "local" conflicts by the countries that survived the breakup of the Soviet Union or of being sold into the indiscriminate hands of other countries seeking to become nuclear powers.

For Curry it is immoral to be MAD but not to be NUTs. Curry is willing to accept the argument that MAD, a strategy in which the entire civilian populations of opposing countries are held hostage, is inherently immoral. "The critics of MAD," he says, "are correct: Nothing can justify the intentional and indiscriminate mass slaughter of millions of bystanders."[82] But he denies that that was ever the operational policy of the United States. The actual targets, he claims, have been military, political, and economic centers. Moreover today's advanced nuclear technology can be targeted so accurately and the damage limited to such precise areas that the strategic use of nuclear weapons is thinkable within "the moral requirements of the Just War tradition."[83] Thus Curry concludes, "there is nothing inherently immoral about nuclear weapons or nuclear war. . . . Weapons are instruments of human intentionality. As such, they can be instruments of peace or instruments of aggression and injustice; they can be used discriminately or indiscriminately. Nuclear weapons are no different. They do not lie outside of the realm of intentionality. Therefore, it is because we affirm the dignity of the human person and because we value peace and justice—and because others do not—that we prepare for war. This is the way it has always been. Nuclear weapons have, after all, changed nothing."[84] Curry offers us a classic argument from the genre of cosmological ethics: *the way things are is the way things ought to be.* Ethics is interpreted as conformity to "reality."

Curry ends by condemning the naive utopianism of Jonathan Schell's call to "reinvent politics," to create a world where all people are equal and national sovereignty has given way to the unity of world government. Schell's vision too closely approximates the vision of the Kingdom of God to be realizable. "Good intentions and imagination are no substitute," for realism Curry tells us, in a world where God's kingdom is "not yet."[85] Curry's position here is not uniquely evangelical, one can find both Catholics and mainline Protestants who have argued for a similar "Christian realism."[86] I do not intend to go into the nuances of these arguments here. My purpose is to illustrate the logic of apocalyptic MAD-ness. Once you enter into the realist story, you have to be prepared to kill in order to heal, and the story is so powerful that it is even able to coopt and assimilate the Gospel into its sacral world-view. This is done by "doubling." That is, the Christian still thinks of himself or herself as one who follows the Sermon on the Mount, but develops a second self to deal with the "reality" of the sinful world on its own terms. From within this "realist" story, Schell's views seem hopelessly utopian but these same "realists" see nothing utopian about "limited nuclear war." What is utopian (in the pejorative sense of illusory), given the history of warfare, is the view that war can be limited once it breaks out. This is a risk that realists are willing to take, because for them survival is an unworthy goal. Edward Norman suggests that modern Pacifist Christians, who are not willing to kill for certain values, have really paganized Christianity, succumbing to overly optimistic or utopian views of human nature.[87] But the optimism about human possibilities that derives from the Renaissance and the Enlightenment, or even that derived from Marxism, are not pagan forms of optimism but are rather derived from the utopianism of the biblical tradition. On the contrary, Norman's fatalistic views of human nature, typical of realists, echo paganism. In Norman's view the "sanctity of human life . . . is an ancient pagan concept that has undergone a modern revival. . . . But there is nothing very sacred about human beings: we are corrupted and in need of redemption. It is not human life but God who is sacred."[88] This of course is nonsense. For the Christian story, like the Jewish, affirms that humans are created in the image of the God who is without image and thus share in the transcendence or sanctity of God, even in their "unredeemed" state.[89] "The preservation of values by armed conflict against militant opposition," says Norman, "is not murder." Life is worth living, he would argue, only if certain values like freedom and justice are defended, even unto death. I would agree that survival by itself is not sufficient. But the realist confuses finding a story worth dying for with finding a story worth killing for. The path of self-transcendence however lies in finding a story worth dying for that forbids you to kill for it, but more importantly, makes it impossible for you to offer any legitimate reasons for killing.

Arguments that suggest that killing is necessary to defend human dignity lost whatever plausibility they once had with the emergence of nuclear weapons. It is Curry who is "hopelessly utopian" (in the pejorative sense) to suggest that words like *weapon* and *war* still have a coherent strategic meaning in a nuclear age. Weapons are instruments used to enable one side or the other to win a war. It is "hopelessly utopian" to think a nuclear war can be won by the use of weapons whose limited use cannot be guaranteed and is not even likely, and whose full use makes human survival unlikely. As Norman points out, warfare from the ancient world on through the Middle Ages right into the modern period has tended to be total. "Whole civilizations were eliminated, whole peoples wiped out."[90] Realists say certain "spiritual values" must be defended *at all costs*. But, as the Gandhian tradition of nonviolence argues, some values cannot be defended at all costs without destroying the very values one seeks to defend. Realists have a contempt for survival and for Schell's emphasis on survival. Although I would agree that survival is not enough, Schell cannot be dismissed that easily—especially by Christian theologians who wish to avoid falling into a Manichaean-Docetist dualism that sacrifices fleshly values to spiritual values as if the body were an incidental problem. Schell is right. Altruism is a positive value only when it involves a sacrifice for the greater good of others. But it is utter Manichaean Gnosticism to be willing to sacrifice the whole of humanity and all living things to "spiritual values." Both Judaism and Christianity—and I would argue also Buddhism—are committed to embodied value. Physical survival of the human community is not irrelevant to the question of value.

Hal Lindsey, in his best selling book *The Late Great Planet Earth*, represents the other type of apocalyptic MAD-ness. Unlike Curry's realism, which offers a perspective he could share with his non-Christian or secular counterparts in nuclear strategy, Lindsey's literalism offers a biblical view of a coming Armageddon that only like-minded believers could share. Lindsey objects to all allegorical or symbolic readings of the Scriptures and insists the prophets and the Book of Revelation must be understood literally as predicting the future, especially the end of the world. He then goes on to identify various names and events referred to in the prophets and the Book of Revelation with current countries and events, using a tortuous combination of linguistic, geographical, and historical exegesis that makes traditional allegorical exegesis look tame. Russia is identified with the land of *Gog, Cush* becomes the black African nations, *Put* is identified with Libya, "Gomer and all it hordes" is said to be the entire collection of Iron Curtain countries, *the King of the South* is Egypt, *the Kings of the North* are China, "the yellow peril," and the revival of the *Roman Empire*, by an amazing feat of literal imagination, is identified with the European common market countries, and so on. Lindsey stretches the meaning of the word *literal* to encompass a mode of exegesis that as Neuhaus says, in another context, "is not unlike that of those who in other cultures forecast future events by reading the entrails of doves and rats. Bible study is reduced to a kind of reading of entrails."[91]

Lindsey reads the prophetic tradition and the Book of Revelation as predicting a final apocalyptic battle between the forces of light and the forces of darkness, in which "it is the presence of this reborn nation of Israel . . . that excites a great enemy from the uttermost north of Palestine to launch an attack upon them which sets off the last war of the world. This war is to be ended with such a display of divine intervention that a great many of the surviving Gentiles and Jews put their whole trust in the true Messiah, Jesus Christ."[92] In this great apocalyptic battle the "Asian horde" from China will be responsible for the destruction of a third of the human race. This prediction in Revelation 9:18, he argued, is "an accurate first-century description of twentieth-century thermonuclear war."[93] Before the final conflagration occurs, however, first the faithful witnesses to Jesus will be magically removed from the earth. They will suddenly disappear, snatched up into heaven in the "rapture." Then the full nuclear holocaust will occur, and "as the battle of Armageddon reaches its awful climax and it appears that all life will be destroyed on earth—in this very moment Jesus Christ will return to save man from self extinction." Thus Lindsey transforms the most terrifying moment of suicidal annihilation for the whole human race into an event to be looked forward to by all true believers. "As history races toward this moment," he asks, "are you afraid or looking with hope for deliverance? The answer should reveal to you your spiritual condition. One way or another history continues in a certain acceleration toward the return of Christ. Are you ready?"[94] Or again, "In other words, Christ is going 'to loose' the atoms of the galaxy in which we live. No wonder there will be a great roar and an intense heat and fire. Then Christ will put the atoms back together to form a new heaven and earth."[95]

Such is the suicidal logic of apocalyptic MAD-ness. This fanciful analysis hardly needs refutation. In terms of Lindsey's own literal apocalyptic reading of the Bible, it should be sufficient to quote the comment of Jesus in Matthew's Gospel: "Heaven and earth will pass away, but my words will not pass away. But about that day and hour no one knows, neither the angels of heaven, nor the Son, but only the Father" (Matthew 24:35–36)." Why should we believe Hal Lindsey knows what no one but God knows? Lindsey's exegesis is nothing short of obscene. He engages in a form of scriptural exegesis that Augustine once appropriately condemned as *fantastica fornicatio*, which might politely be translated "mental masturbation," or less politely as "fucking the sacred symbols." His identification of the nuclear annihilation of the world with the second coming of Jesus, as the triumph of Christian messianism (over the world as a whole and over Judaism in particular), illustrates the demonic suicidal allure of the myth of life through death. It represents nothing less than a total demonic perversion and pagan inversion of the holy, of the "good news" of the biblical tradition.

The Apocalypse as Utopian Madness

If Lindsey gave us a sacral and literally apocalyptic reading of the book of Revelation, Jacques Ellul offers a utopian reading shaped by the experience of the holy. Rather than announcing the catastrophic end of history as our fate, the Apocalypse is, he argues, the revelation of God's freedom at work in history as mediated by radical human hope. Whereas Curry and Lindsey offer us sacral apocalyptic views that are ethically disabling, Ellul offers a utopian view of apocalypse, that is ethically enabling. In Ellul's view, the Apocalypse is to be taken seriously, but not literally, for its speaks in the language of exotic symbol precisely because it speaks of the ultimate paradox of the presence of "the Eternal in Time, of the action of the End in the Present, the discovery of the New Eon, not at the end of time, but in this present history."[96] The very structure of the book, he argues, displays the intersection of time with eternity.

Ellul divides the book of Revelation into five parts each of which is organized around a series of sevens. Parts One (Chapters 2–4) and Two (Chapters 5–7) refer to the seven churches and the seven seals and are said to deal with the relation of the word of God to the church and in history. Parts Four (Chapter 14:6—Chapter 18) and Five (Chapter 19—Chapter 22:5) are said to deal with the word of God from the perspective of eternity as revealed in the seven bowls of last judgment and the seven visions leading to the New Jerusalem. Significantly, says Ellul, between time and eternity stands Part Three (Chapter 8—Chapter 14:5), which proclaims the death, resurrection, and incarnation of Jesus Christ announced by the seven trumpets. Between history and God's judgment stands the lamb who was slain, the suffering servant (Jesus as an embodiment of the people Israel)[97] on whom fell the judgments that would have otherwise fallen on humanity. Thus through the suffering and death of the servant, salvation comes to the whole human race.

In many ways the key section of the Apocalypse, for Ellul, is the second part, the opening of the seven seals, which reveals, he insists, the role of the word of God in history and the role of the witnesses to that word. History, it seems, is like a scroll that can be read and understood only when all seven seals are broken by the Lamb, who alone is able to break these seals and reveal the meaning of history (5:4–5). As the first four seals are broken the four horses are set in motion. The first is the white horse (who reappears in 19:11ff. bearing the Messiah), which represents the conqueror; that is, the word of God in history. Next come the red, black, and pale horses, representing the demonic powers unleashed in politics (e.g.,war), economics (represented by famine and scarcity; i.e., "a day's pay for a ration of wheat," Revelation 6:6), and in nature (i.e., pestilence and death). History, argues Ellul, is made up of the ravages of these last three horses, limited only by the power of the white horse, the conqueror. Were it not for the white horse of the word of God, history would be totally enclosed in the demonic. It is only this word that limits evil and keeps history open to transcendence.

The Book of Revelation, we could say, is to the New Testament what Job is to the Tanakh (i.e., Hebrew Bible)—they are both books of desolation and hope. Both recognize two incongruous facts. Much of human history is ruled by the demonic and is meaningless and yet there are clear signs of transcendence at work in history, desacralizing the demonic in the name of the sanctity of human dignity and the sanctity of creation. Neither book accepts the order of this world as sacred and meaningful. Both view attempts to justify the sacred order of this world at the expense of human dignity as demonic. Both call into question the sacred order of this world in the name of the holy.

In the Book of Revelation, the dragon is the symbol of the demonic. It manifests its power on earth through the two beasts. The first beast incarnates the demonic in political power (the beast with seven heads bearing the crowns of kingship). The second, which looks like a lamb but makes a noise like a dragon, mimics the word of God, promising salvation—but in fact brings slavery and death. This second beast, Ellul argues, is the demonic word, manifest today through mass media as the mythic propaganda of a technological society: "making the world and all its people worship the first beast [i.e., political authority]" (13:12). And the number of the second beast, 666, is not difficult to decipher, he tells us, for it is simply the finite seeking to become infinite and absolute by multiplying itself— seeking to destroy the wholeness of the number 7, which symbolizes the unity of God (3 = trinity) and creation (4 = the four directions of the created order). The two beasts seek to sacralize the created order. They seek to absolutize the finite and close it off from transcendence through a new religiosity whose power can be broken and limited only by the transcendent word of God borne by the witnesses.

When the fifth seal is opened, it discloses the witness and prayer of the martyrs who bear the word of God in history, each of which is given a long white robe (6:9ff.). The witnesses, far from being morally disabled by events beyond their control are the ones who introduce the audacious desacralizing freedom of the word of God, the Wholly Other, into history, tipping the balance toward hope and meaning. The sixth seal then releases the angels of destruction, but their hand is stayed until all the witnesses have been sealed with the seal of God, so that they might be "passed over" at the final judgment (7:2–3). Not being in complicity with the demonic they do not need to undergo separation. These witnesses, says Ellul, are the covenant communities of hope, Judaism and Christianity (the twelve tribes of Israel and a huge uncountable number from every nation, 7:4–9).

Out this vision of the seven seals Ellul constructs his theological ethic of apocalyptic hope. It is a vision of the two communities of apocalyptic hope (Judaism and Christianity) called to assume the vocation of witnesses (martyrs) to the word of God and bearers of that transcendent freedom in the world. Through the witness of these holy communities, the demonic is limited in history and freedom and justice are manifest in the human city in anticipation of the city of God. Where Curry and Lindsey offer a religious vision that is ethically disabling, in which humanity cannot fundamentally change the way things are and must accept an ethic of realism and apocalyptic resignation, Ellul offers an ethically enabling vision in which those who live through apocalyptic hope can intervene in history, desacralize its sacred orders, and introduce hope and freedom into human existence. Ellul's form of apocalyptic hope is utopian.

The seventh seal, when it is finally opened, brings the silence in heaven for about half an hour (8:1). This marks the beginning of the Incarnation and the third or middle part of the Apocalypse, where time and eternity meet. It is characterized by the child born of a woman but attacked by the dragon (Chapter 12), but also the death and resurrection of the two witnesses murdered by the demonic powers, dead for three and a half days and then raised back to life (Chapter 11). Only after the reconciliation accomplished by the two witness[98] does judgment come.

The judgment of creation occurs under the sign of the rainbow (10:1), the covenant of Noah and the divine promise "Never Again." Ellul carefully notes that when the seven bowls of last judgment are finally cast, the suffering of humanity that follows represents the suffering of those who love their slavery to the demonic powers and hate to be separated from them. He points out that the Greek word for judgment is *krisis* and means "to separate." He then notes that, according to Genesis, God created by *separating* light from dark, night from day, etc. The Fall, he says, is the fall into complicity with the demonic, which confuses the work of the creature and the Creator, taking the former for the latter. Hence the separation of the human from the demonic is an act of sanctification, that creative act whereby God restores order out of chaos and confusion; that is, new creation.

Thus, for Ellul, when the final judgment occurs, not humanity but only the demonic powers are condemned to the lake of fire and eternal destruction (19:10). Before the final destruction of Babylon (the symbol of all earthly cities and the dwelling place of the demonic) all the people are called out of the city (18:4), and they stand at a safe distance and weep (18:9, 11, 15, 17). The apocalypse represents the collapse of the horizons of the cities of world as structured by the sacred-demonic. The new city that replaces it is a secular city, one that realizes the utopianism of Babel. A city in which there is "no temple," because God, being all in all, is the light that illuminates the secular. The New Jerusalem is a city that embraces the pluralism of the holy. It is a city whose public square is a light to the nations. Into this new city all the nations and all the kings of the earth, the very ones who opposed the word of God in history, shall bring their treasures (21:22– 27). It is a city in which nothing profane is permitted but only those whose names are inscribed in the book of the lamb, those created in the image of the God who is without image; namely, the whole human race. Once the demonic powers have been removed, creation automatically becomes a new creation.

Storytelling: Public Policy Ethics as Utopian Madness

Ellul understands the Apocalypse through the work of a narrative imagination guided by the experience of the holy. The absolute division of a demonic sacral order that divides the world into permanent enemy camps (the saved and the damned), such as we encountered in Lindsey and Curry, is replaced with a vision of unity-in-diversity, in which Jews and Christians witness to a final vision of salvation that includes the whole human race—all the nations of the earth.

What both Curry and Lindsey have in common is a sacral reading of the biblical tradition that pits the children of light against the children of darkness in a battle for life and death and legitimates that battle with an appeal to the "biblical story" and "biblical values." Neither can find a place for welcoming the stranger or loving one's enemy in the actual life of Christians. Both Curry's "realism" and Lindsey's "literalism" force those who accept their readings of history into a demonic doubling, in which faithfulness to the biblical story as they understand it, requires and even encourages being prepared to kill in order to heal and to slay in order to make alive.

The mythos of the modern world is pervasively shaped by a sacral imagination of both apocalypse and utopia, giving rise to the morally incapacitating Janus-faced myth I outlined in the Introduction. Like manic-depressives we live with the MAD-ness of our mood swings. This sacral Janus-faced myth enslaves us to the real, for when we are in a utopian mood we embrace a technobureaucratic vision of utopia as Disneyland, a place where our every wish is fulfilled. In such a mood we have no desire to change anything. And when we succumb to the apocalyptic fears that haunt the borders of our consciousness and lurk in the dark world of our dreams, then we feel terrified and overwhelmed, as if our fantasyland has turned into some kind of science-fiction horror story. Then we feel it is too late, we feel we can do nothing. The utopianism of the sacred always ends by dividing the world into opposing camps and marshalling its military resources to protect its utopia against the invasion of the enemy. As such, its utopianism always leads to a literal apocalypse.

In a world where MAD-ness is normative, sanity itself appears as madness. In contrast to those possessed by the sacred and its demonic, dualistic logic, there is the divine madness of those possessed by the holy and its audacious pluralistic logic that defends the dignity of the stranger. As Ellul's exegesis of the Book of Revelation shows, the Apocalypse need not be read through the eyes of a sacral imagination that legitimates killing in order to heal. For it can be read through an imagination shaped by the holy, which vindicates the covenant of Noah as well as the covenants of Moses and Jesus, by affirming the utopian promise of Babel as good news for the whole human race. Ellul's exegesis of the Apocalypse, shaped by the experience of the holy, gives us an apocalyptic vision that liberates Apocalypse from every demonic dualism or literalism that promises a "final solution" to the human condition. Ellul's exegesis translates apocalyptic hope into a utopian ethic appropriate to an unfinished world where desolation reigns and yet—and yet neither hope nor the future is abandoned to despair. Apocalypse, as Ellul understands it, is ethically enabling, for it inspires prophetic hope and Jobian audacity, a utopian madness capable of introducing a transforming presence into the world.

The difference between a sacral ethic of realism and a utopian ethic grounded in the holy is a difference in structuring the dialectical relation between the two realms or kingdoms. It represents a problem faced by all two-kingdom traditions, not just Christianity. The realist argues that the dialectic between the cosmological and anthropological realms *must be internalized* within the holy community. Such a community needs to compromise its utopian vision and accommodate itself to the reality of human sinfulness or in the Buddhist case it would be to human enslavement to illusion. To make this dialectic internal to the holy community presupposes that the holy community must think and act, at least in part, as if it were a sacred society. The utopian vision however insists that the dialectic between the two orders *must be kept external* to the community, that to be holy means being really separate from the surrounding society. This separateness is not so much physical as it is a matter of embodying radically alternate values capable of calling society into question. It must stand in tension with society, inserting the negating power of transcendence and otherness into the world of realism and necessity.

When the dialectic between the two realms is internalized, as it is in the realist position, you end up with, at best, an ethic of paradox such as Martin Luther advocated. Such an ethic is resigned to having to compromise with the world, learning to live within two separate (right- and left-handed) stories at the same time—having to live with the contradiction of being at the same time both a saint and a sinner. As we have seen, Luther's ethic of paradox forces a doubling that for all practical purposes accommodates the vision of the holy community to the necessities of a sacred society. As such it is scarcely more than a disguised version of a sacral ethic. There is another alternative—one embraced by both Hauerwas and Ellul. This alternative transforms an ethic of paradox from an ethic of resignation (i.e., accommodation to the "real") into a utopian ethic of the holy capable of desacralizing and transforming the cosmological order of a sacred society, even one that masquerades as secular. This alternate model places the dialectical tension *in the external relation* between the holy community and the larger society rather than internalizing it in the ethic of the community. For both Ellul and Hauerwas, in the holy community the end of history is already made present, and the holy community is meant to embody *now* the very way of life that is promised for the end time. That is what gives the holy community its utopian power. This strategy generates a different kind of ethic of paradox. Instead of inviting a doubling and accommodation between two orders it combines the sectarian emphasis on separateness with an emphasis on paradox. The paradox then becomes living the purity of sectarian vision right in the middle of the sacral world rather than attempting to either leave the world or accommodate oneself to it. In this model the holy community confronts the larger society with an alternate way of life that calls the sacred order of society into question, opening up the possibility of utopian transformation. In the history of Christianity, this strategy is closer to Benedictine monasticism than to the radically sectarian traditions. The Benedictines always retained their ties to the larger world in spite of their separateness and thus had a profound transforming effect upon the world. The same could be said of the Jewish synagogue tradition and the Buddhist sangha tradition, both of which remained separate and yet in the world. It is the inserting of the alien way of life, the otherness of the holy community right into the middle of an established sacred order that has the power to desacralize or secularize it and open it up to theonomous or utopian transformation.

Whether we are speaking of the Buddhist sangha, the Jewish synagogue, or the Christian church (or other kindred communities), what makes the holy community utopian is that it lives a radically alien way of life, a way of life that embodies the transcending Ought, which stands in judgment of the way things are (the Is of sacred order) and calls that order into question. As soon as the holy community internalizes the dialectical tension between Is and Ought, so as to replace utopianism with realism, it compromises this ethic and no longer has anything new to say to the larger society.[99] Religious realists, such as Curry, have no trouble talking policy in the naked public square because they talk the language of that square. But they have nothing unique to offer the world because their message is essentially the same as that of their secular counterparts. An ethic of realism inevitably ends up futurizing and privatizing the religious ethical vision. On the one hand, it puts the realization of peace and justice off into some distant future out of reach and, on the other hand, offers the consolation of a private inner peace. "The true 'peace' of Christianity," says Edward Norman (a theological advocate of realism), "is an interior serenity."[100]

To have something to say in the naked public square other than what it already knows, the holy community must remain a community of strangers. A naked public square filled with communities of strangers has the potential to transform the naked square into an empty square, open to the infinite and utopian transformation. The task of a holy community in the naked public square is to learn the language of technological utopianism, not to accommodate oneself to it, but as Gabriel Vahanian would say, to expropriate that language to express the authentic utopianism of new creation. An appropriate strategy for a holy community is to first *appropriate* the language of the public square, then *contradict* it, but only to *expropriate* its language to express the utopianism of transcendence. If once Christianity expropriated the language of naturalism to express transcendence in supernatural terms, so today the task of the holy communities that inhabit the naked public square is to likewise expropriate the language of technological utopianism. Therefore the task is not to reject the Janus-faced myth of apocalypse and utopia but to rehabilitate and transform it into an authentic theonomous language for the realization our humanity—to liberate it from the sacral imagination and claim it for the holy.

To the realists in the naked public square, whether religious or secular, the utopian language of a holy community seems totally alien and completely mad because utopians seem willing to risk the sacrifice of everything of value through of a naive failure to account for the "depravity" of the "enemy." And from the utopian viewpoint, what passes for sanity in the naked public square is the ultimate demonic MAD-ness that is prepared to kill in order to heal and slay to make alive. The MAD-ness of the realist is the self-contradictory madness of being prepared to annihilate *everything* of value to "preserve" certain values. Thus, as we began so do we end—by noting that the marketplace of the naked public square is inhabited by two types of "madmen," the Nietzschean *Übermensch* on the one hand and the twin figures of Job and John of Patmos on the other.

In charge of the naked public square we will find the descendants of Nietzsche's madman who came to declare God dead and replace him with the *Übermensch* who lives by the will to power. Living in a world without horizons, a world of cultural relativism, they propose a politics of realism, a MAD balance of terror, as the essence of human wisdom. Living in a world of relativism, they propose to settle the issue by an arbitrary leap into an absolutized defense of their particular way of life. Nietzsche's madman asked: "How shall we, the murderers of all murderers, comfort ourselves? What was holiest and most powerful of all . . . has bled to death under our knives. Who will wipe this blood off us? What water is there for us to clean ourselves. What festivals of atonement, what sacred games shall we have to invent. Is not the greatness of this deed too great for us? Must not we ourselves become gods simply to seem worthy of it?"[101]

We know now what games the descendants of Nietzsche's madman invented. We know now what games the new gods who live by the will to power invented. They were first played at Auschwitz and Hiroshima. The object of the game is to kill in order to heal, to assume total control over life and death. If being a god is being in control then no one is more totally in control of his or her life than the suicidal person who believes that suicide is "the final solution." We have now entered a civilizational era in which this private fantasy has become a public and collective fantasy. We live in a world of realists who offer us a "final solution" to the ambiguity of the human predicament. Nietzsche's *Übermensch* and Nietzsche's madman are one and the same being. This Nietzschean superior human being is the technological self that assumes its utopian transvaluation of all values can be accomplished through an autonomous will to power. It is no accident that such Nietzschean selves can never leave off from giving in order to receive. This self, which is always trying to fill the naked public square with the works of his or her own ego, ends up trapped in the cycle of eternal return, of eternal repetition. For a self-transcendence that is not empty, that is not open to the infinite, can produce only an infinitizing (or absolutizing) of the self, in which its will to power proceeds from deicide to homicide. The will to power and its violence is never the midwife of the utopian but always and ever returns us to the world of necessity and self-destruction—the wheel of eternal repetition.

There are those who think that the MAD-ness of our civilization has dissipated with the fall of the Iron Curtain and the dissolution of the Soviet Union. But it remains to be seen whether these changes are profound or merely surface changes. Psychologically, we seem to have been given a reprieve, Nuclear annhilation may seem to us less imminent than at any other time since Hiroshima and Nagasaki. Yet whether nuclear annihilation is viewed as imminent or relatively remote is more likely a symptom of a shift in the manic-depressive rhythms of the Janus-faced myth that governs our era than of any truly utopian change. There are still enough nuclear weapons in their silos to more than complete our annihilation. And with the break up of the Soviet Union there is less control over these weapons than before—and more possibilities for their mindless use. But the MAD-ness of our era is not determined by whether such weapons are ever used. The bomb simply brings into dramatic relief the madness that pervades our everyday world. The MAD-ness is in our methods—our technobureaucratic methods. Our dehumanizing technobureaucratic methods conjoined with our various sacral (dualistic) narratives governed by a Nietzschean will to power feed the conflicts that divide us, both within and between nations—conflicts that have tempted us (and will tempt us again) to seek "final solutions."

In addition to Nietzsche's madman, however, we will also find another type of madman dwelling in the public square: the madman who like Job has the audacity to challenge all sacred authority in the name of human dignity; the madman who confronts the sacral ethic of life through death with an ethic of secular holiness, a utopian ethic of *life against death*. This type of madman is like Abraham standing in the breach between Sodom and Gommorah and their apocalyptic destiny or like Jacob and Job, wrestling with God and humans as with a stranger, so as to ensure that human dignity prevails. Such persons are also like Job and John of Patmos insisting that though injustice reigns in the world and the demonic submerges much of human history in the abyss of meaninglessness, still there is Emmanuel, the God who is with us, the God who affirms the human dignity and rebukes all *apologies* that would seek to give meaning to the demonic and the meaningless.

The descendants of Job and John of Patmos who dwell in the naked public square, like the madmen in Elie Wiesel's plays and novels, display an audacious madness. A mystical and prophetic madness. This is the madness of those who refuse to surrender to the mythos of the demonic, of those who have the chutzpah to welcome the stranger and defend the dignity of the stranger in a world in which sanity is defined as the mutual assured destruction of all strangers. As Zalman says to his rabbi, in Wiesel's *Zalman or the Madness of God:* "We are the imagination and madness of the world— we are imagination gone mad. One has to be mad today to believe in God and in man—one has to be mad to believe. One has to be mad to want to stay human. Be mad, Rabbi, be mad!"[102]

Once, says Irving Greenberg, the madness of the holy was announced by the prophet who proclaimed, "Thus says the Lord." Then the destruction of the second temple brought an end to prophecy, and the prophet was replaced by the rabbi who wrestled with God and other human beings, and won the authority to speak on behalf of both. And then came the Shoah to shatter the authority of both prophet and rabbi, and now we are left only with the storyteller. Chief among the storytellers of our time are those who have literally descended into the abyss of the demonic and have lived to tell their tale—the survivors of Auschwitz and Hiroshima. Of all the storytellers of our time they above all have a "survivor's mission" to speak.

Elie Wiesel offers us a model for understanding the holy mission of all survivors. It is said that after the Buddha experienced his enlightenment he experienced one final temptation. He was tempted not to speak of his experience to others. Having experienced that which cannot be imagined he doubted that it could be spoken of. But out of his compassion for the suffering of the world he overcame his doubt and began to tell his story. Not because the story could capture the experience but in hope that the story could lead others to have their own experiences of emptiness. Wiesel's own story not only recapitulates the audacious anger of Job and the prophetic audacity of Jeremiah but also the compassion of the Buddha, the compassion that conquers silence. Having lived through the time of the demonic inver-

sion of the holy, the awe that silenced Wiesel was the awfulness of the
Shoah, the immensity of the demonic and not the divine. But Wiesel
is one of those rare persons who has descended into the abyss not
only to encounter the demonic but also the divine, and if the desolation of the demonic tempted him to silence, his openness to the
infinite, to the compassion of the infinite, left him, like Jeremiah,
Siddhartha and Job, compelled to give birth to the word and to story.
After ten years of silence, he tells us, he began to tell stories.[103]

Stories, at least stories rooted in an openness to the infinite, are
always utopian stories. They are stories that link us to the past even
as they open the present to a new future. They are unfinished stories
that invite our participation in the drama of life. "You can invent a
novel, but not a story," says Wiesel, "You think you invented it, but
you didn't. . . . Whatever I have, I have received. Whatever I give
belongs to who knows how many generations of Jewish scholars and
dreamers and poets. I have received the words, and in combining
them I am simply fulfilling the function of a messenger, which is to
me as important as that of a storyteller. In fact the storyteller is important only as a messenger."[104] Within his or her own tradition, the
storyteller is a bridge between the living and the dead. But if the
stories he or she tells are rooted in an openness to the infinite, these
stories will have one thing in common with other stories so rooted—
they will be stories that offer us a utopian invitation to welcome the
stranger. Insofar as our post-Shoah storytellers are faithful to their
calling, their stories will invite us to the utopian task of passing over
and coming back. And the storyteller will be a builder of bridges not
only between the past and the future but across religions and cultures. His or her stories will build bridges over the abyss of the demonic and bind strangers to each other in newly created worlds of
common (public) experience. Although those who are the survivors
of Auschwitz and Hiroshima are the first among equals in carrying
out the task of telling and sharing stories, it is a task to which all of us
are invited as we come to identify with these strangers. Living in the
time after Auschwitz and Hiroshima and living through their stories,
we too can become survivors and share in the survivor mission of
being messengers who have recovered from our traditions the utopian ethic of welcoming the stranger and the audacious obligation to
stand in the breach between the stranger and the demonic.

As we look forward to the coming of the millennium, storytelling and the sharing of our individual and communal stories will have
to form the foundation of public policy for a postmodern world. *Postmodern* is a word I use reluctantly because it is used so frequently and

ambiguously. But I have come to realize that *postmodern* is our symbol for the utopian, it evokes our openness to the infinite and desire for a new world. Public policy in the next millennium will grow out of the new public world that will be created among people who share their stories, even as they come to understand themselves as participants in an unfinished story. To project that policy in any detail would be to impose our present world on the future. But the new world we seek, if it is to emerge, must emerge as a common human enterprise, a common task, a sharing of stories across religions and cultures. The good we seek and the practices and institutions that will embody this good must emerge out of the utopian process of passing over and coming back. The good we seek is a good internal to the process. There are no shortcuts. The good place (*eu-topos*) we seek is no permanent place in which to dwell. It occurs, however, wherever two or three, or more are gathered to welcome the stranger. It occurs wherever the sacred walls of community are breached by the utopian experience of communion with the stranger. There the naked public square becomes empty of all (ethnocentric-religocentric) self and filled with the diversity of *otherness*. The utopian world we seek will be created by the virtues required for making the journey into other religions and cultures. Chief among these virtues is the virtue of hospitality to the stranger. It is the stranger at our door who invites us to become new creatures in a new world where each speaks his or her own language and yet each is understood by all.

Epilogue: The Secular University, Religious Studies, and Theological Ethics After Auschwitz and Hiroshima

The challenge of Babel is the challenge of pluralism in an emerging global technological civilization. Either we see it as an invitation to a utopian new beginning to be brought about through the quest for mutual understanding (i.e., passing over and coming back) or a threat continually tempting us to seek a technological "final solution." After Auschwitz and Hiroshima, the choice is either apocalypse or utopia. If we fail to discover the human dignity of strangers we risk undergoing the final indignity of a nuclear holocaust.

Although I was educated in Catholic parochial schools as a child, all my higher education experience as a student and most of it as a professor has been in secular universities. In this setting the university professor was held up as a model of "objectivity." What this meant was that, for the most part, my teachers appeared so neutral that I had no idea what they were committed to or believed in—outside of "examining the issues" and "thinking for yourself." Those ideals, of course, have great value and should not be abandoned. However, after Auschwitz and Hiroshima one has to ask, Is that enough? The privatizing of ethical and religious insight is as dangerous as unrestrained pontification on the part of professors. Does not the appearance of objective neutrality in the classroom leave many of our students with the impression that only "facts" and "skills" are worthy of being taught? When it comes to values, does not the silence of "objectivity" itself teach an eloquent lesson; namely, that values are a matter of personal preference? To treat ethics as a "private" affair is of course a contradiction of their very nature of the subject matter. Nevertheless, too often, I fear, we leave students with the impression that having a right to an opinion means that one opinion is as good as another. Why should they think otherwise if their professors do not think it important to take a stand on those values they think are essential to our future as a human community? The final betrayal may occur when not only professors of law and medicine or political science and sociology, but also philosophy and religion, take refuge in the mastery of facts and technical or methodological skills.

No civilization that has the power to destroy itself can afford the luxury of such a laissez-faire view of education. A civilization that has no wisdom to pass on to the next generation about what makes life valuable and worthwhile is a civilization preparing its own demise. After Auschwitz and Hiroshima we can no longer afford the luxury of such a naive world-view, which tends to reduce knowledge to facts and skills and treat values as personal preferences that we are free to select from, as if we were shopping in some intellectual supermarket. Professors need to be models of persons who understand and are prepared to be answerable for the social consequences of their views and require this of their students as well. We can no longer afford to live in a world where everything is "a matter of opinion" or personal preference.

The answer, of course, must not be to respond to relativism by teaching new forms of absolutism. In this book I have tried to identify a pattern of wisdom in our religions and cultures that finds a middle path between these two extremes—one that surrenders to the questions and welcomes strangers and their stories. We need to recognize and judge the values implicit in all our storied worlds against the "unseen measure" of human dignity, especially that of the stranger. I have tried to make a case for the utopian promise of Babel, arguing for the viability of a pluralistic cross-cultural ethic of human dignity, human rights, and human liberation that is at once both religious and secular. I am only too aware that this is a vulnerable thesis. I have had the audacity to trespass on a number of areas of specialization in religious studies without being an "expert" in these areas. I have engaged in a theology of culture and not just a theology of texts. I have engaged in an interpretation of narrative traditions as living elements within the emerging horizon of a global culture. Therefore, I have ventured to draw on religious themes and stories from different religions and cultures not simply in terms of their indigenous historical and cultural contexts from the past but also as if they are in some sense part of my heritage, speaking to me as a human being living in the closing decade of the second millennium. I do this because I am convinced that that is in fact the case. The mark of a profound story is that it transcends its textual history—living narrative traditions continually provide new insights into the ever-shifting historical horizons of the human condition. Moreover, great narratives achieve their status as "classics" by illuminating the human condition for anyone who is human, across cultures and religions—anyone, that is, who has the patience to appropriate the insights such narratives offer.

It is misleading to understand religious experiences and religious narratives as confined to tightly sealed and mutually exclusive cultural containers. As we have seen, in midlife Tolstoy underwent a profound conversion to the Christianity of Jesus' Sermon on the Mount, which has its roots in the Jewish tradition of welcoming the stranger. This conversion, it turns out, was precipitated by a Christianized version of the life of the Buddha that had made its way into the lives of the saints. Gandhi, in turn, was led to seek the wisdom of nonviolence in the Bhagavad Gita out of his encounter with writings of Tolstoy, especially those on the Sermon on the Mount. Finally, Martin Luther King, Jr., was inspired to go beyond Tolstoy's passive interpretation of the Sermon on the Mount by Gandhi's insights, derived from the Gita, for Gandhi emphasized the need to actively fight injustice through the audacity of nonviolent resistance, especially through organized civil disobedience. What this history reveals is that beyond our religious histories is a history of religion rooted in the convergence of such classical stories as those of Abraham, Jacob, and Job, and of Siddhartha, Arjuna, and Jesus. This history has given rise to a cross-cultural and interreligious ethic of audacity on behalf of the stranger, an ethic of human dignity, human rights, and human liberation.

What this history reveals is that these religious narratives are essentially unfinished stories that invite the participation of the hearer in their further completion. Such narratives have the power to transcend the differences between religious communities, not by eliminating those differences but by building bridges of unity-in-diversity. Gandhi did not become a Christian, and Martin Luther King, Jr., did not become a Hindu. Nevertheless, because of the insight each gained through sharing in the other's story, not only Hindus and Christians but countless others have embraced an ethic of audacity on behalf of strangers. The life stories of Gandhi and King have themselves become part of the ongoing cross-cultural convergence of narratives. Their stories have inspired both "secularists" and those of diverse religious commitments in many cultures to unleash a transcultural social revolution of secular holiness in defense of human dignity.

The time is past when we can regard either secular or religious narrative traditions as providing us with privileged cognitive positions. Secular language and "the secular world-view" do not provide us with some neutral frame of reference or Archimedian viewpoint from which we can safely and without bias analyze all our diverse storied worlds any more than our religious worlds do. As I have argued, the secular world is just one more particular storied world alongside our other storied worlds. Whether this secular world is divine or demonic depends largely on the religious imagination that implicitly or explicitly shapes it. For the holy and the secular are not antithetical but mutually complement each other even as they contravene the sacred. Where the sacral imagination operates within the parameters of a nondialectical dualism that creates a social world in which all who are different are regarded as profane and less than human, the narrative imagination structured by the experience of the holy desacralizes such social worlds and welcomes the stranger. The experience of the holy structures a narrative imagination that can envision the possibility of interdependence (unity-in-diversity) in a pluralistic secular world. The paradox of our age is that it requires a holy secularity. Pragmatically that holy secularity is found in those human rights organizations (whether religious or secular) that champion the dignity of strangers. Intellectually, that holy secularity finds a hospitable home in departments of religious studies, within the curriculum of the humanities—especially, but not exclusively, in secular universities and colleges. For even many religious colleges and universities now have "secular" religious studies departments rather than theology departments.

The academic study of religion is at the same time both a secular and a religious activity. The humanities exist to explore the meaning of human existence as illuminated by the great classical narratives of human experience, religious and secular. Theology as I understand it incontestably belongs to the humanities, for its task is to wrestle with the ever-elusive question of human identity. Knowledge of God and of ourselves, says Calvin, echoing the theology of Augustine, is so closely intertwined that which one precedes and brings forth the other is difficult to discern. But the Augustinian formulation does not articulate the complexity of that truth as well as the story of Jacob wrestling with the stranger (Genesis 32:23–32). For what the Genesis story makes clear is that self-knowledge is never just a private affair between God and the individual. On the contrary, only when we wrestle with the stranger, whether it is our neighbor or our enemy, can we begin to grasp both who we are and who or what God/transcendence is. This complexity makes theology an inherently ethical discipline. The ethical measure of a theology is whether or not it welcomes the stranger and audaciously protects the dignity and well-being of the stranger.

When we wrestle with the stranger, as the biblical story of Jacob implies (Genesis 32:23–32), we wrestle with the infinite—with the unfathomability of both the divine and the human. We wrestle with the God who can neither be named nor imaged and, paradoxically, in whose image we are created. The moment that realization dawns upon us we come to realize that the stranger is not just "the other." In that moment we realize we are strangers even to ourselves. Neither God nor our selves can be named and imaged. Our human dignity lies in the paradox of our essential openness to the infinite such that we can never be reduced and confined to the finite to which we surely belong. When we wrestle with the God who refuses to give a name we become strangers to ourselves and so are able to identify with the experience of the stranger. This enables us to welcome the stranger into our lives as the one whose very strangeness or otherness mediates the presence of a wholly other/transcendence. Through the story of Jacob's encounter with the stranger we come to learn that wrestling with the one who is alien or different does not have to lead to violence and the conquest of the other. It can lead instead to mutual respect. Jacob is the victor, he prevails, but the stranger is not defeated and blesses Jacob before departing. There is a lesson for doing theology and ethics in this story. Theology is not so much a matter of metaphysics as it is a task of reflecting on our encounter with the other as the occasion for understanding our relationship to the wholly other/transcendence. Through this double encounter we come to understand ourselves and what is required of us. Theology is rooted in our experience of alienation, for our experience of being a stranger (even to ourselves) opens us up to the possibility of welcoming the stranger as the holy other.

The quest of the humanities is the quest for insight into what it means to be human. The humanities embody two of the most important characteristics of secular holiness: (1) surrender to the questions (giving rise to the audacity to question all things) and (2) openness to strangers from diverse times and places who have a story to tell. The humanities are "set apart" (i.e., *qadosh* or holy) within the university as those disciplines and areas of study that seek to illuminate and protect the holy as disclosed in the unfathomability of human dignity. In so doing, the humanities go beyond analysis and description to engage in prescription; that is, to engage in ethics. In the humanities, especially in philosophy and theology (as academic disciplines),

we attempt to describe not only what is but to say what ought
to be.

Nothing undermines the teaching of ethics as much as the normless "supermarket" approach that lays out diverse views indif-
ferently. The humanities have a normative responsibility—a responsibility not only to sympathetically understand but also to critically
evaluate and to be audacious in their defense of human dignity. The
humanities ought to measure all world views by the measure of human dignity—the Socratic *unseen measure* of all things human. Our
task is the Socratic one of the examined life, which begins with a
knowledge of ignorance, a knowledge that forces us to recognize that
the human can never be fully fathomed or fully known—that we will
always be, in some sense, strangers even to ourselves. Through the
humanities we attempt to distill from such human experiences in
their moments of greatness the wisdom to live more humanly. Theology of culture as I have been pursuing it in this book reflects such an
understanding—an understanding of theology not as a confessional
discipline but a professional discipline. Its task is not confessing the
truth as seen through one narrative tradition but rather professing
the wisdom that can be discerned through a comparative study of the
great narrative traditions. It seeks the wisdom that comes from wrestling with the stranger. In this context the story of Israel (i.e., Jacob) is
as much my story as is the story of Siddhartha or Jesus or Arjuna—no
matter which narrative tradition I personally identify as "my own."

Religious studies is a product of the alienation produced by a
secular consciousness that is itself the product of both urbanization
and of the experience of the holy. This modern secular consciousness
alienates me sufficiently from my own tradition to be in a position to
be both critical of my own and sympathetic to the traditions of others.
To engage in religious studies, including theology of culture, within
the context of the humanities requires that I desacralize all sacred
traditions, beginning with my own, through a surrender to the critical
questions of the scholar who seeks to understand. The purpose of
these questions is not to profane these traditions but to secularize
them. Secularizing the sacred narrative traditions of the stranger
makes it possible for me to enter into these strange worlds, these
other worlds, and see reality through the eyes of the stranger in order
to come back with new insight into my own religion and culture. As
long as these traditions are considered sacred, they can be approached only by their own initiates. But the wisdom to be learned
from the religious experiences of human beings is too valuable to be

held captive by the traditions in which they originate. To desacralize these narrative traditions, therefore, is not to desecrate them but to treat them as holy. A holy story welcomes the stranger and the stranger's questions. A holy story and its meanings cannot be owned or possessed by any one person or community any more than the experience of the holy itself. Once they are desacralized the narrative worlds of the stranger become narrative worlds open to strangers— open to anyone who is human.

The phenomenological intentionality (i.e., seeking to understand the meaning of human action from the perspective of the actor's intentions) that is central to religious studies simply makes explicit what is unique to the intentionality of the humanities in general. From such a point of view it is never sufficient to study the social and psychological factors that led Shakespeare to write his plays, for example. As helpful as such "scientific" approaches may be for establishing a hermeneutical context, one must still come to grips, finally, with the unique insights and meanings embodied in Shakespeare's plays themselves. And so it is with all great narratives, including great religious narratives.

If, as Alasdair MacIntyre argues, the narrative form of *the quest* is the key to the formation of the virtuous life, then the spiritual adventure or quest of our time, the adventure of passing over and coming back, is essential to human virtue in our pluralistic world. Religious studies as part of the humanities has an essential role to play in that adventure. As Mircea Eliade argues in *The Quest*,[1] the comparative study of religions is the hermenutical key to the emergence of a new humanism, a humanism required by the pluralistic Babel of an emerging world civilization.

The danger of modern secular technological civilization, according to Eliade, is spiritual impoverishment—the smothering of the sacred beneath a veneer of secularity that creates an inability to understand the variety of sacred worlds that have shaped, and continue to shape, our humanity. This inability cuts off modern individuals from a sense of participation in life as a meaningful drama. And yet, he suggests, the sacred lies hidden in every secular culture, just waiting to be awakened. That is the spiritual task of the academic study of religion as Eliade envisioned it. "A considerable enrichment of consciousness," he tells us, "results from the hermeneutical effort of deciphering the meaning of myths, symbols, and other traditional religious structures; in a certain sense, one can even speak of the inner transformation of the researcher and hopefully of the sympathetic reader. What is called the phenomenology and history of religions can be considered among the very few humanistic disciplines that are at the same time propeaedeutic and spiritual techniques."[2]

Eliade was right to see the secular study of religion as a religious activity but his definition of religion as "the sacred" in opposition to the profane/secular made it difficult for him to see that the religious task in the manner I have been proposing. For I have been proposing that the holy and the secular are dialectically related and stand in opposition to the non-dialectical dualism of the sacred/profane. The holy secularizes and humanizes sacred worlds. Therefore I would argue that the spiritual task of the study of religion lies not in the awakening of the sacred hidden beneath the profane to overcome the secular, but rather in discovering that the study of religion as a secular activity is itself a manifestation of another kind of religious experience—the experience of the holy. It is only through secular technological or socio-historical consciousness made possible by the modern social sciences in the nineteenth and twentieth centuries that we have access to the multiple religious worlds of human meaning that Eliade would have us explore humanistically.

Eliade calls for nothing less than a *Second Renaissance* that would give birth to a "new humanism" through a "total hermeneutics"—a humanism that would transcend Western culture to grasp the depth and breadth of the possibilities of our humanity in cross-cultural perspective, especially through attention to the religious experiences of Asia and of the primal religions.[3] "Contrary to the natural sciences and to a sociology that strives to follow their model, hermeneutics ranges itself among the living sources of a culture. For, in short, every culture is constituted by a series of interpretations and revalorizations of its 'myths' or its specific ideologies."[4] Culture itself is a form of "creative hermeneutics." We become, to a large degree, what we interpret ourselves to be. "One could say that the Reformation and the Counter-Reformation constituted vast hermeneutics, intense and sustained efforts to revaluate the Judeo-Christian tradition by an audacious reinterpretation."[5]

Creative hermeneutics is not so much a total break with the past as it is a revealing of latent meanings that were not previously seen and whose recognition changes human consciousness. It is a technique, both academic and spiritual, that "ought to produce in the reader an action of *awakening.*"[6] This hermeneutics, Eliade argues, could produce not only a new world culture but a new phenomenology of mind whose therapeutic implications are nothing less than the liberation of our cultural (technopoetic) creativity.

Nearly all the contemporary philosophies and ideologies recognize that man's [and woman's] specific mode of being in the universe inevitably forces him [or her] to be a creator of culture. Whatever the point of departure for an analysis that seeks a definition of man [i.e., of the human] . . . one comes explicitly or implicitly, to characterize man as a creator of culture (i.e., language, institutions, techniques, arts, etc.). And all the methods of liberation of man—economic, political, psychological— are justified by their final goal: to deliver man from his chains or his complexes in order to open him to the world of the spirit and to render him [and her] *culturally creative*.[7]

"Today history is becoming truly universal for the first time, and so culture is in the process of becoming 'planetary.' The history of man from paleolithic to present times is destined to occupy the center of humanist education, whatever the local or national interpretations. The history of religions can play an essential role in this effort toward a *planétisation* of culture."[8] In a technological civilization, Eliade suggests, this is the direction some theologies of culture are moving in.

No doubt, Eliade was thinking especially of Paul Tillich's theology of culture and the seminar he and Tillich had recently engaged in together on theology and the history of religions. The theology of culture that I am proposing owes a debt to both even as it seeks to chart a path that goes beyond their proposals to embrace a model of theology of culture inspired by the work of Gabriel Vahanian. For Vahanian's theology of culture inspired the central theme of this work—the utopian promise of Babel. His theology has enabled me to see in the story of Babel the possibility of a new world of unity-in-diversity in which each speaks his or her own language yet each is understood by all. The world that Vahanian envisions is a world in which each of us has no other God than the God of others, the God who comes to us through the stranger—*God Anonymous*.[9] As we bring this millennium to an end and look forward to a "postmodern" world, therein lies a utopian vision that might carry us beyond apocalypse to discover a new heaven and a new earth.

Appendix: The United Nations Universal Declaration of Human Rights

PREAMBLE

Whereas recognition of the inherent dignity and of the equal and inalienable rights of all members of the human family is the foundation of freedom, justice and peace in the world,

Whereas disregard and contempt for human rights have resulted in barbarous acts which have outraged the conscience of mankind, and the advent of a world in which human beings shall enjoy freedom of speech and belief and freedom from fear and want has been proclaimed as the highest aspiration of the common people,

Whereas it is essential, if man is not to be compelled to have recourse, as a last resort, to rebellion against tyranny and oppression, that human rights should be protected by the rule of law,

Whereas it is essential to promote the development of friendly relations between nations,

Whereas the peoples of the United Nations have in the Charter reaffirmed their faith in fundamental human rights, in the dignity and worth of the human person and in the equal rights of men and women and have determined to promote social progress and better standards of life in larger freedom,

Whereas Member States have pledged themselves to achieve, in cooperation with the United Nations, the promotion of universal respect for the observance of human rights and fundamental freedoms,

Whereas a common understanding of these rights and freedoms is of the greatest importance for the full realization of this pledge,

Now, Therefore,

THE GENERAL ASSEMBLY PROCLAIMS

THIS UNIVERSAL DECLARATION OF HUMAN RIGHTS as a common standard of achievement for all peoples and all nations, to the end that every individual and every organ of society, keeping this Declaration constantly in mind, shall strive by teaching and education to promote respect for these rights and freedoms and by progressive measures, national and international, to secure their universal and effective recognition and observance, both among the peoples of Member States themselves and among the peoples of territories under their jurisdiction.

Article 1. All human beings are born free and equal in dignity and rights. They are endowed with reason and conscience and should act towards one another in a spirit of brotherhood.

Article 2. Everyone is entitled to all the rights and freedoms set forth in this Declaration, without distinction of any kind, such as race, colour, sex, language, religion, political or other opinion, national or social origin, property, birth or other status.

Furthermore, no distinction shall be made on the basis of the political, jurisdictional or international status of the country or territory to which a person belongs, whether it be independent, trust, non-self-governing or under any other limitation of sovereignty.

Article 3. Everyone has the right to life, liberty and security of person.

Article 4. No one shall be held in slavery or servitude; slavery and the slave trade shall be prohibited in all their forms.

Article 5. No one shall be subjected to torture or to cruel, inhuman or degrading treatment or punishment.

Article 6. Everyone has the right to recognition everywhere as a person before the law.

Article 7. All are equal before the law and are entitled without any discrimination to equal protection of the law. All are entitled to equal protection against any discrimination in violation of this Declaration and against any incitement to such discrimination.

Article 8. Everyone has the right to an effective remedy by the competent national tribunals for acts violating the fundamental rights granted him by the constitution or by law.

Article 9. No one shall be subjected to arbitrary arrest, detention or exile.

Article 10. Everyone is entitled in full equality to a fair and public hearing by an independent and impartial tribunal, in the determination of his rights and obligations and of any criminal charge against him.

Article 11. (1) Everyone charged with a penal offence has the right to be presumed innocent until proved guilty according to law in a public trial at which he has had all the guarantees necessary for his defence.

(2) No one shall be held guilty of any penal offence on account of any act or omission which did not constitute a penal offence, under national or international law, at the time when it was committed. Nor shall a heavier penalty be imposed than the one that was applicable at the time the penal offence was committed.

Article 12. No one shall be subjected to arbitrary interference with his privacy, family, home or correspondence, nor to attacks upon his honour and reputation. Everyone has the right to the protection of the law against such interference or attacks.

Article 13. (1) Everyone has the right to freedom of movement and residence within the borders of each state.

(2) Everyone has the right to leave any country, including his own, and to return to his country.

Article 14. (1) Everyone has the right to seek and to enjoy in other countries asylum from persecution.

(2) This right may not be invoked in the case of prosecutions genuinely arising from non-political crimes or from acts contrary to the purposes and principles of the United Nations.

Article 15. (1) Everyone has the right to a nationality.

(2) No one shall be arbitrarily deprived of his nationality nor denied the right to change his nationality.

Article 16. (1) Men and women of full age, without any limitation due to race, nationality or religion, have the right to marry and to found a family. They are entitled to equal rights as to marriage, during marriage and at its dissolution.

(2) Marriage shall be entered into only with the free and full consent of the intending spouses.

(3) The family is the natural and fundamental group unit of society and is entitled to protection by society and the State.

Article 17. (1) Everyone has the right to own property alone as well as in association with others.

(2) No one shall be arbitrarily deprived of his property.

Article 18. Everyone has the right to freedom of thought, conscience and religion; this right includes freedom to change his religion or belief, and freedom, either alone or in community with others and in public or private, to manifest his religion or belief in teaching, practice, worship and observance.

Article 19. Everyone has the right to freedom of opinion and expression; this right includes freedom to hold opinions without interference and to seek, receive and impart information and ideas through any media and regardless of frontiers.

Article 20. (1) Everyone has the right to freedom of peaceful assembly and association.

(2) No one may be compelled to belong to an association.

Article 21. (1) Everyone has the right to take part in the government of his country, directly or through freely chosen representatives.

(2) Everyone has the right of equal access to public service in his country.

(3) This will of the people shall be the basis of the authority of government; this will shall be expressed in periodic and genuine elections which shall be by universal and equal suffrage and shall be held by secret vote or by equivalent free voting procedures.

Article 22. Everyone, as a member of society, has the right to social security and is entitled to realization, through national effort and international co-operation and in accordance with the organization and resources of each State, of the economic, social and cultural rights indispensable for his dignity and the free development of his personality.

Article 23. (1) Everyone has the right to work, to free choice of employment, to just and favourable conditions of work and to protection against unemployment.

(2) Everyone, without any discrimination, has the right to equal pay for equal work.

(3) Everyone who works has the right to just and favourable remuneration ensuring for himself and his family an existence worthy of human dignity, and supplemented, if necessary, by other means of social protection.

(4) Everyone has the right to form and to join trade unions for the protection of his interests.

Article 24. Everyone has the right to rest and leisure, including reasonable limitation of working hours and periodic holidays with pay.

Article 25. (1) Everyone has the right to a standard of living adequate for the health and well-being of himself and of his family, including food, clothing, housing and medical care and necessary social services, and the right to security in the event of unemployment, sickness, disability, widowhood, old age or other lack of livelihood in circumstances beyond his control.

(2) Motherhood and childhood are entitled to special care and assistance. All children, whether born in or out of wedlock, shall enjoy the same social protection.

Article 26. (1) Everyone has the right to education. Education shall be free, at least in the elementary and fundamental stages. Elementary education shall be compulsory. Technical and professional education shall be made generally available and higher education shall be equally accessible to all on the basis of merit.

(2) Education shall be directed to the full development of the human personality and to the strengthening of respect for human rights and fundamental freedoms. It shall promote understanding, tolerance and friendship among all nations, racial or religious groups, and shall further the activities of the United Nations for the maintenance of peace.

(3) Parents have a prior right to choose the kind of education that shall be given to their children.

Article 27. (1) Everyone has the right freely to participate in the cultural life of the community, to enjoy the arts and to share in scientific advancement and its benefits.

(2) Everyone has the right to the protection of the moral and material interests resulting from any scientific, literary or artistic production of which he is the author.

Article 28. Everyone is entitled to a social and international order in which the rights and freedoms set forth in this Declaration can be fully realized.

Article 29. (1) Everyone has duties to the community in which alone the free and full development of his personality is possible.

(2) In the exercise of his rights and freedoms, everyone shall be subject only to such limitations as are determined by law solely for the purpose of securing due recognition and respect for the rights and freedoms of others and of meeting the just requirements of morality, public order and the general welfare in a democratic society.

(3) These rights and freedoms may in no case be exercised contrary to the purposes and principles of the United Nations.

Article 30. Nothing in this Declaration may be interpreted as implying for any State, group or person any right to engage in any activity or to perform any act aimed at the destruction of any of the rights and freedoms set forth herein.

Notes

Preface

The Death of God (New York: Braziller, 1957, 1959, 1960, 1961). *Wait Without Idols* (New York: Braziller, 1964). *No Other God* (New York: Braziller, 1966). *God and Utopia: The Church in a Technological Civlization* (New York: Seabury Press, 1977). *Dieu anonyme* (Paris: Desclée de Brouwer, 1989). *L'utopie chrétienne* (Paris: Desclée de Brouwer, 1922).

Prologue: The Challenge of Babel—From Alienation to Ethics After Auschwitz and Hiroshima

1. All biblical quotations are from *The New Revised Standard Version*. (Nashville: Thomas Nelson Publishers, 1989), unless otherwise noted.
2. Richard Schwartz, *Judaism and Global Survival* (New York: Atara Publishing Co., 1987), p. 13. Schwartz's source for this claim is J.H. Hertz, *The Pentateuch and Haftorahs* (London: Soncino Press, 1958), p. 504.
3. "Chutzpah," for those unfamiliar with the term, should not be pronounced the way it looks. The "CH" should be pronounced as an aspirated "H" and the first syllable (chutz), should rhyme with "foots," not "huts."
4. I use the spelling a-theist to indicate someone who neither believes nor disbelieves in the existence of God but simply does not see the relevance of such beliefs. I retain the spelling atheist for those for whom the nonexistence of God is an active (one might even say dogmatic) belief.
5. Paul Tillich, "Üeber die Idee einer Theologie der Kultur" in *Kanstudien* (Berlin: Pan Verlag, Rolf Heise, 1920). This essay is found in translation in *What is Religion?*, translated by James Luther Adams (New York: Harper & Row, Harper Torchbooks, 1969).

Chapter 1. Technology and the Dialectics of Apocalypse and Utopia

1. Richard Erdoes, *A.D. 1000: Living on the Brink of Apocalaypse* (New York: Harper and Row, 1988), p. 1.
2. *The City of God*, XX, 7–9. Eric Voegelin, *The New Science of Politics* (Chicago: University of Chicago Press, 1952), p. 109. See especially Chapters 3 and 4, for a discussion of Augustine and Joachim.

3. Voegelin, *The New Science of Politics*, pp. 111–114. Voegelin's most important work is his five volume *Order and History* (Baton Rouge: Louisiana State Univ. Press, 1956–1987).

4. From *The Gay Science* by Friedrich Nietzsche in *The Portable Nietzsche*, ed. Walter Kaufmann (New York: Viking Press, 1954 and 1968), pp. 95–96. *The Gay Science* was first published in 1882.

5. Herbert Richardson, *Toward and American Theology* (New York: Harper and Row, 1967), p. 16.

6. Ibid., p. 17. It is important in the development of this chapter to remember that the Greek term *techné* has two overlapping meanings, suggesting, for example, both the "art" of the poet and the "skill" of the blacksmith.

7. The term *techniques of the human* is suggested by Gabriel Vahanian in *God and Utopia: The Church in a Technological Civilization* (New York: Crossroad Books, Seabury Press, 1977).

8. Within a century of the invention of the term *utopia* by More, the word "came to denote general programs and platforms for ideal societies. . . . The line between a utopian system and political and social theory often became shadowy." Cf. Frank E. Manuel and Fritzie P. Manuel, *Utopian Thought in the Western World* (Cambridge, Mass.: Belknap Press of Harvard University Press, 1979), especially the introduction.

9. *Verbal condition* is more precise, because it suggests that the human being as "subject" is an event that occurs in the act of realizing a "predicate." The human is not static but dynamic; that is, verbal. Whitehead has built an entire metaphysics of process on this observation.

10. Vahanian, *God and Utopia*, p. 50.

11. Alfred North Whitehead, *Modes of Thought* (New York: Free Press, 1938 and 1966), p. 22.

12. Maurice Merleau-Ponty, *Signs* (Evanston, Ill.: Northwestern University Press), p. 91.

13. The priority of "theoria" to "praxis" here is a purely logical one. Historically these have often been reversed. Herbert Richardson has argued persuasively that this distinction is dissolved by the American pragmatic approach to science, which is inherently technological. So he argues: "Whereas theoretical science develops experiments that lead us to perceive nature as an autonomous order with its own intrinsic intentionalites. Pragmatic experiments generate a perception of nature as open to receive human intentions, as receptive to, even inviting, technological transformation." Cf. "Pragmatic Science and Man" in *Projections: Shaping an American Theology for the Future* (New York: Doubleday and Co., 1970) pp. 109–133. All of which is to say, that in a technological society, science itself becomes utopian.

14. Nietzsche, *The Gay Science*, pp. 98–99.

15. Alfred North Whitehead, *The Aims of Education* (New York: The Free Press, 1929 and 1957), p. 12.

16. Ibid., p. 13.

17. Cf. Manfred Stanley, *The Technological Conscience* (New York: The Free Press, 1978).

18. Ibid., p. xiii.
19. Ibid., p. xiii.
20. Ibid., p. xiv.
21. Cf. Karl Mannheim, *Ideology and Utopia* (New York: Harcourt, Brace and World, 1936), especially Chapter 4.
22. Stanley, *The Technological Conscience*, p. 53.
23. Jacques Ellul, *The New Demons* (New York: Crossroad Books, Seabury Press, 1973 and 1975), pp. 48ff.
24. Friedrich Nietzsche, *Thus Spoke Zarathustra*, in *The Portable Nietzsche*, p. 198.
25. The Procrustean and Protean models utilized in this chapter are based on a distinction in Eric Voegelin's work between the "cosmological" and "anthropological" styles of human existence. This distinction will be treated more fully in Chapter 4. The mythological labels were first suggested to me by the psychological work of Robert Jay Lifton, who describes the modern self as "Protean."
26. Nietzsche, *The Gay Science*, p. 95.
27. Nietzsche, *Thus Spoke Zarathustra*, pp. 217–219. In focusing on "The Night Song" here I am following the lead of Eric Voegelin in his treatment of Nietzsche in *Science, Politics and Gnosticism* (Chicago: Henry Regnery Company, 1969).
28. Merleau-Ponty, *Signs*, p. 88.
29. Lonergan's main works are *Insight: A Study of Human Understanding* (New York: Philosophical Library; London: Darton, Longman and Todd, 1957) and *Method in Theology* (New York: Herder and Herder, 1972).
30. A virtually unconditioned truth is a truth whose conditions are met when the relevant questions have been successfully answered. Also, Lonergan considers himself to have isolated the invariant structural dynamic of knowing, because every oversight or error can be discovered and corrected only by reactivating this dynamic, and every protest against this theoretical characterization must itself peform these operations of "attending," "understanding," "judging," and "deciding."
31. The Procrustean and Protean models parallel not only Eric Voegelin's distinctions between cosmological and anthropological order but also Paul Tillich's distinctions between heteronomy and autonomy in ethics. Lonergan's model of shifting horizons would meet the requirement for Tillich's third type of ethic: theonomy. See Chapter 4 for a full discussion of these themes.
32. *The New Demons*, p. 117.
33. "Search for an Image," in *Images of the Future*, ed. Robert Bundy (Buffalo: Prometheus Books, 1976), pp. 24 and 25.
34. Jacques Ellul, *Apocalypse: The Book of Revelation* (New York: Seabury Press, 1977), p. 24.
35. See Vahanian, *God and Utopia*.
36. Ibid., p. 38. The *novum* referred to here should be understood as that which is genuinely new and not just the kind of change that is superfi-

cial. The novum clearly must not be equated with some ideology of progress. On the contrary *novum* suggests "new creation," new beginnings, the grace or forgiveness that enables one to start afresh. It approximates what Ellul would characterize as the eruption of the apocalyptic or eschatological end (i.e., God) here in this present moment that makes possible a transcending and transforming freedom.

37. Vahanian tends to treat *apocalypse* and *eschatology* as terms with opposing meanings between which one must choose, whereas Ellul tends to virtually equate these terms.

38. *God and Utopia*, p. 49.

39. Even as supernaturalism once appropriated and expropriated the language of nature.

40. Jacques Ellul, *The Ethics of Freedom* (Grand Rapids, Michigan: William B. Eerdmans Publishing Co., 1976), p. 164.

41. *God and Utopia*, p. 44.

42. Ibid., p. 137.

43. Ibid., p. 137.

44. Ibid., pp. 45, 46, 54.

45. Ibid., p. 71.

46. Ibid., p. 137.

47. Mannheim, *Ideology and Utopia*, especially Chapter 4. "The Utopian Mentality."

48. Ibid., pp. 262–263.

49. Ibid., p. 213.

50. Ibid., p. 217.

51. Ibid., pp. 192 and 199.

52. Richard John Neuhaus, *The Naked Public Square* (Grand Rapids, Mich.: William B. Eerdmans, 1984).

Chapter 2. The Narrative Ambivalence of a Technological Civilization: Apocalypse or Utopia?

1. Harvey Cox, *The Secular City* (New York: Macmillan, 1965), 1st Edition p. 1.

2. Ibid., p. 4.

3. Ibid., p. 17.

4. Ibid., p. 17.

5. Ibid., p. 30.

6. Ibid., p. 35.

7. Ibid., pp. 35.

8. Ibid., p. 174.

9. Ibid., p. 175.

10. Ibid., p. 175–176.

11. Ibid., p. 177.

12. Ibid., p. 21.

13. Ibid., pp. 109.

14. Ibid., p. 155.

15. Richard Rubenstein, *The Cunning of History: The Holocaust and the American Future* (New York: Harper Colophon Books, 1975), pp. 94–95.

16. Ibid., p. 7.

17. Ibid., p. 2.

18. Ibid., p. 4–5.

19. Ibid., p. 6.

20. Ibid., p. 16.

21. Ibid., p. 17.

22. Ibid., p. 17.

23. Ibid., p. 21.

24. Ibid., p. 87.

25. Ibid., p. 88.

26. Ibid., p. 88.

27. Ibid., p. 89.

28. Ibid., p. 90.

29. Ibid., pp. 90–91.

30. Ibid., p. 91

31. Ibid., p. 29.

32. Ibid., p. 30.

33. Ibid., p. 31.

34. Ibid., p. 31.

35. Ibid., p. 92.

36. Ibid., p. 93.

37. Ibid., p. 93.

38. Ibid., p 97.

39. Jacques Ellul, *The Technological Society* (New York: Random House, Vintage Books, 1964) and *The Political Illusion* (New York: Vintage Books, Random House, 1967).

40. Ellul, *The New Demons*.

41. Ibid., p. 203.

42. Throughout this study, when I speak of a technological society, I shall have Ellul's meaning in mind—a society dominated of technique and efficiency.

43. Ellul, *The Technological Society*, p. xxv.

44. Jacques Ellul, *The Political Illusion*, p. 66.

45. Ellul, *The Technological Society*, p. 141.

46. Ellul, *The New Demons*, p. 48.

47. Ibid., p. 47.

48. Ibid. See Chapter 3, "The Sacred Today."

49. Jacques Ellul, *To Will and to Do* (Philadelphia: Pilgrim Press, 1969), p. 193.

50. Jacques Ellul, *Hope in Time of Abandonment* (New York: Seabury Press, 1973), p. 42.

51. Ellul, *The New Demons*, p. 52.

52. Jacques Ellul, *Autopsy of Revolution* (New York: Alfred A. Knopf, 1971), pp. 160–161.

53. Ellul, *The Technological Society*, p. 427.

54. Jacques Ellul, *The Meaning of the City* (Grand Rapids, Mich.: William B. Eerdmans, 1970), pp. 1–10.

55. Ibid., p. 16.

56. Ibid., p. 13.

57. Elie Wiesel, *One Generation After* (New York: Avon Books, 1965, 1967, 1970), p. 9.

58. Irving Greenberg, "Cloud of Smoke, Pillar of Fire: Judaism, Christianity, and Modernity After the Holocaust," in *Auschwitz: Beginning of a New Era?* ed. Eva Fleischner (New York: KTAV Publishing House, 1977), pp. 37–38. The order of these two paragraphs is inverted from the order of the original text.

59. Arthur A. Cohen, *The Tremendum* (New York: Crossroad, 1981), p. 17.

60. Ibid., p. 17–18.

61. Ibid., p. 18.

62. Ibid., p. 14.

63. Ibid., p. 18–19.

64. Ibid., p. 19.

65. Ibid., p. 20.

66. Ibid., p. 21.

67. Ibid., p. 22.

68. Ibid., p. 36.

69. Ibid., p. 36.

70. Ibid., p. 22.

71. Ibid., pp. 41–42.

72. Ibid., p. 41.

73. Ibid., pp. 43–44.

74. Ibid., p. 30.

75. Ibid., p. 32.

76. Ellul, *Apocalypse*, p. 98.

Chapter 3. From Auschwitz to Hiroshima: The Apocalyptic Dark Night

1. Rosemary Ruether, *Faith and Fratricide* (New York: Seabury Press, 1979), pp. 193–194.

2. Edward Flannery, *The Anguish of the Jews* (New York: Mac Millan, 1965), pp. 49ff.

3. For a full account of this narrative tradition of supersession, see Ruether's *Faith and Fratricide*.

4. Flannery, *The Anguish of the Jews*, p. 92.

5. Franklin Littell, *The Crucifixion of the Jews* (New York: Harper and Row, 1975), p. 104.

6. Lucy Dawidowicz, *The War Against the Jews, 1933–1945* (New York: Holt, Rinehart and Winston, 1975), p. 21.

7. Ibid., p. 21, quoting Hitler's *Mein Kampf.*

8. Paul Althaus, in *The Ethics of Martin Luther* (Philadephia: Fortress Press, 1972), makes the point that, according to Luther, God's grace and wrath are present in both kingdoms (see Chapter 3, especially pp. 53 and 54 and also 81). But the subtle ways in which that is true seem not to have undermined Luther's basic insistence on unquestioning obedience to secular authority.

9. Ibid., p. 74.

10. Ibid., p. 137.

11. Elie Wiesel, *One Generaton After* (New York: Avon Books, 1965), p. 10.

12. Robert Jay Lifton, *The Nazi Doctors: Medical Killing and the Psychology of Genocide* (New York: Basic Books, 1986).

13. Ibid., p. 4.

14. Ibid., p. 5.

15. Ibid., p. 129.

16. Ibid., p. 17.

17. Ibid., p. 16.

18. Ibid., p. 150.

19. Ibid., p. 418.

20. Ibid., p. 419.

21. Ibid., p. 423.

22. Ibid., p. 423.

23. See Chapters 4 and 5 of my book *Narrative Theology After Auschwitz* for a detailed discussion this subject.

24. Lifton, *The Nazi Doctors*, p. 196.

25. Ibid., p. 196.

26. Ibid., p. 426–427.

27. Ibid., p. 464.

28. Ibid., p. 421.

29. Ibid., p. 422.

30. Ibid., pp.423–424.

31. Cohen, *The Tremendum*, p. 19.

32. Note here that I give priority to myth and the power of ideation (the realm of Marx's superstructure) rather than to the social-institutional infrastructure. The tendency of the social sciences, Marxist and non-Marxist, has been to give priority to political and economic factors and to see mythic narratives and ideas as dependent variables. But the history of anti-Judaism/anti-Semitism I think is overwhelming evidence that the mythological-ideational can have the force of an independent variable with the power to alter the infrastructure of society. Although economic and political factors help explain the waxing and waning of anti-Semitism, no infra-

structural factors are persistent enough throughout this long history to explain the continued and pervasive influence of anti-Judaism and anti-Semitism. On the contrary the myth alone can bring coherence to this dark history. Nothing is more symbolically expressive of the autonomy of myth than Hitler's insistence on diverting trains that could have carried troops to the front during the last months of the war in order to send as many Jews to the death camps as possible. There was absolutely no political, military, or economic advantage to such a policy. In fact it was self-destructive. And yet it alone allowed Hitler to live out his own vision of his mythic destiny.

33. Lifton's reference to Luther in relation to the problem of doubling is limited to a perceptive footnote on the dialectical tradition in Germany in which he suggests, quite correctly as we shall see, that doubling may be related to Luther's concept of a God "who works by contraries" (p. 428).

34. Gerhard Ebeling, *Luther: An Introduction to his Thought* (Philadelphia: Fortress Press, 1964 and 1970), pp. 236–237. Emphasis added.

35. *Augustine's Confessions*, trans. Rex Werner (New York: Mentor-Omega, New American Library, 1963), p. 42.

36. *Pagan* is a term I reserve for all religions rooted in the myths that suggest the gods demand the sacrifice of living beings, whether human or animal. All such narratives suggest in one way or another that further life is possible only if some being's life is sacrificed. Such demands sacralize death and are ultimately demonic.

37. Richard Rubenstein, *After Auschwitz* (Indianapolis: Bobbs-Merrill, 1966), p. 125. Rubenstein also points out (p. 54) that Dean Gruber, a minister who saved many Jewish lives during the Holocaust himself, believed that "for some reason it was part of God's plan that the Jews died, God demands our death daily." Despite their religious and political opposition, says Rubenstein, it is frightening to see that both Dean Gruber and Eichmann both served their masters with "complete and utterly unquestioning fidelity."

38. Peter Wyden, *Day One: Before Hiroshima and After* (New York: Simon and Schuster, 1984), p. 212.

39. Greenberg, "Cloud of Smoke, Pillar of Fire."

40. The United States has harbored tribalisms and racisms and imperialisms as vicious as any around the world. The point here is not that the United States has always acted better than other ethnocentric nations but rather that when it did act like other nations it had to explain the inconsistency because its dominant narrative traditions offered no legitimation for such actions as did those of the Nazis and of Meijji Japan.

41. The Hiroshima statistics are from Richard Rhode's *The Making of the Atomic Bomb* (New York: Simon and Schuster, 1986), pp. 734 and 740. The Auschwitz statistic is from Lucy Dawidowicz's *The War Against the Jews*, p. 149.

42. Lifton, *The Nazi Doctors*, p. 171. My "average" figures are a rough calculation based on 2 to 3 million deaths at Auschwitz over a period of three years.

43. Jonathon Schell, *The Fate of the Earth* (New York: Avon Books, 1982), pp. 47 and 54.

44. Ibid., p. 3.

45. Robert Jay Lifton and Richard Falk, *Indefensible Weapons: The Political and Psychological Case Against Nuclearism* (New York: Basic Books,1982), p. 148.

46. See David Duncan and Carl Sagan, *A Path Where No Man Thought: Nuclear Winter and the End of the Arms Race* (New York: Random House, 1990), p. 107.

47. W. B. Yeats, "The Second Coming," in *Selected Poems and Two Plays of William Butler Yeats,* ed. M. L. Rosenthal (New York: Macmillan, 1962), p. 91.

48. Robert Jay Lifton, *Death in Life* (New York: Basic Books, 1967). p. 404.

49. Ibid., p. 408.

50. Ibid., p. 26.

51. Richard Rhodes, *The Making of the Atomic Bomb* (New York: Simon Schuster, 1986), pp. 571–572.

52. Ibid., p. 572.

53. Ibid., p. 572.

54. From Donne's *Holy Sonnets,* in *The Norton Anthology of English Literature,* Vol. 1, (New York: W. W. Norton and Co., 1962), p. 785.

55. Wyden, *Day One*, p. 109.

56. Ibid., pp. 148 and 68.

57. Ibid., p. 150. The conclusion of Oppenheimer, reported by his assistant, on recalling a discussion of the issue of the Chicago protestors with Oppenheimer.

58. Ibid., pp. 148–149.

59. Ibid., p. 157.

60. Ibid., p. 176.

61. Ibid., p. 134.

62. Mircea Eliade, *Cosmos and History* (New York: Harper and Row, 1959), pp. 139ff.

63. R. C. Zaehner, *Hindu Scriptures,* (New York & London: Dutton and Dent, Everyman's Library, 1938, 1966), p. 297.

64. I thank my colleague in Asian religions Nathan Katz for checking the Sanskrit and confirming this for me.

65. Zaehner, *Hindu Scriptures,* pp. 297–298.

66. *The Song of God: Bhagavad Gita* translated by Swami Prabhavananda and Christopher Isherwood, (New York: Mentor, New American Library, 1944, 1951, 1972), p. 122. R. C. Zaehner's translation reads: "Were he to slaughter [all] these worlds, slays nothing. He is not bound." *Hindu Scriptures*, p. 319.

67. *Holy Sonnets*, pp. 787–788.

68. Elie Wiesel, *A Jew Today* (New York: Random House, 1978), p. 155. There is a striking affinity between the Babylonian story of Gilgamesh wrestling with his double, the stranger Enkidu, and Jacob wrestling with the stranger. In both cases no one is defeated and the contest ends with an

affirmative mutual respect. See the epilogue of *Narrative Theology after Ausch-witz* or a fuller discussion of this.

69. A. Alvarez, *The Savage God: A Study in Suicide* (New York: Random House, 1970, 1971, 1972).

70. A *koan* is a verbal puzzle the Zen master gives a disciple to meditate upon day and night until the rational mind is exhausted and defeated and "lets go," at which point enlightenment is experienced and with it the true nonrational meaning of the *koan*.

71. Heinrich Dumoulin, S.J., *A History of Zen Buddhism* (Boston: Beacon Press, 1963), pp. 258–259.

72. Robert Bellah, *Tokugawa Religion: The Cultural Roots of Modern Japan* (New York: The Free Press, 1957, 1985), p. 90.

73. Ibid., p. 90. Bellah, quoting Kawakami Tasuke.

74. Ibid., p. 91.

75. Ibid., p. 93.

76. Ibid., p. 94.

77. Ibid., p. 98.

78. Ibid., pp. 180–181.

79. Robert Bellah, *Beyond Belief* (New York: Harper and Row, 1970.), p. 71.

80. Quoted in Kosuke Koyama's *Mount Fujui and Mount Sinai: A Critique of Idols* (Maryknoll, N.Y.: Orbis Books, 1984), p. 18.

81. Edwin Hoyt, *Japan's War* (New York: Da Capo Press, 1986), p. 11.

82. Koyama, *Mount Fuji and Mount Sinai*, p. 34.

83. Bellah, *Beyond Belief*, pp. 95–96. Japanese Buddhists were as un-questioningly obedient as German Christians were in Nazi Germany. "The majority of those in Japan's world of religion gave their complete cooperation and approval to all government policies from the Meijji Restoration until the end of the 2nd World War, and both Buddhism and Christianity were no exception. As a matter of fact, they were in the very mainstream of this tendency." ["Buddhism and Peace in Modern Japan" by Tsuyoshi Nakano in *Buddhism and Leadership For Peace* (Tokyo: Soka University Peace Research In-stitute, 1986), p. 84.] For an excellent analysis of Buddhist movements and their accommodation to the state in Meijji Japan, see Winston Davis, "Buddh-ism and the Modernization of Japan" in *History of Religions*, Vol. 28, No. 4, May 1989, pp. 305–339.

84. Robert Jay Lifton, *The Future of Immortality, and Other Essays for a Nuclear Age* (New York: Basic Books, 1987), pp. 5–6.

85. Lifton and Falk, *Indefensible Weapons*, p. 251.

86. Ibid., p. 179.

87. Ibid., p. 8–9.

88. We should recognize in these two realms, morality and action, the realms of private and public life, as mirrors of Luther's two kingdoms and its philosophical equivalent, Kant's distinction between noumenal and phenom-enal realms.

89. Schell, *The Fate of the Earth*, p. 195.
90. Ibid., p. 198.

Chapter 4. The Ethical Challenge of Auschwitz and Hiroshima to Technological Utopianism

1. History and society are not themselves empirical realities. No one has ever "seen" either. Both are conceptual realities abstracted from diverse experiences and evidences. At the existential level the experience of being within history, society or transcendence is analagous. In each case we know we are part of a larger movement or reality because we respond to certain symbols that makes us feel part of this larger reality that defines the horizon of (and inspires) our actions.

2. Mircea Eliade, *Cosmos and History: The Myth of Eternal Return* (New York: Harper and Row, 1959).

3. Eric Voegelin, *Order and History*, vol. 3, *Plato and Aristotle* (Baton Rouge: Louisiana State University Press, 1957). See especially his discussion of the "The Models of Soul and Society," pp. 108ff.

4. In Judaism this inwardness is first revealed in the psalms and in the Exilic prophets, especially Jeremiah. For Judaism, openness to the infinite takes the form of an eschatological consciousness in which all things are passing away. In Buddhism it takes the form of a psychological (i.e., meditative) penetration of the ontological level to grasp the radical impermanence of all things. Both result in the radical openness of the self to the temporal dimension.

5. Voegelin, *The New Science of Politics*, p. 75. See discussion on the discovery of the soul pp. 67–75.

6. Transcendence in this sense must not be confused with the "ineffable" which is that which cannot be seen but can be imagined, as when the Upanishads imagine that there is an invisible essence "Brahman" that pervades all things or when neo-Platonism imagines reality "emanating" from the One.

7. See Stanley Hauerwas, *Truthfulness and Tragedy* (Notre Dame, Ind.: University of Notre Dame Press, 1977), pp. 25ff.

8. Bernard Lonergan, *A Second Collection* (Philadelphia: Westminster Press, 1974), p. 92.

9. Peter Berger, *The Sacred Canopy* (New York: Anchor Books, Doubleday & Co., 1967), pp. 6–7.

10. Gabriel Vahanian, *God and Utopia: The Church in a Technological Civilization* (New York: Seabury Press, 1976), p. 137. This awareness is most dramatically represented in the works of two nineteenth century figures, Kierkegaard and Nietzsche. Both rejected Hegel's attempt to create a metaphysics, or perhaps we should say a natural theology of history. They rejected his attempt to reduce history to nature, to reduce the multiplicity of cultures

strung out through time to a single dialectically unfolding, all-encompassing essence. From radically different perspectives (in some respects) both Kierkegaard and Nietzsche insisted that a human being is not a *fixed animal* defined by an *essential human nature*. Both insisted that *existence precedes essence*, and hence history is the realm of freedom that cannot be defined in advance, like the unfolding of an oak tree from an acorn. To be human is to choose one's self, to transvalue all values, to shape one's self and world in terms of as yet unrealized possibilities.

11. By *mediated meaning*, I mean the capacity to live in the world of the imagination. Human language does more than communicate, it mediates remembered worlds and anticipates future worlds, and it imagines and interprets the world of immediate experience, so that even that world is mediated. Our interpretations always stand between us and "reality."

12. Martin Heidegger, *The Question Concerning Technology and Other Essays* (New York: Harper Colophon Books, 1977), p. 34.

13. Vahanian, *God and Utopia*, p. 86.

14. The idea of management embodied in the modern concept of public or social policy is both ethically powerful and ethically dangerous. In formulating a social ethic understood as a management ethic there are two fundamental models we might consider. The first is a centralized model, though which one would seek to impose some design for the total control of society and all the contingencies of life. This would be grandiose, totalitarian, and tragic. In the second case, however, we have a decentralized model of institutional pluralism in which management is understood not on the model of "control of others" but of "self-control." In this case management does for each institution what self-control does for the individual, that is, it enables the exercise of responsibility. In this model, management has the ethical task of making institutions self-transcending and hence able to respond and be called to responsibility for their actions.

15. An extremely useful analysis of the metaphors of nature in Western thought has been done by Robert A. Nisbet, in *Social Change and History* (New York: Oxford University Press, 1969).

16. Paul Tillich, "Ueber die Idee einer Theologie der Kultur," in *Kanstudien* (Berlin: Pan Verlag, Rolf Heise, 1920). This essay is found in translation in *What Is Religion*, trans. James Luther Adams (New York: Harper and Row, Harper Torchbooks, 1969).

17. Ibid., p. 160.

18. Ellul, *The Political Illusion*, p. 234.

19. Tillich, *What Is Religion?* p. 180.

20. Ibid., p. 178.

21. Ibid., p. 156. Tillich followed Fichte's division of the sciences into (1) thinking (logic and mathematics), (2) empirical (roughly comparable to the natural, social, and historical sciences), and (3) cultural or normative, including both *theoria* (i.e., epistemology, aesthetics, metaphysics) and *praxis* (i.e., law, political science, ethics). See Chapter 4 of James Luther Adam's *Paul Tillich's Philosophy of Culture, Science and Religion* (New York: Schocken Books,

1965). Although Tillich was referring explicitly to the last category, his point applies to the historical and social sciences as well.

22. Tillich, *What Is Religion?* p. 158.

23. Ibid., p. 157.

24. Vahanian, *God and Utopia.*

25. Tillich, *What Is Religion?* p. 165.

26. Ibid., p. 165.

27. John Dunne, *The Way of All the Earth* (New York: Mac Millan, 1972), pp. 121ff.

28. Jacques Ellul, *The Presence of the Kingdom* (New York: Seabury Press, 1967), pp. 134 and 135.

29. All religions make some use of both types of language; it is a matter of which is primary. Buddhists, of course, do use metaphor, even as Hindus use the language of negation. But in Buddhism the language of negation is dominant, and analogy and metaphor must be subjugated to it. For Hinduism, on the whole, the inverse is true.

30. Lewis Mumford, *The Myth of the Machine The Pentagon of Power* (New York: Harcourt, Brace, Jovanovich, Inc., 1964, 1970), pp. 396–400.

31. See the essays on religious resurgence in Islam by Lous J. Cantori, Jamal Sanad and Mark Tessler, Gregory Rose and Richard Norton in *Religious Resurgence and Politics in the Contemporary World*, ed. Emile Sahliyeh (Albany: State University of New York Press, 1990).

32. H. Richard Niebuhr, *Christ and Culture* (New York: Harper and Row, Torchbooks, 1951).

33. Paul Tillich, "The Significance of the History of Religions for the Systematic Theologian," in *The Future of Religions*, ed. Jerald C. Brauer (New York: Harper and Row, 1966), p. 82.

34. Ibid., p. 83.

35. Ibid., p. 89.

36. Ibid., p. 90.

37. Lewis Mumford, *Technics and Civilization* (New York: Harcourt, Brace, & World, Inc., 1934, 1964), pp. 81–96.

38. One must acknowledge that the Japanese sense of racial superiority was reinforced by a felt need to defend the Asian world against the arrogant imperialistic assumptions of white Europeans who somehow felt the whole world should belong to them, including Asia.

39. Dunne, *The Way of All the Earth*, p. 151.

40. Tillich, "The Significance of the History of Religions for the Systematic Theologian," in *The Future of Religion*, p. 87.

Chapter 5. Utopian Ethics: From Human Dignity to Human Rights and Human Liberation

1. Irving Greenberg, "Cloud of Smoke, Pillar of Fire," p. 38.

2. Anson Laytner, *Arguing with God: A Jewish Tradition* (Northvale, N.J.: Jason Aronson Inc., 1990), pp. xvi and xvii.

3. Belden C. Lane, "Hutzpa K'lapei Shamaya: A Christian Response to the Jewish Tradition of Arguing with God," *The Journal of Ecumenical Studies* 23 no. 4 (Fall 1986): 567 and 568. I have standardized the transliteration of *hutzpa* with a "*ch*" and modified quotations from Lane accordingly.

4. Mordechai Rotenberg, *Dialogue with Deviance: The Hasidic Ethic and the Theory of Social Contraction* (Philadelphia: Institute for the Study of Human Issues, 1983), p. 14.

5. The quotations from Job are from Marvin Pope's Anchor Bible translation.

6. Jacob Neusner, *Invitation to the Talmud* (New York: Harper and Row, 1973), p. xviii.

7. From the Babylonian Talmud, tract Baba Metzia, IV, 59b cited by Raphael Patai in *Gates to the Old City* (New York: Avon Books, 1980), pp. 244–245 and quoted in Lane, "Hutzpa K'Lapei Shamaya."

8. Wiesel, *A Jew Today*, p. 6.

9. Ibid., p. 6.

10. Ibid., p. 146.

11. Elie Wiesel, *The Trial of God* (New York: Schocken Books, 1979).

12. Ibid., p. 154.

13. Ibid., p. 161.

14. Ibid., from the introduction entitled The Scene.

15. Robert McAfee Brown, *Elie Wiesel: Messenger to All Humanity* (Notre Dame, Ind.: University of Notre Dame Press, 1983), p. 154.

16. Emil Fackenheim, *God's Presence in History* (New York: Harper Torchbooks, 1970), p. 76.

17. Wiesel, *A Jew Today*, p. 147–148.

18. Greenberg, "Cloud of Smoke, Pillar of Fire," p. 55.

19. Fackenheim, *God's Presence in History*, p. 6.

20. Masao Abe, *The Emptying God: A Buddhist-Jewish-Christian Conversation*, ed. John B. Cobb, Jr., and Christopher Ives (Maryknoll, N.Y.: Orbis Books, 1990), pp. 50–51.

21. Ibid., p. 51.

22. Ibid., p. 47.

23. Ibid., p. 9.

24. Ibid., p. 181.

25. Ibid., pp. 48–49.

26. Ibid., p. 52.

27. Ibid., p. 52.

28. Lifton, *Death in Life*, p. 373.

29. See Greenberg's "Cloud of Smoke, Pillar of Fire," p. 27.

30. The Asian response to such tragedy, if I understand Robert Lifton's study of Hiroshima survivors (*Death in Life*) correctly, is *mono no aware*, the experience of "sad beauty"—a kind of resigned aesthetic transcendence of the tragic. And yet one Japanese anthologist of Hiroshima poetry noted that

some of this poetry could be compared with that of Job and suggested that these poets "will emerge from Hiroshima like prophets." *Death in Life*, p. 440.

31. Abe, *The Emptying God*, p. 181.

32. Ibid., pp. 181 and 185. Abe does not provide a biblical reference for his claim that God told Moses that he could not see his face and live. Deuteronomy seems to suggest that Moses was the exception to that rule, being the only person who throughout his life knew God face to face (Deuteronomy 34:10).

33. Greenberg, "Cloud of Smoke, Pillar of Fire," p. 37. The order of these two paragraphs is inverted from the order of the original text.

34. Wiesel, *One Generation After*, p. 220.

35. Eliezer Berkovitz, *Faith After the Holocaust* (New York: KTAV Publishing House Inc., 1973), pp.141 and 133.

36. Rubenstein, *The Cunning of History*, p. 93.

37. Ibid., p. 93.

38. Cohen, *The Tremendum*, p. 22. For an analysis of the relationship between genocide and omnicide by contemporary Jewish authors see *Confronting Omnicide: Jewish Reflections on Weapons of Mass Destruction*, edited by Daniel Landes (Northvale, N.J.: Jason Aronson Inc., 1991).

39. Fackenheim, *God's Presence in History*, p. 84.

40. Irving Greenberg, "The Third Great Cycle of Jewish History" in *Perspectives* (National Jewish Center for Learning and Leadership, September 1981, p. 8).

41. Ibid., p. 9.

42. Ibid., p. 10.

43. Ibid., p. 10.

44. Cox, *The Secular City*, pp. 30–31.

45. R. J. Vincent, *Human Rights and International Relations* (New York: Cambridge University Press, 1986), p. 13.

46. Peter Berger, "On the Obsolescence of the Concept of Honor," in *Revisions*, ed. Stanley Hauerwas and Alasdair MacIntyre (Notre Dame, Ind.: University of Notre Dame Press, 1983) p. 173.

47. Ibid., p. 175.

48. Ibid., p. 176.

49. By the criteria I have established neither Sophocles nor Mencius would be as important for the emergence of human rights as Abraham, Job, or Jeremiah, or Siddhartha for that matter. For the traditions of Sophocles and Mencius did not give rise to holy communities that represent a continuing social and historical witness to the emptiness or imagelessness of the self and hence its dignity and equality.

50. Berger, "On the Obsolescence of the Concept of Honor," p. 176.

51. Ibid., p. 180–181.

52. Eric Voegelin's discussion of the Nicomachean Ethics (1158b29–1159a13) of Aristotle, in *The New Science of Politics*, p. 77.

53. Eventually, Christians adapted this Jewish insight to the gentile world by using the Greek language of metaphysics to speak of being created

in the image of a trinitarian God. Like a Buddhist *koan*, the doctrine of the trinity defied the imagination, even as the doctrine of the incarnation affirmed that the human self, undistorted by sin, is a perfect image of the God who cannot be imaged. This insight however stood in tension with the hierarchical structure of Greek metaphysical thinking. To the degree that this way of thought influenced how Christians thought about God, Christianity drifted back into a cosmicization of the social order. This tension can be seen in the difference between Origen and Augustine's accounts of the trinity. Origen's account is ambiguous. One side of his thought suggests that, because the son emanates from the father, the son is less than the father, and likewise the spirit is less than the son. Augustine, on the other hand, grasps that the trinity must not be thought of in terms of physical metaphors of "emanation" (e.g., such as the sun's rays) but in spiritual terms, whose metaphors are the relations of mind to itself (e.g., memory, intelligence, and will). The result is that in the trinitarian God, all persons (divine and human) are equal. But even in Augustine this realization stands in tension with his use of a hierarchical metaphysics of creation.

54. *The Platform Scripture* (New York: St. John's University Press, 1963), p. 31. The context for this statement is one in which Hui-neng, who became the sixth patriarch of Zen, was seeking to be admitted to the monastery. A priest asks him where he is from, when he admits to being from the south, the master asks: "You are a barbarian. How can you become a Buddha?" to which Hui Neng replies: "Although people are distinguished as northerners and southerners, there is neither north nor south in the Buddha-nature."

55. *The Confessions*, p. 235.

56. Insofar as Christianity and (to a lesser degree) Judaism allowed itself to seduced by the Greek metaphysical tradition it of course tended to reduce "God" to an "Eternal Being," which denies the essential biblical experience of God as temporal-historical and without image. We find this tension in Augustine. The conflict between "Being" and the "Infinite" represents the fundamental conflict between the cosmological imagination and the experience of the holy. In Christianty, with the Protestant Reformation, the holiness of God did break free of the metaphysical imagination of being, but only partially and with ambivalence.

57. Vincent, *Human Rights and International Relations*, p. 82.

58. Nirmala S. Salgado, "Equality and Inequality in the Religious and Cultural Traditions of Hinduism and Buddhism," in *Equality and the Religious Traditions of Asia*, ed. R. Siriwardena (New York: St. Martins Press, 1987), p. 63. The dharma that would have lasted a thousand years, it was said, would now last only five hundred years.

59. Ibid., "Jewish Perspectives on Equality," p. 137.

60. Henry Rosmont, Jr., "Why Take Rights Seriously? A Confucian Critique," in *Human Rights and the World's Religions*, ed. Leroy S. Rouner (Notre Dame, Ind.: University of Notre Dame Press, 1988), p. 177.

61. W. Theodore de Bary, "Neo-Confucian and Human Rights," in *Hu-*

man *Rights and the World's Religions,* ed. Leroy S. Rouner (Notre Dame, Ind.: University of Notre Dame Press, 1988), p. 188.

62. Catholicism is not quite as severe as Protestantism in that it offers the possibility both of the merit of the saints and the prayers of the faithful as ways in which individual inadequacies of those faced with divine judgment after death can be assisted by the community of faith.

63. Rotenberg, *Dialogue with Deviance,* p. 14.

64. Ibid., p. 26.

65. Ibid., p. 26.

66. Ibid., p. 26.

67. Like Christianity, the Buddhist sangha began as a holy community whose success has continually tempted it to assume the form of a sacred society. See Trevor Ling's *The Buddha: Buddhist Civilization in India and Ceylon* (New York: Penguin Books, 1973) and also *Buddha, Marx and God* (New York: St. Martin's Press, 1966 and 1979).

68. Rubenstein, *The Cunning of History,* p. 92.

69. Dunne, *The Way of All the Earth,* p. ix.

70. Ibid., p. ix–x.

71. Ibid., p. xii–xiii.

72. Cohen, *The Tremendom,* p. 36.

73. Wilfred Cantwell Smith, *Toward a World Theology,* pp. 6–11.

74. Doumoulin, *A History of Zen Buddhism,* p. 259.

75. John Carman, "Duties and Rights in Hindu Society" in *Human Rights and the World's Religions,* p. 117. Harvey Cox would suggest that because the people give this constitution to themselves it represents an ethics based on consensus. Max Stackhouse argues that it shows that this is not an authentic rights tradition because the rights are not truly inalienable or transcendent. I would argue that the phrasing reflects being caught between the genuine experience of inalienable human dignity and the lack of either a religious or secular vocabulary for identifying its transcendent character.

76. Carman, ibid., p. 127.

Chapter 6. Beyond Technopolis: The Utopian Promise of Babel

1. Lonergan, *Insight: A Study in Human Understanding,* p. 179.

2. Lonergan, *Method in Theology,* p. 106.

3. Lonergan believes he has isolated the invariant structural dynamic of knowing in this process because every oversight or error can be discovered and corrected only by reactivating this dynamic, and every protest against this account of the noetic act must itself perform these operations of attending, understanding, judging, and deciding.

4. Robert Doran, *Psychic Conversion and the Theological Foundations: Toward a Reorientation of the Human Sciences* (Chico, Calif.: Scholars Press, 1981), p. 9.

5. Ibid., p. 14.

6. Eric Voegelin, *The New Science of Politics*, p. 78. Doran seems to treat this differentiation as two (historical *and* soteriological) but Voegelin, at least in his later work, treats these as components of one differentiation. History, as a symbolic mode of existence, begins with the soteriological event of the Exodus. "History is not a merely human but a divine-human process." See Voegelin's *The Ecumenic Age* (Baton Rouge: Louisiana State University Press, 1974) p. 304.

7. The Western religious experience of revelaton is sometimes viewed as unique. Consequently a distinction between *religion* and *revelation* is often made. Religion represents human striving (striving "in vain" it is usually suggested) to reach out and grasp the infinite; whereas revelation is the gracious movement of the infinite toward the human, in which the infinite seeks out the human and not vice versa. This distinction might be thought to be illustrated by the difference between the Buddhist eightfold path and the ten commandments of Judaism. Whereas the eightfold path begins with human striving and one's duties to self and others (right views, intention, speech, action, livelihood) and finally culminates in meditation (right effort, mindfulness, concentration or *samadhi*), which opens the self to the infinite, the ten commandments begin with the infinite (the first three being concerned with God) and then moves toward one's duties to others (the remaining seven).

However, although the distinction between *religion* and *revelation* does illuminate a peculiar emphasis of Western religion, it is hardly a distinction exclusive to Western religion. Augustine of Hippo, for instance, asked in his work on *The Trinity*: How can I seek the God which I do not know? His development of the doctrine of the trinity in response to this question explicated on the theoretical level what he had first learned on the experiential level, as reported in his *Confessions*. Drawing an analogy to the biblical revelation, he argued that his own seeking of God was already a manifestation of the graciousness of the trinitarian God (i.e., the God of history who acts in time) seeking him out, even before he was conscious of it, so as to awaken in him the desire for wisdom that set him on his quest. For God set him on fire with a passion for wisdom (the passion of *caritas* or selfless love) that drew him beyond his passions for the pleasures of the world (*cupiditas*, ego-centered passion). The orienting passion of *caritas* that set him on a quest that led to his conversion or turning to the infinite was thus due to the infinite turning first toward him, seeking him out, and making him restless until he found his true rest in God.

This same distinction between orienting and disorienting desire is found in Buddhism, which distinguishes between *tanha* (the desires of ego-centered craving) and *samma sankappa* (the desires "based on selflessness and love") (K. N. Jayatilleke, "A Recent Criticsm of Buddhism," in *Facts of Buddhist Thought* (Kandy Ceylon: Buddhist Publ. Society, 1979), reprinted from "A Recent Criticism of Buddhism," *University of Ceylon Review*, Vol. XV, $^3/_4$, 1957; Vol. XIII $^2/_3$, 1955, p. 14.) "A wide gulf . . . exists between the two," said K. N.

Jayatilleke, "Desires are narrow and selfish . . . while selflessness and Love [*metta*] are boundless" (ibid., p. 14). I think it is reasonable to conclude that the orienting desire that set Augustine on his ten-year quest for wisdom and the orienting desire that set Siddhartha on his seven-year quest for wisdom (both seeking an answer to the questions of mortality, morality, and meaning) are typologically the same; namely, in theological terms, that of grace. The agape (boundless love) is already present in the erotic desire (eros) that initiates the seeking. The goal and the path are one. If the difference between religion and revelation is the difference between seeking and being sought, then all three anthropological traditions I have identified—Judaism, Christianity, and Buddhism—exemplify, from a phenomenological perspective, both religion and revelation. The difference is simply that very often Buddhism does not consciously differentiate this dimension; it does not ask for an origin of the desire for liberation, whereas Judaism and Christianity begin with a consciousness of the origin as initiated by the infinite. I do not mean to suggest that there is an implicit theism in Buddhism. This is impossible, at least given the classical definition of God. I mean to suggest only that, phenomenologically, both share an analogous type of experience that may be open to different reflective theorizations.

    8. Doran, *Psychic Conversion*, p. 13.

    9. Lonergan, *Method in Theology*, p. 6.

    10. Doran, *Psychic Conversion*, p. 102, quoting Bernard Lonergan, *Insight*, Chapter 12. What Lonergan and Doran described as alienation here, I would describe as double alienation—an alienation from alienation. Alienation is a graced condition, the flight from alienation (i.e., double alienation) leads to ideology. Ideology is the pretense that we are not alienated and that we can have a home in the world. But because it is built on a denial of our fundamental experience of alienation it is always implicitly totalitarian and violent—it has to reinforce its status with the threat of violence.

    11. I am indebted to Karl Mannheim's *Ideology and Utopia* for this definition of *ideology*.

    12. Daniel Bell, *The Cultural Contradictions of Capitalism* (New York: Basic Books, 1976), pp. xi-xxix.

    13. Robert Doran, "Suffering Servanthood and the Scale of Values," in *Lonergan Workshop*, volume 4 (Chico, Calif.: Scholars Press, 1983), p. 51.

    14. Ibid., p. 61.

    15. Ibid., pp. 58 and 59.

    16. Ibid., p. 57.

    17. Lonergan, *Insight*, pp. 226ff.

    18. Doran, *Psychic Conversion*, p. 102, quoting Lonergan, *Method in Theology*, p. 55.

    19. Lonergan, *Method in Theology*, p. 55.

    20. Doran, *Psychic Conversion*, p. 21, quoting Lonergan, "Creating and Healing in History," in *A Third Collection* (New York: Paulist Press, 1985), pp. 100–109.

    21. Lonergan, *Method in Theology*, p. 243.

22. Doran, *Psychic Conversion*, p. 19.

23. Ibid., pp. 67–68.

24. Ibid., pp. 20 and 68.

25. Ibid., p. 67.

26. Ibid., p. 68.

27. Frederick Crowe S.J., *The Lonergan Enterprise* (Cambridge: Cowley Publications, 1980), pp. 90 and 91.

28. See Chapter 3 of my book *Narrative Theology After Auschwitz: From Alienation to Ethics* (Mpls: Fortress Press, 1992) for a fuller discussion of narrative truth. Quotations from Augustine's *Confessions* in this paragraph can be found on pp. 56 & 57 of Rex Werner's translation.

29. Doran, *Psychic Conversion*, p. 69, quoting Lonergan, *Method in Theology*, p. 31.

30. Ibid., p. 72.

31. Ibid., p. 74.

32. Ibid., p. 29. Doran defines *psyche* as the "sensitive sequence of sensations, memories, images, emotions, conations, associations, bodily movements, and spontaneous intersubjective responses. These constitute what we call the psyche" (p. 182)

33. See Doran's *Subject and Psyche* (Lanham, M.D.: University Press of America, 1980).

34. Both Jung and Doran talk about the wholenss of the self, but I am inclined to think of the self rather as an openness to the infinite. The term *wholeness* seems to suggest a closure that would short-circuit this openness.

35. Doran, *Psychic Conversion*, p. 176.

36. Ibid., pp. 176–177.

37. Ibid., p. 178.

38. Ibid., p. 178.

39. Ibid., p. 180.

40. Ibid., p. 181.

41. Lifton, *The Nazi Doctors*.

42. Ibid., p. 306.

43. Ibid., p. 307.

44. Doran, *Psychic Conversion*, p. 150.

45. Ibid., p. 192.

46. Ibid., p. 200.

47. This is the reason I take Augustine's surrender to the questions at age 19 as a more authentic conversion than his later experience in the garden at age 32, where (as he says in Book 8) all his doubts were "swept away" such that he could later persecute rather than welcome the stranger who differed with him.

48. I am indebted to Manfred Stanley, of the Maxwell School at Syracuse University, for this analogy.

49. Neuhaus, *The Naked Public Square*, p. 85.

50. Ibid., p. 85, quoting John Courtney Murray, "Return to Tribalism," *Catholic Mind* (January 1962).

51. Ibid., p. 87.

52. Lifton and Falk, *Indefensible Weapons*, pp. 137ff.

53. Alasdair MacIntyre, *After Virtue* (Notre Dame: University of Notre Dame Press, 1981), 2nd Edition p. 88.

54. Ibid., p. 68.

55. Ibid., p. 69.

56. Ibid., p. 69.

57. Ibid., p. 69.

58. Ibid., p. 71.

59. Ibid., p. 59.

60. See Chapter 8 of ibid.

61. I say *at least* two, because an ethic of welcoming the stranger will require that we be open to more than two stories as relevant to the ethical life.

62. Richard H. Schwartz, *Judaism and Global Survival* (New York: Atara Publishing Co., 1987), p. 13.

63. Jeffrey Stout, *Ethics After Babel* (Boston: Beacon Press, 1988), p. 7.

64. Peter Berger, in *The Homeless Mind*, by Peter Berger, Birgitte Berger, and Hansfried Kellner (New York: Vintage Books, Random House, 1973.), p. 42.

65. Ibid., pp. 49–50.

66. Albert Speer, *Inside the Third Reich* (New York: Macmillan, 1970), p. 33. For an extended discussion of Albert Speer in terms of narrative ethics and professional ethics see my book *Narrative Theology After Auschwitz*.

67. Stout, *Ethics After Babel*, pp. 75–76.

68. Ibid., pp. 80–81.

69. Ibid., p. 188.

Chapter 7. A Utopian Vision: Narrative Ethics in a MAD World

1. Lewis Mumford, *The City in History* (New York: Harcourt, Brace and World, 1961), p. xi.

2. Neuhaus, *The Naked Public Square*, p. vii.

3. Ibid., pp. 8–9.

4. Ibid., p. 88–89.

5. Ibid., p. 9.

6. See MacIntyre, *After Virtue*, Chapter 9 and Stout, *Ethics After Babel*, Chapter 7, "Moral Abominations."

7. Neuhaus, *The Naked Public Square*, p. 15.

8. Ibid., p. 19.

9. Ibid., p. 17.

10. Ibid., p. 18.

11. Ibid., p. 60.

12. Ibid., p. 188.

13. Ibid., p. 76.

14. Ibid., pp. 76–77.

15. Ibid., p. 92.

16. Ibid., p. 116.

17. Ibid., p. 174.

18. Ibid., p. 146.

19. Ibid., p. 121. Neuhaus quoting Novak.

20. Michael Novak, *The Spirit of Democratic Capitalism* (New York: American Enterprise Institute and Simon and Schuster, 1982), p. 52.

21. Ibid., p. 52.

22. Ibid., p. 53.

23. Ibid., p. 54.

24. Ibid., pp. 54–55.

25. Neuhaus, *The Naked Public Square*, p. 121.

26. Max Stackhouse, *Creeds, Society and Human Rights* (Grand Rapids, Michigan: William B. Eerdmans Publishing Co., 1984), pp. 4–5.

27. Ibid., p. 5.

28. Rubenstein, *The Cunning of History*, p. 89.

29. Max Stackhouse, "The World Religions and Political Democracy: Some Comparative Reflections," *Religion and Society* 29, no. 4. (December 1982): 19–49. See the section "The A-Social World of Buddhism," pp. 35–40. Stackhouse seems to be unaware of the significant body of literature that now exists, correcting the Weberian stereotype with a rich understanding of the social and political dimensions of Buddhism. To say that the sangha is asocial and otherwordly is like saying that Benedictine monasticism is asocial and otherworldly. It has an initial plausability that upon closer examination can be shown to completely miss the truth.

30. Trevor Ling, *The Buddha* (New York: Penguin Books, 1973). See Chapters 3 and 4 and especially Chapter 7, "The New Society."

31. K. N. Jayatilleke, "The Practical Policy of Buddhism Towards Racism and Caste," in *Facets of Buddhist Thought* (Kandy Ceylon: Buddhist Publication Society, 1979), pp. 43–44.

32. Taitetsu Unno, "Personal Rights and Contemporary Buddhism," in *Human Rights and the World's Religions*, ed. Leroy S. Rouner (Notre Dame, Ind.: University of Notre Dame Press, 1988), p. 131.

33. Ling, *The Buddha*, p. 157.

34. Ibid., p. 163.

35. Robert A. F. Thurman, "Social and Cultural Rights in Buddhism," in *Human Rights and the World's Religions*, pp. 155 and 154.

36. See my "A Case for Corporate and Management Ethics," *California Management Review* 23, no. 4 (Summer 1981).

37. In the early Benedictine tradition each monastery had considerable autonomy. By the time of the Cluniac reforms in the eleventh century this was no longer true. Authority became centralized in an international corporate social structure.

38. Ling, *The Buddha*, p. 161.

39. Greenberg, *The Third Great Cycle*, p. 6.

40. Robert Thurman, "Social and Cultural Rights in Buddhism," p. 148.

41. Stanley Hauerwas, *The Peaceable Kingdom* (Notre Dame, Ind.: University of Notre Dame Press, 1983), p. 144.

42. Ibid., p. 144.

43. Ibid., p. 144.

44. MacIntyre, *After Virtue*, p. 263.

45. Ibid., p. 219.

46. Ibid., pp. 222.

47. Ibid., pp. 219.

48. Ibid., p. 223.

49. Ibid., p. 187.

50. Ibid., p. 187–188.

51. Ibid., p. 189–190.

52. Ibid., p. 191.

53. Ibid., p. 191.

54. Ibid., p. 194.

55. Ibid., p. 194–195.

56. Ibid., p. 195. In the first edition MacIntyre actually claimed: "it is one of the tasks of government to make its citizens virtuous" (p. 182).

57. This is not an attempt to subordinate Job to a Christian Christology. On the contrary the point would be that the God of the covenant has always been "God with us," who inspires an audacious chutzpah on behalf of human dignity.

58. See Chapter 1 of my *Narrative Theology After Auschwitz: From Alienation to Ethics* for a discussion of these themes in relation to Paul's letter to the Romans, especially Chapter 11, where Paul tells gentiles that if they are arrogant enough to think themselves better than the Jews they will be cut off from the holy root of the natural olive tree of Judaism onto which they have been grafted by their faith.

59. Reinhold Niebuhr, *Moral Man and Immoral Society* (New York: Charles Scribner's Sons, 1960), p. 91.

60. Ibid., p. 49.

61. Ibid., pp. 95ff.

62. Stanley Hauerwas, *Against the Nations* (Minneapolis: Winston Press, 1985), p. 188.

63. Ibid., p. 185.

64. Ibid., p. 188.

65. Ibid., p. 196.

66. Ibid., p. 123.

67. Ibid., p. 127.

68. Ibid., p. 197. Hauwerwas suggests that in "the meal provided by the Lord of history [i.e., communion or eucharist] we discover our particularity is not destroyed but enhanced by the coming of the stanger." I wish that were true. But I do not see how it can be as long as that meal is restricted

to "believers" and dispensed by a bureaucratic expert (priest or minister), as if God's gracious transcendence can be owned and parceled out. Both traditional baptismal and eucharistic practices in Christianity succumbed very early to the pagan sacralism of the mysteries (i.e., sacraments) whose purpose was to separate those who are sacred from those who are profane so as to diminish and domesticate the God whose love, like the rain, falls on the just and the unjust alike.

69. Hauerwas, *The Peaceable Kingdom*, p. 144.

70. Berkovitz, *Faith After the Holocaust*, p. 139.

71. Ibid., p. 139.

72. M. K. Gandhi, *The Science of Satyagraha* published by (Bombay: Anand T. Hingorani, 1970) and distributed by (Weare, N.H.: Greenleaf Books), p. 6.

73. Dunne, *The Way of All the Earth*, p. 54.

74. Ibid., p. 53.

75. Rubenstein, *The Cunning of History*, p. 93.

76. Myron S. Augsburger and Dean C. Curry, *Nuclear Arms: Two Views on World Peace* (Waco, Texas: Word Books, 1987), pp. 106–107. My references are to that portion of the book written by Curry, who takes a pro-nuclear war "realist" position.

77. Ibid., p. 108.

78. Ibid., p. 111.

79. Ibid., p. 111.

80. Ibid., p. 112.

81. Ibid., p. 126.

82. Ibid., p. 138.

83. Ibid., pp. 142.

84. Ibid., p. 143.

85. Ibid., pp. 143–144.

86. See Novak and Neuhaus's essays in *Ethics and Nuclear Arms: European and American Perspectives*, ed. Raymond English (Washington, D.C.: Ethics and Public Policy Center, 1985). Edward Norman's article fits into this camp as well.

87. Ibid., pp. 111–121.

88. Ibid., p. 116.

89. "It is precisely in this that God proves his love for us," says Paul, "that while we were still sinners, Christ died for us. . . . For if when we were God's enemies, we were reconciled to him by the death of his Son, it is all the more certain that we who have been reconciled will be saved by his life" (Romans 5: 8 and 10).

90. *Ethics and Nuclear Arms*, p. 115.

91. Neuhaus, *The Naked Public Square*, p. 15.

92. Hal Lindsey, *The Late Great Planet Earth* (New York: Bantam Books, 1970), p. 41.

93. Ibid., p. 71.

94. Ibid., p. 157.

95. Ibid., p. 168.

96. Ellul, *Apocalypse*, p. 24.

97. In Ellul's view the life of Jesus as suffering servant cannot be separated from the historical people Israel; that is, the Jews and their suffering.

98. That is, those who make up the body of the suffering servant, Jews and Christians.

99. For a more detailed discussion of the dialectics of two kingdom ethics see Chapter 5 of my *Narrative Theology After Auschwitz*.

100. Norman, in *Ethics and Nuclear Arms*, p. 119.

101. Nietzsche, from the *Gay Science*, pp. 95–96.

102. Brown, *Elie Wiesel*, p. 213. Brown is quoting Wiesel's play.

103. Wiesel, *A Jew Today*, p. 14.

104. Brown, p. 44, quoting from Wiesel's, *Victory*, p. 24.

Epilogue: The Secular University, Religious Studies, and Theological Ethics After Auschwitz and Hiroshima

1. Mircea Eliade, *The Quest* (Chicago: University of Chicago Press, 1969).

2. Ibid., Preface.

3. Ibid., Chapter 4.

4. Ibid., p. 61.

5. Ibid., p. 61.

6. Ibid., p. 62.

7. Ibid., p. 67.

8. Ibid., p. 69.

9. This is a translation from the title of Vahanian's new book *Dieu anonyme ou la peur des mots* (Paris: Desclee de Brouwer, 1989).

Index